The
Alaska
Almanac®

FACTS ABOUT ALASKA

21st Edition

~

Alaska Northwest Books™
Anchorage • Seattle • Portland

~

First edition published 1976
Twenty-first edition
Previously published as FACTS ABOUT ALASKA: The ALASKA ALMANAC®

ISBN 0-88240-491-1
ISSN 0270-5370
Key title: The Alaska Almanac

Cover and interior design: Michelle Taverniti
Cover illustration: Mindy Dwyer
Editor: Tricia Brown
Compiler: Ann Chandonnet
Page composition/editorial assistance: Fay L. Bartels
Maps: Gray Mouse Graphics
Permissions/credits for illustrations and photographs are on page 234.

Alaska Northwest Books™
An imprint of Graphic Arts Center Publishing Company
P.O. Box 10306, Portland, OR 97296-0306
800-452-3032

Printed on acid-free recycled paper in the United States of America

A Note to Our Readers

With this twenty-first edition of
The Alaska Almanac®, Alaska Northwest
Books™ again welcomes Mr. Whitekeys
and his wacky bits of Alaska wisdom. For
over a decade, thousands of Alaskans and
visitors to Alaska have enjoyed an evening
of music and comedy with Whitekeys and
his irreverent singing, dancing cast at
Anchorage's Fly By Night Club. The
originator of the infamous Whale Fat
Follies, Mr. Whitekeys brings his distinctive, bizarre insights on real life in the
Northland—from bears to politics—to
the pages of The Alaska Almanac®.
—the editors of Alaska Northwest Books™

American
Guidance Systems
of Minnesota sent a package
of educational materials to the
Annette Island School District in
Metlakatla, Alaska. The company
filled out a Customs declaration
form just in case Alaska was
not a part of the U.S.A.

Contents

Acknowledgments

This edition of The Alaska Almanac® *has been compiled and updated from information supplied by many helpful state and federal offices, organizations, and experts.*

The editors gratefully acknowledge:
Duncan Adams
Alaska Bureau of Vital Statistics
Alaska Center for the Book
Alaska Department of Labor
Alaska Division of Tourism
Alaska Journal of Commerce
Alaska Newspapers Inc.
Anchorage Convention & Visitors Bureau
Anchorage Daily News
Annual Report of Lands Under Control of the U.S. Fish and Wildlife Service as of September 30, 1997
Marlene Blessing
Delon A. Brown, Alaska Agricultural Statistics Service, Palmer
George M. Constantino, Chief, Division of Refuges, U.S. Department of the Interior, Fish and Wildlife Service
R.N. DeArmond
Epicenter Press
Fairbanks Convention & Visitors Bureau
Fairbanks Daily News-Miner
Sylvia Fields, Skagway Convention & Visitors Bureau
Lt. J.M. Fitzgerald, U.S. Coast Guard
Becki Gray, Usibelli Coal Mine Inc.
Anne Haydon, Health Program Manager, Alaska Department of Health & Social Services, Division of Public Health
Margaret E. Holland, Legislative Liaison, Central Region, Alaska Department of Transportation and Public Facilities
Sara Juday
Juneau Convention & Visitors Bureau
Jim Kelly, Director of Communications, Alaska Permanent Fund Corporation
Ketchikan Visitors Bureau, *Experience Alaska: Ketchikan Area Guide, 1997*
Klondike Gold Rush Centennial Committee of Washington State
Karen Kolivosky, Communications Manager, Fairbanks Convention & Visitors Bureau
Steve J. McGroarty, Northern Regional Manager, Alaska Department of Natural Resources, Division of Mining and Water Management
Steve McMains, Alaska Oil and Gas Conservation Commission
Jeneane Moore, Administrative Associate, Alaska Court System
Ken Morris, Public Relations Director, Anchorage Convention & Visitors Bureau
Older Persons Action Group Inc.
John Quinley, National Park Service
Rose Ragsdale
Kathryn Reid, Volunteer Coordinator Policy & Planning, Alaska Department of Natural Resources, Division of Parks & Outdoor Recreation
Herman Savikko
Seward Convention & Visitors Bureau
Debi Shade
Bill Sherwonit
Skagway Centennial Committee
Tom Sokolowski, Chief, West Coast/Alaska Tsunami Warning Center
State of Alaska, Department of Administration, Division of Senior Services
Sharon Svarny-Livingston, Executive Director, Unalaska/Port of Dutch Harbor Convention & Visitors Bureau
Kate A. Swalling, External Affairs, AT&T Alascom
Pat R. Wendt, Executive Director, Hostelling International-Anchorage
Ellen Wheat
Mr. Whitekeys
Camille Whitmire
Greg Williams, State Demographer, Alaska Department of Labor
Linda Wilson, Alaska Miners Association Inc.
Arnold Woodard, Alaska Sled Dog & Racing Association
1997 Medical Directory of the Alaska State Medical Association

Mr. Whitekeys wishes to acknowledge the assistance of the *Anchorage Daily News,* Ken Bell, Randy Brandon, Heather Brock, Kathy Gliva, Jenny Haggar, Clint Lillibridge, Rich Owens, and Maynard and Kathy Smith.

Miscellaneous Facts About Alaska

Motto: *"North to the Future."*
Nickname: *"The Last Frontier."*
State capital: *Juneau.*
Purchased from Russia: *1867.*
Organized as a territory: *1912.*
Entered the Union: *Jan. 3, 1959; 49th state.*
Governor: *Tony Knowles.*
Land area: *570,373.6 square miles, or about 365,000,000 acres—largest state in the union; one-fifth the size of the Lower 48.**
State population: *607,800 from July 1996 estimate.*
Largest city in population: *Anchorage, population 254,000 from June 1997 estimate.*
Largest city in area: *Sitka with 4,710 square miles, 1,816 square miles of which is water. Juneau is second, with an area of 3,108 square miles.*
Typical Alaskan: *According to 1993 Alaska Department of Labor figures, the median age for males is 29.7 years and 29.6 for females. About 52 percent of Alaskans are male, the highest percentage of any state.*
Per capita personal income per resident: *$24,513 in 1996, tenth highest in the nation.*
Area per person: *Approximately 0.93 square mile for each person in Alaska. New York State has .003 square mile per person.*
Arts funding: *In 1996, the National Endowment for the Arts (NEA) made direct and indirect grants to Alaskans of more than $595,000.*
Highest/lowest temperatures: *Highest 100°F at Fort Yukon, 1915. Lowest –80°F at Prospect Creek Camp, 1971.*
Heaviest annual snowfall: *974.5 inches at Thompson Pass near Valdez, during the winter of 1952–53.*

Tallest mountain in North America: *Mount McKinley, 20,320 feet.*
Miles of shoreline: *33,904—twice the length of the Lower 48.*
Tourism: *German-speaking Europe provides the largest number of international visitors to Alaska.***
Farthest north city in the U.S.: *Barrow, 350 miles north of the Arctic Circle.*
World's largest and busiest seaplane base: *Lake Hood, in Anchorage, accommodating more than 800 takeoffs and landings on a peak summer day.*
Largest contiguous state park in the nation: *Wood-Tikchik State Park, with 1.6 million acres of wilderness.*
World's largest concentration of bald eagles: *Along the Chilkat River, just north of Haines. As many as 3,000 bald eagles can gather here in fall and winter.*
America's biggest earthquake: *Occurred March 27, 1964, Good Friday. Measuring 8.6 on the Richter scale (has since been revised upward to 9.2—the strongest ever recorded in North America), the earthquake devasted much of southcentral Alaska.*
Second greatest tide range in North America: *38.9 feet near Anchorage in Upper Cook Inlet.*
World's largest producer of zinc: *Red Dog Mine in the Northwest Arctic Borough of Alaska.*
Greatest concentration of glaciers in the nation: *In Alaska, 5 percent of the state—approximately 29,000 square miles—is covered by glaciers, 128 times more area than in the rest of the U.S.*

*Revised land area from U.S. Census Bureau, 1996.
**Anchorage Convention & Visitors Bureau, June 1997.

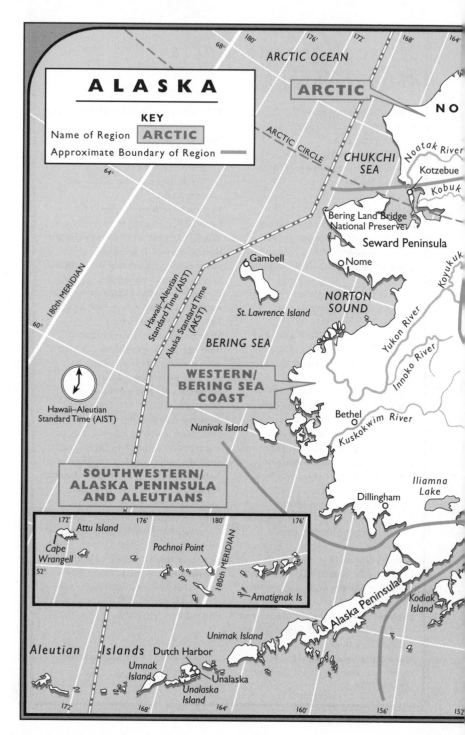

ALASKA

KEY

Name of Region ARCTIC

Approximate Boundary of Region ——

ARCTIC OCEAN

ARCTIC

N O

ARCTIC CIRCLE

CHUKCHI SEA

Noatak River

Kotzebue

Kobuk

Bering Land Bridge National Preserve

Seward Peninsula

Nome

Koyukuk

NORTON SOUND

Gambell

St. Lawrence Island

Yukon River

Innoko River

BERING SEA

WESTERN/ BERING SEA COAST

Bethel

Kuskokwim River

Nunivak Island

Hawaii–Aleutian Standard Time (AIST)

Hawaii–Aleutian Standard Time (AIST)

Alaska Standard Time (AKST)

180th MERIDIAN

Iliamna Lake

Dillingham

SOUTHWESTERN/ ALASKA PENINSULA AND ALEUTIANS

Attu Island

Cape Wrangell

Pochnoi Point

180th MERIDIAN

Amatignak Is

Alaska Peninsula

Kodiak Island

Unimak Island

Aleutian   Islands   Dutch Harbor

Umnak Island

Unalaska

Unalaska Island

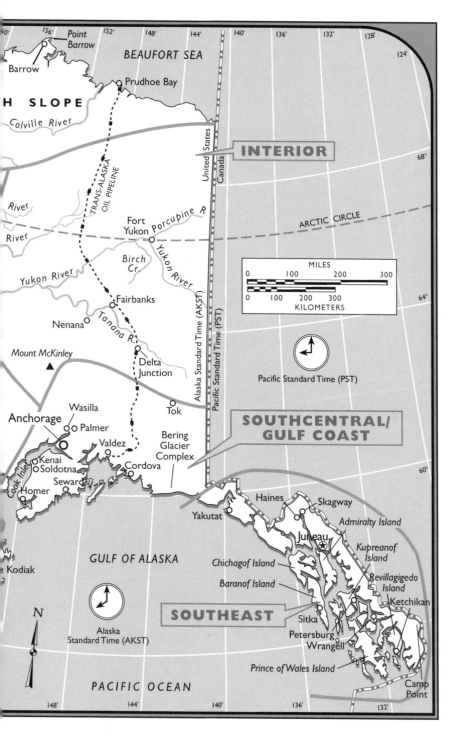

Point Barrow
BEAUFORT SEA
Barrow
Prudhoe Bay
H SLOPE
Colville River
INTERIOR
River
TRANS-ALASKA OIL PIPELINE
United States
Canada
ARCTIC CIRCLE
River
Fort Yukon
Porcupine R
Yukon River
Birch Cr.
Yukon River
Fairbanks
Nenana
Tanana R.
Alaska Standard Time (AKST)
Pacific Standard Time (PST)
Mount McKinley
Delta Junction
Tok
Wasilla
Anchorage
Palmer
Valdez
Bering Glacier Complex
Kenai
Soldotna
Cordova
Seward
Homer
Cook Inlet
MILES
0   100   200   300
0   100   200   300
KILOMETERS

Pacific Standard Time (PST)

SOUTHCENTRAL/ GULF COAST

Haines
Skagway
Yakutat
Admiralty Island
Juneau
Kupreanof Island
GULF OF ALASKA
Chichagof Island
Baranof Island
Revillagigedo Island
Ketchikan
Kodiak
SOUTHEAST
Sitka
Petersburg
Wrangell
N
Alaska Standard Time (AKST)
Prince of Wales Island
Camp Point
PACIFIC OCEAN

156' 152' 148' 144' 140' 136' 132' 128' 124'
68°
64°
60°
148' 144' 140' 136' 132'

Agriculture

Agriculture in Alaska ranges from backyard gardens to 3,000-acre farms. Extremes of weather and a short growing season challenge cultivation in the state, but certain crops—notably potatoes and carrots—thrive in the cool soil temperatures. Overall, climatic conditions are not the greatest impediments to Alaska farming. More significant hurdles are high production costs and competition from the Lower 48.

Alaska's commercial farming is concentrated in two major regions: the Matanuska Valley, northeast of Anchorage, which in 1996 contributed 56 percent of the state's value of farm production, and the Tanana Valley, which was responsible for 39 percent.

Total Acreage of Alaska Cropland by Region

Region	Percent
Tanana Valley	56.3
Matanuska Valley	35.4
Kenai Peninsula	8.0
Southeast & Southwestern Alaska	0.3

An estimated 15 million to 18 million acres in Alaska are believed to be arable, but only 920,000 acres—less than one-half of 1 percent of the state—are currently considered land in farms. In 1996, crops covered 31,322 acres; the balance was in pasture and uncleared land.

Total market value of Alaska's agricultural products in 1996 was $29,340,000—less than in 1995. Feed crops accounted for $2.1 million of total market receipts, and vegetables (including potatoes), were $3.03 million of the total.

Greenhouse and nursery industries—a substantial portion of the state's agricultural picture—amounted to $18.2 million, or 62 percent of total cash receipts for 1996.

Over 98 percent of the barley grown in 1996 was harvested in the Tanana Valley. Total production netted 285,000 bushels, yielding 41 bushels per acre. Production value for the 1996 barley crop was roughly $926,000, down from the 1995 crop of $1,228,000. Harvest of oats yielded 45 bushels per acre for a total of only 31,500 bushels at an estimated value of $79,000. This reflects an increase from 70,200 bushels valued at $179,000 in 1995.

Another Alaska agricultural enterprise is the raising of reindeer. Officials estimate there are 23 herds in Western Alaska, or a total of approximately 27,000 head. Most of the reindeer are located on the Seward Peninsula and Nunivak Island, where they contribute significantly to the local economies. Among the by-products of reindeer is the powder made from clipped antlers, most of which is exported to the Far East. Sales related to reindeer were valued at $961,000 in 1996, down $249,000 from 1995.

The annual milk production in 1996 totaled 13,500,000 pounds, an increase of 1,600,000 pounds from 1995. Dairy products brought in $2.61 million in 1996, down from 1995. Economic stresses continue to reduce the number of farmers involved in this capital-intensive industry. In 1989, 1,600 cows produced nearly 2.7 million gallons of milk. By 1996, the number of cows decreased to 800. Only 11 dairies are now operating in the state.

The small vegetable gardens of the Russian fur traders are believed to constitute the first Alaskan agriculture. Gold rush days saw growing interest in local farming possibilities, but it wasn't

A new ultimate reference book on Alaskan gardening contained this statement: "Crapapples . . . are among Alaska's lovliest flowering trees."

The New Deal in Alaska

The Matanuska Valley experiment of the Great Depression era is a classic illustration of the difficulties besetting Alaska farming. In 1934, with considerable fanfare, the federal government invited people from poor rural areas of the northern Midwest to help found an agricultural colony in the picturesque valley between the Chugach and Talkeetna mountain ranges, 45 miles northeast of Anchorage. No sooner had the colonists arrived [in 1935] than Alaska's fickle climate greeted them with unseasonable rains throughout May and June. The newcomers lived in tents while helping government workers erect frame houses and other buildings. Meanwhile, their children succumbed to epidemics of measles and scarlet fever. Some families grew discouraged and gave up. . . . The colony survived but never flourished. Soil quality was uneven, colonists quarreled over the best land, bureaucratic regulation stifled initiative, and most settlers found 40 acres too little to make a go of things. In 1939 an early snow destroyed 80 percent of the grain and vegetable harvest. . . . In 1948 only 40 of the original 202 pioneer families remained.—Harry Ritter, Alaska's History

until 1935 that there was a concerted effort to introduce commercial growing. President Franklin Roosevelt's New Deal resettlement plan transplanted 202 farm families from the Midwest to the Matanuska Valley, where they were to create a food source for the territory. Although most produce comes from Outside, local farmers still supply Anchorage and nearby military installations with some fresh produce and dairy products. The growing season averages 115 days; there are some days with over 19 hours of sunlight in the summer (which help produce giant-sized vegetables).

The Tanana Valley growing season is shorter than that of the Matanuska Valley, with about 95 frost-free days. Because growing season temperatures are warmer in the Tanana Valley, many experts consider the area to have greater agricultural potential. Barley and oats are raised for grain and hay. Most Alaska-grown grain is used for domestic livestock feed. All are

spring varieties, since few winter types survive the cold.

Beef, pork, hay, eggs and fresh produce are produced throughout the Railbelt region and are easily transported to major markets. (The Railbelt region consists of the areas linked by the Alaska Railroad, from Seward north to Fairbanks.) Umnak and Unalaska Islands provide grazing area for 1,000 sheep, down considerably from 27,000 in 1970.

Across Alaska, the pressure of urban development is reducing the number of acres available for farming. At the same time, the state is attempting to increase the number of farms through sales of agriculture tracts. Farming is also used by many individuals as a supplement to other income. In 1996, there were 510 farms with annual sales of $1,000 or more.

Since 1978, state land sales have placed more than 165,000 acres of potential agricultural land into private ownership. Most of this acreage is in the Delta Junction area,

Crops	Acres Harvested	1996 Crop Value
Hay (14.4 tons)*	20,200	$2,736,000
Potatoes (129 cwt.)*	630	2,490,000
Barley, for grain (285 bushels)*	6,900	926,000
Vegetables (except potatoes)	332	1,385,000
Oats, for grain (31.5 bushels)*	700	79,000

*Volume in thousands
Source: Alaska Agricultural Statistics Service

where tracts of up to 3,200 acres were originally sold by lottery for grain farming. The Nenana area is among those under consideration for future agricultural development.

Additional information is available from the Alaska Agricultural Statistics Service, P.O. Box 799, Palmer 99645; (907) 745-4272.

Air Travel

Alaska is the "flyingest" state in the Union; the only practical way to reach many areas of rural Alaska is by airplane. According to the Federal Aviation Administration, Alaska Region, in early 1996 there were 10,681 registered pilots, 1 out of every 58 Alaskans, and 9,698 registered aircraft, 1 for every 59 Alaskans. Alaska has approximately 6 times as many pilots per capita and 14 times as many airplanes per capita as the rest of the United States.

According to the FAA, Alaska has 325 airports, plus 1,100 recorded landing areas and 102 seaplane bases. That puts Alaska sixth, behind Texas, Illinois, California, Pennsylvania and Florida, in the number of airports in the state. Of the seaplane bases, Lake Hood in Anchorage is the largest and busiest in the world. On a yearly basis, an average of 234 takeoffs and landings occur daily, and more than 800 on a peak summer day. Merrill Field in Anchorage recorded 184,759 flight operations during 1995. Anchorage International Airport will see more than 5 million passengers pass through in 1998. Anchorage International is the number-one airport in the U.S. for cargo traffic, based on all-cargo aircraft landed weights. In 1996, 10.5 billion pounds of cargo moved through the airport.

Anchorage is becoming a hub for air-cargo carriers, with more than a dozen companies, both domestic and international, zeroing in during the early months of 1997. In fiscal 1996, AIA counted 26,674 revenue landings of cargo aircraft, up from 23,566 a year ago.

Pilots who wish to fly their own planes to Alaska should have the latest United States government flight information publication, *Alaska Supplement. Flight Tips for Pilots in Alaska* is available from the Federal Aviation Administration, 222 W. Seventh Ave., No. 14, Anchorage 99513-7587.

Scheduled passenger service is available to dozens of Alaskan communities (*see* Intrastate Service, this section). Contact the airlines for current schedules and fares.

Air taxi operators are found in most Alaskan communities, and aircraft can be chartered to fly you to a wilderness spot and pick you up later at a prearranged time and location. Most charter operators charge an hourly rate either per plane load or per passenger (sometimes with a minimum passenger requirement); others may charge on a per-mile basis. Flightseeing trips to area attractions are often available at a fixed price per passenger. Charter fares range from $140 to $175 per person (four-person and up minimum) for a short flightseeing trip, to $350 an hour for an eight-passenger Cessna 404.

A wide range of aircraft is used for charter and scheduled passenger service in Alaska. The larger interstate airlines— Alaska, Continental, Northwest, Reno Air, United and Delta—use jets (Douglas DC-8, DC-10, Boeing 727, 737, 757, 767); Reeve Aleutian flies Electra, Boeing 727 and YS-11. Prop jets and single- or twin-engine prop planes on wheels, skis and floats are used for most intrastate travel. A few of the types of aircraft flown in Alaska are: 19-passenger de Havilland Twin Otter, 10-passenger Britten–Norman Islander,

In 1995, an Alaska Permanent Fund dividend check purchased 2.57 round-trip tickets to Hawaii. In 1996 the dividend was worth 2.74 tickets. The 1997 check is estimated to be worth 3.37 tickets. The state government obviously knows how much its residents like to leave the state.

7-passenger Grumman Goose (amphibious), DC–3, 4-passenger Cessna 185, 9-passenger twin-engine Piper Navajo Chieftain, 5- to 8-passenger de Havilland Beaver, 3- to 4-passenger Cessna 180, 5- to 6-passenger Cessna 206 and single-passenger Piper Super Cub.

INTERNATIONAL SERVICE.

Several international carriers provide Alaska either cargo or passenger service through the Anchorage gateway. The list includes: Aeroflot, Air China, Alaska Airlines (to Russia and Mexico), Asiana, Cathay, China Airlines, ERA Aviation, Federal Express, Korean Airlines, Nippon Cargo Airlines, Northwest Airlines, Singapore Airlines, United Airlines and United Postal Service.

INTERSTATE SERVICE. U.S.

carriers providing interstate passenger service: Alaska Airlines, Continental Airlines, Delta Air Lines, ERA Aviation,

Northwest Airlines, Peninsula Airways, Reeve Aleutian Airways, Reno Air, Southcentral Air and United Airlines. These carriers also provide freight service between Anchorage and Seattle.

INTRASTATE SERVICE. From

Anchorage. Alaska Airlines, 4750 International Road, Anchorage 99502. Serves Cordova, Fairbanks, Gustavus/ Glacier Bay, Juneau, Ketchikan, Kotzebue, Nome, Petersburg, Prudhoe Bay, Sitka, Wrangell and Yakutat. Additional routes served on a contract basis by local carriers.

Alaska Island Air, P.O. Box 220374, Anchorage 99522. Serves Willow.

Arctic Transportation Services, 5701 Silverado Way, Anchorage 99518.

Delta Air Lines, 3830 W. International Airport Road, Anchorage 99502. Serves Fairbanks.

ERA Aviation, 6160 S. Airpark Drive, Anchorage 99502. E-mail: info@era-aviation.com. Serves Cordova, Homer, Iliamna, Kenai, Kodiak, Seward, Valdez and Whitehorse.

Ketchum Air Service, Box 670, Valdez 99686; (907) 835-3789. Serves Anchorage, Columbia Glacier, Cordova, McKinley, Valdez and remote fishing.

PenAir, 6231 Collins Way, Anchorage 99502. Serves Aniak, Dillingham, Dutch Harbor, King Salmon, McGrath, St. George, St. Marys, St. Paul and Unalakleet.

Reeve Aleutian Airways Inc., 4700 W. International Airport Road, Anchorage 99502. Serves the Alaska Peninsula, Aleutian Islands and Pribilof Islands. Serves Bethel, Kotzebue, McGrath, Nome and many other bush communities in Alaska.

Southcentral Air, 135 Granite Point Court, Kenai 99611. Serves Dog Fish, Homer, Kenai, Port Graham, Seldovia, Soldotna and Windy Bay.

Yute Air, 4706 Harding Drive, Anchorage; (907) 243-7000. Serves Aniak, Bethel, Kenai, King Salmon, Kotzebue and Nome.

From Barrow. Cape Smythe Air, P.O. Box 549, Barrow 99723. Serves Brevig Mission, Elim, Golovin, Shishmaref, Teller, Wales and White Mountain.

By the 1930s, the airplane had replaced the dog team as carrier of U.S. mail to many Alaska villages. From Winging It! by Jack Jefford

From Fairbanks. Frontier Flying Service, 3820 University Ave., Fairbanks 99709. Serves Allakaket, Anaktuvuk Pass, Bettles, Fort Yukon, Galena, Huslia, Kaltag, Kotzebue, Nome and Ruby.

Larry's Flying Service, P.O. Box 2348, Fairbanks 99707. Serves Denali National Park and Preserve (McKinley Park airstrip).

Warbelow's Air Ventures, Inc., 3758 University Ave., Fairbanks 99709. Serves Ambler, Central, Chalkyitsik, Circle, Eagle, Fort Yukon, Galena, Hughes, Huslia, Kaltag, Kobuk, Koyukuk, Nulato, Rampart, Shungnak, Tanana and Utopia.

From Glennallen. Gulkana Air Service, P.O. Box 342, Glennallen 99588. Serves Anchorage.

From Haines. L.A.B. Flying Service, P.O. Box 272, Haines 99827. Serves Hoonah, Juneau and Skagway.

From Juneau. Air North Charter, 1873 Shell Simmons Drive, Juneau 99801; (907) 789-2007. Serves Dawson, Fairbanks, Juneau, Old Crow and Whitehorse.

Coastal Helicopters, 2355 Ka-See-An Drive, Juneau 99801; (907) 789-5600. Serves fishermen, skiers, photographers.

Loken Aviation, 8955 Yandukin Drive, Juneau 99801; (907) 789-3331. Serves wilderness cabins, Native villages and fishing lodges.

Wings of Alaska, 1873 Shell Simmons Drive, Suite 119, Juneau 99801. Serves Angoon, Elfin Cove, Gustavus/Glacier Bay, Haines, Hoonah, Kake, Pelican, Skagway and Tenakee.

From Kenai. Southcentral Air Inc., 135 Granite Point Court, Kenai 99611. Serves Anchorage, Dog Fish, Homer, Port Graham, Seldovia, Seward, Soldotna and Windy Bay.

From Ketchikan. Ketchikan Air Service, P.O. Box 6900, Ketchikan 99901. Serves Hyder and Stewart, British Columbia.

Temso Helicopters, Inc., P.O. Box 5057, Ketchikan 99901. Serves Craig, Hydaburg, Klawock, Metlakatla and other Southeast points.

From Kodiak. Island Air Service, 2295 Mill Bay Road, Kodiak 99615; (800) 504-2327.

Sea Hawk Air, 5279 W. Rezanof, Kodiak 99615; (800) 770-HAWK.

Uyak Air Inc., 211 Marine Way, Kodiak 99615; (800) 303-3407.

From Nome. Bering Air Inc., P.O. Box 1650, Nome 99762. Serves Kotzebue and points in western Alaska.

From Skagway. L.A.B. Flying
Service, (907) 983-2471.
Skagway Air Service, (907) 983-2218.
Temsco, (907) 9833-2900.

From Talkeetna. K2 Aviation, Box
545, Talkeetna 99676; (907) 733-2291.
Serves Anchorage, Kantishna, McKinley
and glacier landings.

From Tanana. Tanana Air Service,
P.O. Box 60713, Fairbanks 99706. Serves
Eagle, Fairbanks, Huslia, Manley Hot
Springs, Nenana, New Minto and Rampart.

From Tok. 40-Mile Air Ltd., P.O. Box
539, Tok 99780. Serves Boundary, Chicken,
Delta Junction, Eagle, Fairbanks and
Tetlin.

Alaska-Canada
Boundary In 1825, Russia,
in possession of Alaska, and Great Britain,
in possession of Canada, established the
original boundary between Alaska and
Canada. The demarcation was to begin at
54°40' north latitude, just north of the
mouth of Portland Canal, follow the canal
to 56° north latitude, then traverse the
mountain summits parallel to the coast as
far as 141° west longitude. From there it
would conform with that meridian north
to the Arctic Ocean. The boundary line
along the mountain summits in southeastern Alaska was never to be farther
inland than 10 leagues—about 30 miles.

After purchasing Alaska in 1867, the
United States found that the wording about
the boundary line was interpreted differ-
ently by the Canadians. They felt the measurements should be made inland from the
mouths of bays, while Americans argued
the measurements should be made from
the heads of the bays. In 1903, however, an
international tribunal upheld the American
interpretation of the treaty, providing
Alaska the 1,538-mile-long border it has
with Canada today. The southeastern
Alaska border is 891 miles long, and 181
miles of that border is over water. If the
Canadians had won their argument they

would have had access to the sea, and
Haines, Dyea and Skagway now would be
in Canada.

The 20-foot-wide vista—a swath of
land cleared 10 feet on each side of the
boundary between southeastern Alaska,
British Columbia and Yukon Territory—
was surveyed and cleared between 1904
and 1914. Portions of the 710-mile-long
boundary were again cleared in 1925, 1948,
1978 and 1982 by the International Boundary Commission. Monument and vista
maintenance of 1978 and 1982 was conducted by the Canadian section of the
commission and by the U.S. section in
1983, 1984 and 1985.

The Alaska-Canada border along the
141st meridian was surveyed and cleared
between 1904 and 1920. Astronomical
observations were made to find the meridian's intersection with the Yukon River;
then, under the direction of the International Boundary Commission, engineers
and surveyors of the U.S. Coast and Geodetic Survey and the Canadian Department
of the Interior worked together north and
south from the Yukon. The vista extends
from Demarcation Point on the Arctic
Ocean south to Mount St. Elias in the
Wrangell Mountains (from there the
border cuts east to encompass southeastern
Alaska). This part of the border stretches
for 647 miles in one of the world's longest
straight lines, varying less than 50 feet
along its entire length.

Monuments are the actual markers of
the boundary and are located so they tie in
with survey networks of both the United
States and Canada. Along the Alaska
boundary most monuments are 2$\frac{1}{2}$-foot-
high cones of aluminum-bronze set in concrete bases or occasionally cemented into
rock. A large pair of concrete monuments
with a pebbled finish mark major boundary
road crossings. Because the boundary is not
just a line but in fact a vertical plane dividing land and sky between the two nations,
bronze plates mark tunnel and bridge
crossings. Along the meridian, 191 monuments are placed, beginning 200 feet from
the Arctic Ocean and ending at the south
side of Logan Glacier.

Alaska Highway (SEE ALSO HIGHWAYS)

The Alaska Highway runs 1,520 miles through Canada and Alaska from Milepost 0 at Dawson Creek, British Columbia, through Yukon Territory to Fairbanks, Alaska. Until this overland link between Alaska and the Lower 48 was built in 1942, travel to and from Alaska was primarily by water.

History. The highway was built to relieve Alaska from the hazards of shipping by water and to supply a land route for equipment during World War II.

By agreement between the governments of Canada and the United States, the highway was built in eight months by the U.S. Army Corps of Engineers and was dedicated in November 1942. Crews worked south from Delta Junction, Alaska, north and south from Whitehorse, Yukon Territory, and north from Dawson Creek, British Columbia.

The building of the highway was recognized as one of the greatest engineering feats of the 20th century. Two major sections of the highway were connected on Sept. 23, 1942, at Contact Creek, Milepost

Driving the Alaska Highway

Sometimes referred to as the Alcan, the Alaska Highway is a two-lane road that winds and rolls across the wilderness. It is open and maintained year-round. Some sections of road have no centerline, and some stretches of narrow road have little or no shoulder. The best driving advice on these sections is to take your time, drive with your headlights on at all times, keep to the right on hills and corners and drive defensively.

There are relatively few steep grades on the Alaska Highway. The most mountainous section of highway is between Fort Nelson, British Columbia, and Watson Lake, Yukon Territory, where the highway crosses the Rocky Mountains.

Almost the entire length of the Alaska Highway is asphalt-surfaced, ranging from poor to excellent condition. Some rugged stretches exist with many chuckholes, gravel breaks, hardtop with loose gravel, deteriorated shoulders and bumps.

Watch for frost heaves on all portions of the highway. This rippling effect in the pavement is caused by the alternate freezing and thawing of the ground.

Drive slowly in sections of frost heaves to avoid breaking an axle or trailer hitch.

Travelers should keep in mind that road conditions are subject to change. Be alert for bumps and holes in the road; some are signed or flagged, but many are not.

Watch for construction crews along the Alaska Highway. Extensive road construction may require a detour, or travelers may be delayed while waiting for a pilot car to guide them through the construction. Motorists may also encounter some muddy roadways at construction areas if there were heavy rains while the roadbed was torn up.

Dust and mud are generally not a problem, except in construction areas and on a few stretches of the highway.

Don't drive too fast on gravel. Gravel acts just like many little ball bearings, and you could lose control of your vehicle. Driving fast on gravel is also hard on your tires, raises dust and throws rocks at oncoming cars. Heavy rain on a gravel road generally means mud. Considerable clay in the road surface means it can be very slippery when wet.

Gas, food and lodging are found along the Alaska Highway on an average of every 20 to 50 miles. The longest stretch without services is about 100 miles. Not all businesses are open year-round, nor are most services available 24 hours a day. Regular, unleaded and diesel gasoline and propane fuel are available along the highway. Both government campgrounds and commercial campgrounds are located along the Alaska Highway.

588.1, where the 35th Engineer Combat Regiment working west from Fort Nelson met the 340th Engineer General Service Regiment working east from Whitehorse. The last link in the highway was completed on Nov. 20, 1942, when the 97th Engineer General Service Regiment, heading east from Tanacross, met the 18th Engineer Combat Regiment, coming northwest from Kluane Lake, at Milepost 1200.9. A ceremony commemorating the event was held at Soldiers Summit on Kluane Lake, and the first truck to negotiate the entire highway left that day from Soldiers Summit and arrived in Fairbanks the next day.

After World War II, the Alaska Highway was turned over to civilian contractors for widening and graveling, replacing log bridges with steel and rerouting at many points. Road improvements continue on the Alaska Highway today.

Preparation for Driving the Alaska Highway.

Make sure your vehicle and tires are in good condition before starting out. A widely available item to include is clear plastic headlight covers to protect your headlights from flying rocks and gravel.

You might also consider a wire-mesh screen across the front of your vehicle to protect paint, grill and radiator from flying rocks. These may be purchased ready-made, or you may manufacture your own.

For those hauling trailers, a piece of 1/4-inch plywood fitted over the front of your trailer offers protection from rocks and gravel.

You'll find well-stocked auto shops in the North, but may wish to carry the following for emergencies: flares; first-aid kit; mosquito repellent; trailer bearings; good bumper jack with lug wrench; a simple set of tools, such as hammer, screwdrivers, pliers, wire, crescent wrenches, socket and/ or open-end wrenches, pry bar; electrician's

tape; small assortment of nuts and bolts; fan belt; one or two spare tires (two spares for traveling any remote road); and any parts for your vehicle that might not be available along the way. Include an extra few gallons of gas and also water, especially for remote roads. You may also wish to carry a can of brake fluid, power steering fluid and automatic transmission fluid. You do not, however, want to overload your vehicle with too many spare parts.

Along the Alaska Highway, dust is at its worst during dry spells, following heavy rain (which disturbs the road surface) and in construction areas. If you encounter much dust, check your air filter frequently. To help keep dust out of your vehicle, try to keep air pressure in the car by closing all windows and turning on the fan. Filtered heating and air-conditioning ducts in a vehicle bring in much less dust than open windows or vents. Mosquito netting placed over the heater/fresh-air intake and flow-through ventilation will help eliminate dust.

Alcoholic Beverages

The legal age for possession, purchase and consumption of alcoholic beverages is 21 in Alaska. As of 1995, any person under the age of 21 found guilty of consuming alcohol as a minor can have his or her driver's license suspended for 90 days.

Any business that serves or distributes alcoholic beverages must be licensed by the state. The number of different types of licenses issued is limited by the population in a geographic area. Generally one license of each type may be issued for each 3,000 persons or fraction thereof. Licensed premises include bars, some restaurants and clubs. Packaged liquor, beer and wine are sold by licensed package stores. Licenses are renewed biennially.

Recreational site licenses, caterer's

55 years ago

The Alaska Canada Military Highway, dubbed the "Alcan," opened for military traffic in November 1942. Built in just over eight months, the highway spanned 1,400 miles of wilderness.

permits and special events permits allow the holder of a permit or license to sell at special events, and allow nonprofit fraternal, civic or patriotic organizations to serve beer and wine at certain activities.

State law allows liquor outlets to operate from 8 A.M. to 5 A.M., but provides that local governments can impose tighter restrictions.

Local governments may also ban the sale of, or otherwise restrict, alcoholic beverages. Bethel, Hughes, Huslia, Iliamna, Kotzebue, Nondalton, Port Alexander, Red Devil, St. Marys and Unalakleet have banned the sale of all alcoholic beverages.

The following communities have banned possession and/or the sale and importation of alcoholic beverages (knowingly bringing, sending or transporting alcoholic beverages into the community). Contact the ABC Board at (907) 277-8638 for more information. Or check http://www.revenue.state.ak.us/abc.htm

Akiak	Kiana
Alakanuk	Kipnuk
Allakaket	Kivalina
Ambler	Kobuk
Anaktuvuk Pass	Kokhanok
Angoon	Kongiganak
Atka	Kotlik
Atmautluak	Koyuk
Atqasuk	Kwethluk
Barrow	Kwigillingok
Birch Creek	Lower Kalskag
Brevig Mission	Manokotak
Buckland	Marshall (Fortuna)
Chalkyitsik	Mekoryuk
Chefornak	Minto
Chevak	Mountain Village
Deering	Napakiak
Diomede	Napaskiak
Eek	Newtok
Elim	Nightmute
Emmonak	Noatak
Gambell	Noorvik
Golovin	Nuiqsut
Goodnews Bay	Nunapitchuk
Grayling	Pilot Station
Hooper Bay	Platinum
Kaktovik	Point Hope
Kasigluk	Point Lay

Quinhagak	Stevens Village
Russian Mission	Tanacross
St. Marys	Tatitlek
St. Michael	Teller
Savoonga	Tetlin
Scammon Bay	Togiak
Selawik	Toksook Bay
Shageluk	Tuluksak
Shaktoolik	Tuntutuliak
Sheldon Point	Tununak
Shishmaref	Upper Kalskag
Shungnak	Wainwright
Stebbins	Wales

Alyeska
Pronounced Al-YES-ka, this Aleut word means "the great land" and was one of the original names of Alaska. Mount Alyeska, a 3,939-foot peak in the Chugach Mountains south of Anchorage, is the site of the state's largest ski resort.

Alyeska Tramway
The 60-passenger aerial tram at Alyeska Resort, completed in 1993, was designed to accommodate residents and visitors who had yet to enjoy the view of Turnagain Arm and Glacier Valley from the summit of Mount Alyeska.

Two tramcars take skiers and sightseers from the base of the mountain to the 2,300-foot level at a rate of about 26 miles per hour—about a 5-minute ride.

Designed by Von Roll Tramways, Inc., of Switzerland, the tramway took nearly two years to build. It is the shortest and steepest tramway in North America. The slope averages 25.55 degrees, although there are some areas at 38.17 degrees.

We asked a bookstore owner what Alaskans are most likely to read. She replied, "You mean other than *Playboy?*"

Amphibians

In Alaska, there are three species of salamander, two species of frog and one species of toad. In the salamander order, there are the rough-skinned newt, long-toed salamander and northwestern salamander. In the frog and toad order, there are the boreal toad, wood frog and spotted frog. The northern limit of each species may be the latitude at which the larvae fail to complete their development in one summer. While some species of salamander can overwinter as larvae in temperate southeastern Alaska, the shallow ponds of central Alaska freeze solid during the winter. All but the wood frog, *Rana sylvatica,* which with its shortened larval period is found widespread throughout the state and north of the Brooks Range, are found primarily in southeastern Alaska.

Anchorage (SEE ALSO REGIONS OF ALASKA)

Anchorage is located on a broad peninsula in Cook Inlet, defined by Knik Arm and Turnagain Arm, and bordered to the east by the Chugach Mountains. Anchorage and the Kenai Peninsula comprise the region Alaskans call "Southcentral," a region milder in climate than the Interior, with average temperatures of 15°F in January and 58°F in July, and an average snowfall of about 70 inches a year.

Name Game

Congress authorized a railroad to be built from the ocean port of Seward to Fairbanks in the Interior in 1914, and the anchorage at the mouth of Ship Creek was chosen as the construction camp and headquarters for the Alaskan Engineering Commission. The name Anchorage was confirmed by the federal government with the establishment of a postal office in 1915; it had earlier been variously called "Knik Anchorage," "Ship Creek" and "Woodrow." ✍

Anchorage's daylight has a daily maximum of 19 hours, 21 minutes in summer and reaches a minimum of 5 hours, 28 minutes in winter.

Anchorage's population was 1,856 in 1920, and remained at a few thousand until after World War II.

In 1994, Anchorage, Alaska's most populous city, broke the quarter million mark for the first time ever; in 1997 it is home to 254,000 people (about 42 percent of the state's population).

Anchorage suffered millions of dollars in damage in a devastating earthquake on March 27, 1964, originally measured at 8.6 on the Richter scale, but later upgraded to 9.2—the strongest ever recorded in North America. (*See also* Earthquakes)

Sometimes called the "Air Crossroads of the World," Anchorage is a major gateway for international travelers. Surrounded by dense spruce, birch and aspen forests, it is just a step away from the wilderness and multiple recreational opportunities. Anchorage also serves as a jump-off point for tourists— heading 200 miles north to visit Denali National Park

and Mount McKinley, North America's highest mountain; or south 52 miles to view Portage Glacier, one of the state's most-visited sights; or even to one of Alaska's bush locations for hunting, fishing, skiing, hiking, nature photography or sightseeing.

Although bear and moose may occasionally wander the city's highways and byways, Anchorage offers many of the attractions of any large metropolis, such as art galleries, museums, libraries, cultural diversity, music—including a symphony orchestra, opera and dance—and theaters big enough to stage productions by national touring companies. Anchorage has more than 200 churches and approximately 80 schools, including the University of Alaska Anchorage and Alaska Pacific University. Restaurants offer everything from fine dining and ethnic cuisine to fast food. Accommodations are offered at over 70 hotels, motels and approximately 100 bed-and-breakfasts.

Contact the Anchorage Convention and Visitors Bureau for a free visitor's guide, maps and additional information, 524 W. Fourth Ave., Anchorage 99501; phone (800) 478-1255; e-mail acvb@alaska.net; home page http://www.alaska.net/~acvb.

Antiquities Laws

(*SEE ALSO* NATIONAL HISTORIC PLACES) State and federal laws prohibit excavation or removal of historic and prehistoric cultural materials without a permit. Nearly all 50 states have historic preservation laws; Alaska's extends even to tidal lands, thereby making it illegal to pick up artifacts on the beach.

It sometimes is difficult to distinguish between historic sites and abandoned property. Old gold-mining towns and cabins, plus areas such as the Chilkoot and Iditarod Trails, should always be considered historic sites or private property. Also, cabins that appear to be abandoned may in fact be seasonally used trapping cabins where the structure and possessions are vital to the owner.

Alaska law prohibits the disturbance of fossils, including prehistoric animals such as mammoths.

Archaeology (*SEE ALSO*

BERING LAND BRIDGE) Alaska has a long and rich archaeological history. The first human migrants to North and South America some 40,000 to 15,000 years ago came first to Alaska, crossing over the now-submerged ice-age Bering Land Bridge that connected Siberia to Alaska.

Some of the oldest archaeological materials that demonstrate human occupation of Alaska come from Trail Creeks Cave north of Nome, where a 15,000-year-old cracked bison leg bone and bone point were found. Better evidence can be found for human occupation from 11,000 years ago. Small hunting tools have been found throughout Alaska, probably belonging to nomadic hunting and gathering peoples. The archaeological record

becomes more complicated about 4,000 years ago, when it reveals cultural patterns characteristic of Alaska Native groups still extant at the time of contact with the white man.

In 1993, the presence of what may be the oldest documented site of human habitation in North America was discovered. Called the Mesa Site, it is located about 150 miles north of the Arctic Circle in the foothills of the Brooks Range. The 11,700-year-old hunting site is perched atop a 200-foot mesa overlooking the surrounding plain. It was likely in use for 2,000 years as a hunters' lookout for prey such as caribou.

There is still much to discover about Alaska's prehistory. Many archaeological sites are small, representing the camps of wandering hunters and gatherers; some sites, especially along the coast where rich natural resources allowed people to become more sedentary and established, are large and deep. Where permafrost occurs, preservation of even the most perishable organic materials offers a wealth of information on life in the past. There are several thousand known archaeological sites in the state. One of the most famous is the 500-year-old Utkeaviq Site at Barrow, where the "frozen family" was unearthed from Mound 44 in the Birnirk archaeological site during 1982–83.

Archaeological excavations, or digs, are almost always confined to the summer months. The University of Alaska in both Fairbanks and Anchorage frequently sponsors digs, as do several state and federal agencies. Recent excavations have taken place near Unalaska, Tok, Kodiak, Fairbanks, Prince William Sound, Point Franklin and on the Kenai Peninsula.

Participants, who will be required to pay a fee, are invited to take part in a dig on Afognak. Inquire with the Afognak Native Corporation, Box 1277, Kodiak 99615; (800) 770-6014; e-mail dig@afognak.com.

At the Point Franklin dig near Wainwright, artifacts unearthed included a seal scratcher (used by a hunter to trick a seal at its breathing hole), 300-year-old mukluks and a 1,000-year-old spearhead.

Arctic Circle (SEE ALSO

DAYLIGHT HOURS) The Arctic Circle (see map, pages 8–9) is the latitude at which the sun does not set for one day at summer solstice and does not rise for one day at winter solstice. The latitude, which varies slightly from year to year, is approximately 66°34' north from the equator and circumscribes the northern frigid zone.

A solstice occurs when the sun is at its greatest distance from the celestial equator. On the day of summer solstice, June 20 or 21, the sun does not set at the Arctic Circle, and because of refraction of sunlight, it appears not to set for four days. Farther north, at Barrow (the northernmost community in the United States), the sun does not set from May 10 to August 2.

At winter solstice, December 21 or 22, the sun does not rise for one day at the Arctic Circle. At Barrow, it does not rise for 67 days.

Arctic Winter Games The Arctic Winter Games

are held every two years in mid-March for northern athletes from Alaska, northern Alberta, Greenland, Northwest Territories, Russia and Yukon Territory. The first games were held in 1970 in Yellowknife, Northwest Territories, and have since been held in Fairbanks and Whitehorse, Yukon Territory. The 1998 games will take place in March at Yellowknife.

In 1996, 1,100 athletes and 60 coaches from Alaska participated in the games. Competition includes alpine skiing, badminton, cross-country skiing, curling, dog mushing, figure skating, basketball, broomball, gymnastics, silhouette shooting, ski biathlon, snowshoeing, table tennis and volleyball. Cultural events and performances encourage participation by people of all ages.

Aurora Borealis

The Phenomenon. The aurora borealis (northern lights) is produced by charged electrons and protons striking gas particles in the earth's upper atmosphere. The electrons and protons are released through sunspot activity on the sun and emanate into space. A few drift the one- to two-day course to earth, where they are pulled to the most northern and southern latitudes by the planet's magnetic forces.

The color of the aurora borealis varies, depending on how hard the gas particles are being struck. Auroras can range from simple arcs to draperylike forms in green, red, blue and purple. The lights occur in a pattern rather than as a solid glow, because electric current sheets flowing through gases create V-shaped potential double layers. Electrons near the center of the current sheet move faster, hit the atmosphere harder and cause the different intensities of light observed in the aurora.

Displays take place as low as 40 miles above the Earth's surface, but usually begin about 68 miles above and extend hundreds of miles into space. They concentrate in two bands roughly centered above the Arctic Circle and Antarctic Circle (the latter known as aurora australis) that are about 2,500 miles in diameter. In northern latitudes the greatest occurrence of auroral displays is in the spring and fall months, owing to the tilt of the planet in relationship to the sun's plane, but displays may occur on dark nights throughout the winter.

If sunspot activity is particularly intense and the denser-than-usual solar wind heads to earth, the resulting auroras can be so great that they cover all but the tropical latitudes.

Some observers claim that the northern lights make a sound similar to the rustle of taffeta, but scientists say the displays cannot be heard in the audible frequency range.

Residents of Fairbanks, which is located on the 65th parallel, see the aurora borealis an average of 240 nights a year. The University of Alaska Fairbanks issues weekly aurora forecasts each winter.

Photographing the
Aurora Borealis. To capture the

northern lights on film, you will need a 35mm camera that has both adjustable f-stop and shutter speed, a sturdy tripod, a locking-type cable release (some 35mm cameras have both *time* and *bulb* settings, but most have *bulb only,* which calls for use of the locking-type cable release) and a camera with an f/3.5 lens (or faster).

f-stop	ASA 200	ASA 400
f1.2	3 sec.	2 sec.
f1.4	5	3
f1.8	7	4
f2	20	10
f2.8	40	20
f3.5	60	30

It is best to photograph the lights on a night when they are not moving too rapidly. And, as a general rule, photos improve if you manage to include recognizable subjects in the foreground—trees and lighted cabins being favorites of many photographers. Set your camera up at least 75 feet back from the foreground objects to make sure that both the foreground and aurora are in sharp focus.

Normal and wide-angle lenses are best. Try to keep your exposures under a minute—a 10- to 30-second exposure is generally best. The lens openings and exposure times are only a starting point, since the amount of light generated by the aurora is inconsistent. (For best results, bracket widely.)

Ektachrome 200 and 400 color film can be push-processed in the home darkroom or by most custom-color labs, allowing use of higher ASA ratings (800, 1200 or even 1600 on the 400 ASA film, for example). Kodak will push-process film if you include an ESP-1 envelope with your standard film-processing mailer. (Consult your local camera store for details.)

A few notes of caution: Protect the camera from low temperatures until you are ready to make your exposures. Some newer cameras, in particular, have electrically controlled shutters that will not function properly at low temperatures.

Three-hatch baidarka, *ca. 1909.* From Baidarka by George Dyson

Wind the film slowly to reduce the possibility of static electricity, which can lead to streaks on the film. Grounding the camera when rewinding can help prevent the static-electricity problem. (To ground the camera, hold it against a water pipe, drain pipe, metal fence post or other grounded object.) Follow the basic rules and experiment with exposures.

The first photographs to show the aurora borealis in its entirety were published in early 1982. These historic photographs were taken from satellite-mounted cameras specially adapted to filter unwanted light from the sunlit portion of the earth, which is a million times brighter than the aurora. From space, the aurora has the appearance of a nearly perfect circle.

Baidarka

The *baidarka* (also spelled bidarka or bidarkee), or Aleut kayak, is a portable decked boat made of skins (usually seal) stretched over wood frames. The *baidarka* (a Russian term for the skin boat) was widely used by Aleuts and Alaskan coastal Natives for transportation and hunting in areas associated with Russian influence. *Baidarkas* were the only form of kayak commonly built with three

A Coast Guard survey of Alaskan boating safety concluded that approximately 50 percent of all man-overboard accidents resulted from the victim trying to relieve himself over the side of the vessel.

hatchways, and generally had a forked bow, whereas most other kayaks did not.

Baleen (SEE ALSO BASKETS AND WHALES AND WHALING)

Baleen (often mistakenly called whale "bone") hangs from the upper jaw of baleen whales in long, fringed, bonelike strips. Baleen whales, such as humpback, bowhead, minke and gray, feed by taking in seawater and filtering small fish, plankton and the tiny, shrimp-like creatures called krill through the baleen. Baleen is made of keratin, a substance found in human fingernails. The outer edge of baleen is hard; the inside edges of the baleen plates form a fringe of coarse bristles that is similar in appearance to matted goat hair.

The number of plates along an adult humpback's jaw, the largest of the baleen whales, varies from 600 to 800 (300 to 400 per side); the roof of the mouth is empty of plates. The bowhead whale has 600 plates, some of which reach 14 feet or more in length. Baleen varies in thickness and texture. Baleen from humpback whales is coarse; sei whales have finely textured baleen.

Baleen was once used for corset stays, Venetian blinds, hairbrushes and buggy whips. It is no longer of significant commercial use, although Alaska Natives use brownish black bowhead baleen to craft fine baskets and model ships to sell.

Barabara

Pronounced buh-RAH-buh-ruh, this traditional Aleut or Eskimo dwelling is built of sod supported by driftwood or whale ribs.

Baranov, Alexander

Alexander Andreyevich Baranov (1747–1819), sometimes called "Lord of Alaska," was manager of the Russian American fur-trading company and the first governor of Russian Alaska.

A failed Siberian fur businessman, Baranov seemed an unlikely choice for overseeing the expansion of the Russian American empire when he arrived in Kodiak in 1790. But his aggressiveness and tough political skills proved indispensable. Within seven years, he had eliminated all competitors and secured the entire south Alaska coast, from the Aleutian Islands to Yakutat, for the Russian-American Company.

Learning to handle a *baidarka* and navigate a seagoing sloop, he established Fort St. Michael at remote Sitka Bay in 1799 and, in 1804, reestablished the post following its destruction by Tlingit warriors.

Baranov was a pragmatic ruler. He encouraged marriage between European men and Native women. The settlement's need for clerks and artisans led him to require basic schooling for all children. Lacking military support to exclude British and American ships from Alaskan waters, he cultivated cordial relations with foreign captains. By the time he retired in 1818, Russian influence in the North Pacific stretched from Siberia to Fort Ross in northern California.

Baranov died of fever aboard ship en route to St. Petersburg in 1819.

Barrow (SEE ALSO MUSEUMS)

Situated 350 miles north of the Arctic Circle, Barrow is the northernmost city in the United States and the largest Inupiat Eskimo community in the world.

Barrow was called Utqiagvik by its Inupiat founders. Because of its key location at the junction of the Chukchi and Beaufort Seas, Barrow became an important whaling site. The town remains today a center of subsistence whaling and harvesting of other land and water species.

More than 4,200 people live in this harsh, polar environment, unconnected to any other community by road. Within the 21-square-mile city limits, however, there are 28 miles of roadway covering three distinct areas of settlement: the traditional

Inupiat community of Barrow, the former Naval Arctic Research Laboratory and portions of the Distant Early Warning (DEW) Line station.

Barrow is the seat of government of the North Slope Borough, and serves as a regional center for the 89,000-square-mile borough. It is also the corporate headquarters for the Arctic Slope Regional Corporation and the Ukpeagvik Inupiat Corporation, which were established under the Alaska Native Claims Settlement Act.

Barrow has a strong and growing tourist industry. Visitors are attracted by everything from traditional whaling celebrations to polar bear watching, northern lights and the midnight sun. A monument across from the airport is dedicated to Will Rogers and Wiley Post, commemorating the 1935 airplane crash that happened 15 miles to the south of Barrow and killed the famous duo.

Baseball

Presently, there are six teams playing baseball in Alaska, making up two leagues. The Alaska Baseball League consists of the Fairbanks Goldpanners, Anchorage Bucs and Hawaiian Island Movers. The Alaska Central Baseball League includes the Anchorage Glacier Pilots, Kenai Peninsula Oilers and Mat–Su Miners. Baseball season opens in June and runs through the end of July. Each team plays a round-robin schedule with the other Alaska teams, in addition to scheduling games with visiting Lower 48 teams.

The Anchorage Bucs began playing during the 1981 season. They defeated Team USA in 1991, defeated the Moscow Red Devils in 1992 and won the Alaska League championship several times. In 1993, the Bucs were recognized as America's number-one summer collegiate team.

The Anchorage Glacier Pilots are entering their 28th year. This semi-pro team drafts talented collegiate athletes from all over the U.S. Over 80 former players have gone on to play in the major leagues. The Pilots consistently finish in the top seven at the annual NBC Championships in Wichita, Kansas.

The caliber of play in Alaska is some of the best nationwide at the amateur level. Major league scouts rate Alaska baseball at A to AA, visiting each season to check out the talent for possible recruitment.

The list of major league players who were once on Alaskan teams is impressive, and includes stars Tom Seaver, Chris Chambliss and Dave Winfield. Some 20 former Bucs now playing in the majors include Wally Joyner, Mike McFarlane, Bobby Jones and Jeff Kent.

Baskets (SEE ALSO BALEEN AND NATIVE ARTS AND CRAFTS)

Native basketry varies greatly according to materials locally available. Athabascan Indians of the Interior, for example, weave baskets from willow root gathered in late spring. The roots are steamed and heated over a fire to loosen the outer bark. Weavers then separate the material into fine strips by pulling the roots through their teeth.

Eskimo grass baskets are made in river delta areas of southwestern Alaska from Bristol Bay north to Norton Sound and from Nunivak Island east to interior Eskimo river villages. The weavers use very fine grass harvested in fall. A coil basketry technique is followed, using coils from $1/8$ to $3/4$ inch wide. Seal gut, traditionally dyed with berries (today with

Tlingit spruce-root basket. From Indian Baskets of the Pacific Northwest and Alaska by Allen Lobb, Art Wolfe and Barbara Paxson

commercial dyes), is often interwoven into the baskets.

Baleen, a glossy, hard material that extends in slats from the upper jaw of some types of whales, is also used for baskets. Baleen basketry originated about 1905 when Charles D. Brower, trader for a whaling company at Point Barrow, suggested, after the decline of the whalebone (baleen) industry for women's corsets, that local Eskimo men make the baskets as a source of income. The baskets were not produced in any number until 1916. The weave and shape of the baskets were copied from the split-willow Athabascan baskets acquired in trade. A decorative "knob" of ivory is often added. Later, baleen baskets were also made in Point Hope and Wainwright.

Most birch bark baskets are made by Athabascan Indians, although a few Eskimos also produce them. Commonly, they are shaped as simple cylinders, or canoe shapes, held together with spruce root lashings. Sometimes the birch bark is cut into thin strips and woven into diamond or checkerboard patterns. Birch bark is usually collected in spring and early summer; large pieces free of knots are preferred. Birch bark baskets traditionally were used as cooking vessels; food was placed in them and hot stones added. Birch bark baby carriers also are still made, chiefly for collectors.

Among the finest of Alaskan baskets are the tiny, intricately woven Aleut baskets made of rye grass, which in the Aleutians is abundant, pliable and very tough. The three main styles of Aleut baskets—Attu, Atka and Unalaska—are named after the islands where the styles originated. Although the small baskets are the best known, Aleuts also traditionally made large, coarsely woven baskets for utilitarian purposes.

Tlingit, Haida and Tsimshian Indians make baskets of spruce roots and cedar bark. South of Frederick Sound, basket material usually consists of strands split from the inner bark of red cedar. To the north of the sound, spruce roots are used. Maidenhair ferns are sometimes interwoven into spruce root baskets to form patterns resembling embroidery. A large spruce root basket may take months to complete.

Examples of Alaska Native basketry may be viewed in many museums within the state, including the University of Alaska Museum, Fairbanks; the Anchorage Museum of History and Art, Anchorage; the Sheldon Jackson Museum, Sitka; and the Alaska State Museum, Juneau.

Prices for Native baskets vary greatly. A fine-weave, coiled beach grass basket may cost from $100 to $500; birch bark baskets, which look like trays, may range from $35 to $125; willow root trays may cost $800; finely woven Aleut baskets may cost $200 to $800; cedar bark baskets may range from $30 to $80; and baleen baskets range in price from $600 to more than $2,200 for medium-sized baskets. These prices are approximate and are based on the weave, material used, size and decoration added, such as beads, embroidery or ivory.

Beadwork (SEE ALSO NATIVE ARTS AND CRAFTS) Eskimo and Indian

women create a variety of handsomely beaded items. Before contact with Europeans, Indian women sometimes carved beads of willow wood or made them from seeds of certain shrubs and trees. Glass seed beads became available to Alaskan Athabascan Indians in the mid-19th century, although some types of larger trade beads were in use earlier. Beads quickly became a coveted trade item. The *Cornaline d'aleppo*, an opaque red bead with a white center, and the faceted Russian blue beads were among the most popular types.

The introduction of small glass beads sparked changes in beadwork style and design. More colors were available, and the

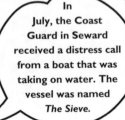

In July, the Coast Guard in Seward received a distress call from a boat that was taking on water. The vessel was named *The Sieve.*

smaller, more easily maneuvered beads made it possible to work out delicate floral patterns impossible with larger trade beads.

Historically, beads were sewn directly onto leather garments or other items with the overlay stitch. Contemporary beadwork is often done on a separate piece of felt that is not visible once the beads are stitched in place.

Alaskan Athabascan beadworkers sometimes use paper patterns, often combining several motifs and tracing their outline on the surface to be worked. The most common designs include flowers, leaves and berries, some in very stylized form. Many patterns are drawn simply from the sewer's environment. Since the gold rush, magazines, graphic art, advertising and patriotic motifs have inspired Athabascan beadworkers, although stylized floral designs are still the most popular.

Designs vary regionally, as do the ways in which they are applied to garments or footgear. Skilled practitioners execute beadwork so distinctive it can be recognized at a glance.

Bears (See also Mammals and McNeil River State Game Sanctuary)

Three species of bear inhabit Alaska: the black, the brown/grizzly and the polar bear. Most of Alaska can be considered bear country, and for those wishing to spend time in Alaska's great outdoors, bear country becomes "beware" country. Sows are extremely aggressive if their young are around, and bears will guard a moose kill against all passersby. Bear behavior should always be considered unpredictable at best. Bear scat or a large concentration of flies in one area are signs for hikers to watch for and retreat from. The Alaska Department of Fish and Game publishes *The Bears and You,* recommended reading for hikers and campers.

Black Bears. Black bears are usually jet black or brown with a brown-yellow muzzle, and weigh from 100 to 200 pounds as adults. The brown color phase can sometimes be confused with grizzlies, but black bears are generally smaller and lack the grizzly's distinct shoulder hump. Black bear

Brown/grizzly bears range throughout much of Alaska. From *Alaska's Accessible Wilderness* by Bill Sherwonit

habitat covers three-fourths of Alaska, with high concentrations found in Southeast, Prince William Sound and the coastal mountains and lowlands of southcentral Alaska. Low to moderate densities are found in interior and western Alaska. Their range coincides with that of semi-open forests, and though omnivorous, their diet consists mainly of vegetation due to the difficulty of getting meat or fish. Black bears often spend their lives within five miles of their birthplace and will frequently return to their home range if transplanted. They easily climb trees, with both cubs and adults using trees as a place of escape. Cubs are generally born in late January or February weighing 8 to 10 ounces, and while average litter size is two cubs, three or four is not unusual. Black bears den up in winter for up to six months, but are not true hibernators. Their body temperature remains high, and they awaken easily—even in midwinter.

Brown/Grizzly Bears. Fur colors of brown/grizzly bears vary from blond to black with shades of brown and gray in between. As adults, they can weigh over 1,000 pounds, but are usually smaller; size depends on sex, age, time of year and geographic location. Coastal bears, referred to as "browns" or "brownies," are the largest living omnivorous land mammals in the world and grow larger than Interior "grizzlies." Browns or grizzlies are found in most of Alaska, with the exception of islands in the extreme southeastern part of the state. The lowest populations are found in the northern Interior and the Arctic. Their range is wherever food is abundant, but they prefer open tundra and grasslands. Diet consists of a wide variety of plants and animals, including their own kind, and humans under some circumstances. In their realm, grizzlies are king and fear no other animal except man with a firearm. While attacks on humans are the exception, when they occur the results are tragic. These bears are also tremendously strong and have been seen carrying—off the ground— an 800-pound moose. One to two hairless cubs are usually born in late January or February weighing 8 to 10 ounces, and sows have been known to adopt orphaned cubs. Time of year and duration of denning varies with the location and physical condition of the bear, and can be up to six months of the year. Dens are frequently on hillsides or on mountain slopes.

Polar Bears. The only areas on a polar bear not covered with heavy, white fur are its eyes and large, black nose. The bear, seemingly aware that his nose gives him away to prey, will hold a paw up to hide it when hunting. An adult polar bear weighs 1,500 pounds or more and has a long neck with a proportionately small head. Their habitat is the Canadian–eastern Alaska

Arctic and the western Alaska Arctic–eastern Russia, the latter being home to the world's largest polar bears. Their range is the arctic ice cap, and they are more numerous toward the southern edge of the ice pack. Occasionally they will come ashore, but generally stay near the coast. While ashore they eat some vegetation, but their diet consists primarily of ringed seals, walrus, stranded whales, birds and fish. Cannibalism of cubs and young bears by older males is not unusual. Polar bears are strong swimmers, and reports exist of swimming bears seen 50 miles from the nearest land or ice. When swimming, they use their front paws for propulsion and trail their rear paws. Mother bears have been seen with a cub hanging onto their tail, towing it through the water. Cubs are born in December with two being the common litter size. They weigh about a pound at birth and remain with their mother for about 28 months. Usually only pregnant sows den up, for an average of six months in the winter. Polar bears need stable, cold areas for denning, and dens in Alaska have been found 30 miles inland, along the coast, on offshore islands, on shorefast ice and on drifting sea ice.

Bering, Vitus Vitus

Jonassen Bering (1681–1741) is credited as the first European to discover Alaska. A

Danish captain serving Russia under the crown of Peter the Great, Bering was in command of an expedition to find out if the continents of Asia and America were connected and to claim new lands for Russia.

He piloted his first expedition in 1728 through the strait that now bears his name, concluding that Asia and America were not joined. On that voyage, however, he never saw the fog-shrouded Alaska mainland. The expedition was considered a failure.

In June 1741, Bering set sail again as captain of the ill-fated *St. Peter*. Also on board was the German naturalist Georg Steller; biologists still refer to the Steller sea lion and Steller's jay as a consequence of his field work on the journey. A second ship piloted by Aleksei Chirikov accompanied the *St. Peter*.

During the voyage, Bering and Chirikov lost contact in foul weather, never to meet again. In July both ships sighted southern Alaska. On July 16, Steller led a landing party on what is now Kayak Island at Cape St. Elias, just east of Prince William Sound.

Short of food and weakened with scurvy, Bering was anxious to set sail for Kamchatka before winter. Against the advice of Steller, the explorer sailed for home. In heavy seas the *St. Peter* ran aground on a rocky island off the Siberian coast, since known as Bering Island. Twenty sailors, including Bering, died of scurvy. The remaining sailors survived by eating fish and seals, eventually built a boat from the wreckage of the *St. Peter* and returned to Russia.

Bering's voyage not only laid the basis for Russian claims to Alaska but also opened the fur trade. His crews brought back many pelts, among them 800 sea otter skins. By the late 1700s, the Russian fur trade had become the richest fur enterprise in the world, setting the stage for the extinction of Steller's sea cow by 1768 and the near-extinction of the sea otter in the 1820s.

Bering Land Bridge

The Bering Land Bridge, which joined eastern Siberia and western Alaska, is thought by most archaeologists to be the route by which man came to the New World between 40,000 and 15,000 years ago. The land bridge rose as the formation of massive glaciers during the ice ages caused the sea levels to fall, creating an arctic grassland up to 900 miles wide called Beringia. Early migrants probably crossed Beringia in pursuit of prey such as the woolly mammoth and mastodon. While the two continents were connected, plants, animals and man migrated into Alaska, and perhaps down ice-free corridors to populate other parts of the western hemisphere. Even after the glaciers melted and the sea level rose, many of the indigenous peoples on both sides of the Bering Strait remained united by family ties, common traditions and common environments, and until the Cold War used skin boats to cross the 55 miles of ocean separating the two continents, a practice that recently has been revived.

Recognizing the need to preserve the unique archaeological record, both discovered and undiscovered, that the area holds, the U.S. Congress created Bering Land Bridge National Preserve. The National Park Service manages the preserve. Straddling the Arctic Circle on the Seward Peninsula, the 2.5-million-acre preserve features ecological, geological, anthropological and historical processes rather than places. The low profile of the preserve's landscape gives a sense of unobstructed vastness and exposure to the elements.

Road access ends 400 miles from Bering Land Bridge National Preserve, but the information superhighway now leads right to it. The BLBNP's home page (http://www.nps.gov/bela) gives a detailed look at the region.

Berries
Wild berries abound in Alaska, with the circumboreal lingonberry/lowbush cranberry (*Vaccinium vitis-idaea*) being the most widespread. Blueberries of one species or another grow in most of the state. Some 50 other species of wild fruit are found in Alaska, including strawberries, raspberries, cloudberries, salmonberries, crowberries, nagoonberries and crab apples. Highbush cranberries (which are not really

cranberries) can be found on bushes even in the dead of winter, and the frozen berries provide a refreshing treat to the hiker.

The fruit of the wild rose, or rose hip, is not strictly a berry but is an ideal source of vitamin C for bush dweller and city resident alike. A few hips will provide as much of the vitamin as a medium-sized orange. The farther north the hips are found, the richer they are in vitamin C.

Lingonberry/ Lowbush Cranberry (*Vaccinium vitis-idae*). From *Alaska Wild Berry Guide and Cookbook*

Alaska does have one poisonous berry, the baneberry. Sometimes called doll's eyes or chinaberries, baneberries may be white or scarlet in color. As few as six berries can induce violent symptoms of poisoning in an adult.

Billiken

This smiling ivory figure with a pointed head, though long a popular Northland souvenir, is not an Eskimo invention. The billiken was patented in 1908 by Florence Pretz of Kansas City.

A small, seated, Buddha-like figure, the original billiken was manufactured by the Billiken Company of Chicago and sold as a good luck charm. Thousands of these figurines were sold during the 1909 Alaska-Yukon-Pacific Exposition in Seattle.

Billikens vanished soon afterward from most Lower 48 shops; however, someone had brought them to Nome, and the Eskimos of King Island, Little Diomede and Wales began carving ivory replicas of the billikens.

A popular notion contends that rubbing a billiken's tummy brings good fortune.

Birds

Authorities at the Anchorage Audubon Society acknowledge 430 bird species in Alaska. If unsubstantiated sightings are included, the species total increases.

Thousands of ducks, geese and swans wing north to breeding grounds each spring. Millions of seabirds congregate in nesting colonies on exposed cliffs along Alaska's coastline, particularly on the Aleutian Islands, and on islands in the Bering Sea.

Migratory birds reach Alaska from many corners of the world. Arctic terns travel up to 22,000 miles on their round trip each year from Antarctica. Others come from South America, Hawaii, the South Pacific islands and Asia.

Each May one of the world's largest concentrations of shorebirds funnels through the Copper River Delta near Cordova. Waterfowl such as trumpeter swans and the world's entire population of dusky Canada geese breed there.

Other key waterfowl habitats include the Yukon–Kuskokwim Delta, Yukon Flats, Innoko Flats and Minto Lakes. During migration, huge flocks gather at Egegik, Port Heiden, Port Moller, Izembek Bay, Chickaloon Flats, Susitna Flats and Stikine Flats.

Raptors, led by the bald eagle, range throughout the state. The largest gathering of eagles in the world takes place in Alaska every winter between October and February. In 1972, the Chilkat Bald Eagle Preserve was set aside to protect the 3,000 eagles that assemble at the site along the Chilkat River near Haines.

Alaska has three subspecies of peregrine falcon: arctic, American and Peale's. Arctic and American peregrine falcons join the Eskimo curlew, Aleutian Canada goose, spectacled eider and short-tailed albatross on the endangered or threatened species list for the state. The Steller's eider and the dusky Canada goose are now being considered for the endangered or threatened species list by the U.S. Fish and Wildlife Service.

Following is a list of some geographically restricted birds whose origins are in Siberia or Asia, as well as a few of the state's more well-known species:

Over 3,000 eagles may gather at the Chilkat River near Haines each fall to feed on salmon. From *Alaska's Birds* by Robert H. Armstrong

Aleutian Tern. Breeds in coastal areas, marshes, islands, lagoons, rivers and inshore marine waters. Nests only in Alaska on the ground in matted, dry grass. Casual sightings in southeastern Alaska in spring and summer, and in northern Alaska in summer.

Arctic Tern. Breeds in tidal flats, beaches, glacial moraines, rivers, lakes and marshes. Nests in colonies or scattered pairs on sand, gravel, moss or in rocks. The arctic tern winters in Antarctica, bypassing the Lower 48 in its 20,000-mile round-trip migration. Common sightings in southeastern, southcoastal and western Alaska in spring, summer and fall, and in southwestern Alaska in spring and fall.

Arctic Warbler. Found in willow thickets. Nests on the ground in grass or moss in willow thickets. Common sightings in the Alaska Range, the Seward Peninsula and the Brooks Range in spring, summer and fall.

Bald Eagle. Found in coniferous forests, deciduous woodlands, rivers and streams, beaches and tidal flats, rocky shores and reefs. Nests in old-growth timber along the coast and larger mainland rivers. In treeless areas, nests on cliffs or on the ground. There are more bald eagles in Alaska than in all the other states combined, and sightings commonly occur in southeastern, southcoastal and southwestern Alaska year-round.

Bluethroat. Nests on the ground in shrub thickets in the uplands and the foothills of western and northern Alaska.

Casual sightings in southwestern Alaska in spring and fall.

Emperor Goose. Nests near water in grassy marsh habitat on islands or banks or in large tussocks. The bulk of the world's population nests in the Yukon–Kuskokwim Delta, with a few others nesting farther north to Kotzebue Sound and a few more in eastern Siberia. Rarely is an emperor goose seen east or south of Kodiak. Common sightings in southwestern Alaska in spring, fall and winter, and in western Alaska in spring, summer and fall.

Horned Puffin. Nests on sea islands in rock crevices or in burrows among boulders, on sea cliffs and on grassy slopes. Breeds inshore, in marine waters and on islands. Common sightings in southwestern and western Alaska in spring, summer and fall.

Pacific Loon. Breeds in coniferous forests or in lakes on tundra, and nests on projecting points or small islands. Folklore credits the loon with magical powers, and several legends abound. Common sightings in southeastern and southcentral Alaska in spring, fall and winter, and in southwestern, central, western and northern Alaska in spring, summer and fall.

Red-faced Cormorant. Habitat includes inshore marine waters. Nests in colonies on ledges of sea cliffs, small piles of rocks and shelves on volcanic cinder cones. In North America this bird appears only in Alaska. Common sightings in southcoastal and southwestern Alaska year-round.

Arctic tern near the Mendenhall Glacier, Juneau.
From *Alaska's Birds* by Robert H. Armstrong

Red-legged Kittiwake. Breeds in the Pribilof Islands, and on Buldir and Bogoslof Islands in the Aleutians. Nests on cliff ledges and cliff points. Common sightings near breeding areas in southwestern Alaska in summer.

Whiskered Auklet. A small gray diving seabird with white whiskers. It nests only in the Aleutians, particularly at the eastern end of Unalaska Island and on nearby Baby Islands.

White Wagtail. Found in open areas with short vegetation usually along the Seward Peninsula coast. Nests near or on the ground in crevices or niches in old buildings. Casual sightings in central Alaska in spring, and in southwestern Alaska in spring and summer.

About 10 million swans, geese and ducks also nest in Alaska each year, making the state "critical" habitat for North America's waterfowl. In North America some species and subspecies use Alaska as their exclusive nesting grounds, while over half the North American population of other species nests in the state.

Five chapters of the National Audubon Society are based in Alaska: the Anchorage Audubon Society, Inc. (Alaska–Hawaii Regional Office, P.O. Box 101161, Anchorage 99510), the Juneau Audubon Society (P.O. Box 021725, Juneau 99802), the Arctic Audubon Society (P.O. Box 82098, Fairbanks 99708), the Kenai Audubon Society (P.O. Box 3371, Soldotna 99669) and the Kodiak Audubon Society (Box 1756, Kodiak 99615). In addition to trying to help people increase their knowledge of birds, the groups (except for Fairbanks) coordinate over 20 annual Christmas bird counts around the state. The Fairbanks Bird Club (P.O. Box 81791, Fairbanks 99708) conducts the annual Christmas count for that area.

Bird-watchers gather during the first week of May for the Copper River Delta Shorebird Festival in Cordova and the Kachemak Bay Shorebird Festival in Homer. Ketchikan holds an annual rufous hummingbird festival.

Blanket Toss
As effective as a trampoline, the blanket toss (or *nalukataq*) features a walrus hide blanket grasped by a number of people in a circle. They toss a person on the blanket as high as possible for as long as that person can remain upright. Every true Eskimo festival and many non-Native occasions include the blanket toss, which was originally used to allow Eskimo hunters to spot game, such as walrus and seal, in the distance. Depending on the skill of the person being tossed and the number of tossers, a medium-weight person might typically go 20 feet in the air.

Boating

(SEE ALSO CRUISES AND FERRIES) Travel by boat is an important means of transportation in Alaska, where highways cover only about one-third of the state. Until the advent of the airplane, boats were often the only way to reach many parts of Alaska. Most of Alaska's supplies still arrive by water, and in Southeast—where precipitous terrain and numerous islands make road building impossible—water travel is essential.

According to the U.S. Coast Guard, there are approximately 40,300 vessels registered in Alaska. Of these, 20,376 are between 16 and 26 feet, and 3,859 are between 26 and 40 feet.

Moorage. To accommodate the needs of this fleet, there are approximately 8,000 rental slips plus 2,000 transient slips available at public small-boat harbors in Alaska. According to the state, actual service capacity is somewhat greater because of the transient nature of many boats and certain management practices allowing "double parking." There are also harbors at various remote locations; no services other than moorage are provided at these harbors.

Local governments have the major responsibility for operating public floats, grids, docks, launching ramps and associated small-boat harbor facilities throughout the coastal areas of the state. Moorage facilities constructed by the state are intended for boats up to a maximum of 100 feet, with a limited number of facilities for larger vessels where large boats are common. With the exception of Ketchikan, Sitka and Juneau, there are no private marine facilities.

Recreational Boating. Alaska ranks 16th nationally in per capita ownership of recreational boats. Recreational boating opportunities in Alaska are too numerous

and varied to list here; Alaska has thousands of miles of lakes, rivers and sheltered seaways. For information about boating within national forests, parks, monuments, preserves and wildlife refuges, contact the appropriate federal agency. For travel by boat in southeastern Alaska's Inside Passage and the sheltered seaways of southcentral Alaska's Prince William Sound—or elsewhere in Alaska's coastal waters—NOAA nautical charts, pilot guides and tidal current tables are available. *(See Information Sources)*

Sea kayakers from around the world are drawn to Alaska to paddle its sheltered waterways and challenge its open coast. Kayakers in Alaska can visit tidewater glaciers and natural hot springs, meeting whales and sea otters along the way.

Inland boaters will find hundreds of river and lake systems suitable for traveling by boat, raft, kayak or canoe. Canoe routes have been established on the Kenai Peninsula (contact Kenai National Wildlife Refuge, P.O. Box 2139, Soldotna 99669); in Nancy Lake State Recreation Area (contact Superintendent, Mat–Su District, HC32, Box 6706, Wasilla 99687); and on rivers in the Fairbanks and Anchorage areas (contact Bureau of Land Management, 1150 University Ave., Fairbanks 99709, and 222 W. Seventh Ave., No. 13, Anchorage 99513).

Travel by water in Alaska requires extra caution. Weather changes rapidly and is often unpredictable; it's important to be prepared for the worst. Alaska waters, even in midsummer, are cold. A person falling overboard may

> Anchorage's mayor expanded the official annual "Scoop the Poop Day" to an official "Scoop the Poop Week" in 1997. Spokesperson Barbara Campbell said, "Twenty-two tons of dog poop per day is dropped in this town. And I don't think a lot of it is getting picked up."

become immobilized by the cold water in only a few minutes. And since many of Alaska's water routes are far from civilization, help may be a long way off.

Persons inexperienced in traveling Alaska's waterways might consider hiring a charter boat operator or outfitter. Guides offer local knowledge and provide all necessary equipment. The Division of Tourism (Box 110801, Juneau 99811) maintains current lists of such services. Recreation information on both state and federal lands is available at the three Alaska Public Lands Information Centers: 605 W. Fourth Ave., Suite 105, Anchorage 99501; 250 Cushman St., Suite 1A, Fairbanks 99701; and P.O. Box 359, Tok 99780.

Bore Tide (SEE ALSO TIDES) A
bore tide is a steep, foaming wall of water formed by a flood tide surging into a constricted inlet. In Cook Inlet, where maximum tidal range approaches 40 feet, incoming tides are further compressed in Knik and Turnagain Arms and tidal bores may sometimes be seen. Though 1- to 2-foot-high bores are more common, spring tides in Turnagain Arm may produce bore tides up to 6 feet high, running at speeds of up to 10 knots, and even higher bores have been reported when unusually high tides come in against a strong southeast wind. Good spots to view bore tides in Turnagain Arm are along the Seward Highway, between 26 and 37 miles south of Anchorage; they can be expected to arrive there approximately 2 hours and 15 minutes later than the tide book prediction for low tide at Anchorage.

Breakup (SEE ALSO NENANA
ICE CLASSIC) Breakup occurs when melting snows raise the level of ice-covered streams and rivers sufficiently to cause the ice to break apart and float downstream. Breakup  is one of two factors determining the open-water season for river navigation, the second being the depth of the river.

Peak water conditions occur just after breakup.

The navigable season for the Kuskokwim and Yukon Rivers is June 1 through September 30; the Nushagak River, June 1 through August 31; and the Noatak River, late May through mid-June.

Breakup is a spectacular sight-and-sound show. Massive pieces of ice crunch and pound against one another as they push their way downriver racing for the sea, creating noises not unlike many huge engines straining and grating. The spine-tingling sound can be heard for miles. It marks the finale of winter and the arrival of spring in Alaska.

Sometimes great ice jams occur, causing the water to back up and flood inhabited areas. This natural phenomenon occurred at Fort Yukon in spring 1982 and at McGrath in 1990.

Bunny Boots Bunny boots,
also called vapor barrier boots, are large, insulated rubber boots that protect feet from frostbite. Black bunny boots are generally rated to −20°F, while the more common white bunny boots are even warmer and have been used in the most extreme conditions, including the heights of Mount McKinley, even though they're cumbersome for climbing. They are no longer made but are still in demand. Used bunny boots cost at least $50 to $150.

Bus Lines Scheduled bus service
is available in summer to and within Alaska, although buses don't run as frequently as in the Lower 48. (Local transit service is also available in some major communities.) Services may be infrequent; consult current schedules.

Alaska Sightseeing/Cruise West, 513 W. Fourth Ave., Anchorage 99501. Provides service between Anchorage, Denali National Park and Preserve, Columbia Glacier, Fairbanks, Prince William Sound and Valdez.

Alaskon Express, 745 W. Fourth Ave., Anchorage 99501; (800) 780-6652. Provides service between Anchorage, Haines, Skagway and Whitehorse.

Denali Express/McKinley Tours, 405 L St., Anchorage 99501. Provides service between Anchorage and Denali.

Eagle Custom Tours, 329 F St., Anchorage 99501. Provides service between Anchorage, Portage Glacier, the Matanuska Valley, Denali Natonal Park and Preserve and the Kenai Peninsula on a charter basis only.

Gray Line of Alaska, 745 W. Fourth Ave., Anchorage 99501. Provides local city sightseeing tours, travel between Anchorage, Denali National Park, Fairbanks, Dawson, Prudhoe Bay, Skagway, Valdez, Ketchikan, Juneau and Whitehorse.

Princess Tours, 519 W. Fourth Ave., Anchorage 99501; (800) PRINCESS. Provides sightseeing excursions and tours throughout Alaska, as well as several hotels.

Seward Bus Lines, P.O. Box 1338, Seward 99664. Provides daily service between Anchorage, Cooper Landing and Seward.

Westours Motorcoaches, 547 W. Fourth Ave., Anchorage 99501. Provides service throughout Alaska and the Yukon.

White Pass and Yukon Motorcoaches, 300 Elliott Ave. W., Seattle, WA 98119. Provides service between Skagway, Haines, Valdez, Glennallen, Whitehorse and Anchorage.

Bush
Originally used to describe large expanses of wilderness beyond the fringes of civilization, inhabited only by trappers and prospectors, "bush" has come to stand for any part of Alaska not accessible by road. A community accessible only by air, water, sled or snow machine is considered a bush village, and anyone living there is someone from the bush.

The bush is home to most of Alaska's Native people and to many individuals who live on homesteads, operate mines or work as guides, pilots, teachers, trappers or fishermen.

The term "bush" is also applied to the small planes and their pilots who service areas lacking roads. Bush planes are commonly equipped with floats and skis to match terrain and season. For their oftentimes courageous air service, Alaskan bush pilots have become modern frontier heroes.

Cabin Fever
Cabin fever is a state of mind blamed on cold, dark, winter weather when people are often housebound. It is characterized by depression, preoccupation, discontent and occasionally violence and has been described as "a 12-foot stare in a 10-foot room."

Cabin fever is commonly thought to afflict miners and trappers spending a lonely winter in the wilderness, but, in truth, these people are active and outdoors enough to remain content. It is more likely to strike the snowbound, city dwellers who do not ski or mush dogs, or the disabled. The arrival of spring or a change of scene usually relieves the symptoms.

Cabins (SEE ALSO CAMPING; NATIONAL FORESTS; AND STATE PARK SYSTEM)
Rustic cabins in remote Alaskan places can be rented from the Forest Service, the Bureau of Land Management (BLM), the Alaska State Parks and the U.S. Fish and Wildlife Service. The modest price ($25 to $50 per night per cabin) makes this one of the best vacation bargains in Alaska. Visitors should prepare for rigorous backcountry travel and be ready to provide emergency shelter should they be unable to reach their cabin for any reason.

Almost 200 Forest Service cabins are scattered through the Tongass and Chugach National Forests in southeastern and south-central Alaska. Some are located on salt water, others on freshwater rivers, streams or lakes. Some of the cabins can be reached by boat or trail, but because of the remote locations, visitors frequently arrive by chartered aircraft.

The average cabin is 12 by 14 feet and is usually equipped with a table, an oil or

Mulcahy View Cabin in Shuyak Island State Park. From *Alaska's Accessible Wilderness* by Bill Sherwonit

wood stove and wooden bunks without mattresses. Most will accommodate a group of four to six. There is no electricity. Outhouses are down the trail a little way. Visitors need to bring their own food, bedding, cooking utensils and stove fuel. In addition, it's advisable to have a gas or propane stove for cooking, a lantern and insect repellent. Splitting mauls are provided on site for cutting firewood. Since firewood is scarce and often wet, visitors should carry a supply of dry wood. Reservations may be made in person or by mail. Payment must accompany the reservation. Permits for use are issued on a first-come, first-served basis, up to 179 days in advance. Length of stay for some cabins is limited.

For reservations and information on **Chugach National Forest** cabins, contact: Alaska Public Lands Information Center (APLIC), 605 W. Fourth Ave., Anchorage 99501; (907) 271-2737.

For reservations and information on **Tongass National Forest** cabins, contact: USDA Forest Service Information Center, 101 Egan Drive, Juneau 99801.

The **Forest Service** recommends that visitors contact the Information Center and request a copy of the *Recreation Cabins* booklet. It's a good idea to do this at least six months before the date of desired occupancy. The booklet contains the applications for cabin use plus tips on planning a stay.

The **Bureau of Land Management** has 11 public-use cabins in the White Mountains National Recreation area east of Fairbanks used primarily by winter recreationists (only three cabins are accessible during summer months). Cabins must be reserved prior to use and a fee is required. Contact the BLM Support Center, 1150 University Ave., Fairbanks 99709-3844; (907) 474-2350.

The **U.S. Fish and Wildlife Service** maintains public-use cabins within the Kodiak National Wildlife Refuge. Contact the Refuge Manager, 1390 Buskin River Road, Kodiak 99615.

Alaska State Parks maintains 38 public-use cabins throughout the state. For reservations and information contact the Department of Natural Resources Public Information Center, 3601 C St., Suite 200, Anchorage 99503-5929; (907) 269-8400; TDD (907) 269-8411; fax (907) 269-8901. Open 11 A.M. to 5 P.M. weekdays.

Cache
Pronounced "cash," this small storage unit is built to be inaccessible to marauding animals. A cache is basically a miniature log cabin mounted on stilts. It is reached by a ladder that bears, dogs, foxes and other hungry or curious animals can't climb. Extra precautions include wrapping tin around the poles to prevent climbing by clawed animals and extending the floor a few feet in all directions from the top of the poles to discourage those clever enough to get that high.

Squirrels are the most notorious of Alaska's cache-marauding critters. To be truly animal-proof, a cache should be built in a clearing well beyond the 30-foot leaping distance a squirrel

According to an Anchorage video rental spokesman, "Alaskan video rental customers aren't particularly known for their discriminating taste. If it's a choice between *King Pin* and *Sense and Sensibility*, there's no question which one they're gonna choose."

can manage to jump from a treetop.

Bush residents use the cache as a primitive food freezer for game and fish in winter. A cache may also store furs from a trapline, extra fuel and bedding. Size is determined by need. Sometimes a cache will be built between three or four straight trees growing close together.

Like "mush" (*marché*), the word "cache" is borrowed from French-Canadian voyageurs.

Calendar of Annual Events

January • **Anchorage**—All Alaska Juried Art Show; Hatcher Cup Series, Hatcher Pass Lodge; Nastar Ski Races, Alyeska; Russian New Year's Ball; Sled Dog Races; Folk Festival. **Anchor Point**—Snow Rondi Fest. **Bethel**—Sled Dog Races. **Fairbanks**—Ski Joring and Sled Dog Races. **Glennallen**—Copper Basin 300 Sled Dog Race. **Haines**—Dalton Trail 30 Sled Dog Race; Snow Machine Rally. **Homer**—Snow Machine Races. **Juneau**—Alascom Ski Challenge; Rainier Downhill Challenge Cup; state legislature convenes. **Kodiak**—Russian Orthodox Masquerade Ball; Russian Orthodox Starring Ceremony. **Seward**—Polar Bear Jump Festival. **Sitka**—Alaska Airlines Basketball Tournament; Russian Christmas and Starring. **Soldotna**—Sled Dog Races; Winter Games. **Unalaska**—Russian New Year's Masquerade. **Willow**—Winter Carnival.

February • **Anchorage**—Fur Rendezvous; Iron Dog Iditarod; Northern Lights Women's Invitational; Sled Dog Races; World Masters Cross Country Ski Championships. **Big Lake**—Winter Carnival. **Cordova**—Iceworm Festival. **Fairbanks**—Festival of Native Arts; Ski Joring; Yukon Quest Sled Dog Race. **Homer**—Winter Carnival. **Juneau**—Taku Rendezvous. **Ketchikan**—Festival of the North. **Knik**—Iditabike; Iditaski Nordic Ski Race. **Nenana**—Nenana Ice Classic; Tour de Minto Sled Dog Race. **Nome**—Dexter Creek Sled Dog Race; Gold Rush Classic Snow Machine Race; Heart Throb Biathlon. **Palmer**—Sled Dog Races. **Petersburg**—Devil's Thumb Days Festival. **Sitka**—Basketball Tournament. **Soldotna**—Ski Joring; Sled Dog Races; Winter Games. **Tok**—Sled Dog Races. **Valdez**—Ice Climbing Festival; Winter Carnival. **Wasilla**—Iditarod Days. **Wrangell**—Tent City Days.

March • **Anchorage**—Iditarod Trail Sled Dog Race begins; International Ice Carving Competition; Native Youth Olympics. **Chatanika**—Chatanika Days. **Dillingham**—Beaver Round Up. **Fairbanks**—Athabascan Old-Time Fiddling Festival; Festival of Native Arts; Ice Art Competition; Sled Dog Races; Winter Carnival. **Juneau**—Rainier Downhill Challenge Cup; Sourdough Pro/Am Ski Race; Southeast Championships. **Kodiak**—Comfish Alaska; Pillar Mountain Golf Classic. **Nome**—Miners and Mushers Ball; Basketball Tournament; Bering Sea Golf Classic; Month of Iditarod Sled Dog Races; Snow Machine Race. **North Pole**—Winter Carnival. **Skagway**—Buckwheat Ski Classic; Windfest Winter Festival. **Tok**—Race of Champions Sled Dog Race. **Valdez**—Winter Carnival. **Wasilla**—Iditarod Days.

(continued)

More Calendar of Annual Events

April • **Anchorage**—Alyeska Spring Carnival; Native Youth Olympics. **Barrow**—Spring Festival. **Cordova**—Copper River Shorebird Festival. **Craig/Klawock**—Salmon Derby. **Fairbanks**—International Curling Bonspiel. **Girdwood**—Alyeska Spring Carnival. **Haines**—Alaska State Community Theater Festival. **Juneau**—Folk Festival; Ski to Sea Race. **Kotzebue**—Arctic Circle Sunshine Festival. **Seward**—Gray Whale Watch Weekends. **Sutton**—Coal Miner's Ball. **Unalaska**—Tanner Crab Roundup Festival; Easter Egg Hunt. **Valdez**—World Extreme Ski Championships. **Whittier**—Crab Festival.

May • **Anchorage**—Saturday Market begins; Irish Music Festival. **Anchor Point**—Anchor River King Salmon Derby. **Delta Junction**—Buffalo Wallow Square Dance Jamboree. **Homer**—Center for Alaska Coastal Studies Beach Walk; Halibut Derby begins; Shorebird Festival. **Juneau**—Jazz and Classics Festival; Ski to Sea Relay Race. **Kodiak**—Chad Ogden Ultramarathon; Crab Festival and Fishing Derby. **Nome**—Annual Polar Bear Swim in the Bering Sea. **Palmer**—Colony Days. **Petersburg**—Little Norway Festival; Salmon Derby. **Savoonga**—Walrus Festival, St. Lawrence Island. **Seldovia**—Fishing Derby. **Seward**—Exit Glacier 5K and 10K runs. **Sitka**—Salmon Derby. **Skagway**—Centennial Ball. **Talkeetna**—Miners' Day Festival. **Valdez**—Prince William Sound Regatta of Ships; Halibut Derby begins.

June • **Anchorage**—Juneteenth; Family Kite Day; Mayor's Midnight Sun Marathon; Run for Women. **Barrow**—Nalukataq Whaling Festival. **Fairbanks**—Air Show; Midnight Sun Baseball Game; Midnight Sun Run; Northern Inua; Summer Folk Fest and Solstice Preview; Tanana River Raft Classic; Yukon 800 Marathon Boat Race. **Haines**—Cowboy Beauty Contest. **Homer**—Halibut Derby. **Juneau**—Pedal Plod and Paddle Triathlon. **Ketchikan**—Garden Tour. **Kodiak**—Freedom Days. **Nenana**—River Daze. **Nome**—ARCO–Jesse Owens Games; Midnight Sun Softball Tournament, Festival and Raft Race. **Palmer**—Colony Days. **Sitka**—Salmon Derby; Summer Music Festival; Writers' Symposium. **Skagway**—Summer Solstice. **Unalaska**—Dutch Harbor Remembrance Day. **Valdez**—Halibut Derby; Whitewater Weekend. **Whittier**—Three-Headed Fish Derby.

July • Fourth of July celebrations take place in most towns and villages. **Anchorage**—Bluegrass and Folk Festival; Canine Frisbee Festival. **Big Lake**—Fishing Derby; Regatta Water Festival. **Chugiak-Eagle River**—Bear Paw Festival. **Dawson City**—Yukon Gold Panning Championship. **Delta Junction**—Softball Tournament. **Fairbanks**—Golden Days; Renaissance Faire; Summer Arts Festival; World Eskimo-Indian Olympics. **Homer**—Halibut Derby. **Hope**—EMS 5-K Run and Crafts Bazaar. **Kodiak**—Bear Country Music Festival. **Kotzebue**—Northwest Native Trade Fair. **Naknek**—Fishtival. **Nome**—Anvil Mountain Run. **Seldovia**—Salmon Shuffle Run. **Seward**—Halibut Tournament; Mount Marathon Race; Silver Salmon Derby; Softball Tournaments. **Sitka**—Fourth of July Celebration (four days).

(continued)

More Calendar of Annual Events

July continued • **Skagway**—Soapy Smith's Wake. **Soldotna**—Progress Days. **Talkeetna**—Moose Dropping Festival; Salmon Derby. **Valdez**—Prince William Sound Music Festival. **Wasilla**—Water Festival. **Wrangell**—Logging Show.

August • **Anchorage**—Military Open House and Air Show; Governor's Picnic. **Anchor Point**—Salmon Derby. **Chena Hot Springs**—Northern Brewers Microfest. **Copper Valley**—Kenny Lake Fair. **Cordova**—Silver Salmon Derby. **Dillingham**—Silver Salmon Derby. **Eagle River**—Alaskan Scottish Highland Games. **Fairbanks**—Iditafoot Race; Summer Arts Festival; Tanana Valley Fair. **Haines**—Bald Eagle Music Festival; Southeast Alaska State Fair. **Juneau**—Golden North Salmon Derby. **Ketchikan**—Alaska Seafest; Blueberry Festival; Silver Salmon Derby. **Kodiak**—Pilgrimage to St. Herman's Monk's Lagoon; Rodeo and State Fair. **Ninilchik**—Kenai Peninsula State Fair. **Palmer**—Alaska State Fair. **Seward**—Silver Salmon Derby; Softball Tournament; Tok Run. **Skagway**—Dyea Dash. **Soldotna**—Silver Salmon Derby. **Talkeetna**—Bluegrass Festival. **Tanana**—Valley Fair. **Tok**—Mainstreet Alaska Sourdough Potlatch. **Unalaska**—Pink Salmon Derby. **Valdez**—Theater Conference Gold Rush Days. **Wrangell**—Coho Derby.

September • **Anchorage**—Oktoberfest; UAA Crafts Fair. **Cordova**—Salmon Derby. **Dillingham**—Fall Fair. **Fairbanks**—Equinox Marathon and Relay; **Homer**—Labor Day Seafood Festival. **Kenai**—Silver Salmon Derby. **Ketchikan**—Salmon Derby. **Kodiak**—Silver Salmon Derby; State Fair and Rodeo. **Nome**—Great Bathtub Race. **Petersburg**—Salmon Derby. **Seward**—Fall Classic 5K and 10K runs. **Skagway**—Klondike Trail of '98 Road Relay. **Tanana**—Rampart Labor Day Race. **Valdez**—Silver Salmon Derby. **Whittier**—Silver Salmon Derby. **Wrangell**—Silver Salmon Derby.

October • **Anchorage**—Alaska Federation of Natives Convention. **Fairbanks**—Oktoberfest. **Haines**—Alaska Day Fest. **Kodiak**—Oktoberfest. **Petersburg**—October Arts Festival. **Sitka**—Alaska Day Festival. **Unalaska**—Unalaska Pride Bulb Sale.

November • **Anchorage**—Alascattalo Parade; Great Alaska Shootout; Museum Crafts and Book Festival; Symphony of Trees. **Cordova**—Community Christmas Festival. **Delta Junction**—Winter Carnival. **Fairbanks**—Athabascan Fiddling Festival; Northern Invitational Curling Spiel; Sled Dog Races. **Haines**—Bald Eagle Festival. **Kenai**—Christmas Comes to Kenai Celebration. **Ketchikan**—Christmas Festival of Lights; Singing in the Rain Festival.

December • **Anchorage**—Alyeska New Year's Eve Extravaganza; Seawolf Hockey Classic; Swedish Christmas at Oscar Anderson House. **Barrow**—Christmas Festival. **Cordova**—North Country Faire. **Fairbanks**—The Nutcracker; Ski Joring and Sled Dog Races. **Ketchikan**—Festival of Lights Holiday Ball. **Kodiak**—Harbor Stars Boat Parade. **Nome**—Firemen's Carnival. **North Pole**—Candle Lighting Ceremony. **Palmer**—Colony Christmas. **Sitka**—Christmas Boat Parade. **Talkeetna**—Bachelor Society Ball and Wilderness Women Contest; Christmas Lighting. **Whittier**—Animals' Christmas. ✍

Camping (SEE ALSO CABINS; CHILKOOT TRAIL; HIKING; NATIONAL FORESTS; NATIONAL PARKS, PRESERVES AND MONUMENTS; NATIONAL WILDLIFE REFUGES; AND STATE PARK SYSTEM)

Numerous public and privately operated campgrounds are found along Alaska's highways. Electrical hookups and dump stations are scarce. The dump station at Russian River campground is available for Chugach National Forest visitors. Alaska's backcountry offers virtually limitless possibilities for wilderness camping. Get permission before camping on private land. If the land is publicly owned, it's worthwhile to contact the agency that manages the land regarding regulations and hiking/camping conditions.

The U.S. Forest Service maintains 26 campgrounds in the Tongass and Chugach National Forests, most with tent and trailer sites and minimum facilities. Most campgrounds are available on a first-come, first-served basis, and stays are limited to 14 days, except in Russian River campground, where the limit is three days during the salmon run. Campground fees are $8 to $16 per night depending upon facilities, which can include firegrates, pit toilets, garbage pickup, picnic tables and water. Most campgrounds are open from Memorial Day through Labor Day, weather permitting.

For further information about camping in the Chugach National Forest, contact Alaska Public Lands Information Center, 605 W. Fourth Ave., Suite 85, Anchorage 99501. For camping information for the Tongass National Forest, contact Forest Service Information Center, 101 Egan Drive, Juneau 99801.

The state's Division of Forestry requires burning permits for open burning in most areas of interior and southcentral Alaska. Permits are not required if fires are in approved burn barrels or are used for emergency signaling.

The National Park Service (Alaska Regional Office, 2525 Gambell St., Anchorage 99503) at Denali National Park and Preserve offers one walk-in campground, three campgrounds accessible by private vehicles and three campgrounds accessible only by shuttle bus.

Denali National Park has a reservation system for three campgrounds and all shuttle bus transportation services in the park. Reservations for 25 percent of the shuttle bus seats and 25 percent of the campsites in Riley Creek, Savage River and Teklanika River Campgrounds can be made by calling (907) 272-7275 or (800) 622-7275. The hours of operation for the reservation system are 8 A.M. to 6 P.M. Monday through Friday, and 9 A.M. TO 5 P.M. Saturday and Sunday (Alaska time). The remaining bus seats and campsites can be reserved in person up to two days in advance at the Denali Visitor Center, as in previous years.

The shuttle bus fee ranges from $12 (to Toklat) to $30 (to Kantishna). Payment can be made by MasterCard, VISA or American Express, and up to eight tickets may be reserved at a time.

Reservations for a majority of the shuttle bus seats and campsites in all campgrounds, including those in Sanctuary River, Igloo Creek and Wonder Lake, are available in advance by phone. The remaining bus seats and campsites will be available for reservation in person, up to two days in advance. It is no longer possible to obtain shuttle bus tickets or campsite reservations at the Alaska Public Lands Information Centers in Anchorage and Fairbanks.

Situated near the park entrance and open year-round are Riley Creek, for tents and trailers, and Morino, for walk-in tent campers. The other campgrounds are open between May and September, depending on weather. Brochures may be obtained from Denali National Park and Preserve, P.O. Box 9, Denali Park 99755. Reservations should be made well in advance by contacting Denali National Park at (907) 683-2215. The toll-free out-of-state number for bus and campground reservations is (800) 622-7275.

Glacier Bay and Katmai National Parks each offer one campground for walk-in campers, and Katmai now requires reservations. Backcountry camping is permitted in Denali, Glacier Bay, Katmai and Klondike Gold Rush National Parks, as well as other national parks and monuments.

Wood–Tikchik State Park's vast wilderness attracts kayakers, backpackers and anglers. From Alaska's Accessible Wilderness by Bill Sherwonit

Alaska State Parks (3601 C St., Suite 200, Anchorage 99503) maintains the most extensive system of roadside campgrounds and waysides in Alaska. All are available on a first-come, first-served basis. Fees are charged and a yearly pass is offered. Call (907) 269-8400, 11 A.M. to 5 P.M. Monday through Friday. Brochure available.

U.S. Fish and Wildlife Service (State Office, 1011 E. Tudor, Anchorage 99503) has several wildlife refuges open to campers, although most are not accessible by highway. The Kenai National Wildlife Refuge (P.O. Box 2139, Soldotna 99669) has several campgrounds accessible from the Sterling Highway linking Homer and Anchorage.

The Bureau of Land Management (222 W. Seventh Ave., No. 13, Anchorage 99513) maintains 11 campgrounds in interior Alaska. In 1994, BLM opened its first fully developed campground on the Dalton Highway at Mile 180 (5 miles north of Coldfoot). Fees vary by location. Brochures describing BLM campgrounds are available.

The **Alaska Public Lands Information Centers** provide information on all state and federal campgrounds in Alaska, along with state and national park passes and details on wilderness camping. Visit or contact one of the following centers: 605 W. Fourth Ave., Anchorage 99501, (907) 271-2737; P.O; Box 359, Tok 99780, (907) 883-5677; 250 Cushman, Suite 1A, Fairbanks 99701, (907) 451-7352. For a recording of state parks area conditions, call (907) 762-2278.

Private Campgrounds. For information, contact the Alaska Campground Owners Association, Box 84884, Fairbanks 99708; (907) 883-5877.

Chambers of Commerce (SEE ALSO CONVENTION AND VISITORS BUREAUS AND INFORMATION CENTERS) **Alaska State Chamber,** 217 Second St., Suite 201, Juneau 99801,

An Anchorage Safeway store advertised a Super Saver special on "Salad Bowels" for only $3.69 each!

(907) 586-2323; 415 E St., Suite 201, Anchorage 99501, (907) 278-2722.

Anchor Point Chamber, P.O. Box 610, Anchor Point 99556; (907) 235-2600.

Anchorage Chamber, 441 W. Fifth Ave., Suite 300, Anchorage 99501; (907) 272-2401.

City of Barrow, P.O. Box 629, Barrow 99723; (907) 852-5222.

Bethel Chamber, P.O. Box 329, Bethel 99559; (907) 543-2911.

Big Lake Chamber, P.O. Box 520067, Big Lake 99652; (907) 892-9230.

Chugiak–Eagle River Chamber, 11401 Old Glenn Highway, Eagle River 99577; (907) 694-4702.

Greater Copper Valley Chamber, P.O. Box 469, Glennallen 99588; (907) 822-5555.

Cordova Chamber, P.O. Box 99, Cordova 99574; (907) 424-7443.

Delta Chamber, P.O. Box 987, Delta Junction 99737; (907) 895-5068.

Dillingham Chamber, P.O. Box 348, Dillingham 99576; (907) 842-5115.

Greater Fairbanks Chamber, 709 Second Ave., Fairbanks 99701; (907) 452-1105 or (907) 456-5774.

Funny River Chamber, HC 1, Box 1424, Soldotna 99669; (907) 262-7711.

Haines Chamber, P.O. Box 1449, Haines 99827; (907) 766-2202.

Healy Chamber of Commerce, Box 437, Healy 99743; (907) 683-4636.

Homer Chamber, P.O. Box 541, Homer 99603; (907) 235-7740.

Greater Juneau Chamber, 124 W. Fifth St., Juneau 99801; (907) 586-6420.

Greater Kenai Chamber, 402 Overland, Kenai 99611; (907) 283-7989.

Greater Ketchikan Chamber, P.O. Box 5957, Ketchikan 99901; (800) 770-3300.

Kodiak Area Chamber, P.O. Box 1485, Kodiak 99615; (907) 486-5557.

56 years ago

In 1941, only 75,000 residents lived in all of the Alaska Territory, and only 100 airfields— all unpaved— served about 200 airplanes.

City of Kotzebue, P.O. Box 46, Kotzebue 99752; (907) 442-3401.

City of Nenana, P.O. Box 00070, Nenana 99760; (907) 832-5441.

Nome Chamber, P.O. Box 240, Nome 99762; (907) 443-3879.

North Peninsula Chamber, P.O. Box 8053, Nikiski 99635; (907) 776-8369.

North Pole Community Chamber, P.O. Box 55071, North Pole 99705; (907) 488-2242.

Greater Palmer Chamber, P.O. Box 45, Palmer 99645; (907) 745-2880.

Petersburg Chamber, P.O. Box 649, Petersburg 99833; (907) 772-3646.

Greater Prince of Wales Chamber, P.O. Box 497, Craig 99921; (907) 826-2353.

Seldovia Chamber, Drawer F, Seldovia 99663; (907) 234-7890.

Seward Chamber, P.O. Box 749, Seward 99664; (907) 224-3094.

Greater Sitka Chamber, P.O. Box 638, Sitka 99835; (907) 747-8604.

Skagway Chamber, P.O. Box 194, Skagway 99840; (907) 983-1898.

Soldotna Chamber, P.O. Box 236, Soldotna 99669; (907) 262-9814.

Sutton Chamber, P.O. Box 24, Sutton 99674; (907) 745-4527.

Talkeetna Chamber, P.O. Box 334, Talkeetna 99676; (907) 733-2330.

Tok Chamber, P.O. Box 389, Tok 99780; (907) 883-5887.

Unalaska/Port of Dutch Harbor Chamber, P.O. Box 833, Dutch Harbor 99692; (907) 581-4242.

Valdez Chamber, P.O. Box 512, Valdez 99686; (907) 835-2330.

Greater Wasilla Chamber, 1801 Parks Highway, #C18, Wasilla 99654; (907) 376-1299.

Wrangell Chamber, P.O. Box 49, Wrangell 99929; (907) 874-3901.

Cheechako Pronounced
chee-CHA-ko, or chee-CHA-ker by some

old-time Alaskans, the word means tenderfoot or greenhorn. According to *The Chinook Jargon,* a 1909 dictionary of the old trading language used by traders from the Hudson's Bay Company in the early 1800s, the word cheechako comes from combining the Chinook Indian word *chee,* meaning new, fresh or "just now," with the Nootka Indian word *chako,* which means to come, to approach or to become.

Chilkat Blanket

Dramatic, bilaterally symmetrical patterns, usually in black, white, yellow and blue, adorn these heavily fringed ceremonial blankets.

The origin of the Chilkat dancing blanket is Tsimshian. Knowledge of the weaving techniques apparently diffused north to the Tlingit, where blanket-making reached its highest form among the Chilkat group. Visiting traders coined the blanket's name during the late 19th century.

Time, technical skill and inherited privileges were required to weave Chilkat blankets and other ceremonial garments.

Woman in Chilkat blanket, circa 1900. From *The Alaska Heritage Seafood Cookbook* by Ann Chandonnet

High-ranking men and women wore the blankets as cloaks. Portions of worn blankets, or smaller weavings, were made into dance aprons and tunics.

Yarn for Chilkat dancing blankets was spun primarily from the wool of the mountain goat. The designs woven into Chilkat blankets consist of geometric totemic shapes that can be reproduced by the method known as twining. (Early blankets are unadorned or display geometric patterns lacking curvilinear elements.) Often, totemic crests on painted house posts and the designs woven into garments were quite similar. Female weavers reused pattern boards of wood painted with a design by men.

A few weavers are producing Chilkat blankets and the related Raven's Tail blankets today.

Chilkoot Trail (*SEE ALSO* GOLD *AND* SKAGWAY) The Chilkoot Trail, which spans 33 miles from Dyea, just north of Skagway, over Chilkoot Pass to Lake Bennett, British Columbia, was one of the established routes taken by would-be prospectors to Yukon Territory goldfields during the Klondike gold rush of 1897–98. Thousands of gold stampeders climbed the tortuous trail over Chilkoot Pass that winter. Those who reached Lake Bennett built boats to float down the Yukon River to Dawson City.

Today, the steep and rocky Chilkoot Trail is part of Klondike Gold Rush National Historical Park and is climbed each year by approximately 3,000 backpackers. The Chilkoot Trail begins about 5 miles from Skagway on Dyea Road. There are a dozen campgrounds along the trail and ranger stations on both the Alaska and British Columbia portions of the trail (the trail crosses the international border at 3,739-foot Chilkoot Pass, 16.5 miles from the trailhead). Highlights include Slide Cemetery near the remains of the town of Dyea at the start of the trail; the Golden Stairs, a 45-degree climb to the summit; and numerous relics, left by prospectors, still visible along the trail. The trail ends at Bennett, 8 miles from the nearest roadway.

For more information, contact Klondike Gold Rush National Historical Park, Box 517, Skagway 99840; (907) 983-2921.

Chill Factor

The wind's chill factor can lower the effective temperature many degrees. While Alaska's regions of lowest temperatures also generally have little wind, activities such as riding a snow-mobile or even walking can produce the same effect on exposed skin.

Temperature (Fahrenheit)	Wind Chill Temperature at Selected mph		
10	20	30	45
40	28	18	13	10
30	16	4	−2	−6
20	4	−10	−18	−22
10	−9	−25	−33	−38
0	−21	−39	−48	−54
−10	−33	−53	−63	−70
−20	−46	−67	−79	−85
−30	−58	−82	−94	−102
−40	−70	−96	−109	−117

The wind's chill factor, when severe, can lead to frostnip (the body's early-warning signal of potential damage from cold—a "nipping" feeling in the extremities), frostbite (formation of small ice crystals in the body tissues) or hypo-thermia (dangerous lowering of the body's core temperature). Other factors that combine with wind chill and bring on these potentially damaging or fatal effects are exposure to wetness, exhaustion and lack of adequate clothing.

Chitons

Chitons are oval-shaped marine mollusks with shells made up of eight overlapping plates. The gumboot and the Chinese slipper chiton are favorite Alaskan edible delicacies. The gumboot, named for the tough, leathery, reddish brown covering that hides its plates, is the largest chiton in the world. It is prized

as traditional food by southeastern Alaska Natives.

Climate (SEE ALSO WINDS)

Alaska's climate zones are maritime, transition, continental and arctic. With the exception of the transition zone along western Alaska, the zones are divided by mountain ranges that form barriers to shallow air masses and modify those deep enough to cross the ranges. The Brooks Range inhibits southward movement of air from the Arctic Ocean, thus separating the arctic climate zone from the Interior. The Chugach, Wrangell, Aleutian and Alaska mountain ranges often limit northward air movement and dry the air before it reaches the Interior's continental zone.

Other meteorologic/oceanographic factors affecting Alaska's climate zones are air temperature, water temperature, cloud coverage, and wind and air pressure. The amount of moisture that air can hold in a gaseous state is highly dependent on its temperature. Warm air can contain more water vapor than cold air. Therefore, pre-cipitation, as rain or snow or in other forms, is likely to be heavier from warm than from cold air. Water temperatures change more slowly and much less than land temperatures. For this reason, coastal area temperatures vary less than those farther inland.

Climate Zones. The maritime climate zone includes Southeast, the Northern Gulf Coast and the Aleutian Chain. Temperatures are mild—relatively warm in the winter and cool in summer. Precipitation is heavy, 50 to 200 inches annually along the coast and up to 400 inches on mountain slopes. Storms are frequently from the west and southwest, resulting in strong winds along the Aleutian Islands and the Alaska Peninsula. Amchitka Island's weather station has recorded some of the windiest weather in the state, followed by Cold Bay. Frequent storms with accompanying high winds account for rough seas with occasional waves to 50 feet in the Gulf of Alaska, particularly in fall and winter.

The transition zone is, in effect, two separate zones. One is the area between the coastal mountains and the Alaska Range, which includes Anchorage and the Matanuska Valley. Summer temperatures are higher than those of the maritime climate zone, with colder winter temperatures and less precipitation. Temperatures, however, are not as extreme as in the continental zone.

Another transition zone includes the west coast from Bristol Bay to Point Hope. This area has cool summer temperatures that are somewhat colder than those of the maritime zone, and cold winter temperatures similar to the continental zone. Cold winter temperatures are partly due to the sea ice in the Chukchi and Bering Seas.

The continental climate zone covers the majority of Alaska except the coastal fringes and the Arctic Slope. It has extreme temperatures and low precipitation. There are fewer clouds in the continental zone than elsewhere, so there is more warming by the sun during the long days of summer and more cooling during the long nights of winter. Precipitation is light because air masses affecting the area lose most of their moisture crossing the mountains to the south.

The Arctic, north of the Brooks Range, has cold winters, cool summers and desert-like precipitation. Prevailing winds are from the northeast off the arctic ice pack, which never moves far offshore. Summers are generally cloudy and winters are clear and cold. The cold air allows little precipitation and inhibits evaporation. Because continuous permafrost prevents the percolation of water into the soil, the area is generally marshy with numerous lakes. (*See also* Permafrost)

The chart on pages 46–47 shows normal average monthly temperatures and precipitation for 14 communities in Alaska. Included are annual temperatures and precipitation and mean seasonal snowfall. The chart is based on data from NOAA and the Alaska state climatologist.

Climate Records. Highest temperature: 100°F, at Fort Yukon, June 27, 1915.

Lowest temperature: –80°F, at Prospect Creek Camp, Jan. 23, 1971.

Most precipitation in one year: 332.29 inches, at MacLeod Harbor (Montague Island), 1976.

Most monthly precipitation: 70.99 inches at MacLeod Harbor, November 1976.

Most precipitation in 24 hours: 15.2 inches, in Angoon, Oct. 12, 1982.

Least precipitation in a year: 1.61 inches, at Barrow, 1935.

Most snowfall in a season: 974.5 inches, at Thompson Pass, 1952–53.

Most monthly snowfall: 297.9 inches, at Thompson Pass, February 1953.

Most snowfall in 24 hours: 62 inches, at Thompson Pass, December 1955.

Least snowfall in a season: 3 inches, at Barrow, 1935–36.

Highest recorded snow pack (also highest ever recorded in North America): 356 inches on Wolverine Glacier, Kenai Peninsula, after the winter of 1976–77.

Highest recorded wind speed: 139 mph, at Shemya Island, December 1959.

Coal (*See also* Minerals and

Mining) About half of the coal resource of the United States is believed to lie in Alaska. The demonstrated coal reserve base of the state is over 6 billion short tons, identified coal resources are about 160 billion short tons, and hypothetical and speculative resource estimates range upward to 6 trillion short tons. The regions containing the most coal are northwestern Alaska, Cook Inlet–Susitna Lowland and the Nenana Trend. Geologists estimate that

(Continued on page 48)

Alaska magazine reported that "Real Alaskans know the ideal time to till your garden, plant the seeds, and harvest the vegetables falls on the same day."

Average Temperatures (Fahrenheit) and Precipitation (Inches)

	ANCHORAGE	BARROW	BETHEL	COLD BAY	FAIRBANKS	HOMER	JUNEAU
January							
Temperature	14.9	−13.4	6.7	28.6	−10.1	22.7	24.2
Precipitation	0.80	0.20	0.81	2.71	0.55	2.23	3.98
February							
Temperature	18.7	−17.8	6.0	27.4	−3.6	24.7	28.4
Precipitation	0.86	0.18	0.71	2.30	0.41	1.78	3.66
March							
Temperature	25.7	−15.1	13.3	29.9	11.0	28.0	32.7
Precipitation	0.65	0.15	0.80	2.19	0.37	1.57	3.24
April							
Temperature	35.8	−2.2	23.6	33.3	30.7	35.4	39.7
Precipitation	0.63	0.20	0.65	1.90	0.28	1.27	2.83
May							
Temperature	46.6	19.3	39.9	39.6	48.6	42.8	47.0
Precipitation	0.63	0.16	0.83	2.40	0.57	1.07	3.46
June							
Temperature	54.4	34.0	50.5	45.7	59.8	49.3	53.0
Precipitation	1.02	0.36	1.29	2.13	1.29	1.00	3.02
July							
Temperature	58.4	39.3	55.0	50.5	62.5	53.4	56.0
Precipitation	1.96	0.87	2.18	2.50	1.84	1.63	4.09
August							
Temperature	56.3	37.9	52.9	51.5	56.8	53.3	55.0
Precipitation	2.31	0.97	3.65	3.71	1.82	2.56	5.10
September							
Temperature	48.4	30.5	45.2	47.7	46.5	47.6	49.4
Precipitation	2.51	0.64	2.58	4.06	1.02	2.96	6.25
October							
Temperature	36.6	13.5	29.4	39.6	25.1	37.5	42.2
Precipitation	1.86	0.51	1.48	4.45	0.81	3.41	7.64
November							
Temperature	21.2	−1.7	16.8	34.4	2.7	28.6	33.0
Precipitation	1.08	0.27	0.98	4.33	0.67	2.74	5.13
December							
Temperature	16.3	−11.2	8.5	31.0	−6.5	24.3	27.1
Precipitation	1.06	0.17	0.95	3.16	0.73	2.71	4.48
Annual							
Temperature	35.9	9.4	29.0	38.3	26.9	37.4	40.6
Precipitation	15.37	4.67	16.90	35.84	10.37	24.93	52.86
Mean Seasonal Snowfall (inches)	69.0	28.0	47.0	62.0	68.0	58.0	100.0

Average Temperatures and Precipitation (continued)

KETCHIKAN	KING SALMON	KODIAK	McGRATH	NOME	PETERSBURG	VALDEZ	
33.9	14.9	29.9	–8.7	7.0	27.6	20.5	**January** Temperature
14.01	1.11	9.52	0.81	0.88	9.31	5.63	Precipitation
38.9	14.8	30.5	–2.6	3.9	31.1	24.1	**February** Temperature
12.36	0.82	5.67	0.74	0.56	7.85	5.08	Precipitation
38.9	22.4	32.9	10.2	8.6	34.7	29.2	**March** Temperature
12.22	1.06	5.16	0.75	0.63	7.19	4.06	Precipitation
42.8	30.2	37.5	26.5	17.6	40.4	37.1	**April** Temperature
11.93	1.07	4.47	0.73	0.67	6.94	2.89	Precipitation
48.6	42.4	43.5	44.5	35.6	47.2	45.2	**May** Temperature
9.06	1.25	6.65	0.84	0.58	5.92	2.74	Precipitation
54.0	50.0	49.6	55.3	45.9	53.0	51.8	**June** Temperature
7.36	1.54	5.72	1.56	1.14	5.00	2.64	Precipitation
58.0	54.7	54.4	58.7	51.5	55.8	54.9	**July** Temperature
7.80	2.10	3.80	2.16	2.18	5.36	3.77	Precipitation
58.4	53.9	55.2	54.3	50.2	55.0	53.5	**August** Temperature
10.60	2.96	4.03	2.87	3.20	7.57	5.73	Precipitation
53.6	47.2	50.0	44.2	42.5	50.3	47.2	**September** Temperature
13.61	2.75	7.18	2.19	2.59	11.15	7.99	Precipitation
46.3	32.4	40.7	24.7	28.0	43.5	38.1	**October** Temperature
22.55	1.98	7.85	1.24	1.38	16.83	8.23	Precipitation
39.0	22.0	34.4	4.4	15.9	35.6	27.4	**November** Temperature
17.90	1.45	6.89	1.18	1.02	11.99	6.09	Precipitation
35.4	15.9	30.8	–6.0	7.3	30.5	22.9	**December** Temperature
15.82	1.19	7.39	1.12	0.82	10.66	6.65	Precipitation
45.5	33.5	40.8	25.5	26.2	42.1	37.7	**Annual** Temperature
155.22	19.28	74.33	16.18	15.64	105.77	61.50	Precipitation
37.0	46.0	80.0	93.0	56.0	102.0	320.0	Mean Seasonal Snowfall (inches)

(Continued from page 45)

perhaps 80 percent of Alaska's coal underlies the 23-million-acre National Petroleum
Reserve on the North Slope. Although the
majority of the coals are of bituminous and
subbituminous ranks, anthracite coal does
occur in the Bering River and Matanuska
fields. In addition to the vast resource base
and wide distribution, the important selling
points for Alaska coal are its extremely low
sulfur content and access to the coast for
shipping.

Exploration, technology and economics
will ultimately determine the marketability
of Alaska's coal resources. Large-scale exploration programs have been conducted in
most of Alaska's coalfields by private industry and state and federal governments. New
coal developments such as Dimond Chuitna
on the Beluga reserves west of Anchorage on
Cook Inlet are seeking new markets for their
coal. Wishbone Hill Mine near Palmer is
expected to produce 1 million metric tons
of clean coal per year. Production continues
in the Nenana coalfield. The Arctic Slope
Regional Corporation is working to develop
its coal reserves in northwestern Alaska.

Alaska's production of coal in 1996 was
1.5 million short tons and came exclusively
from the Usibelli Coal Mine near Healy. Of
that amount, one-half was burned in interior Alaska power plants, and the remainder
was shipped to Korea.

Conk
Alaskans apply this term to
a type of bracket
fungus. The platelike
conks grow on dead
trees. When dry and
hard, conks are
snapped off and used
to paint on.

Constitution of Alaska
One of the most remark-
able achievements in the long battle for
Alaskan statehood was the creation of the
constitution of the state of Alaska in the
mid-1950s. Statehood supporters believed
that creation of a constitution would
demonstrate Alaska's maturity and

readiness for statehood, so in 1955 the
territorial legislature appropriated $300,000
for the cost of holding a Constitutional
Convention in Fairbanks.

For 73 days in 1955–56, a total of
55 elected delegates from all across the
territory of Alaska met in the new Student
Union Building (now called Constitution
Hall) on the University of Alaska campus.
William A. Egan, a territorial legislator and
former mayor of Valdez, who later became
the first governor of the state of Alaska, was
president of the convention. Under his
leadership, the disparate group of Alaskans
hammered out a document that is considered a model for a state constitution.

The National Municipal League calls the
brief 14,000-word document drafted by the
convention delegates "one of the best, if not
the best, state constitutions ever written."
By an overwhelming margin the people of
Alaska approved the new constitution at
the polls in 1956, paving the way for the
creation of the 49th state in 1959.

Continental Divide
(*SEE ALSO* MOUNTAINS) The Continental
Divide extends into Alaska. Unlike its
portions in the Lower 48, which divide the
country into east-west watersheds, the
Continental Divide in Alaska trends
through the Brooks Range, separating
watersheds that drain north into the
Arctic Ocean and west and south into the
Bering Sea.

According to *Alaska Science Nuggets*,
geologists used to regard the Brooks Range
as a structural extension of the Rocky
Mountains. Recent thinking, however,
assumes the range to be 35 million to
200 million years older than the Rockies.
The Alaska Range is comparatively young,
only about 5 million years old.

Convention and Visitors Bureaus and Information Centers
Anchorage Convention
and Visitors Bureau, 524 W. Fourth Ave.,
Anchorage 99501; (907) 276-4118.

Home page: http://www.alaska.net/~acvb; e-mail acvb@alaska.net.

Begich–Boggs Visitors Center, P.O. Box 129, Girdwood 99587; (907) 783-2326.

Bethel Visitor Center, P.O. Box 388, Bethel 99559; (907) 543-2798.

Big Lake Visitor Information Center, P.O. Box 520067, Big Lake 99652; (907) 892-9030.

Greater Copper Valley Visitor Information Center, P.O. Box 469, Glennallen 99588; (907) 822-5555.

Cordova Visitors Center, P.O. Box 391, Cordova 99574; (907) 424-7443.

Delta Junction Visitor Information Center, P.O. Box 987, Delta Junction 99737; (907) 895-5068.

Fairbanks Convention and Visitors Bureau, 550 First Ave., Fairbanks 99701; (907) 451-1724 or (800) 327-5774.

Haines Visitor Information Center, City of Haines, P.O. Box 518, Haines 99827; (907) 766-2234.

Homer Chamber of Commerce, Box 541, Homer 99603-0541; (907) 235-7740.

Juneau Convention and Visitors Bureau, 76 Egan Drive, Suite 300, Juneau 99801-1753; (907) 586-1737.

Kachemak Bay Convention and Visitors Association, Box 1001, Homer 99603-1001; (907) 235-8897.

Kenai Visitor Information Center, P.O. Box 1991, Kenai 99611-6935; (907) 283-1991 or (800) 535-3624; e-mail kptmc@alaska.net.

Ketchikan Convention and Visitors Bureau, 131 Front St., Ketchikan 99901; (907) 225-6166.

Kodiak Island Convention and Visitors Bureau, 100 Marine Way, Kodiak 99615; (907) 486-6545.

Nome Convention and Visitors Bureau, P.O. Box 240, Nome 99762; (907) 443-5535.

Petersburg Visitor Information, P.O. Box 649, Petersburg 99833; (907) 772-4636.

Seward Visitor Information Cache, P.O. Box 749, Seward 99664; (907) 224-8051.

Sitka Convention and Visitors Bureau, P.O. Box 1226, Sitka 99835; (907) 747-5940.

Skagway Convention and Visitors Bureau, P.O. Box 415, Skagway 99840; (907) 983-2854.

Tok Visitor Center, P.O. Box 389, Tok 99780; (907) 883-5775.

Unalaska/Port of Dutch Harbor Convention and Visitors Bureau, Box 545, Unalaska 99685; (907) 581-2612.

Valdez Convention and Visitors Bureau, P. O. Box 1603, Valdez 99686; (907) 835-4636 or (800) 770-5954.

Wrangell Convention and Visitors Bureau, P.O. Box 1078, Wrangell 99929; (907) 874-3800.

Cook, Captain James

James Cook (1728–79) went to sea as an apprenticed seaman, entering the British Royal Navy at the age of 27. He rose in rank by merit and was sent on two scientific expeditions—the first to the South Pacific (1768–71) and the second to Antarctica (1772–75).

In July 1776, the British Admiralty instructed Captain Cook to proceed to the northwest coast of North America and attempt to find the Northwest Passage—a hoped-for sea link from the Pacific to the Atlantic.

The *Resolution* and *Discovery* sailed from Plymouth via Cape of Good Hope, New Zealand, Tahiti and the Hawaiian Islands, arriving at Nootka Sound on Vancouver Island on March 30, 1778. From then until October 3,

The Anchorage Convention and Visitors Bureau reports that a business executive would not discuss having his convention in Alaska because "our bylaws say we have to meet in the United States."

Cook cruised northward and westward along the coast to the Arctic Ocean, sketching the chief features of this coast, practically unknown to Europeans before this historic voyage. He named many features of the coast, including Turnagain Arm, where land blocked his ships and they were forced to "turn again."

Failing to find the Northwest Passage, Captain Cook left Unalaska in the Aleutians on October 27. Cook returned to Hawaii, the Big Island, where he was killed by local residents on Feb. 14, 1779. His accounts of the voyage were published in 1784–85 in three volumes and a large atlas.

This pioneering navigator and explorer is commemorated in Alaska by Cook Inlet (named by Vancouver for his predecessor) and Mount Cook. A statue of Cook stands in Anchorage, facing the Knik Arm of Cook Inlet.

Coppers (SEE ALSO POTLATCH)

Coppers (*tinnehs*) are beaten copper plaques that were important symbols of wealth among the Pacific Northwest Coast Natives.

Coppers are shaped something like a keyhole or a shield, are usually 2 or 3 feet long and weigh approximately 40 pounds. Coppers varied in value from tribe to tribe.

Early coppers were made of ore from the Copper River area, although western traders quickly made sheet copper available. Some scholars believe that Tlingit craftsmen shaped placer copper into the desired form themselves, while others maintain that coppers were forged by Athabascans. The impressive plaques were engraved or carved in relief with totemic crests.

The value of coppers increased as they were traded or sold, and their transfer implied that a potlatch would be given by the new owner. Coppers were given names, such as "Cloud," "Point of Island" or "Killer Whale," and were spoken of in respectful terms. They were thought of as powerful, and their histories were as well known as those of the noblest families.

Coppers were often broken and destroyed during public displays and distribution of wealth. Some parts of the

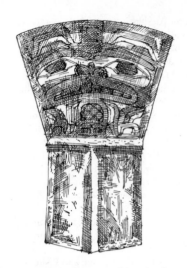

Coppers, symbols of Native wealth and rank, were shield-shaped copper plaques weighing up to 40 pounds. From *The Great Alaska Nature Factbook* by Susan Ewing

coppers were valued nearly as much as the whole.

To this day, certain coppers that were part of museum collections for years are still valued highly by some tribes, and are displayed as symbols of wealth and prestige during marriage ceremonies and potlatches.

Cost of Living (SEE ALSO INCOME)

How expensive is it to live in Alaska? Has the cost of living in Alaska increased? The answers to these questions depend on the cost of living measurements used. According to the Alaska Department of Labor's Research and Analysis section, the Consumer Price Index (CPI) best reflects how prices have changed in a particular place. For comparative pricing, cost-of-living measurements such as American Chamber of Commerce Researchers Association's (ACCRA, see page 51) reflect cost differences among several cities.

The urban/rural cost differential in food studies shows an interesting contrast between Alaska and other areas of the U.S. Other surveys show that in the Lower 48 large urban areas tend to have higher food costs than less populated areas. The opposite is true in Alaska. The cost of food and other basics such as fuel is higher in rural communities than in the state's urban centers like Anchorage, Juneau, Fairbanks and Ketchikan. The highest food costs are found in isolated communities supplied primarily by air.

Alaska's sheer size, lack of a comprehensive road network and distance from the contiguous 48 states make personal and business transportation costly. Air travel, which may be a luxury for residents in other states, becomes a necessity for Alaskans living in places such as Barrow, Nome or Dillingham. A typical living cost for these residents usually includes the high cost of transportation just to leave town.

Likewise, shipping goods as well as providing services and medical care to more remote areas in Alaska is expensive, especially when there is little or no competition to keep prices down. And because agriculture and industry in Alaska is limited, most food, construction materials and consumption items are shipped in from Outside, adding to their cost.

Food. In a December 1996 Cost of Food study conducted by the University of Alaska Cooperative Extension Study, the U.S. Department of Agriculture and SEA Grant, food prices fluctuated greatly among cities and towns within the state. Prices on the average were less expensive in the larger cities, such as Anchorage, and very expensive in bush communities. Food costs for the more isolated communities of Bethel and St. George can range between 147 percent and 220 percent more than Anchorage. For example, a week's worth of groceries for a family of four (with elementary school-children) in December 1996 cost $98.05 in Anchorage, $144.14 in Bethel and $215.79 in St. George.

Housing. Though housing costs are considered high in Alaska, other states nationwide reflect comparable prices.

Gasoline. The average cost for one gallon of unleaded gasoline (from a third quarter 1996 survey

by American Chamber of Commerce Researchers Association (ACCRA) was: Juneau, $1.44; Anchorage, $1.34; Fairbanks, $1.41; Kodiak, $1.69.

Taxes. Sample city and borough taxes (compiled in 1992) were: Juneau, 4 percent sales; Anchorage, none; Fairbanks, none; Nome, 4 percent sales; Dillingham, 5 percent sales; Wrangell, 7 percent sales. There is no state income tax in Alaska.

Larger communities such as Anchorage, Cordova and Haines may impose property taxes. Special taxes are issued in some communities, for example: 10 percent tobacco and 8 percent hotel/motel taxes in Anchorage; 2 percent tax on raw fish in the Aleutians East Borough; and 1 percent salmon tax in Yakutat.

Personal income. The cost of living in Alaska is high, and so is personal income. In 1996, the annual per capita personal income for Alaska was $24,513, which positioned Alaska as the tenth highest in the nation in income standings.

For more information, contact the Alaska Department of Labor, Research and Analysis section, P.O. Box 21149, Juneau 99802-1149.

Courts
The Alaska court system operates at four levels: the supreme court, court of appeals, superior court and district court. The Alaska judiciary is funded by the state and administered by the supreme court.

The five-member supreme court, established by the Alaska Constitution in 1959, has final appellate jurisdiction of all actions and proceedings in lower courts. It sits monthly in Anchorage and Fairbanks, quarterly in Juneau and occasionally in other court locations.

The three-member court of appeals was established in 1980 to relieve the supreme court of some of its ever-increasing caseload. The supreme court retained its ultimate authority in all cases, but concentrated its attention on civil appellate matters, giving authority in criminal and quasi-criminal matters to the court of appeals. The court of appeals has appellate jurisdiction in certain superior court proceedings and jurisdiction to review district court decisions. It meets regularly in Anchorage and travels occasionally to other locations.

The superior court is the trial court with original jurisdiction in all civil and criminal matters and appellate jurisdiction over all matters appealed from the district court. The superior court has exclusive jurisdiction in probate and in cases concerning minors. There are 32 superior court judges.

The district court has jurisdiction over misdemeanor violations and violations of ordinances of political subdivisions. In civil matters, the district court may hear cases for recovery of money, damages or specific personal property if the amount does not exceed $50,000. The district court may also inquire into the cause and manner of death, as well as issue marriage licenses, summonses, writs of habeas corpus, and search and arrest warrants. District court criminal decisions may be appealed directly to the court of appeals or the superior court. There are 17 district court judges.

Administration of the superior and district courts is divided by region into four judicial districts: First Judicial District, Southeast; Second Judicial District, Nome-Kotzebue; Third Judicial District, Anchorage-Kodiak-Kenai; and Fourth Judicial District, Fairbanks.

District magistrates serve rural areas and help ease the workload of district courts in  metropolitan areas. In criminal matters, magistrates may enter judgment of conviction upon a plea of guilty to any state misdemeanor and may try state misdemeanor cases if the defendant waives his right to a district court judge. Magistrates may also hear municipal ordinance violations and state traffic infractions without the consent of the accused. In civil matters, magistrates may hear cases for recovery of money, damages or specific personal property if the amount does not exceed $5,000.

Selection of Justices, Judges and Magistrates.

Supreme court justices and judges of the court of appeals, superior court and district court are appointed by the governor from candidates submitted by the Alaska Judicial Council. All justices and judges must be citizens of the United States and have been residents of Alaska for at least five years. A justice must be licensed to practice law in Alaska at the time of appointment and have engaged in active law practice for eight years. A court of appeals judge must be a state resident for five years immediately preceding appointment, have been engaged in the active practice of law not less than eight years immediately preceding appointment and be licensed to practice law in Alaska. Qualifications of a superior court judge are the same as for supreme court justices, except that only five years of active practice are necessary. A district court judge must be 21 years of age, a resident for at least five years, and (1) be licensed to practice law in Alaska and have engaged in active practice of law for not less than three years immediately preceding appointment, or (2) have served for at least seven years as a magistrate in the state and have graduated from an accredited law school.

The chief justice of the supreme court is selected by majority vote of the justices, serves a three-year term and cannot succeed him- or herself.

Each supreme court justice and each judge of the court of appeals is subject to approval or rejection by a majority of the voters of the state on a nonpartisan ballot at the first general election held more than three years after appointment. Thereafter, each justice must participate in a retention election every 10 years. A court of appeals judge must participate every eight years.

Superior court judges are subject to approval or rejection by voters of their judicial district at the first general election held more than three years after appointment. Thereafter, it is every sixth year. District court judges must run for retention in their judicial districts in the first general election held more than two years after appointment and every fourth year thereafter.

District magistrates are appointed for an indefinite period by the presiding superior court judge of the judicial district in which they will serve.

Alaska State Supreme Court, 1959–1996: Justices and Tenure.

Harry O. Arend, 1960–1965
George F. Boney, 1968–1972
Chief Justice, 1970–1972
Robert Boochever, 1972–1980
Chief Justice, 1975–1978
Alexander Bryner, 1997–
Edmond W. Burke, 1975–1996
Chief Justice, 1981–1984
Allen T. Compton, 1980–
Chief Justice, 1996–1997
Roger G. Connor, 1968–1983
John H. Dimond, 1959–1971
Robert L. Eastaugh, 1994–
Robert C. Erwin, 1970–1977
Ms. Dana Fabe, 1996–
James M. Fitzgerald, 1972–1975
Walter H. Hodge, 1959–1960
Warren W. Matthews, 1977–
Chief Justice, 1987–1990
Daniel A. Moore, Jr., 1983–1996
Chief Justice, 1992–1996
Buell A. Nesbett, 1959–1970
Chief Justice, 1959–1970
Jay A. Rabinowitz, 1965–1977
Chief Justice, 1972–1975; 1978–1981;
1984–1987; 1990–1992

Alaska State Court of Appeals, 1980–1996: Judges and Tenure.

Alexander O. Bryner, 1980–1997
Chief Judge, 1980–1997
Robert G. Coats, 1980–
Chief Judge, 1997–
David Mannheimer, 1990–
James K. Singleton, Jr., 1980–1990

Cruises (*See also* Boating and Ferries)

There are many opportunities for cruising Alaska waters, aboard either charter boats, scheduled boat excursions or luxury cruise ships.

Charter boats are readily available in southeastern and southcentral Alaska. Charter boat trips range from daylong fishing and sightseeing trips to overnight and longer customized trips or package tours. There is a wide range of charter boats, from simple fishing boats to sailboats, yachts and mini-class cruise ships.

In summer, scheduled boat excursions— from day trips to overnight cruises—are available at the following locations: Ketchikan (Misty Fiords); Sitka (harbor and area tours); Bartlett Cove and Gustavus (Glacier Bay); Juneau (Lynn Canal); Valdez and Whittier (Columbia Glacier, Prince William Sound); Seward (Resurrection Bay, Kenai Fjords); Homer (Kachemak Bay); and Fairbanks (Chena and Tanana Rivers).

For details and additional information on charter boat operators and scheduled boat excursions, contact the Alaska Division of Tourism, P.O. Box 110801, Juneau 99811.

From May through September, 16 cruise lines carry visitors to Alaska via the Inside Passage. Cruise lines include Carnival, Radisson Diamond and World Explorer. For the phone numbers of the companies, contact Cruise Lines International, (212) 921-0066 There's also a bewildering array of travel options. Both round-trip and one-way cruises are available, or a cruise may be sold as part of a packaged tour that includes air, rail and/or motorcoach transportation. (*See* Bus Lines)

Prices vary. A 7- to 11-day Inside Passage cruise costs $1,839 to $4,189. Booking by February 14 can yield substantial savings.

Because of the wide variety of cruise trip options, it is wise to work with a travel agent.

Following is a partial list of cruise ships serving Alaska in the 1997–98 season:

Alaska Sightseeing/Cruise West, Suite 700, Fourth & Battery Building, Seattle, WA 98121; (206) 441-8687. *Sheltered Seas*

(90 passengers); 5- or 6-day daylight cruise between Ketchikan and Juneau. *Spirit of Glacier Bay* (58 passengers); 4- or 5-day cruise between Juneau and Glacier Bay. *Spirit of Alaska* (84 passengers), *Spirit of Discovery* (82 passengers) and *Spirit of '98* (101 passengers); 7-night cruises between Seattle and Juneau. A 10-night adventure cruise is available on three ships. Alaska Sightseeing also offers an all-Alaska adventure cruise on the *Spirit of Alaska,* Ketchikan to Juneau, 7 nights.

Clipper Cruise Lines, 7711 Bonhomme Ave., St. Louis, MO 63105-1965; (314) 727-2929. *Yorktown Clipper* (138 passengers); 7-day round-trip cruise between Juneau and Ketchikan, and a 14-day cruise from Juneau to Seattle.

Cunard/NAC Lines, 555 Fifth Ave., New York, NY 10017; (212) 880-7500. *Sagafjord* (618 passengers); 11-day cruise between Vancouver, British Columbia, and Anchorage. *Crown Dynasty;* 7-day cruise between Vancouver and Seward. *Sea Goddess;* 7-day cruises between Vancouver, British Columbia, and Anchorage.

Holland America Westours Inc., 300 Elliott Ave. W., Seattle, WA 98119; (800) 426-0327. MS *Nieuw Amsterdam* (1,214 passengers), MS *Noordam* (1,214 passengers), SS *Rotterdam* (1,114 passengers), MS *Ryndam* (1,266 passengers) and the *Westerdam*; 3-, 4- and 7-night round-trip cruises from Vancouver, British Columbia.

Norwegian Cruise Line, 2 Alhambra Plaza, Coral Gables, FL 33134; (800) 327-7030. *Royal Odyssey* (775 passengers)

and *Windward* (1,246 passengers); 7-day cruises between Vancouver, British Columbia, and Anchorage and 10-day cruises from San Francisco to Skagway.

Princess Cruises, 2815 Second Ave., Suite 400, Seattle, WA 98121; (206) 728-4202 or (800) PRINCESS. *Dawn Princess* (2,000 passengers); *Sun Princess* (2,000 passengers); *Golden Princess* (620 passengers); 7-day round-trip Inside Passage cruises between Vancouver, British Columbia, and Seward. *Fair Princess* (620 passengers); 12-day round-trip Inside Passage cruises from San Francisco. *Regal Princess* and *Crown Princess* (1,590 passengers); 7-day cruises between Vancouver, British Columbia, and Anchorage. *Sky Princess* (1,200 passengers) and *Star Princess* (1,500 passengers); 7-day round-trip Inside Passage cruise from Vancouver, British Columbia.

Regency Cruises, 260 Madison Ave., New York, NY 10016; (212) 972-4499. MV *Regent Sea* (729 passengers), *Regent Star* (706 passengers) and *Regent Sun* (836 passengers); 7 days between Vancouver, British Columbia, and Whittier.

Royal Caribbean International, 903 South America Way, Miami, FL 33132; (800) 791-RCCL. *Sun Viking* (726 passengers); 7 days between Vancouver, British Columbia, and Skagway.

Special Expeditions, 720 Fifth Ave., New York, NY 10019. *Sea Bird* (70 passengers) and *Sea Lion* (70 passengers); 11-day wilderness cruises between Prince Rupert, British Columbia, and Sitka.

World Explorer Cruises, 555 Montgomery St., San Francisco, CA 94111; (800) 854-3835. *Universe Explorer* (739 passengers); 7- and 14-day round-trip cruises between Vancouver, British Columbia, and Seward.

In 1996 an FDA regulation prohibited a Washington state company from claiming that tap water drawn directly from Sitka's water utility was "pure glacier water." The company responded by saying, "If we have to put in that it's just regular municipal supply water—regular drinking water—then we lose the entire niche already."

Dalton Highway

(*SEE ALSO* HIGH-WAYS) The 414-mile-long Dalton Highway begins at Milepost 73.1

on the Elliott Highway. Call (907) 456-ROAD for road and weather conditions.

This all-weather gravel road bridges the Yukon River, crosses the Arctic Circle at Mile 115.3, and climbs the Brooks Range. At Atigun Pass (Mile 246.8) it crosses a continental divide, the highest highway pass in

Alaska. Then the road passes through tundra plains before reaching the Prudhoe Bay oil fields at Deadhorse on the coast of the Arctic Ocean. Public travel for the final 8 miles may be restricted.

The highway was named for James Dalton, a post–World War II explorer who played a large role in the development of North Slope oil and gas industries. It was built as a haul road for supplies and to provide access to the northern half of the 800-mile trans-Alaska oil pipeline during construction. Originally called the North Slope Haul Road, it is still often referred to as the "Haul Road."

The Dalton Highway is open to all vehicles, but is not maintained. Services are limited to Yukon Ventures (Mile 56) and Coldfoot Services (Mile 175). Proceed with caution.

Daylight Hours (SEE ALSO ARCTIC CIRCLE)

Maximum (at Summer Solstice, June 20 or 21)

	Sunrise	Sunset	Hours of Daylight
Adak	6:27 A.M.	11:10 P.M.	16:43 hrs
Anchorage	3:21 A.M.	10:42 P.M.	19:21 hrs
Barrow	May 10	Aug. 2	84 days continuous
Fairbanks	1:59 A.M.	11:48 P.M.	21:49 hrs
Juneau	3:51 A.M.	10:09 P.M.	18:18 hrs
Ketchikan	4:04 A.M.	9:33 P.M.	17:29 hrs

Minimum (at Winter Solstice, December 21 or 22)

	Sunrise	Sunset	Hours of Daylight
Adak	10:52 A.M.	6:38 P.M.	7:46 hrs
Anchorage	10:14 A.M.	3:42 P.M.	5:28 hrs
Barrow	*	*	0:00 hrs
Fairbanks	10:59 A.M.	2:41 P.M.	3:42 hrs
Juneau	9:46 A.M.	4:07 P.M.	6:21 hrs
Ketchikan	9:12 A.M.	4:18 P.M.	7:06 hrs

*From November 18 through January 24—a period of 67 days—there is no daylight in Barrow.

Diamond Willow
Fungi, particularly *Valsa sordida Nitschke*, are generally thought to be the cause of diamond-shaped patterns in the wood grain of some willow trees. There are 33 varieties of willow in Alaska, at least five of which can develop diamonds. They are found throughout the state, but are most plentiful in river valleys. Diamond willow, stripped of bark, is used to make lamps, walking sticks and novelty items.

Dog Mushing (SEE ALSO IDITAROD TRAIL SLED DOG RACE AND YUKON QUEST INTERNATIONAL SLED DOG RACE)
In many areas of the state where snow machines had nearly replaced the working dog team, the sled dog has returned, due in part to a rekindled appreciation of the reliability of nonmechanical transportation. In addition to working and racing dog teams, many people keep two to 10 sled dogs for recreational mushing.

Sled dog racing is Alaska's official state sport. Races ranging from local club meets to world championships are held throughout the winter.

Championship speed races are usually run over two or three days, with the cumulative time for the heats deciding the winner. Distances for the heats vary from about 12 to 30 miles. The size of dog teams also varies, with mushers using anywhere from seven to 20 dogs in their teams. Since racers are not allowed to replace dogs in the team, most finish with fewer than they started with (attrition may be caused by anything from tender feet to sore muscles).

Sprint mushing is divided into limited and open classes. Limited class ranges from three to 10 dogs and from 3 to 12 miles per day. Open class racing has no limit on the number of dogs and ranges from 10 to 30 miles a day.

Long-distance racing (the Yukon Quest, the Iditarod) pits racers not only against one another, but also against the elements. Sheer survival can quickly take precedence over winning when a winter storm catches a dog team in an exposed area. Stories abound of racers giving up their chance to finish "in the money" to help out a fellow musher who has gotten into trouble. Besides the weather, long-distance racers also have to contend with moose attacks on the dogs, sudden illness, straying off the trail and sheer exhaustion. With these and other challenges to overcome, those who finish

have truly persevered against the odds.

Purses range from trophies only to a peak of $45,000 for the largest sprint purse at the Open World Championship Sled Dog Race. A purse is split between the finishers. The richest purse in sled dog racing is the Iditarod. In the last couple of years, due to the controversy over humane treatment of dogs in races, several significant sponsors withdrew from support of the sport, reducing the size of the purses. The Iditarod purse, for example, was $350,000 in 1995, but $300,000 in 1996. For information about dog mushing, call the Alaska Dog Mushers Association in Fairbanks, (907) 457-6874 or e-mail *Mushing Magazine* at mushing@polarnet.com.

See statistics below for two of the biggest championship races. Other major races around the state follow on page 57.

Open World Championship Sled Dog Race, Anchorage

Scheduled during Fur Rendezvous in February. Best elapsed time in three heats over three days, 25 miles each day. Purse is split among the top 15 finishers. Winners of the previous 10 years are:

| | Elapsed Time (minutes:seconds) | | | | |
	Day 1	Day 2	Day 3	Total	Purse
1988 Charlie Champaine	103:53	92:00	89:33	285:26	$30,000
1989 Roxy Wright-Champaine	87:30	90:32	89:22	266.84	50,000
1990 Charlie Champaine	89:00	96:13	94:01	279:14	50,000
1991 Charlie Champaine	89:10	94:49	95:43	279:42	70,000
1992 Roxy Wright-Champaine	87:30	89:35	92:22	269:42	70,000
1993 Roxy Wright-Champaine	87:44	90:45	93:21	271:50	75,000
1994 Ross Saunderson	86:26	90:24	*	176:50	50,000
1995 Ross Saunderson	84:19	88:57	85:07	258:23	45,000
1996 Cancelled due to lack of snow					
1997 Axel Gasser	95:47	99:09	102:03	296:59	45,000

*Trail conditions shortened race to two heats.
Source: Alaska Sled Dog and Racing Association

Open North American Sled Dog Race Championship, Fairbanks

Held in March. Best elapsed time in three heats over three days; 20 miles on Days I and 2; 28 miles on Day 3.* Purse is split among the top 15 finishers. Winners of the previous 10 years are:

		Elapsed Time (minutes:seconds)			
	Day I	Day 2	Day 3	Total	Purse
1988 Marvin Kokrine	63:52	66:16	95:42	225:49	$30,000
1989 Roxy Wright-Champaine	62:10	62:42	92:07	216:59	44,000
1990 Charlie Champaine	62:47	67:38	95:40	226:05	45,000
1991 Ross Saunderson	60:12	63:53	97:44	221:50	46,000
1992 Roxy Wright-Champaine	66:17	65:59	94:29	226:46	52,000
1993 Roxy Wright-Champaine	64:48	64:06	95:36	224:31	58,000
1994 Ross Saunderson	**	63:16	91:12	154:28	49,000
1995 Amy Streeper	61:42	65:29	94:48	221:59	46,940
1996 Amy Streeper	68:58	63:17	90:29	222:45	32,500
1997 Neil Johnson	64:06	64:53	94:25	223:24	22,500

*Times have been rounded off.
**Time not counted because locked gate delayed the first three mushers.

Clark Memorial Sled Dog Race, Soldotna to Hope, 100 miles. Held in January.

Copper Basin 300, Glennallen. Held in January, covering 300 miles over two to three days.

Iditarod Trail Sled Dog Race. (See Iditarod Trail Sled Dog Race)

Junior North American Championships, Fairbanks. For children under 18. Held in March. Three heats, one- to eight-dog classes.

Junior World Championship Race, Anchorage. Three heats in three days. Held in February.

Kusko 300, Bethel to Aniak. Held in January.

Limited North American Championships, Fairbanks. Three heats over three days; one- and two-dog ski joring. Held in March.

Tok Race of Champions, Tok. Two heats in two days, 20.5 miles a day. Held in March.

Willow Winter Carnival Race, Willow. Two heats in two days, 18 miles each day. Held in January.

Women's World Championship Race, Anchorage. Three heats in three days, 12 miles each day. Held in February.

Yukon Quest International Sled Dog Race. (See Yukon Quest International Sled Dog Race)

Earthquakes (SEE ALSO

WAVES) Between 1899 and mid-1996, 10 Alaska earthquakes occurred that equaled or exceeded a magnitude of 8 on the Richter scale. During the same period, more than 75 earthquakes took place that were of magnitude 7 or greater.

Alaska averages 1,000 earthquakes a year that measure 3.5 or more on the Richter scale. In May 1995 alone, the Alaska Earthquake Information Center detected and located 540 earthquakes in Alaska. The largest of these measured 5.5 and was located 16 miles southwest of Anchorage.

The West Coast/Alaska Tsunami Warning Center is responsible for warning coastal residents of Alaska, Washington, Oregon, California and British Columbia about any earthquake that could generate a tsunami. According to the Center, Alaska's earthquake activity typically follows the same pattern from month to month, interspersed with sporadic swarms, or groups of small earthquakes, and punctuated every decade or so by a great earthquake and its aftershocks. Alaska is the most seismic of all the 50 states, and the most seismically active part of the state is the Aleutian Islands arc system. Seismicity related to this system extends into the Gulf of Alaska and northward into interior Alaska to a point near

Mount McKinley. These earthquakes are largely the result of underthrusting of the North Pacific plate. Many earthquakes resulting from this underthrusting occur in Cook Inlet—particularly near Mount Illiamna and Mount Redoubt—and near Mount McKinley. North of the Alaska Range, in the central interior, most earthquakes are of shallow origin.

The earthquake that created the highest seiche, or splash wave, ever recorded occurred on the evening of July 9, 1958, when a quake with a magnitude of 7.9 on the Richter scale rocked the Yakutat area. A landslide containing approximately 40 million cubic yards of rock plunged into Gilbert Inlet at the head of Lituya Bay. The gigantic splash resulting from the slide sent a wave 1,740 feet up the opposite mountainside, denuding it of trees and soil down to bedrock. It then fell back and swept through the length of the bay and out to sea. One fishing boat anchored in Lituya Bay at the time was lost with its crew of two; another was carried over a spit of land by the wave and soon after foundered, but its crew was saved. A third boat anchored in the bay miraculously survived intact.

The most destructive earthquake to strike Alaska occurred at 5:36 P.M. on Good Friday, March 27, 1964. Registering between 8.4 and 8.6 on the Richter scale in use at the time, its equivalent moment magnitude has since been revised upward to 9.2, making it the strongest earthquake ever recorded in North America. With its primary epicenter deep beneath Miners Lake in northern Prince William Sound, the earthquake spread shock waves that were felt 700 miles away. The earthquake and seismic waves that followed killed 131 persons, 115 of them Alaskans. Of the 131 deaths, 119 were caused by the tsunami that resulted from the earthquake.

The 1964 earthquake released 10 million times more energy than the atomic bomb that devastated Hiroshima in World War II, and 80 times the energy of the San Francisco earthquake of 1906. It also moved more earth farther, both horizontally and vertically, than any other earthquake ever recorded except the 1960 Chilean earthquake. In the 69-day period after the main quake, there were 12,000 jolts of 3.5 magnitude or greater.

The highest sea wave caused by the 1964 earthquake occurred when an undersea slide near Shoup Glacier in Port Valdez triggered a wave that toppled trees 100 feet above tidewater and deposited silt and sand 220 feet above salt water.

During June 1996, the Alaska Earthquake Information Center located 567 earthquakes in or near Alaska. The largest of these was a major earthquake on June 9

Earthquake damage in downtown Anchorage, 1964. From *Alaska's History* by Harry Ritter

with a magnitude of 7.9, the largest earthquake to have occurred in North America in more than 10 years. The earthquake was felt sharply at Adak and Atka; minor damage was reported at Adak. This quake generated minor tsunamis in Alaska and other locales in the Pacific Basin. Through the end of June, 118 aftershocks of magnitude 4 or larger were recorded and many hundreds of smaller aftershocks were observed on seismic records.

The seismic energy radiated by the June 9 earthquake was about 30 times that generated by the January 1995 Northridge earthquake in California or the January 1994 Kobe, Japan, quake, both of which had magnitudes around 7.2. For comparison, the 1964 Good Friday earthquake released about 1,000 times the energy of the Northridge and Kobe quakes.

To learn more about earthquakes, visit the University of Alaska Fairbanks web site at http://www.giseis.alaska.edu/Seis/. For the latest earthquake and tsunami updates, contact the WC/ATWC Web page at http://www.alaska.net./~ATWC.

Economy (*See also* Cost of Living; Employment; *and* Exports and Imports)

Few states in the union have experienced the boom-and-bust cycles that have characterized Alaska's resource-rich economy. Driven by the oil, timber, mining, fishing and tourism industries, Alaska's economy expands when it is able to export its goods and services abroad or to the Lower 48. The peaks and troughs in Alaska's economy are seasonal and often dependent upon events outside the state's borders.

The oil and gas industry is by far the major player in the Alaskan economy. In terms of revenue to the state, no industry is as important to Alaska's economy as oil. About $2 billion a year, or 85 percent of every state dollar, is generated by taxes and royalties on North Slope crude oil. When oil prices are high, so are state revenues. For every $1 per barrel increase in the price of oil, the state collects $150 million from royalty and severance taxes. Nearly 85 percent of the state budget is paid for by oil revenues and more than 20 percent of all jobs in the state are directly dependent on state government spending. The Alaska economy suffered a major blow with the drop in oil prices in 1986; few industries were spared during the recession. The recovery that began in 1989 was spurred on in part by higher oil prices. The *Exxon Valdez* oil spill cleanup effort added about $2 billion to the state's economy over 18 months. The fortunes of Alaska's oil industry, and therefore many sectors of the economy, are dependent on world oil prices.

Alaska's economy grew for the ninth straight year in 1996, propelled by an expanding services sector, a solid visitor season and a growing hard-rock mining industry. However, job growth was slower than at any time during the 1990s. Timber and fishing industry woes, combined with federal government downsizing and a slower construction season dampened stronger economic performance. Continued consolidation in Alaska's oil industry added to sluggish employment growth in the state.

The biggest contributor to Alaska's job growth and economic performance in 1996 was services. Health care, business and professional services, and social services agencies, particularly those providing job training and vocational rehabilitation services, experienced healthy employment increases last year. Amusement and recreation services posted another solid year.

Fueled by new eating and drinking establishments and growth in miscellaneous retailers, retail employment was the second-largest contributor to private sector growth in 1996. Eating and drinking establishments posted a third consecutive year of job growth.

After three strong years, Alaska's construction industry slipped in performance. Hotel employment fell as some of Alaska's larger hotels cut back on their level of service, including cutting restaurant service and cutting staff during seasonal slowdowns in operations.

The oil industry suffered from the after-effects of the ARCO layoff, continued downsizing at Alyeska Pipeline, and consolidation at oil field service companies.

The economic reverberations from the oil industry's woes were felt throughout the state.

On the non-oil mining front, 1996 saw several hard-rock mining projects come into production so that by year-end, the industry posted an impressive 30 percent employment gain.

Alaska's public sector lost 1,000 jobs in 1995 due to federal government downsizing taking its toll on several federal agencies, including the Bureau of Land Management, the Forest Service and the Department of Transportation. State government employment held steady.

According to the *Alaska Economic Trends* (April 1997), Alaska's economy will continue to grow, though slowly, during 1997. The industries that will be driving this growth are hard rock mining, services, trade and the visitor sector. On the negative side, contraction in Alaska's public sector employment, segments of the oil and gas industry and manufacturing will offset gains in other industries. The cumulative effect will be sluggish overall growth.

There are 166,000 moose in Alaska. Each one produces approximately 400 "moose nuggets" per day. The price of a moose nugget swizzle stick is $.99. Therefore, this renewable resource has a potential economic value of $17,995,230,000 per year.

Education (SEE ALSO SCHOOL DISTRICTS *AND* UNIVERSITIES AND COLLEGES)

According to the 1993–94 *Alaska Education Directory*, Alaska has 467 public schools. The Bureau of Indian Affairs operated rural schools in Alaska until 1985.

The state Board of Education has seven members appointed by the governor. (In addition, two nonvoting members are appointed by the board to represent the military and public school students.) The board is responsible for setting policy for education in Alaska schools and appoints a commissioner of education to carry out its

 decisions. The public schools are controlled by 54 school districts, and each school district elects its own school board. There are 20 Regional Education Attendance Areas that oversee education in rural areas outside the 34 city and borough school districts.

Any student in grades kindergarten through 12 may choose to study at home through the unique state-operated correspondence school, the Alyeska Central School, which also serves traveling students, GED students, migrant students and students living in remote areas. Home study has been an option for Alaskan students since 1939.

The state Department of Education also operates the Alaska Vocational Technical Center at Seward and a number of other education programs ranging from adult basic education to literacy skills.

Alaskans between 7 and 16 years old are required to attend school. According to state regulations, a student must earn a minimum of 21 high school credits to receive a high school diploma. The state Board of Education has stipulated that four credits must be earned in language arts, three in social studies, two each in math and science, and one in physical education or health. Local school boards set the remainder of the required credits.

Since 1976, the state has provided secondary school programs to any community in which an elementary school is operated and one or more children of high school age wish to attend high school. This mandate was the result of a class action suit initiated on behalf of Molly Hootch, a high school–age student. Prior to the Molly Hootch Decree, high school–age students in villages without a secondary school attended high school outside their village. Of the 127 villages originally eligible for high school programs under the Molly Hootch Decree, only a few remain without one.

There were approximately 7,300 teachers and administrators in the public schools and approximately 106,500 students enrolled in K–12 in public schools in 1994–95. The size of schools in Alaska varies greatly, from a 1,900-student high school in Anchorage to one- or two-teacher, one-room schools in remote rural areas.

Sixty-six percent of the school district's operating fund is provided by the state, 23 percent by local governments and 11 percent by the federal government. Alaska's average salary for teachers is among the highest in the nation.

Employment (SEE ALSO ECONOMY)

Alaska's economy grew for the ninth straight year in 1996. However, job growth was slower than at any time during the 1990s. Wage and salary jobs grew by 0.6 percent, slightly more than half of the 1 percent pace set in 1995.

On an annual basis, Alaska's economy added 1,200 jobs in 1996. For most of the 1990s, the economy has added about 5,000 jobs per year. Regionally, job growth varied, with Fairbanks experiencing strong employment gains (2.1 percent), while Gulf Coast employment slipped (–0.7 percent).

Alaska's statewide jobless rate rose 0.5 of a percentage point in 1996 to 7.8 percent. Despite the rate increase, Alaska's annual unemployment rate was below 8 percent for the fourth straight year. While the economy has been creating jobs at a slow rate, Alaska's unemployment rate has managed to stay relatively low due to a combination of factors: first, the number of wage and salary job opportunities available has continued to grow, while net migration to Alaska has slowed. This means that employers increasingly relied upon the state's resident labor force to fill additional jobs. This trend contributed to the overall drop in the unemployment rate.

Alaska's slower job growth was caused

by several events. The oil and gas industry experienced a hard year, beginning in late 1994 with layoffs at ARCO and continuing in 1995 with additional layoffs at Alyeska Pipeline and consolidation at oil field service companies. As the volume of oil flowing from the North Slope declines, Alyeska plans to continue to shrink the size of its workforce. Especially hardest hit by these layoffs were Anchorage and the North Slope.

Meanwhile, civilian and military agencies continued downsizing, shedding 1,000 jobs with troop drawdowns, base closures and agency reductions. In state and local government, employment held steady.

The biggest contributor to job growth in 1996 was services. Engineering, management services and health care were the biggest gainers, boosted by a strong construction season, demand for temporary services and job additions at hospitals and health care facilities, respectively.

Social service agencies, particularly those providing job training and vocational rehabilitation services, experienced a healthy employment increase in 1996. Amusement and recreation services posted another strong year.

Retail expansion that began three years ago leveled off in mid-1995, then fell by 100 jobs in 1996. Eating and drinking establishments posted growth.

After three years of strong performance, the state's construction industry experienced little change in 1996.

Alaska's manufacturing sector led 1996's list of declining industries. A healthy salmon catch propelled Alaska's seafood processors to hire more employees, but low salmon prices offset the gains, and by year's end at least 300 jobs were lost in the seafood processing sector. In the wood products industry, sawmills experienced shutdowns and shift cutbacks, while logging and pulp mill employment suffered when the Ketchikan Pulp Co. closed in March 1997.

On balance, 1996 was a struggle for Alaska's economy, but it still managed to post an employment gain.

Alaska's unemployment rate is best

Alaska Employment by Month 1992–1996

Employees (in thousands)

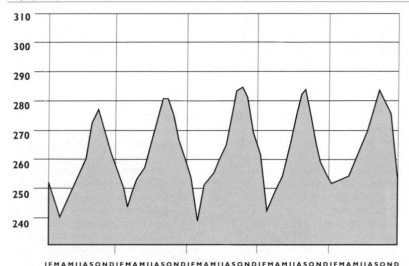

Source: Alaska Dept. of Labor, Research and Analysis Section, April 1997

Average Annual Employment 1983-1996

Employees (in thousands)

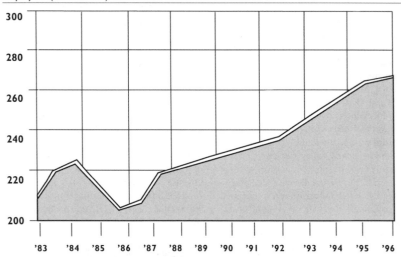

Source: Alaska Dept. of Labor, Research and Analysis Section, April 1997

Alaska Wage and Salary Employment by Industry 1996

Industry	Percent
Government (federal, state, local)	26.9
Services and Miscellaneous	25.6
Trade	21.4
Transportation/Communications	9.1
Finance/Insurance/Real Estate	4.0
Mining (includes oil and gas)	3.5
Manufacturing	2.4
Construction	2.7

Source: Alaska Dept. of Labor, Research and Analysis Section, April 1997

Unemployment Figures for January 1997

Area	Percent
Statewide	9.4
Anchorage	7.2
Fairbanks North Star Borough	9.4
Juneau Borough	8.1
Kodiak Island Borough	12.3
Nome	10.8
Ketchikan Gateway Borough	11.9
Bristol Bay Borough	12.5

characterized by a very seasonal labor market. Increased activity of all types in the summer makes unemployment fairly low, while a lack of activity in the winter months pushes up the unemployment rate. In addition, unemployment figures vary dramatically from one region to another. High unemployment rates in Alaska's rural areas are common. In the Gulf Coast region, for example, the unemployment rate can approach 20 percent in the winter months.

If you're seriously considering a move to Alaska to seek a job, first make a visit and explore the possibilities yourself. Jobs are scarce in Alaska and housing is expensive—there are now, and will be in the foreseeable future, plenty of Alaska residents out of work and anxious to find jobs. For additional information, write: Alaska Department of Labor, Alaska State Employment Service, P.O. Box 3-7000, Juneau 99802. Employment offices are located in most major communities.

Energy and Power

For the purposes of classifying power usage, the state of Alaska can be divided into three major regions, each having similar energy patterns, problems and resources: the Extended Railbelt region, the Southeast region and the bush region. The Extended Railbelt region consists of major urban areas linked by the Alaska Railroad (Seward, Anchorage and Fairbanks). The southcentral area of this region uses relatively inexpensive natural gas in Cook Inlet and hydroelectrical power plants for electrical production and heating. The Fairbanks–Tanana Valley area uses primarily coal, and also oil, to meet its electrical needs. Future electrical demand for the Extended Railbelt region will be met by a combination of hydropower and coal- and gas-fired generators.

The Southeast region relies on hydropower for a large portion of its electrical generation. (Most of the existing hydroelectric power projects in Alaska are located in the Southeast region.) In the smaller communities, diesel generators are used.

The bush region includes all communities that are remote from the major urban areas of the Extended Railbelt and Southeast regions. Electricity in bush communities is typically provided by small diesel generators. Where wind projects are feasible, such as at Lolo Bay and Unalakleet, wind power can be a viable, fuel-saving alternative to diesel-powered generators. Thermal needs in the bush are currently being met almost entirely by heating oil. Wood and kerosene heaters are used to a limited extent. Natural gas is available in Barrow.

Eskimo Ice Cream

Also called *akutak* (Yupik Eskimo word for Eskimo ice cream), this classic Native delicacy, popular throughout Alaska, is traditionally made of whipped berries, seal oil and freshly fallen snow. Sometimes

Soapberry. From *Alaska Wild Berry Guide and Cookbook* by Alaska Northwest Books

shortening, raisins and sugar are added. In different regions, variations are found. One uses the soopalallie berry, *Shepherdia canadensis* (also called soapberry), a bitter species that forms a frothy mass like soapsuds when beaten.

Exports and Imports

The total value of Alaska's exports, excluding air freight, was $5.9 billion in 1996, up from $2.6 billion in 1995.

Alaska-based exports (products of Alaska manufacture) accounted for $2.5 billion of total exports in 1995, up slightly from 1994. Fish and timber account for the greatest portion of Alaska-based exports. Alaska is the nation's largest exporter of fish, accounting for half the total U.S. seafood exports. Most fish goes to Asian markets, though an estimated 20 to 30 percent of the nation's fish exports are Alaskan products that exit indirectly through processors in Seattle and other Lower 48 ports.

Japan was Alaska's number-one customer, accounting for 62 percent, or $1.6 billion, of total exports. Korea imported $164 million in Alaska goods; Taiwan $57 million worth. "With . . . a greater push for value-added products made in Alaska, the repeal of the oil export ban and the emerging markets of the Pacific nations, Alaska is in a great position for the coming century," said Gov. Tony Knowles.

The U.S. Department of Commerce

estimates that every billion dollars in exports represents 18,000 to 22,000 jobs. In Alaska, most of the 25,000 to 28,000 fishing jobs and 2,700 timber jobs rely directly on Alaska's international trade.

The state's most valuable exports, excluding air freight, are: fish, timber, petroleum products, minerals and coal. Air freight, which totaled over $2.6 billion in 1995, is the state's largest export commodity. Air freight is shipped out of Alaska, but is usually produced in other U.S. states or overseas. According to the *Alaska Journal of Commerce,* records show that international air freight out of Alaska has nearly quadrupled since 1990. Runway expansions in 1997 at Anchorage International Airport will make Alaska more attractive to air cargo carriers.

Alaska's imports for 1995 were valued at over $2 billion. Of that total, 90 percent entered Alaska as air cargo, which passes through Anchorage International Airport. Calculation of total imports for the state is difficult because many imports come through Seattle and the Alaska Center for International Business cannot quantify that figure.

Fairbanks

Fairbanks, nicknamed "Alaska's golden heart," is located in Alaska's Interior 200 miles south of the Arctic Circle and 120 miles north of Denali National Park and Preserve.

Long before European explorers and trappers came to the area, Athabascan Indians lived, fished and hunted along the shores of the Yukon and Tanana Rivers, the site of the present-day city.

In 1901, Captain E. T. Barnette traveled up the Yukon River with supplies for a trading post, which he planned to establish farther upriver. But the steamer could not negotiate the fast-moving river, and Barnette was dropped off near what is now First Avenue and Cushman Street in Fairbanks.

In 1902, an Italian prospector named Felix Pedro discovered gold about 16 miles north of Barnette's trading post. Barnette quickly joined the ensuing gold rush, which formed the newest mining community. Barnette's friend, Judge James Wickersham, suggested Fairbanks as the new town's name, in honor of Indiana Senator Charles Fairbanks.

By 1908, Fairbanks was the largest, busiest city in the territory, boasting electric lights, city sewer, fire and police protection, a courthouse and jail, a hospital, school, library and three newspapers.

Today Fairbanks is Alaska's second-largest city, home to 31,633 residents (as of 1996), and the service and supply center for Interior and Arctic industries. A total of 82,435 people live in the Fairbanks North Star Borough. Government, oil, mining, construction and tourism are important elements in the Fairbanks economy, as are Fort Wainwright, the first Army airfield in Alaska, and Eielson Air Force Base. The University of Alaska Fairbanks campus overlooks the city.

Summer temperatures average 62°F, often ranging into the 70s and 80s, with 22 hours of daylight at the solstice, when a Midnight Sun Baseball Game is played after 10:30 P.M. with no artificial lighting. Winter temperatures range from −4°F to −21°F with the lowest-ever temperature recorded at −61°F. The winter snowfall averages 65 inches.

Winter attractions include an international ice-carving competition, sled dog races and northern lights viewing (Fairbanks is considered the best place on earth to view the northern lights). Summer activities include the Golden Days celebration, Tanana Valley Fair (the state's oldest) and the World Eskimo-Indian Olympics

31 years ago

President Lyndon B. Johnson declared flood-stricken Fairbanks a disaster area in August 1967 after a 6-day storm dumped nearly 6 inches of rain in a region that averages 12 inches of rain *a year.*

held annually in July (*see also* World Eskimo-Indian Olympics).

Alaskaland Pioneer Park is a 44-acre park offering a Gold Rush town, historic buildings, food, small shops, entertainment and a Native Village Museum with live demonstrations of Native culture and crafts.

Fairbanks has river rafting, sternwheeler riverboat tours, gold rush sites, dog mushing and aurora-viewing. It is a good jumping-off spot for the Alaska Railroad, Denali National Park and remote wilderness areas. For information, contact the Fairbanks Visitors Bureau, 550 First Ave., Fairbanks 99701; phone (800) 327-5774.

Ferries (SEE ALSO BOATING AND CRUISES)

The state Department of Transportation and Public Facilities, Marine Highway System, provides year-round scheduled ferry service for passengers and vehicles to communities in southeastern, southcentral and southwestern Alaska. The southeastern Alaska ferry system does not connect with southcentral and southwestern Alaska.

A fleet of six ferries on the southeastern system connects Bellingham, Washington, and Prince Rupert, British Columbia, with the southeastern Alaska ports of Hyder/Stewart, Ketchikan, Metlakatla, Hollis, Petersburg, Wrangell, Kake, Sitka, Angoon, Pelican, Hoonah, Tenakee Springs, Juneau, Haines and Skagway. These southeastern communities (with the exception of Hyder, Haines and Skagway) are accessible only by boat, ferry or airplane. The six vessels of the southeastern system are the *Aurora, Columbia, LeConte, Malaspina, Matanuska* and *Taku.*

After falling through the ice of Fairbanks' Chena River, Tim Mayberry recounted, "I kept thinking, 'What a way to die, on a two-bit river on a 10-cent day.'"

Southwest and southcentral Alaska are served by two ferries. The *Tustumena* serves Chenega Bay, Seward, Port Lions, Kodiak, Homer, Seldovia, Cordova and Valdez, with limited summer service to Chignik, False Pass, Akutan, Sand Point, King Cove, Cold Bay and Dutch Harbor. In summer, the *Bartlett* provides service between Valdez, Tatitlek, Cordova and Whittier.

Scheduled state ferry service to southeastern Alaska began in 1963; ferry service to Kodiak Island began in 1964. The first three ferries of the Alaska ferry fleet were the *Malaspina, Matanuska* and *Taku.*

Reservations are required for all sailings. Rates for senior citizens and for passengers with disabilities are available. The address of the main office of the Alaska Marine Highway System is P.O. Box 25535, Juneau 99802-5535; phone (907) 465-3941; or (800) 642-0066 (U.S. and Canada); fax (907) 277-4829.

Nautical Miles Between Ports

Southeastern System

Bellingham–Ketchikan	600
Prince Rupert–Ketchikan	91
Ketchikan–Metlakatla	16
Ketchikan–Hollis	40
Hollis–Petersburg	122
Hollis–Wrangell	95
Ketchikan–Wrangell	89
Wrangell–Petersburg	41
Petersburg–Juneau	108
Petersburg–Kake	59
Kake–Sitka	110
Sitka–Angoon	66
Angoon–Tenakee	33
Tenakee–Hoonah	47
Angoon–Hoonah	60
Hoonah–Juneau (Auke Bay)	45
Sitka–Hoonah	115
Hoonah–Pelican via South Pass	58
Hoonah–Juneau	68
Juneau–Haines	91
Haines–Skagway	13
Juneau (Auke Bay)–Haines	68
Petersburg–Juneau (Auke Bay)	120
Petersburg–Sitka	156
Juneau (Auke Bay)–Sitka	136

(continued)

Nautical Miles Between Ports (continued)

Southwestern System

Seward–Cordova	146
Seward–Valdez	143
Cordova–Valdez	73
Valdez–Whittier	84
Seward–Kodiak	175
Kodiak–Port Lions	27
Kodiak–Homer	126
Homer–Seldovia	16
Kodiak–Sand Point via Sitkinak Strait	353

Embarking Passenger and Vehicle Totals (in thousands) on Alaska Mainline Ferries*

Southeastern System

	Passengers	Vehicles
1986	296.1	76.0
1987	326.6	83.5
1988	344.2	90.7
1989	344.4	89.8
1990	363.1	94.7
1991	368.8	95.2
1992	372.7	97.2
1993	342.6	92.6
1994	348.0	90.8
1995	332.2	88.9
1996	318.9	87.9

Southwestern System

	Passengers	Vehicles
1986	51.8	16.0
1987	52.0	16.5
1988	50.3	16.6
1989	44.2	15.7
1990	50.5	16.5
1991	36.2	12.8
1992	47.8	15.7
1993	48.7	15.7
1994	48.5	15.2
1995	45.4	15.1
1996	46.1	14.8

*Mainline ports for Southeast are: Bellingham, Prince Rupert, Ketchikan, Wrangell, Petersburg, Sitka, Juneau, Haines and Skagway. Mainline ports for southwestern Alaska are: Cordova, Valdez, Whittier, Homer, Seldovia, Kodiak, Seward and Port Lions.

The Malaspina *of the Alaska Ferry fleet, 1989. From* Alaska's History *by Harry Ritter*

Alaska State Ferry Data.

Aurora (235 feet, 14.5 knots): 250 passengers, 44 vehicles, no cabins. Began service in 1977.

Bartlett (193 feet, 12 knots): 190 passengers, 41 vehicles, no cabins. Began service in 1969.

Columbia (418 feet, 17.3 knots): 625 passengers, 158 vehicles, 91 cabins. Began service in 1974.

LeConte (235 feet, 14.5 knots): 250 passengers, 44 vehicles, no cabins. Began service in 1974.

Malaspina (408 feet, 16.5 knots): 500 passengers, 107 vehicles, 84 cabins. Began service in 1963 and was lengthened and renovated in 1972.

Matanuska (408 feet, 16.5 knots): 500 passengers, 108 vehicles, 108 cabins. Began service in 1963.

Taku (352 feet, 16.5 knots): 475 passengers, 83 vehicles, 44 cabins. Began service in 1963.

Tustumena (296 feet, 13.3 knots): 210 passengers, 42 vehicles, 26 cabins. Began service in 1964.

Fires on Wild Land

The 1996 fire season marked 57 years of fire fighting in Alaska. In 1939, fire guards covered only 4 percent of the area needing

protection. Today, no area goes unprotected. Village crews make up the backbone of Alaska's fire-fighting operations.

Fire season starts in April or May, when winter's dead vegetation is vulnerable to any spark. Lightning is the leading cause of wild land fires in Alaska. In June, thunderstorms bring as many as 3,000 lightning strikes a day to the Alaska Interior. By mid-July in a normal year, rainfall in interior Alaska increases.

When wildfires threaten inhabited areas, the Bureau of Land Management's (BLM) Alaska Fire Service (in the northern half of the state) and the State of Alaska Division of Forestry (in the southern half of the state) provide fire protection to lands managed by the BLM, National Park Service, U.S. Fish and Wildlife Service, Native corporations and the state.

All land management agencies in Alaska have placed their lands in one of four protection categories—critical, full, modified and limited. These protection levels set priorities for fire fighting.

With its 570,374 square miles of land, Alaska is more than twice the size of Texas. Most of this vast area has no roads, and transportation for firefighters is usually by airplane. Fire camps are remote. Mosquito repellent is a necessity, but headlamps are not required since the midnight sun shines all night. Aircraft bring in all supplies, even drinking water. Radios are the only means of communication with headquarters.

Black spruce is a fire-dependent species and burns very quickly. Firefighters use chain saws to cut the trees and Pulaskis to cut through the underlying vegetation. It is nearly impossible to transport heavy equipment to fires in remote areas.

Bulldozers are not used because they damage the delicate permafrost layer, leading to dramatic erosion.

Firefighters don't depend on lookout towers in the wilderness to spot wildfires. Today, computers detect the ionization from a lightning strike anywhere in the state, determine the latitude and longitude of the strike and display it on a computer screen. Detection specialists then fly to the areas of greatest risk.

When a fire is reported, computers tell the dispatcher which agency manages the land and whether the fire should be aggressively attacked.

Remote automatic weather stations report weather conditions all over Alaska, enabling weather forecasters to predict thunderstorms in any part of the state. Smoke jumpers and fire-retardant airplanes are pre-positioned close to the predicted thunderstorm activity.

The largest single fire ever reported in Alaska burned 1,161,200 acres 74 miles northwest of Galena in 1957. Unusually dry weather in 1990 made it the most severe fire season on record in Alaska. Lightning was the primary cause of more than 900 fires, with an average of 2,000 strikes a day occurring between June 26 and July 5.

Alaska Wildfires

Calendar Year	No. of Fires	Acres Burned
1986	396	395,169
1987	706	158,851*
1988	639	2,167,795*
1989	485	68,893*
1990	932	3,189,427*
1991	760	1,667,965*
1992	474	150,057*
1993	869	713,116*
1994	643	265,722
1995	421	43,945
1996	724	599,267

*Combined AFS (federal) and state coverage

In 1996, dryer than normal conditions made it difficult to control a wildfire that began near Big Lake (60 miles northwest of Anchorage) and spread for more than a week, burning 37,500 acres and destroying 344 buildings valued at $8.8 million. Fire crews from the Lower 48 were brought in to help fight the blaze, which threatened populated areas. Alaska wildfires have destroyed more acreage in the past, but none have been as economically devastating. President Clinton declared the area a national disaster, qualifying residents for assistance funds.

Fishing COMMERCIAL.
Alaska's commercial fish production is greater in value than that of any other state in the country and also first in volume. In fact, Alaska landings account for about 56 percent of the total seafood production in the United States.

Value and Volume of Alaska Fish and Shellfish Landings*

Year	Value	Volume (in lbs.)
1985	$ 590,751,000	1,184,807,000
1986	752,417,000	1,236,062,000
1987	941,690,000	1,697,547,000
1988	1,339,394,000	2,639,250,000
1989	1,332,000,000	5,213,100,000
1990	1,500,000,000	5,920,000,000
1991	1,216,482,000	5,144,800,000
1992	1,577,421,000	5,637,937,000
1993	1,278,000,000	6,010,000,000
1994	1,346,000,000	5,779,000,000
1995	1,287,000,000	5,746,000,000**

*Source: National Marine Fisheries Service, U.S. Department of Commerce
**Preliminary figures

Commercial fisheries in Alaska during the 1995 season harvested approximately 5.7 billion pounds of seafood, worth about $1.3 billion. This volume is slightly less than that landed in 1994. The breakdown on the various commercial fisheries is as follows:

Salmon. Alaska accounts for 95 percent of the United States commercial landings of Pacific salmon. Over 907 million pounds of Alaska salmon entered fish markets in 1996, with an ex-vessel value of more than $365 million, down from the record catch of 1995.

Fishing boat in Southeast Alaska. From *Journeys Through the Inside Passage* by Joe Upton

With some 1997 exceptions, Alaska's salmon runs are in excellent shape; most spawning stock sizes are very near levels the Alaska Department of Fish and Game considers ideal. Record-breaking commercial catches and all-time-high run sizes are so commonplace in Alaska they are no longer newsworthy, whereas run declines, blockades and even extinctions continue to make news in the Pacific Northwest.

Shellfish. The 1995 (1994–95) shellfish season produced a harvest of approximately 109 million pounds, worth over $265 million to participating fishermen. Total harvest dropped considerably from the previous year, as *C. opilio* tanner (snow) crab landings declined. The decline is attributed to natural mortality and fishing pressure for specific, dominant age-classes. The harvest limit for 1997 was set at 117 million pounds.

Herring. The 1995 commercial herring harvest in Alaska totaled over 99 million pounds. Sac roe fisheries accounted for approximately 90 percent of that total. The total value of the 1995 commercial herring fisheries around the state totaled about $42 million, a significant increase from the previous year's $23 million catch.

Halibut. The 1996 commercial halibut fisheries in Alaska produced a catch of approximately 48.6 million pounds, worth $121 million. Halibut fisheries in Alaska changed from the "24- to 48-hour derby

Ex-vessel Value of Alaska's Commercial Fisheries (in millions of dollars)

Species	1988	1989	1990	1991	1992	1993	1994	1995
Salmon	$744.9	$505.0	$546.8	$312.3	$575	$390	$482	$481
Shellfish	235.6	274.0	352.0	301.4	301	356	314	265
Halibut	66.1	76.1	85.0	91.6	49	60	85	65
Herring	56.0	20.3	27.0	28.6	30	17	22	42
Groundfish	441.1	456.6	482.8	482.6	625	455	443	434

1996 Final Commercial Salmon Harvest (in thousands of fish)

Region	King	Sockeye	Coho	Pink	Chum	Total
Southeast	200	2,790	3,030	64,660	15,800	86,480
Central (Prince William Sound, Cook Inlet, Kodiak, Chignik and Bristol Bay)	184	43,525	1,225	30,560	3,997	79,491
Arctic–Yukon– Kuskokwim	110	120	1,220	490	610	2,550
Western (Alaska Peninsula and Aleutian Islands)	10	3,310	365	2,179	856	6,720
Total	510	49,750	5,840	97,900	21,250	175,250

Source: Alaska Department of Fish and Game, 1997.

style" to an Individual Fishing Quota (IFQ) program beginning March 15, 1995. There are 4,500 holders of an IFQ in 1997. They have eight months to catch the 51 million pounds of halibut allotted.

Groundfish. According to statistics compiled by the National Marine Fisheries Service (NMFS), about 4.5 billion pounds of groundfish were harvested during the 1995 season. This catch was made up largely of pollock from the Bering Sea. Alaska pollock remains the most important species in quantity, accounting for over 30 percent of all the commercial fishery landings in the entire United States. Estimates place the value of Alaska's groundfish landings at more than $434 million, down from 1994.

Alaska's billion-dollar fishing industry faces some hard choices in the future. Too many boats are chasing too few fish, according to some experts. Highly efficient trawlers with huge capacities have emphasized speed and volume fishing, increasing pressure for more and more fish to be harvested.

Nowhere in the industry has the race for fish been as frenzied as for Alaska's groundfish, for which the number of harvesting permits has grown 700 percent over the last decade. Not so long ago, groundfish such as pollock and cod were considered

Top Ten Trophy King Salmon

1. 97 lbs., 4 oz (Kenai River, 1985)
2. 95 lbs., 10 oz. (Kenai River, 1990)
3. 93 lbs., 0 oz. (Kelp Bay, 1977)
4. 92 lbs., 4 oz. (Kenai River, 1985)
5. 91 lbs. 10 oz. (Kenai River, 1988)
6. 91 lbs., 4 oz. (Kenai River, 1987)
7. 91 lbs., 0 oz. (Kenai River, 1995)
8. 89 lbs., 3 oz. (Kenai River, 1989)
9. 89 lbs., 0 oz. (Kenai River, 1994)
10. 88 lbs., 11 oz. (Kenai River, 1980)

low-value species. Groundfish today is a $434 million piece of the fisheries pie. However, groundfish seasons around the state continue to shrink as vessels become more capable of taking the established quotas in shorter periods of time.

What once was a year-round fishery has diminished to just a few weeks a year, despite large catches. Prohibited species and by-catch species concerns will continue to shape the state's groundfish fisheries in the years ahead.

There is growing concern that overexploitation of Alaska's fisheries could result in biological devastation of some species—a problem that New England fisheries now face. In the quest for quick, high-yield catches, there is significant accidental by-catch waste of species such as halibut, salmon and crab. Illegal fishing, questions about the effects of concentrated harvesting during spawning season and habitat pollution add to the potential biological difficulties that the Alaska fishing industry could face.

SPORT. There are 11 sportfishing management areas in Alaska, with varying bag and possession limits and possible special provisions. Current copies of *Alaska Sport Fishing Regulations Summary* are available from the Department of Fish and Game, Box 3-2000, Juneau 99802, or any sportfishing office in the state.

Regulations. A sportfishing license is required for residents and nonresidents 16 years of age or older. (Alaskan residents 60 years of age or older who have been residents one year or more do not need a sportfishing license as long as they remain residents; a special identification card is issued for this exemption.)

Resident sportfishing licenses cost $10, valid for the calendar year issued (nonresident, $50; 1-day nonresident, $10; 3-day nonresident, $15; 14-day nonresident, $30). A resident is a person who has maintained a permanent place of abode within the

Yes Surimi, That's Pollock

Pollock, the largest single-species commercial fishery in the world, is a favorite food fish, not only in Japan, but also in the U.S., where it is made into fish fillets, fish sticks and imitation shellfish (crab, scallops, shrimp). The pollock, which can reach up to 3 feet long and can weigh up to 11 pounds, is filleted, minced and thoroughly washed in chilled water to remove blood, fat and enzymes and increase certain elastic proteins. The water is then pressed out, leaving an odorless, white subtance that has a texture similar to crab meat. To make the final product, color and flavors are added.
—Robert H. Armstrong, *Alaska's Fish*

state for 12 consecutive months and has continuously maintained a voting residence in the state. Military personnel on active duty permanently stationed in the state and their dependents can purchase a nonresident military sportfishing license ($10).

An additional stamp is required for those wishing to fish for king salmon. Cost for residents is $10, for nonresidents, $15.

On Jan. 1, 1999, annual license fees for nonresidents go to $150. Nonresident 14-day licenses rise to $50, and nonresident 3-day licenses to $10. The cost of king salmon tags will also increase.

Nearly all sporting goods stores in Alaska sell fishing licenses. They are also available by mail from the Alaska Department of Revenue, Fish and Game License Section, 1111 W. Eighth St., Room 108, Juneau 99801.

The following sport fish species information includes the best bait or lure and the

The Harbor Bar and Liquor Store in Petersburg advertised, "We sell fishing equipment by the glass, bottle, case or keg."

state record fish weight in pounds
and ounces:

Arctic char: Spoons, eggs; 17 lbs. 8 oz.
Arctic grayling: Small spinners, flies; 4 lbs.
13 oz.
Burbot: Bait; 24 lbs. 12 oz.
Chum salmon: Spoons; 32 lbs.
Cutthroat trout: Eggs, spinners, flies; 8 lbs.
6 oz.
Dolly Varden: Eggs, spinners, flies; 17 lbs.
8 oz.
Halibut: Octopus, herring; 450 lbs.
King salmon: Eggs, herring; 97 lbs. 4 oz.
Kokanee: Spinners, eggs; 2 lbs.
Lake trout: Spoons, plugs; 47 lbs.
Northern pike: Eggs, spoons, spinners;
38 lbs.
Pink salmon: Small spoons; 12 lbs. 9 oz.
Rainbow/Steelhead trout: Flies, lures, eggs;
42 lbs. 3 oz.
Red salmon: Flies; 16 lbs.
Sheefish: Spoons; 53 lbs.
Silver salmon: Herring, spoons; 26 lbs.
Whitefish: Flies, eggs; 9 lbs.

Fish Wheel
The fish wheel is
a machine fastened to a river shore and
propelled by current, which scoops up fish
heading upstream to spawn. Widely used
for subsistence salmon fishing, the fish
wheel provides an easy and inexpensive way
of catching salmon without injuring them.
Contrary to popular belief, Alaska Natives
did not invent the fish wheel. Non-Natives,
probably Scandinavians, apparently first
introduced the fish wheel on the Tanana

*Fish wheel on the Tanana River. From The
Alaska Heritage Seafood Cookbook by
Ann Chandonnet*

River in 1904. Soon after, it appeared on
the Yukon River, where it was used by both
settlers and Natives. It first appeared on the
Kuskokwim in 1914, when prospectors
introduced it for catching salmon near
Georgetown.

Today, subsistence fishing with the use
of a fish wheel is allowed on the Tanana
River, the Copper River, as well as the
Yukon River and its tributaries. Currently,
there are 166 limited-entry permits for the
use of fish wheels by commercial salmon
fishermen on the Yukon River system—
the only district where commercial and
subsistence fishermen use the same gear.
Fishing times with the wheels are regulated.

Prior to its appearance in Alaska, the
fish wheel was used on the East Coast, on
the Sacramento River in California and
on the Columbia River in Washington
and Oregon.

Furs and Trapping
According to the state furbearer biologist,
the major sources of harvested Alaska furs
are the Yukon and
Kuskokwim valleys.

The Arctic provides
limited numbers of
arctic fox, wolverine
and wolf, but the Gulf
Coast areas and Southeast are more
productive. Southeast Alaska is a good
source of mink and otter.

Trapping is seasonal work, and most
trappers work summers at fishing or other
employment. Licenses are required for
trapping. (*See* Hunting section for cost of
licenses.)

State-regulated furbearers are beaver,
coyote, red fox (includes cross, black or
silver color phases), arctic fox (includes
white or blue), lynx, marmot, marten,
mink, muskrat, river (land) otter, squirrel
(parka or ground, flying and red), weasel,
wolf and wolverine. Very little harvest
or use is made of parka squirrels and
marmots.

Prices for raw skins are widely variable
and depend on the buyer, quality, condition
and size of the fur.

Pelts accepted for purchase are beaver,

Living on the Trapline

Trapline life has many inconveniences, from lack of modern facilities like indoor plumbing and electricity, to living with the cold and dark. . . . The thing about trapping is that you have to love it or you couldn't stand it. When you finally get your trails broken out, a big snow falls and again you must break out every mile of trail and clean out every one of one hundred and fifty or so sets. Then a freezing rain falls and the ice-covered traps are incapacitated until you break every one loose again.

Coming home at day's end often means arriving after sunset at a small, dark cabin as cold inside as out. The dogs must be unhitched and picketed, the fire lit, gear packed in, and water fetched or snow started melting. Frozen marten must be hung up to thaw, frozen fish chopped up and cooked for the dogs. After supper we have animals to skin, the dogs to feed, perhaps some repair work or wood-cutting to complete before the aching body can be laid to rest on a spruce-pole bunk. —Julie and Miki Collins, *The Trapline Twins*

coyote, lynx, marten, mink, muskrat, otter, red and white fox, red squirrel, weasel (ermine), wolf and wolverine. Check with a buyer for current market prices.

Geography (SEE MAP,

PAGES 8–9. SEE ALSO GLACIERS AND ICE FIELDS; LAKES; MOUNTAINS; POPULATIONS AND ZIP CODES; REGIONS OF ALASKA; AND RIVERS)

State capital: Juneau.

State population: 607,800

Land area: 570,374 square miles, or about 365,000,000 acres—largest state in the union; one-fifth the size of the Lower 48. Alaska is larger than the three next largest states in the United States combined.

Area per person: Approximately 0.93 square mile per person.

Diameter: East to west, 2,400 miles; north to south, 1,420 miles.

Coastline: 6,640 miles, point to point; as measured on the most detailed maps available, including islands, Alaska has 33,904 miles of shoreline—twice the length of the Lower 48's. Estimated tidal shoreline, including islands, inlets and shoreline to head of tidewater, is 47,300 miles.

Adjacent salt water: North Pacific Ocean, Bering Sea, Chukchi Sea, Arctic Ocean.

Alaska–Canada border: 1,538 miles long; length of boundary between the Arctic Ocean and Mount St. Elias, 647 miles;

Southeast border with British Columbia and Yukon Territory, 710 miles; water boundary, 181 miles.

Geographic center: 63°50' north, 152° west, about 60 miles northwest of Mount McKinley.

Northernmost point: Point Barrow, 71°23' north.

Southernmost point: Tip of Amatignak Island, Aleutian Chain, 51°13'05" north.

Easternmost and westernmost points: It all depends on how you look at it. The 180th meridian—halfway around the world from the prime meridian at Greenwich, England, and the dividing line between east and west longitudes—passes through Alaska. According to one view, Alaska has both the easternmost and westernmost spots in the country! The westernmost is Amatignak Island, 179°10' west; and the easternmost, Pochnoi Point, 179°46' east. On the other hand, if you are facing north, east is to your right and west to your left. Therefore, the westernmost point is Cape Wrangell, Attu Island, 172°27' east; and the easternmost is near Camp Point, in southeastern Alaska, 129°59' east.

Tallest mountain: Mount McKinley, 20,320 feet, and the tallest mountain in North America. Alaska has 39 mountain ranges, containing 17 of the 20 highest peaks in the United States.

Largest natural freshwater lake: Iliamna, 1,150 square miles. Alaska has more than 3 million lakes more than 20 acres in size.

Longest river: Yukon, 1,875 miles in Alaska; 2,298 total. There are more than 3,000 rivers in the state. The Yukon River ranks third in length of U.S. rivers, behind the Mississippi and Missouri Rivers.

Largest island: Kodiak, in the Gulf of Alaska, 3,588 square miles. There are 1,800 named islands in the state, 1,000 of which are located in Southeast Alaska.

Largest city in population: Anchorage, population 254,000 (June 1997 estimate).

Largest city in area: Sitka, with 4,710 square miles, 1,816 square miles of which are water. Juneau is second, with 3,108 square miles.

Glaciers and Ice

Fields The greatest concentrations of glaciers are in the Alaska Range, Wrangell Mountains and the coastal ranges of the Chugach, Coast, Kenai and St. Elias Mountains, where annual precipitation is high. All of Alaska's well-known glaciers fall within these areas. The distribution of glacier ice, according to the U.S. Geological Survey, is shown on the map on page 75.

Glaciers cover approximately 29,000 square miles—or 5 percent—of Alaska, which is 128 times more area covered by glaciers than in the rest of the United States. There are an estimated 100,000 glaciers in Alaska, ranging from tiny cirque glaciers to huge valley glaciers.

Glaciers are formed where, over a number of years, more snow falls than melts. Alaska's glaciers fall roughly into five general categories: alpine, valley, piedmont, ice fields and ice caps. Alpine (mountain and cirque) glaciers head high on the slopes of mountains and plateaus. Valley glaciers are an overflowing accumulation of ice from mountain or plateau basins. Piedmont glaciers result when one or more glaciers join to form a fan-shaped ice mass at the foot of a mountain range. Ice fields develop when large valley glaciers interconnect, leaving only the highest peaks and ridges to rise above the ice surface. Ice caps are smaller glaciers perched on plateaus.

Alaska's better-known glaciers accessible by road are: Worthington (Richardson Highway), Matanuska (Glenn Highway), Exit (Seward Highway), Portage (Seward Highway) and Mendenhall (Glacier Highway). In addition, Childs and Sheridan Glaciers may be reached by car from Cordova, and Valdez Glacier, also accessible by car, is only a few miles from the town of Valdez. The sediment-covered terminus of Muldrow Glacier in Denali National Park and Preserve is visible at a distance along several miles of the park road.

Many spectacular glaciers in Glacier Bay National Park and Preserve, in Kenai Fjords and in Prince William Sound are visible from tour boats or flightseeing.

Glacier ice often appears blue to the eye because it absorbs all the colors of the spectrum except blue, which is scattered back.

Other facts about glaciers: About three-fourths of all the fresh water in Alaska is stored as glacial ice. This is many times greater than the volume of water stored in all the state's lakes, ponds, rivers and reservoirs.

• Longest tidewater glacier in North America is Hubbard, 76 miles long (heads in Canada). In 1986, Hubbard rapidly advanced and blocked Russell Fiord

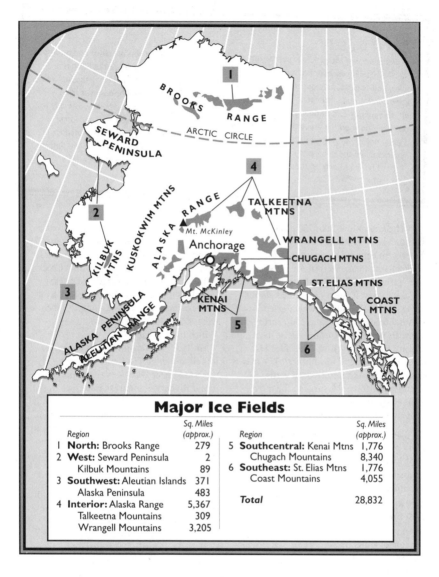

Major Ice Fields

Region	Sq. Miles (approx.)	Region	Sq. Miles (approx.)
1 **North:** Brooks Range	279	5 **Southcentral:** Kenai Mtns	1,776
2 **West:** Seward Peninsula	2	Chugach Mountains	8,340
Kilbuk Mountains	89	6 **Southeast:** St. Elias Mtns	1,776
3 **Southwest:** Aleutian Islands	371	Coast Mountains	4,055
Alaska Peninsula	483		
4 **Interior:** Alaska Range	5,367	**Total**	28,832
Talkeetna Mountains	309		
Wrangell Mountains	3,205		

near Yakutat. Later in the year, the ice dam gave way.

• Longest glacier is Bering (including Bagley Icefield), more than 100 miles long.

• Southernmost active tidewater glacier in North America is LeConte.

• Greatest concentration of tidewater-calving glaciers is in Prince William Sound, with 20 active tidewater glaciers.

• Largest piedmont lobe glacier is Malaspina, 850 square miles; the Malaspina Glacier complex (including tributary glaciers) is approximately 2,000 square miles in area. The largest glacier is the Bering Glacier complex, about 2,250 square miles in size, which includes Bagley Icefield.

• La Perouse Glacier in Glacier Bay National Park is the only calving glacier in North America that discharges icebergs directly into the open Pacific Ocean.

Glacier

The whole front of the glacier is gashed and sculptured into a maze of shallow caves and crevasses, and a bewildering variety of novel architectural forms, clusters of glittering lance-tipped spires, gables, and obelisks, hold out standing bastions and plain mural cliffs, adorned along the top with fretted cornice and battlement, while every gorge and crevasse, groove and hollow, was filled with light, shimmering and throbbing in pale-blue tones of ineffable tenderness and beauty. The day was warm, and back on the broad melting bosom of the glacier . . . many streams were rejoicing, gurgling, ringing, singing, in frictionless channels worn down through the white disintegrated ice of the surface into the quick and living blue, in which they flowed with a grace of motion and flashing of light to be found only on the crystal hillocks and ravines of a glacier. —John Muir, *Travels in Alaska* (1879)

• There are more than 750 glacier-dammed lakes in Alaska; the largest at the present time is 28-square-mile Chakachamna Lake west of Anchorage.

• Variegated Glacier, at Russell Fiord in Yakutat Bay, is the most studied glacier in the world. The glacier, which extends 10 miles from its head to its foot, surprised scientists in 1995 by surging (a rise in forward movement) four years ahead of schedule. By the end of summer 1995, the glacier had moved hundreds of yards. Scientists attribute the surge to the movement of water underneath the glacier rather than climatic conditions.

A miner at Little Creek outside of Nome once sluiced *200 pounds* of gold in 7 hours. That's over 20 times the average Alaskan yearly household income, which is already the highest in the nation!

Gold (*See also* GOLD STRIKES AND RUSHES *AND* MINERALS AND MINING)

The largest gold nugget ever found in Alaska was discovered near Nome. The nugget, weighing 155 troy ounces, was found Sept. 29, 1903, on Discovery Claim on Anvil Creek, Nome District. The nugget was 7 inches long, 4 inches wide and 2 inches thick.

Four other large nuggets have been found in Alaska, one of which also came from the Discovery Claim on Anvil Creek in 1899. It was the largest Alaska nugget found up to that time, weighing 82.2 troy ounces, and was 6¼ inches long, 3¼ inches wide, 1⅜ inches thick at one end and ½ inch thick at the other.

In 1914, the second-largest nugget mined, weighing 138.8 troy ounces, was found near Discovery Claim on Hammond River, Wiseman District. Two of the top five nuggets have been discovered within the last 10 years, with one coming from Lower Glacier Creek, Kantishna District, in 1984, weighing 91.8 troy ounces, and the other from Ganes Creek, Innoko District, in 1986, weighing 122 troy ounces.

If you are interested in gold panning, sluicing or suction dredging in Alaska—for fun or profit—you'll have to know whose land you are on and familiarize yourself with current regulations.

Panning, sluicing and suction dredging on private property, established mining claims and Native lands is considered trespassing unless you have the consent of the owner. On state and federal lands, contact the agency for the area you are interested in for current restrictions on mining.

You can pan for gold for a small fee by visiting one of the gold-panning resorts in Alaska. Commercial resorts rent gold pans and let you try your luck on gold-bearing creeks and streams on their property.

If you want to stake a permanent claim, the state Department of Natural Resources has a free booklet, *Regulations and Statutes Pertaining to Mining Rights of Alaska Lands,* which can be obtained by contacting the department offices in Juneau, (907) 465-2400; Fairbanks, (907) 451-2790; and Anchorage, (907) 762-2518.

According to the Alaska Division of Geological and Geophysical Surveys, Alaska's gold operations produced 161,565 troy ounces in 1996. Estimated 1997 production is expected to be 450,000 ounces.

Following are volumes (in troy ounces) and value figures for recent years of Alaska gold production:

Gold Production in Alaska, 1987–96

Year	Vol. (in troy oz.)	Value
1987	229,700	$104,500,000
1988	265,500	112,837,000
1989	297,900	113,796,000
1990	231,700	89,204,000
1991	243,900	88,291,000
1992	262,500	88,463,000
1993	192,500	68,145,000
1994	182,100	70,300,000
1995	141,882	56,000,000
1996	161,565	60,910,005

The following chart shows the fluctuation in the price of gold (1987–97) after the gold standard was lifted in 1967. Note that these are average annual prices and do not reflect the yearly highest or lowest prices.

Average Annual Price of Gold, per Troy Ounce

1934 to 1967	$ 35.00
1987	447.00
1988	425.00
1989	381.98
1990	385.00
1991	362.03
1992	337.00
1993	354.00
1994	386.00
1995	395.00
1996	377.00
est. 1997	350.00*

*Source: Alaska Division of Tourism

Gold Strikes and Rushes

1848—First Alaska gold discovery (Russian River on Kenai Peninsula)

1861—Stikine River near Telegraph Creek, British Columbia; Wrangell

1872—Cassiar district in Canada (Stikine headwaters country)

1872—Near Sitka

1874—Windham Bay near Juneau

1880—Gold Creek at Juneau

1886—Fortymile discovery

Gold Rush Ancestors

For tracing family members who were part of the gold rush, consult the booklet "How to Find Your Gold Rush Ancestors," available from Alaska's Office of History and Archaeology, Alaska Department of Natural Resources, 3601 C St., Suite 1278, Anchorage 99503; (907) 269-8721.

For Canadian information, write to the Yukon Archives, Box 2703, Whitehorse, YT Y1A 2C6; (403) 667-5321. Canadian mining records are at the Dawson Museum, P.O. Box 303, Dawson, YT Y0B 1G0; (403) 993-5291.

Native Indians, Aleuts and Eskimos can contact the Bureau of Indian Affairs Enrollment Office, P.O. Box 25520, Juneau 99802, phone (907) 586-6735, or the Canadian Department of Indian and Northern Affairs, Room 122, 300 Main St., Whitehorse, YT Y1A 2B5; (403) 667-3353.

Stampeders and their supplies at Dyea, about 1898. From Alaska's History by Harry Ritter

1887—Yakutat areas and Lituya Bay
1893—Mastodon Creek, starting Circle City
1895—Sunrise district on the Kenai Peninsula
1896—Klondike strike, Bonanza Creek, Yukon Territory, Canada
1896—Council (Seward Peninsula)

1898—Anvil Creek near Nome; Atlin district
1898—Hope and Sunrise on Turnagain Arm
1898—British Columbia
1899—Nome beaches
1900—Porcupine rush out of Haines
1902—Fairbanks (Felix Pedro, Upper Goldstream Valley)
1905—Kantishna Hills
1906—Innoko
1907—Ruby
1908—Iditarod
1913—Chisana
1913—Marshall
1914—Livengood

Klondike—the Hammered Water

The word "Klondike," after 1898 one of the most famous place-names in the history of the Northland, comes from tron-diuck, which means "hammered water." It refers to stakes hammered into the bed of the Klondike River at its mouth, where Han Athabascan people annually set their salmon traps and nets. The nets and weirs would be anchored to stakes laboriously driven into the bed of the river. Tron refers to the hefty hammer stones used to pound in the stakes. There are fewer than two dozen Han speakers living today, but this word of theirs, "Klondike," lives on in history because of its association with the lure of northern gold.—Ann Chandonnet, *The Alaska Heritage Seafood Cookbook*

Golf   Golf is a growing part of modern Alaskan life. The Municipality of Anchorage maintains two golf courses—the Anchorage Golf Course on O'Malley Road, an 18-hole all-grass course offering views of the Chugach Range, the city and, on a clear day, Mount McKinley; and a nine-hole course (artificial turf greens) at Russian Jack Springs located at Boniface Parkway and Debarr Road. The newly opened Tanglewood Lakes Golf Club offers a 9-hole all-grass course. Two military courses are open to the public—Eagle Glen Golf Course (18 holes) at Elmendorf Air Force Base, and the 18-hole Moose Run Golf

Gold Rush Centennial

In the summer of 1896, while prospecting on Rabbitt Creek in Canada's Yukon Territory, George Carmack took out a $5 pan of gold—at a time when 10 cents a pan was considered a worthwhile find. Carmack renamed the creek Bonanza and staked claims for himself and his two partners.

When word reached the rest of the world the following spring, more than 100,000 gold-seekers from all over the world set off for the Klondike. Many took routes through Alaska—or eventually stampeded to Alaska strikes.

Centennial events celebrating Northern gold rushes began in 1997. A sample of '98 events follows:

January–June 1, 1998—"Gold Rush Fever," special exhibit at the Anchorage Museum of History and Art.

March—The Buckwheat Ski Classic, a cross-country ski race over the White Pass route, is planned for Skagway; in Nome, dance the night away at the Miners and Mushers Ball.

March 14–15—Chatanika Days. Winter festival featuring outhouse races, long-john contest and more in gold mining town of Chatanika, 30 miles from Fairbanks. (907) 389-2164.

April or early May—Spring crossing of Chilkoot Pass by Seattle Mountaineers.

May 6–9—Centennial Reunion of White Pass & Yukon Route Railroad employees in Skagway.

May–September—Hope & Sunrise Historical Mining Museum shows exhibits about the Turnagain Arm gold rush that preceded the Klondike strike of 1896.

June 15–July 1—Dyea to Dawson Race. Fifty two-person teams, each carrying symbolic gold rush goods, will pack over the Chilkoot Trail to Lake Bennett, where they will begin a 400-mile canoe trip to Dawson.

July 2–8—In Wrangell, centennial of the gold rush via the first route up the Stikine River. In Skagway, Soapy Smith leads the parade on a white horse, and Soapy's Wake is re-enacted.

Sept. 9–12—Alaska Pioneer Convention in Dawson City, Yukon Territory, Canada.

For more information, contact the Alaska Gold Rush Centennial Task Force, (907) 269-8721; the Juneau Convention & Visitors Bureau, (907) 586-2201; or the Skagway Convention & Visitors Bureau, (907) 983-2854. The Alaska Division of Tourism has a complete schedule of Alaska's Gold Rush events. Phone (907) 465-2010; e-mail to GoNorth@Commerce.state.ak.us. Or visit the Klondike Gold Rush Web site at http//Gold.Rush.org.

Course (the oldest golf course in Alaska) at Fort Richardson.

Palmer Municipal Golf Course (18 holes) has a driving range, clubhouse, and rental clubs and carts.

Fairbanks offers the nine-hole Fairbanks Golf and Country Club west of the downtown area, and the nine-hole Chena Bend Golf Course located at Fort Wainwright.

Mendenhall Golf Course in Juneau (nine holes) has a driving range, rental clubs and glacier views.

Every March, Kodiak holds the Pillar Mountain Golf Classic, an irreverent par-70 one-hole match up the side of 1,400-foot Pillar Mountain.

During the summer months, golfers may tee off as late as 10 P.M. Die-hard golfers play in the winter using brightly painted balls. At the annual Lake Louise winter game in Wasilla, played on lake ice, golfers use orange balls that are highly visible on the snow and ice. Nome hosts the Bering Sea Ice Classic Golf Tournament in March and additional golf tournaments in September.

Alaska's northernmost golf course is in Coldfoot, featuring three holes, a driving range and rental clubs. Herds of musk oxen are allowed to "play through."

Other golf courses can be found throughout the state, including Birch Ridge in Soldotna and Settlers Bay in Knik. An occasional private campground will offer putting greens or mini-golf for their guests.

Government (SEE ALSO COURTS AND OFFICIALS) Alaska is represented in the U.S. Congress by two senators and one representative. The capital of Alaska is Juneau.

A governor and lieutenant governor are elected by popular vote for four-year terms on the same ticket. The governor is given extensive powers under the constitution, overseeing 15 major departments: Administration, Commerce and Economic Development, Community and Regional Affairs, Corrections, Education, Environmental Conservation, Fish and Game, Health and Social Services, Labor, Law, Military and Veterans Affairs, Natural Resources, Public Safety, Revenue, and Transportation and Public Facilities.

The legislature is bicameral, with 20 senators elected from 14 senate districts for four-year terms, and 40 representatives from 27 election districts for two-year terms. Under the state constitution, redistricting is accomplished every 10 years, after the reporting of the decennial federal census. The latest redistricting occurred in 1991. The judiciary consists of a state supreme court, court of appeals, superior court, district courts and magistrates.

Alaska is unique among the 50 states in that most of its land mass has not been organized into political subdivisions equivalent to the county form of government. Local

government is by a system of organized boroughs, much like counties in other states. Several areas of the state are not included in any borough because of sparse population. Boroughs generally provide a more limited number of services than cities. There are two classes. First- and second-class boroughs have three mandatory powers: education, land use planning, and tax assessment and collection. The major difference between the two classes is in how they may acquire other powers. Both classes have separately elected borough assemblies and school boards. (Third-class boroughs are no longer permitted in Alaska.) All boroughs may assess, levy and collect real and personal property taxes. They may also levy sales taxes.

Incorporated cities are small units of local government, serving one community. There are two classes. First-class cities, generally urban areas, have six-member councils and a separately elected mayor. Taxing authority is somewhat broader than for second-class cities and responsibilities are broader. A first-class city that has adopted a home rule charter is called a home rule city; adoption allows the city to revise its ordinances, to the extent that the powers it assumes are those not prohibited by law or charter. Second-class cities, generally places with fewer than 400 people, are governed by a seven-member council, one of whom serves as mayor. Taxing authority is limited. A borough and all cities located within it may unite in a single unit of government called a unified municipality.

There are 246 federally recognized tribal governments in Alaska and one community (Metlakatla, originally an Indian reservation) organized under federal law.

In 1995, there were 16 organized boroughs and unified home rule municipalities: three unified home rule municipalities, five home rule boroughs, seven second-class boroughs.

In a candidate questionnaire, Republican senate candidate Jerry Ward pledged that if elected, he would shrink the size of state government and reduce the number of state employees "through nutrition."

Alaska's 149 incorporated cities include 12 home rule cities, 21 first-class cities and 116 second-class cities.

Borough Addresses and Contacts.
Aleutians East Borough. P.O. Box 349, Sand Point 99661; (907) 383-5334.

Municipality of Anchorage. *Contact:* Mayor's Office or Manager's Office, P.O. Box 196650, Anchorage 99519; (907) 343-4431.

Bristol Bay Borough. *Contact:* Borough Clerk, P.O. Box 189, Naknek 99633; (907) 246-4224.

Denali Borough. *Contact:* Mayor, P.O. Box 480, Anderson 99744; (907) 683-1330.

Fairbanks North Star Borough. *Contact:* Clerk, P.O. Box 71267, Fairbanks 99707; (907) 459-1000.

Haines Borough. *Contact:* Borough Secretary, P.O. Box 1209, Haines 99827; (907) 766-2611.

City and Borough of Juneau. *Contact:* City-Borough Manager, 155 S. Seward St., Juneau 99801; (907) 586-5240.

Kenai Peninsula Borough. *Contact:* Borough Clerk, 144 N. Binkley St., Soldotna 99669; (907) 262-4441.

Ketchikan Gateway Borough. *Contact:* Borough Manager, 344 Front St., Ketchikan 99901; (907) 225-6625.

Kodiak Island Borough. *Contact:* Borough Mayor or Borough Clerk, 710 Mill Bay Road, Kodiak 99615; (907) 486-5736.

Lake and Peninsula Borough. P.O. Box 495, King Salmon 99613; (907) 276-3421.

Matanuska–Susitna Borough. *Contact:* Borough Manager, 350 E. Dahlia Ave., Palmer 99645-6488; (907) 745-4801.

North Slope Borough. *Contact:* Borough Mayor, P.O. Box 69, Barrow 99723; (907) 852-2611.

Northwest Arctic Borough. P.O. Box 1110, Kotzebue 99752; (907) 442-2500.

City and Borough of Sitka. *Contact:* Administrator, 304 Lake St., Room 104, Sitka 99835; (907) 747-3294.

City and Borough of Yakutat. Box 160, Yakutat 99689; (907) 784-3323.

Highways (SEE ALSO ALASKA HIGHWAY AND DALTON HIGHWAY)
As of January 1996, the state Department of Transportation and Public Facilities estimated total public road mileage in Alaska at 14,336 centerline miles, including those in national parks and forests (2,539). The state also operates 2,865 miles of ferry routes.

Major Highways in Alaska

	Alaska Route	Year Opened	Total Length (miles)		Open
			Paved	Gravel	
Alaska	2	1942	294		All year
Copper River	10	*	12.4	36	Apr.–Oct.
Dalton	11	1974		415	All year
Denali	8	1957	21.4	114	Apr.–Oct.
Edgerton	10	1923	35		All year
Elliott	2	1959	28	124	All year
George Parks	3	1971	324		All year
Haines	7	1947	44		All year
Klondike	2	1978	15		All year
Richardson	4	1923	272		All year
Seward/Glenn	9&1	1951	308		All year
Steese	6	1928	44	118	All year
Sterling	1	1950	138		All year
Taylor	5	1953		160	Apr.–Oct.
Tok Cutoff	1	1940	123		All year

*Construction on the Copper River Highway—which was to link up with Chitina on the Edgerton—was halted by the 1964 Good Friday earthquake, which damaged the Million Dollar Bridge, and local Cordova citizens who desired semi-isolation.

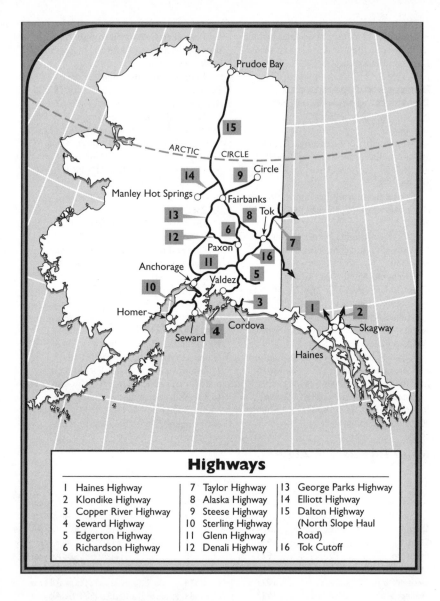

Highways

1	Haines Highway	7	Taylor Highway	13	George Parks Highway	
2	Klondike Highway	8	Alaska Highway	14	Elliott Highway	
3	Copper River Highway	9	Steese Highway	15	Dalton Highway	
4	Seward Highway	10	Sterling Highway		(North Slope Haul	
5	Edgerton Highway	11	Glenn Highway		Road)	
6	Richardson Highway	12	Denali Highway	16	Tok Cutoff	

Highways in Alaska range from six-lane paved freeways to one-lane dirt and gravel roads. Approximately 22 percent of the roads in the Alaska highway system are paved, with the exception of the following major highways that are partial gravel (*see* chart on page 81): Copper River (Alaska Route 10), Dalton (Alaska Route 11), Denali (Alaska Route 8), Elliott (Alaska Route 2), Steese (Alaska Route 6) and Taylor (Alaska Route 5).

The chart on page 81 lists each major highway in Alaska, its route number, the year the highway opened to vehicle traffic and its total length within Alaska (most of the Alaska Highway, Haines Highway and Klondike Highway 2 lie within Canada). Also indicated is whether the highway is open all year or closed in winter.

For weather and updated road conditions, travelers can call (800) 478-7675 for a recorded message, which includes avalanche warnings and weight restrictions on the Alaska highway system.

Hiking

Developed trails suitable for all ability levels may be found near Alaska's larger cities and towns. However, most of Alaska's public recreation lands are wilderness. Trails are nonexistent and hikers must chart their own course using topographic maps and compass. Using both maps and tide tables, it is also feasible to hike along ocean shorelines at low tide.

Hikers in Alaska must plan for cold, wet and rapidly changing weather. Take rain gear. If staying overnight in the backcountry, carry a tent, backpacking stove, first-aid kit and emergency flares. Snow can be encountered in any season.

Plan to bring everything you need with you; some businesses rent canoes and kayaks, but few rent personal gear such as backpacks. Backcountry guides often furnish equipment on escorted expeditions.

Bears inhabit most of Alaska. Read all bear safety information and follow proper procedures for camping and hiking in bear country. You must be completely self-sufficient and responsible for your own safety. (*See* Bears)

Information on hiking in Alaska's national parks and monuments is available from the Alaska Public Lands Information Centers: 605 W. Fourth Ave., Suite 105, Anchorage 99501; 250 Cushman St., Suite 1A, Fairbanks 99701; and P.O. Box 359, Tok 99780; or from park headquarters for the area you're interested in. (*See* National Parks, Preserves and Monuments)

The Alaska Division of Parks (*see* State Park System) has information on hiking on the lands managed by that agency.

51 years ago

In August 1947, Mrs. Barbara (Bradford) Washburn became the first woman to reach the summit of Mount McKinley.

History (SEE ALSO GOLD STRIKES AND RUSHES *AND* RUSSIAN ALASKA)

11,000–6,000 years ago—Human culture in southeastern, Aleutians, Interior and northwestern Arctic Alaska.

6,000 years ago—Most recent migration from Siberia across the land bridge. Earliest migration believed to have taken place up to 20,000 years ago.

5,000–3,000 years ago—Human culture present on the Bering Sea Coast.

1725—Vitus Bering sent by Peter the Great to explore the North Pacific.

1741—On a later expedition, Bering in one ship and Alexei Chirikof in another sight Alaska. Chirikof probably sees land on July 15, a day ahead of his leader, who was perhaps 300 miles or more to the north. Georg Steller goes ashore on Kayak Island, becoming the first European known to have set foot on Alaska soil.

1743—Russians begin concentrated hunting of sea otter, continuing until the species is almost decimated.

1772—A permanent Russian settlement is established at Unalaska.

1774–94—Explorations of Alaska waters by Juan Perez, James Cook and George Vancouver.

1784—First Russian settlement is established on Kodiak Island at Three Saints Bay.

1794—Vancouver sights Mount McKinley.

1799—Alexander Baranof establishes the Russian post known today as Old Sitka. A trade charter is granted to the Russian-American Company.

1821—Russians prohibit trading in Alaska waters by other nations, making the Russian-American Company the sole trading firm.

1824–42—Russian exploration of the mainland leads to the discovery of the Kuskokwim, Nushagak, Yukon and Koyukuk Rivers.

1837—Father Herman, last survivor of the original Russian missionaries to Alaska, dies on Spruce Island near Kodiak.

1845—The Missionary School at Sitka opens, offering the study of the Aleut, Tlingit and Eskimo languages, medicine and Latin.

1847—Fort Yukon is established by Hudson's Bay Company.

1848—American whalers first enter the Arctic Ocean through Bering Strait.

1853—Russian explorer-trappers find the first oil seeps in Cook Inlet.

1855—The U.S. Navy explores the North Pacific around the Aleutian Islands and the Bering Sea.

1859—Baron Edoard de Stoecki, minister and chargé d'affaires of the Russian delegation to the United States, is given authority to negotiate the sale of Alaska.

1860—Russians estimate Native Alaskan Christians at 12,000, with 35 chapels, 9 churches, 17 schools and 3 orphanages in 43 communities.

1866—Alaska's first newspaper *The Esquimeaux,* was published in manuscript at Libbyville.

1867—United States under President Andrew Johnson buys Alaska from Russia for $7.2 million; the treaty is signed March 30 and formal transfer takes place on October 18 at Sitka. Fur seal population begins to stabilize. U.S. Army is given jurisdiction over the Department of Alaska the following year.

1869–70—The *Alaska Times,* the first newspaper to be printed in Alaska, is published in Sitka.

1872—Gold is discovered near Sitka.

1873—Frederick Schwatka conducts a military reconnaissance of Alaska's Interior.

Residential street in Fairbanks in the early 1900s. From Alaska's History *by Harry Ritter*

1878—First salmon canneries established at Klawock and Old Sitka.

1882—First commercial herring fishing begins. U.S. Navy destroys the Tlingit village of Angoon.

1884—An Organic Act gives Alaska its first civil government.

1885—Lieutenant Henry Allen explores the Copper River.

1891—First oil claims staked in Cook Inlet area.

1897–1900—Klondike gold rush in Yukon Territory; heavy traffic through Alaska on the way to the goldfields.

1898—Gold is discovered on Nome beaches. Frank Reid shoots con artist Soapy Smith in Skagway. U.S. Geological Survey begins mapping program of Alaska.

1902—First oil production, at Katalla. Telegraph from Eagle to Valdez is completed.

1906—Peak gold production year. Alaska is granted a nonvoting delegate to Congress; governor's office moves from Sitka to Juneau.

1911—Copper production begins at Kennicott.

1912—Territorial status for Alaska; first terr torial Legislature is convened the following year. Mount Katmai erupts.

1913—First airplane flight in Alaska, at Fairbanks; first

The *Anchorage Daily News* ran an announcement for a Supernatural Lecture which read, "The Inner Peace Movement presents a talk by Neil Gossman on the subjects of ESP, life after death, telepathy, deja vu and deja vu."

automobile trip from Fairbanks to Valdez.

1914—President Wilson authorizes construction of the Alaska Railroad.

1916—First bill proposing Alaska statehood is introduced in Congress. Peak copper production year.

1917—Creation of Mount McKinley National Park. Founding of Wasilla.

1918—Worldwide epidemic of Spanish flu decimates Alaska's Native population. Creation of Katmai National Monument.

1922—First pulp mill starts production at Speel River, near Juneau.

1923—President Warren Harding drives spike completing the Alaska Railroad.

1930—The first "talkie" motion picture is shown in Fairbanks, featuring the Marx Brothers in *The Cocoanuts.*

1935—Matanuska Valley Project, which establishes farming families in Alaska, begins. First Juneau-to-Fairbanks flight.

1936—All-time record salmon catch in Alaska—126.4 million fish. Black Rapids Glacier advances 3 miles in three months, coming within a half mile of the Richardson Highway.

1937—Nell Scott is the first woman appointed to the Alaska Legislature.

1940—Military buildup in Alaska; Fort Richardson, Elmendorf Air Force Base are established. Alaska's population comprises about 40,000 non-Native Alaskans and 32,458 Natives. Pan American Airways inaugurates twice-weekly service between

Matanuska colonists arriving at Palmer Station, 1935. From *Alaska's History* by Harry Ritter

Seattle, Ketchikan and Juneau, using Sikorsky flying boats.

1942—Dutch Harbor is bombed and Attu and Kiska islands are occupied by Japanese forces. Alaska Highway is built—first overland connection to Lower 48.

1943—Japanese forces are driven from Alaska.

1947—Barbara Washburn becomes the first woman to ascend Mount McKinley.

1953—Oil well is drilled near Eureka, on the Glenn Highway, marking the start of modern oil history.

1957—Kenai oil strike.

1958—Statehood measure is passed by Congress; statehood is proclaimed officially on Jan. 3, 1959; first general election is held.

1963—State ferry service to Southeast Alaska begins.

1964—Good Friday earthquake, March 27, causes heavy damage throughout the Gulf Coast region; 131 people lose their lives.

1967—Fairbanks flood.

1968—Oil and gas discoveries at Prudhoe Bay on the North Slope; $900 million North Slope oil lease sale the following year; pipeline proposal follows.

1970—Naomi Uemura makes first solo ascent of Mount McKinley and perishes on his descent. Federal government sets aside 500,000 acres for Chugach State Park.

1971—Congress approves Alaska Native Claims Settlement Act, granting title to 40 million acres of land and providing more than $900 million in payment to Alaska Natives.

1973—The first 1,100-mile sled dog race begins March 3, following part of an old dog team mail route blazed in 1910; it's called the Iditarod Trail Sled Dog Race.

1974—Trans-Alaska pipeline receives final approval; construction buildup begins.

1975—Population and labor force soar with construction of pipeline. Alaska Gross Products hits $5.8 billion— double the 1973 figure.

1976—Voters select Willow area for

new capital site. Iditarod Trail is designated a National Historic Trail by U.S. Congress.

 1977—Completion of the trans-Alaska oil pipeline from Prudhoe Bay to Valdez; shipment of first oil by tanker from Valdez to Puget Sound.

1978—A 200-mile offshore fishing limit goes into effect. President Jimmy Carter withdraws 56 million acres of federal lands in Alaska to create 17 new national monuments.

1979—State of Alaska files suit to halt the withdrawal of 56 million acres of Alaska land by President Carter under the Antiquities Act.

1980—Special session of the Alaska Legislature votes to repeal the state income tax and provides for refunds of 1979 taxes. Legislature establishes a Permanent Fund as a repository for one-fourth of all royalty oil revenues for future generations. Census figures show Alaska's population grew by 32.4 percent during the 1970s. The Alaska Lands Act of 1980 puts 53.7 million Alaska acres into the national wildlife refuge system, parts of 25 rivers into the national wild and scenic rivers system, 3.3 million acres into national forest lands and 43.6 million acres into national park land.

1981—Legislature puts on the ballot a constitutional amendment proposal to limit state spending. Secretary of the Interior James Watt initiates plans to sell oil and gas leases on 130 million acres of Alaska's non-restricted federal land and announces a tentative schedule to open 16 offshore areas of Alaska as part of an intense national search for oil and gas on the outer continental shelf.

1982—Oil revenues for state decrease. Vote for funds to move state capital from Juneau to Willow is defeated. First Permanent Fund dividend checks of $1,000 each are mailed to every six-month resident of Alaska.

1983—Time zone shift: All Alaska, except westernmost Aleutian Islands, moves to Alaska Standard Time, one hour west of Pacific Standard Time. Record-breaking salmon harvest in Bristol Bay. Building permits set a record at just under $1 billion.

1984—State of Alaska celebrates its 25th birthday.

1985—Anchorage receives the U.S. bid for the 1994 Olympics. Iditarod Trail Sled Dog Race is won by Libby Riddles, the first woman to win in the history of the race.

1986—Mount Augustine in lower Cook Inlet erupts. World Championship Sled Dog Race held during Fur Rendezvous is canceled for the first time due to lack of snow. Iditarod Trail Sled Dog Race is again won by a woman, Susan Butcher of Manley.

1987—Iditarod Trail Sled Dog Race is won by Susan Butcher for the second consecutive year.

1988—The first successful solo winter ascent of Mount McKinley by Vern Tejas of Anchorage. The Iditarod Trail Sled Dog Race is won by Susan Butcher for the third year in a row. Anchorage loses its bid for the 1994 Olympics to Norway.

1989—Worst oil spill in U.S. history occurs in Prince William Sound when the *Exxon Valdez* runs aground. Record-breaking cold hits entire state, lasting for weeks. Soviets visit Alaska, and the Bering Bridge Expedition crosses the Bering Strait by dogsled and skis. Mount Redoubt begins erupting in December.

1990—Valdez sets a new record for snowfall. Susan Butcher wins her fourth Iditarod Sled Dog Race. Election upset as Walter J. Hickel becomes governor.

1991—Fairbanks sets a new record for snowfall. Rick Swenson claims fifth Iditarod win.

1992—Alaska celebrates 50th anniversary of the Alaska Highway. One of Alaska's oldest newspapers, the *Anchorage Times,* shuts down. Mount Spurr erupts.

1993—The Department of Fish and Game announces a plan to allow aerial hunting of wolves. Springtime comes early to the Interior, with the second-warmest April on record.

1994—Diseased herring appear in Prince William Sound for the second season. Exxon is found guilty of recklessness in the 1989 oil spill in Prince William

Sound. Alaskan skier Tommy Moe is a gold medalist at the Olympic Games in Norway.

1995—Two Anchorage residents are killed by a grizzly along a trail in a popular hiking area of Chugach State Park.

1996—Princess Tours' Denali Lodge burns down in March, but is rebuilt by June. Alaska's worst wildfire destroys $8.8 million in homes and other buildings.

1997—Legislature approves 71-cent tax increase per cigarette pack. ARCO Alaska and British Petroleum announced plans to develop two more North Slope oil fields.

Holidays in 1998

New Year's Day	January 1
Martin Luther King Day	January 19
Presidents' Day	
—holiday	February 16
—traditional	February 22
Seward's Day*	March 27
Memorial Day	
—holiday	May 25
—traditional	May 30
Independence Day	July 4
Labor Day	September 7
Alaska Day**	October 18
Veterans' Day	November 11
Thanksgiving Day	November 26
Christmas Day	December 25

*Seward's Day commemorates the signing of the treaty by which the United States bought Alaska from Russia, signed on March 30, 1867.

**Alaska Day is the anniversary of the formal transfer of the territory and the raising of the U.S. flag at Sitka on Oct. 18, 1867.

Homesteading (SEE LAND USE)

Hooligan

Smelt, also known as eulachon or candlefish, are known as "ooligan" in southeastern Alaska. The Tlingit dried these oily little fish, inserted a twisted spruce bark wick and used them as candles. The Tlingit caught the 9-inch fish in great numbers, ripened them for several days to speed the release of the oil from the flesh and then rendered their oil in baskets or cooking pots. The flavor and color of the

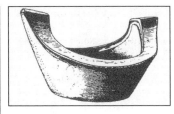

Native bowl used for hooligan grease. From The *Alaska Heritage Seafood Cookbook* by Ann Chandonnet

oil or "grease" were determined by the length of time the fish ripened. The oil was stored in bulb kelp "jars" corked with wooden plugs or in bentwood boxes. Some of the oil was traded with Interior people by packing it over timeworn paths which became known as "grease trails." The Tlingit considered hooligan vital to their diet and gallons of the oil were consumed during the winter as a nutritious dip for dried foods.

Hooligan, now considered a subsistence or sport catch only, are caught by dip netting as they travel upriver to spawn. Hooligan resemble trout in general structure and have a distinctive odor and taste. The flesh is ivory colored, extremely perishable and should be cooked or pickled the same day it is caught.

Hospitals and Health Facilities (SEE ALSO PIONEERS' HOMES)

Alaska has numerous hospitals, nursing homes and other health care facilities.

For a list of emergency medical services, contact the Office of Emergency Medical Services, Division of Public Health, Dept. of Health and Social Services, P.O. Box 110616, Juneau 99811-0616.

MUNICIPAL, PRIVATE AND STATE HOSPITALS, CLINICS AND SPECIALTY FACILITIES.

Anchorage. Alaska Psychiatric Institute (176 beds), 2900 Providence Drive, 99508.

Alaska Surgery Center, 4001 Laurel St., 99508-5396.

Charter North Hospital (80 beds), 2530 DeBarr Road, 99508.

Columbia Alaska Regional Hospital (238 beds), 2801 DeBarr Road, P.O. Box 143889, 99514-3889.

Columbia North Star Hospital (35 beds), 1650 S. Bragaw, 99508.

Providence Alaska Medical Center (345 beds), 3200 Providence Drive, P.O. Box 196604, 99519-6604.

Cordova. Cordova Community Medical Center (23 beds), Box 160, 99574.

Fairbanks. Fairbanks Memorial Hospital (177 beds), 1650 Cowles St., 99701.

Glennallen. Cross Roads Medical Center, P. O. Box 5, 99588.

Homer. South Peninsula Hospital (40 beds), 4300 Bartlett St., 99603.

Juneau. Bartlett Regional Hospital (51 beds), 3260 Hospital Drive, 99801.

Juneau Recovery Unit (15 alcoholism treatment beds), 3250 Hospital Drive, 99801.

Ketchikan. Ketchikan General Hospital (92 beds), 3100 Tongass Ave., 99901.

Kodiak. Providence Kodiak Medical Center (25 beds), 1915 E. Rezanof Drive, 99615.

Palmer. Valley Hospital (36 beds), P.O. Box 1687, 99645.

Petersburg. Petersburg Medical Center (25 beds), Box 589, 99833.

Seward. Providence Seward Medical Center (20 beds), Box 365, 99664.

Sitka. Sitka Community Hospital (24 beds),

209 Moller Drive, P.O. Box 500, 99835.

Soldotna. Central Peninsula General Hospital (62 beds), 250 Hospital Place, 99669.

Valdez. Harborview Developmental Center (state-operated residential center for the mentally handicapped; 80 beds), Box 487, 99686.

Valdez Community Hospital (15 beds), Box 550, 99686.

Wrangell. Wrangell General Hospital (8 beds), Box 1081, 99929.

U.S. PUBLIC HEALTH SERVICE HOSPITALS AND CLINICS.

Anchorage. Alaska Native Medical Center (140 beds), 4315 Diplomacy Drive, 99508.

Barrow. Samuel Simmonds Memorial Hospital (14 beds), Box 29, 99723-0029.

Bethel. Yukon–Kuskokwim Delta Regional Hospital (50 beds), P.O. Box 287, 99559.

Dillingham. Kanakanak Hospital (15 beds), P.O. Box 130, 99576.

Fairbanks. Chief Andrew Isaac Health Center, 1408 19th St., 99701.

Juneau. SEARHC Medical Clinic, 3245 Hospital Drive, 99801.

Ketchikan. PHS Alaska Native Health Center, 3289 Tongass Ave., 99901.

Kodiak. Kodiak Area Native Association, 3449 Rezanof Drive E., 99615.

Kotzebue. Maniilaq Health Center (17 beds), P.O. Box 43, 99752.

Metlakatla. Annette Island Service Unit, P.O. Box 439, 99926.

The *Nome Nugget* reported that you might be a real Alaskan if "you have ever taken the baby's temperature with a turkey thermometer."

Nome. Norton Sound Health Corporation (19 beds), P.O. Box 966, 99762.

Sitka. SEARHC Mount Edgecumbe Hospital (78 beds), 222 Tongass Drive, 99835.

MILITARY HOSPITALS.

Eielson Air Force Base. Eielson Air Force Base Clinic, 354 MOG/SG, 3349 Central Ave., Eielson AFB 99702-2399.

Elmendorf AFB. Headquarters Third Medical Center, 3 MOG/SGHQ, 24800 Hospital Drive, 99506-3700.

Fort Greely. Fort Greely Health Clinic, APO AP 96508.

Fort Richardson. U.S. Army Troop Medical Clinic, 99505.

Fort Wainwright. Bassett Army Community Hospital, 99703.

Ketchikan. Coast Guard Dispensary, 99901.

Kodiak. USCG Support Center, Rockmore-King Medical Clinic, Box 195002, 99619-5002.

Mount Edgecumbe. U.S. Coast Guard Air Station, 611 Airport Road, 99835.

NURSING HOMES.

Anchorage. Mary Conrad Center (90 beds), 9100 Centennial Drive, 99504.

Providence Extended Care Center (224 beds), 4900 Eagle St., 99503.

Fairbanks. Denali Center (90 beds), 1510 19th Ave., 99701.

Juneau. Saint Ann's Care Center (45 beds), 415 Sixth St., 99801.

Ketchikan. General Hospital Long Term Care Unit (46 beds), 3100 Tongass Ave., 99901.

Seward. Wesley Rehabilitation and Care Center (66 beds), Box 430, 99664.

Soldotna. Heritage Place (45 beds), 232 Rockwell Ave., 99669.

Valdez. Harborview Development Center (80 beds), P.O. Box 487, 99686.

CHEMICAL DEPENDENCY TREATMENT CENTERS.

Alaska has 18 chemical dependency centers, located in Anchorage, Eagle River, Fairbanks, Juneau, Palmer, Sitka and Wasilla. For details, call the Alaska State Medical Association, (907) 562-2662.

Hostels

Alaska has 11 Hosteling International member hostels, located in the following communities:

Alyeska International Home Hostel, P.O. Box 10-4099, Anchorage 99510; (907) 783-2099. Located 40 miles south of Anchorage in Girdwood.

Anchorage International Hostel, 700 H St., Anchorage 99501; (907) 276-3635. Located on the corner of Seventh and H streets.

Delta Youth Hostel, P.O. Box 971, Delta Junction 99737; (907) 895-5074. Located 3 miles from Milepost 272 on Richardson Highway.

Hosteling International, Mile 3 Oil Well Road, P.O. Box 39083, Ninilchik 99639.

Juneau International Hostel, 614 Harris St., Juneau 99801; (907) 586-9559. Located four blocks northeast of the capitol building.

Ketchikan Youth Hostel, P.O. Box 8515, Ketchikan 99901; (907) 225-3780. Located in United Methodist Church, Grant and Main streets.

Sheep Mountain Lodge, HCO 3, Box 8490, Palmer 99645; (907) 745-5121. Located at Mile 113.5 of the Glenn Highway.

Sitka Youth Hostel, P.O. Box 2645, Sitka 99835; (907) 747-8356. Located in

Nature's Hot Springs

Native Alaskans were the first to use these naturally occurring hot waters. Aleuts used thermal springs at Adak, Atka, Geyser Bight, Akutan and other islands in the Aleutian chain. The hot springs village site near Port Moller Hot Springs (on the north side of the Alaska Peninsula) has been occupied intermittently over the past 3,000 years. The original Native names—Kruzagampah, Kwiniuk, Hoonah—were changed to Pilgrim, Elim and Tenakee by early miners who used the springs. Miners and trappers were quick to discover the benefits of the hot water for bathing and other uses, and usually provided the first written accounts of the springs.

United Methodist Church, Edgecumbe and Kimsham streets.

Skagway Home Hostel, Box 231, Skagway 99840; (907) 983-2131. Located on Third Avenue near Main Street.

Snow River International Hostel, HRC 64, Box 425, Seward 99664. Located at Mile 16 of the Seward Highway.

Tok International Youth Hostel, P.O. Box 532, Tok 99780. Located 1 mile south of Mile 1322.5 of the Alaska Highway on Pringle Drive.

The hostels in Alyeska, Anchorage, Juneau, Skagway and Seward are open year-round. All others are open only in the summer, and all of the hostels accept reservations by mail. Opening and closing dates, maximum length of stay and hours vary.

Hostels are available to anyone with a valid membership card issued by one of the associations affiliated with Hosteling International. Membership is open to all ages. By international agreement, each youth hostel member joins the association of his own country. A valid membership card, which ranges from $10 to $250 (life), entitles a member to use hostels.

Hostel memberships and a guide to American Youth Hostels can be purchased from the state office (Alaska Council, AYH, Box 240347, Anchorage 99524; (907) 243-3844), national office (American Youth Hostels, 1332 I St. NW, Suite 800, Washington, D.C. 20005) or from most local hostels.

Hot Springs

The Alaska Division of Geological and Geophysical Surveys identifies 124 geothermal areas in the state that include hot springs, fumaroles, geothermal wells or a combination of these. Most geothermal areas (56) occur along the Aleutian volcanic arc, 19 are located in the Southeast panhandle and 49 are scattered throughout mainland Alaska. Most are inaccessible by automobile.

Of the state's 124 geothermal areas, only 19 have experienced any sort of development, and only six hot spring areas provide resort facilities. Resorts with swimming pools, changing rooms, restaurants and lodging are found at Chena Hot Springs (a 62-mile drive east from Fairbanks) and Circle Hot Springs (136 miles northeast by road from Fairbanks). Although not accessible by road, Bell Island Hot Springs (40 air miles northeast of Ketchikan and accessible by boat) and Melozi Hot Springs (200 air miles northwest of Fairbanks) have lodging, pool and accommodations. Less developed is Manley Hot Springs in the small community of the same name at the end of Elliott Highway (160 miles west of Fairbanks). The hot springs are privately owned and a primitive bathhouse is used primarily by local residents. Manley Hot Springs Resort is located near the springs, but its waters are supplied from a geothermal well. The resort does have a pool, restaurant and lodging facilities. Ophir Hot Springs (about 50 miles southwest of Aniak) has a private hunting camp with accommodations and an aboveground hot pool.

There are 11 additional springs with cabins and/or bathing tubs and changing facilities. Most of these are accessible only by boat, plane, snowmobile, dog team, ATV or on foot. Among them is the community of Tenakee Springs on Chichagof Island in southeastern Alaska, which maintains an old bathhouse near the waterfront for public use. The state Marine Highway System provides ferry service to Tenakee Springs. Chief Shakes Hot Springs, near Wrangell, and White Sulfur Hot Springs and Goddard Hot Springs, both near Sitka, all have Forest Service cabins and are accessible by boat or floatplane. Tolovana Hot Springs, 45 miles northwest of Fairbanks, features two cabins and a hot tub. Reservations are required. Visitors can soak and photograph the old buildings that were once an orphanage at Pilgrim Hot Springs, 60 miles from Nome, accessible by road in summer only. Also on the Seward Peninsula is Serpentine Hot Springs, a winter destination by snowmobile from Nome.

Other springs include Baranof Hot Springs on Baranof Island, and Kanuti Hot Springs, about 10 miles west of the Dalton Highway near Caribou Mountain. These springs are used primarily by skiers and mushers in the winter.

A map featuring most of the thermal areas in Alaska can be purchased for $5 from the Alaska Division of Geological and Geophysical Surveys, 794 University Ave., Suite 200, Fairbanks 99701-3645. For a map or more information, call (907) 451-5027.

Hunting
There are 26 game management units in Alaska with a wide variety of seasons and bag limits. Current copies of the *Alaska State Hunting Regulations* with maps delineating game unit boundaries are available from the Alaska Department of Fish and Game (P.O. Box 25525, Juneau 99802) or from Fish and Game offices and sporting goods stores throughout the state.

Regulations. A hunting or trapping license is required for all residents and nonresidents with the exception of Alaska residents under 16 years or older than 60 years of age. A special identification card

Both male and female Dall sheep grow horns. From *Alaska's Mammals* by Dave Smith (text) and Tom Walker (photos)

is issued for the senior citizen exemption.

A resident hunting license (valid for the calendar year) costs $25; trapping license (valid until September 30 of the year following the year of issue), $15; hunting and trapping license, $40; hunting and sportfishing license, $40; hunting, trapping and sportfishing license, $55.

A nonresident (U.S. citizen) and alien hunting license (valid for the calendar year) costs $85; hunting and sportfishing license, $135; hunting and trapping license, $250.

Military personnel stationed in Alaska may purchase a small game hunting license for $25, and a small game hunting and sportfishing license for $40. Military personnel must purchase a nonresident hunting license at full cost ($85) and pay nonresident military fees for big game tags (one-half the nonresident rate), unless they are hunting big game on military property.

Licenses may be obtained from any designated issuing agent or by mail from the Alaska Department of Fish and Game, Licensing Division, P.O. Box 25525, Juneau 99802; (907) 465-2376.

Big game tags and fees are required for residents hunting musk oxen and brown/grizzly bear and

The moose nugget jewelry souvenir manufacturing industry held steady in 1997, although some new producers entered the market and others dropped out. A major distributor explained, "You can only produce so many of those before your self esteem starts to suffer."

for nonresidents and aliens hunting any big game animal. These nonrefundable, non-transferable, metal locking tags (valid for the calendar year) must be purchased prior to the taking of the animal. A tag may be used for any species for which the tag fee is of equal or less value. Fees quoted below are for *each* animal.

All residents (regardless of age), non-residents and aliens intending to hunt brown/grizzly bear must purchase tags (resident, $25; nonresident, $500; alien, $650). Residents, nonresidents and aliens are also required to purchase musk oxen tags (resident, $500 each bull taken on Nunivak Island, $25 each cow from Nelson Island or in Arctic National Wildlife Refuge; nonresident, $1,100; alien, $1,500).

Nonresident tag fees for other big game animals are as follows: deer, $150; wolf or wolverine, $175; black bear, $225; elk or goat, $300; caribou, $325; moose, $400; bison, $450; sheep, $425.

Nonresident alien tag fees for other big game animals are as follows: deer, $200; wolf or wolverine, $250; black bear, $300; elk or goat, $400; caribou, $425; moose, $500; bison, $650; and sheep, $550.

Nonresidents hunting brown/grizzly bear, Dall sheep or mountain goat are required to have a guide or be accompanied by an Alaska resident relative over 19 years of age within the second degree of kinship (includes parents, children, sisters or brothers). Nonresident aliens hunting big game must have a guide. A current list of registered Alaska guides is available for $5 from the Department of Commerce, Division of Occupational Licensing, Big Game Commercial Services Board, Box 11806, Juneau 99811-0806.

Residents and nonresidents 16 years of age or older hunting waterfowl must have a signed federal migratory bird hunting stamp (duck stamp) and a signed state waterfowl conservation stamp. The Alaska duck stamp is available from agents who sell hunting licenses or by mail from the Alaska Department of Fish and Game, Licensing Section.

Trophy Game. Record big game in Alaska as recorded by the Boone and Crockett Club in the latest (1993) edition of *Records of North American Big Game* are as follows:

Black bear: Skull 13 $7/16$ inches long, 8 $9/16$ inches wide (1987).
Brown bear (coastal region): Skull 17 $15/16$ inches long, 12 $13/16$ inches wide (1952).
Grizzly bear (inland): Skull 17 $3/16$ inches long, 9 $5/16$ inches wide (1991).
Polar bear: Skull 18 $1/2$ inches long, 11 $7/16$ inches wide (1963). It is currently illegal for

Traditional Bear Hunt

The traditional Inupiat attached great spiritual significance to the grizzly, whom they called aklaq. While they considered the black bear to be somewhat of a dimwit, they respected and feared the grizzly above all other animals. If a hunter killed one, the skin became the door of his house, and whoever entered was notified of the man's bravery and skill. Considering how bears were hunted in the days before firearms, such a door was no idle boast. A hunter would stalk a bear with a stout bone-tipped spear, or wait in ambush under a cutbank. When the surprised animal would rear up to get a better look at his attacker, the man would dart under the front paws, moving in from the right (since bears are said to be left-handed) and plant his spear on the ground, angling up and inward. As the bear came down to crush the man, he impaled himself. The hunter would dive out of the way and wait for the bear to thrash out his life, and finish him with another spear if needed. . . . Once a bear was killed, there were rules of spiritual etiquette which were strictly followed . . . acts that assured that the bear's spirit would not molest the hunter, and that it would be born again.—Nick Jans, The Last Light Breaking

anyone but an Alaskan Eskimo, Aleut or Indian to hunt polar bear in Alaska.

Bison: Right horn 18 ¹/₈ inches long, base circumference 15 inches; left horn 21 inches long, base circumference 15 ¹/₄ inches; greatest spread 31 ⁷/₈ inches (1977).

Barren Ground caribou: Right beam 50 ⁶/₈ inches, 24 points; left beam 40 ¹/₈ inches, 23 points (1987).

Moose: Right palm length 49 ⁵/₈ inches, width 20 ³/₄ inches; left palm length 49 ⁶/₈ inches, width 15 ⁵/₈ inches; right antler 18 points, left 16 points; greatest spread 77 inches (1978).

Mountain goat: Right horn 11 ⁵/₈ inches long, base circumference 5 ³/₄ inches; left horn 11 ⁵/₈ inches long, base circumference 5 ⁵/₈ inches (1933).

Musk ox: Right horn 26 ⁴/₈ inches; left horn 26 ³/₈ inches; tip-to-tip spread 27 ⁴/₈ inches (1986).

Dall sheep: Right horn 48 ⁵/₈ inches long, base circumference 14 ⁵/₈ inches; left horn 47 ⁷/₈ inches long, base circumference 14 ³/₄ inches (1961).

Hypothermia

(*See also* Chill Factor)
Hypothermia develops when the body is exposed to cold and cannot maintain normal temperatures. In an automatic survival reaction, blood flow to the extremities is shut down in favor of preserving warmth in the vital organs. As internal temperature drops, judgment and coordination become impaired. Allowed to continue, hypothermia leads to stupor, collapse and death. Immersion hypothermia occurs in cold water.

Ice (*See* Glaciers and Ice Fields; Icebergs; Ice Fog; Iceworm; *and* Nenana Ice Classic)

Icebergs (*See also* Glaciers and Ice Fields) Icebergs are formed wherever glaciers reach salt water or a freshwater lake and chunks break off into the water. Some accessible places to view icebergs include Glacier Bay, Icy Bay, Yakutat Bay, Taku Inlet, Endicott Arm, portions of northern

Prince William Sound (College Fiord, Barry Arm, Columbia Bay), Mendenhall Lake and Portage Lake.

If icebergs contain little or no sediment, approximately 75 percent to 80 percent of their bulk may be underwater. The more sediment an iceberg contains, the greater its density, and an iceberg containing large amounts of sediment will float slightly beneath the surface. Glaciologists of the U.S. Geological Survey believe that some of these "black icebergs" may actually sink to the bottom of a body of water. Since salt water near the faces of glaciers may be liquid to temperatures as low as 28°F, and icebergs melt at 32°F, some of these underwater icebergs may remain unmelted indefinitely.

Alaska's icebergs are small compared to the icebergs found near Antarctica and Greenland. One of the largest icebergs ever recorded in Alaska was formed in May 1977, in Icy Bay. Glaciologists measured it at 346 feet long, 297 feet wide and 99 feet above the surface of the water.

Sea Ice. Seawater typically freezes at −1.8°C or 28.8°F. The first indication that seawater is freezing is the appearance of frazil—tiny needlelike crystals of pure ice— in shallow coastal areas of low current or areas of low salinity, such as near the mouths of rivers. Continued freezing turns the frazil into a soupy mass called grease ice and eventually into an ice crust approximately 4 inches thick. More freezing, wind and wave action thicken the ice and break it into ice floes ranging from a few feet to several miles across. In the Arctic Ocean, ice floes can be 10 feet thick. Most are crisscrossed with 6- to 8-foot-high walls of ice caused by the force of winds.

Sea salt that is trapped in the ice during freezing is leached out over time, making the oldest ice the least saline. Meltwater forming in ponds on multi-year-old ice during summer months is a freshwater source for native marine life.

Refreezing of meltwater ponds and the formation of new ice in the permanent ice pack (generally north of 72° north latitude) begins in mid-September. While the ice pack expands southward, new ice freezes to the coast (shorefast ice) and spreads seaward. Where the drifting ice pack grinds against the relatively stable shorefast ice, tremendous walls or ridges of ice are formed, some observed to be 100 feet thick and grounded in 60 feet of water. They are impenetrable by all but the most powerful icebreakers. By late March the ice cover has reached its maximum extent, approximately from Port Heiden on the Alaska Peninsula in the south to the northern Pribilof Islands and northwestward to Siberia. In Cook Inlet, sea ice, usually no more than 2 feet thick, can extend as far south as Anchor Point and Kamishak Bay on the east and west sides of the inlet, respectively. The ice season usually lasts from mid-November to April.

The Navy began observing and forecasting sea ice conditions in 1954 in support of the construction of defense sites along the Arctic coast. In 1969, the National Weather Service began a low-profile sea ice reconnaissance program, which expanded greatly during the summer of 1975 when, during a year of severe ice, millions of dollars of materials had to be shipped to Prudhoe Bay. Expanded commercial fisheries in the Bering Sea also heightened the problem of sea ice for crabbing and bottom fish trawling operations. In 1976, headquarters for a seven-days-a-week ice watch was established at Fairbanks; it was moved to Anchorage in 1981.

The National Weather Service operates a radio facsimile broadcast service that makes current ice analysis charts, special oceanographic charts and standard weather charts available to the public via standard radios equipped with "black box" receivers. Commercial fishing operators, particularly in the Bering Sea, use the radio-transmitted charts to steer clear of problem weather and troublesome ice formations. More information is available from the National Weather Service in Kodiak or Anchorage.

Ice Fog Ice fog develops when air just above the ground becomes so cold, it can no longer retain water vapor and tiny, spherical ice crystals are formed. Ice fog is most common in arctic and subarctic regions in winter when clear skies create an air inversion, trapping cold air at low elevations. It is most noticeable when man-made pollutants are also suspended in the air inversion.

Iceworm Although often regarded as a hoax, iceworms actually exist. These small, threadlike, segmented black worms, usually less than 1 inch long, thrive in temperatures just above freezing. Observers as far back as the 1880s reported that at dawn or dusk or on overcast days, the tiny worms, all belonging to the genus *Mesenchytraeus*, may literally carpet the surface of glaciers. When sunlight strikes them, they burrow back down into the ice; temperatures over 75°F kill them.

The town of Cordova commemorates its own version of the iceworm each February with an Iceworm Festival, when a 100-foot-long, multilegged "iceworm" leads a parade down Main Street. Other activities include an arts and crafts show, ski events, contests, dances, and honorary king and queen.

Iditarod Trail Sled Dog Race (SEE ALSO DOG MUSHING AND YUKON QUEST INTERNATIONAL SLED DOG RACE)

Two of the longest sled dog races in the world take place in Alaska: the Yukon Quest and the Iditarod. The first Iditarod Trail Sled Dog Race, conceived and organized by Joe Redington, Sr., of Knik, and the late Dorothy Page, of Wasilla, was run in 1967 and covered only 56 miles. The race was lengthened in 1973, and the first ever 1,100-mile sled dog race began in Anchorage on March 3, 1973, and ended April 3 in Nome. Of the 34 who started the race, 22 finished. The Iditarod has been run every year since its inception. In 1997, the Iditarod Trail Sled Dog Race marked its 25th anniversary.

In 1976, Congress designated the Iditarod as a National Historic Trail. The official length of the Iditarod National Historic Trail System, including northern and southern routes, is 2,350 miles.

Following the old dog team mail route

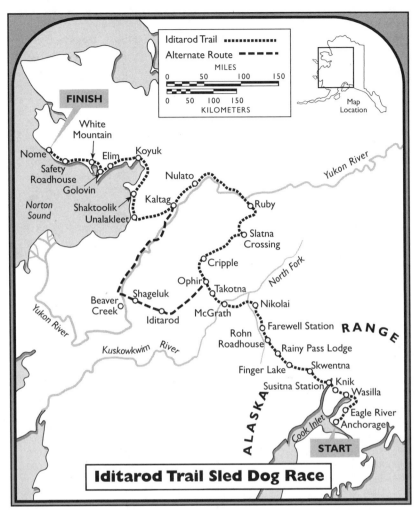

Iditarod Trail ●●●●●●●●●●
Alternate Route ▬ ▬ ▬ ▬

MILES
0   50   100   150

0   50   100   150
KILOMETERS

Map Location

FINISH

White Mountain

Nome
Safety
Roadhouse
Golovin
Elim
Koyuk

Norton Sound

Shaktoolik
Unalakleet

Kaltag

Nulato

Ruby

Yukon River

Slatna Crossing

Cripple

Ophir
Takotna
Shageluk
Beaver Creek
Iditarod
McGrath

Nikolai

North Fork

Farewell Station

R A N G E

Yukon River

Kuskowkwim River

Rohn Roadhouse
Rainy Pass Lodge

Finger Lake
Skwentna

Susitna Station
Knik
Wasilla
Eagle River
Anchorage

A L A S K A

Cook Inlet

START

Iditarod Trail Sled Dog Race

blazed in 1910 from Knik to Nome, the race route crosses two mountain ranges, follows the Yukon River for about 150 miles, runs through several bush villages and crosses the pack ice of Norton Sound.

Strictly a winter trail because the ground is mostly spongy muskeg swamps, the route attracted national attention in 1925 when sled dog mushers, including the famous Leonhard Seppala, relayed 300,000 units of life-saving diphtheria serum to epidemic-threatened Nome. However, as the airplane and snowmobile replaced the sled dog team, the trail fell into disuse. Thanks to

Redington and Page, the trail has been assured a place in Alaska history.

Each year the Iditarod takes a slightly different course, using an alternate southern route in odd years (*see* map above). The route is traditionally described as 1,049 miles long (a figure that was selected because Alaska is the 49th state), but the actual distance run each year is close to 1,100 miles.

In 1997, 53 mushers began the race; nine were scratched. Martin Buser chalked up his third win, taking home a purse of $50,000.

1997 Results

Place	Musher	Days	Hrs.	Min.	Dogs	Prize
1.	Martin Buser	9	08	30	45	$50,000
2.	Doug Swingley	9	11	41	15	44,800
3.	Jeff King	9	15	35	15	36,400
4.	DeeDee Jonrowe	9	18	26	10	31,500
5.	Vern Halter	9	20	58	44	27,300
6.	Lavon Barve	9	21	06	37	24,955
7.	Bill Cotter	9	21	37	28	23,328
8.	Ramy Brooks	9	21	51	09	21,700
9.	Peryll Kyzer	9	22	20	49	20,073
10.	Tim Osmar	9	22	59	28	18,445
11.	John Baker	9	23	09	36	15,470
12.	Sven Engholm	9	23	24	08	13,090
13.	Charlie Boulding	9	23	49	25	11,305
14.	Paul Gebhardt	10	08	59	25	10,115
15.	Ramey Smyth	10	14	11	20	9,520
16.	Mitch Seavey	10	14	31	55	9,240
17.	Linwood Fiedler	10	14	58	20	8,820
18.	Mike Williams	10	15	45	02	8,400
19.	David Sawatzky	10	17	54	00	7,980
20.	Kris Swanguarin	10	19	26	01	7,560

Winners and Times

Year	Musher	Days	Hrs.	Min.	Sec.	Prize
1975	Emmitt Peters, Ruby	14	14	43	45	$15,000
1976	Jerry Riley, Nenana	18	22	58	17	7,000
1977	Rick Swenson, Eureka	16	16	27	13	9,600
1978	Rick Mackey, Wasilla	14	18	52	24	12,000
1979	Rick Swenson, Eureka	15	10	37	47	12,000
1980	Joe May, Trapper Creek	14	07	11	51	12,000
1981	Rick Swenson, Eureka	12	08	45	02	24,000
1982	Rick Swenson, Eureka	16	04	40	10	24,000
1983	Rick Mackey, Wasilla	12	14	10	44	24,000
1984	Dean Osmar, Clam Gulch	12	15	07	33	24,000*
1985	Libby Riddles, Teller	18	00	20	17	50,000
1986	Susan Butcher, Manley	11	15	06	00	50,000
1987	Susan Butcher, Manley	11	02	05	13	50,000
1988	Susan Butcher, Manley	11	11	41	40	30,000
1989	Joe Runyan, Nenana	11	05	24	34	50,000
1990	Susan Butcher, Manley	11	01	53	23	50,000
1991	Rick Swenson, Two Rivers	12	16	34	39	50,000
1992	Martin Buser, Big Lake	10	19	17	15	50,000
1993	Jeff King, Denali Park	10	15	38	15	50,000**
1994	Martin Buser, Big Lake	10	13	02	39	50,000***
1995	Doug Swingley, Simms, MT	09	02	42	19	52,500
1996	Jeff King, Denali Park	09	05	43	13	50,000
1997	Martin Buser, Big Lake	09	08	30	45	50,000+

* Does not include $2,000 in silver ingots for reaching the halfway checkpoint first.
**Does not include $3,000 in silver ingots for reaching the halfway checkpoint first.
*** Does not include $2,500 in gold nuggets for first musher to reach Unalakleet.
 + Does not include Dodge truck.

Igloo

(*SEE ALSO* BARABARA) The word igloo, meaning snowhouse, is from northern and eastern Eskimo (Inupiaq *iglu* or "house"). The stereotypical igloo is a snow block structure that could be quickly built as a temporary trail shelter for Arctic Alaska and Canada Eskimos. Igloos are constructed in a spiral with each tier leaning inward at a greater angle. The entrance is a tunnel with a cold trap. A sleeping platform raises sleepers off the cold floor, while a vent at the top allows in fresh air for ventilation, and an ice window admits light.

Most Alaskan indigenous dwellings were sod igloos, dome- or Quonset-shaped structures whose roof was supported with wood or whale bones and covered with insulating sod.

Income

(*SEE ALSO* COST OF LIVING) On a per capita income basis, Alaska was ranked 12th in the nation at $24,002 per person in 1995, a modest gain from $23,344 per person in 1994. Per capita income is calculated by taking the state's total personal income and dividing it by the state's total resident population. Because it is a relative measure of the entire population, some people believe it is a good yardstick of economic well-being.

Alaska's income picture relative to the rest of the nation has declined. In 1995, the state's per capita income advantage fell to 103 percent of the national average. This was down considerably from the 130 percent of the national average Alaskans enjoyed in 1985. Though Alaska's per capita income has continued to increase, the increase in the cost of living has been greater. For many Alaskans, the shrinking lead in per capita income may no longer be large enough to make up for the state's high cost of living.

Most Alaskans' personal income comes from net earnings, which include wages, salaries and tips. The average monthly wage reached $2,691 in 1995. In the major industry groups, oil and gas reflects the highest monthly average wage of $6,620, according to the Alaska Department of Labor, Research and Analysis Section. Roughly 89 percent of these mining jobs are supplied through the oil and gas industries. High wages, long hours and a mostly full-time workforce explain the industry's top average monthly pay. Low wages and part-time jobs explain retail trade's lowest average monthly wage of $1,463.

Median household income in Alaska in 1995 was $47,954, which ranked Alaska first in the nation. According to the U.S. Census Bureau, 7.1 percent of Alaska's population lived below the poverty level in 1995. Historically, the rate of poverty in Alaska has been considerably higher in rural parts of the state.

Information Sources

Abuse of Adults. Adult Protective Services, Anchorage (800) 478-9996.

Agriculture. State Division of Agriculture, Box 949, Palmer 99645.

Alaska Natives. Alaska Federation of Natives, 411 W. Fourth Ave., Anchorage 99501.

Boating, Canoeing and Kayaking. Alaska Dept. of Transportation and Public Facilities, P.O. Box Z, Juneau 99811; State of Alaska, Division of Parks and Outdoor Recreation, 3601 C St., Suite 1200, Anchorage 99503.

Business. Alaska Department of Commerce and Economic Development, P.O. Box D, Juneau 99811;

The Anchorage Convention and Visitors Bureau reports that an Alaskan visitor at Denali Park actually asked, "What time does the 1 o'clock tour start?"

State Chamber of Commerce, 217 Second St., Suite 201, Juneau 99801.

Census Data. Alaska Department of Labor, Research and Analysis, P.O. Box 107018, Anchorage 99510.

Customs. U.S., (907) 474-0307; Canadian, (403) 862-7230.

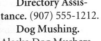

Directory Assistance. (907) 555-1212.

Dog Mushing. Alaska Dog Mushers Association, Box 662, Fairbanks 99707.

Education. Alaska Department of Education, P.O. Box 25535, Juneau 99802.

The Elderly. Division of Senior Service, 3601 C St., Suite 310, Anchorage 99503; (907) 563-5654; elsewhere, (800) 478-9996.

Ferry System. Alaska Marine Highway, P.O. Box 25535, Juneau 99802-5535.

Gold Panning. Alaska Miners Association, 501 W. Northern Lights Blvd., Suite 203, Anchorage 99503.

Handicapped Access. Challenge Alaska, Box 110064, Anchorage 99511; (907) 563-2658. Outdoor recreation programs for persons with disabilities. Sea kayaking, adaptive skiing.

Health. State Department of Health and Social Services, Division of Public Health, P.O. Box H, Juneau 99811.

Highway Information. Alaska State Troopers (for emergencies), (907) 452-1313; Alaska State Highway System, (800) 478-7675.

Historical Archives. Alaska State Archives, Box 6, Juneau 99811; University of Alaska Archives, 3211 Providence Drive, Anchorage 99508.

Housing. State Housing Authority, P.O. Box 10080, Anchorage 99510.

Hunting and Fishing Regulations. State Department of Fish and Game, P.O. Box 3-2000, Juneau 99802. Recorded information: (907) 452-1525.

Job Opportunities. Job Service, 3301 Eagle, Anchorage 99503; State Employment Service, P.O. Box 3-7000, Juneau 99802.

Job Opportunities for People with Disabilities. ASSETS, Inc., 2330 Nichols St., Anchorage 99508; (907) 279-6617.

Labor. State Department of Labor, P.O. Box 25501-5501, Juneau 99802.

Land. Alaska Public Lands Information Centers, 605 W. Fourth Ave., Suite 105, Anchorage 99501; 250 Cushman St., Suite 1A, Fairbanks 99701; P.O. Box 359, Tok 99780; Bureau of Land Management, 222 W. Seventh Ave., No. 13, Anchorage 99513; State Division of Lands, P.O. Box 107005, Anchorage 99510.

Legislature. Legislative Information Office, 716 W. Fourth Ave., Anchorage 99501.

Libraries. Alaska State Library, 344 W. Third Ave., Anchorage 99501.

Made in Alaska Products. Alaska Association of Manufacturers, P.O. Box 142831, Anchorage 99514.

Maps (topographic). U.S. Geological Survey, 4230 University Drive, Room 101, Anchorage 99508; 101 12th Ave., Room 126, Fairbanks 99701.

Medicaid Waivers: Division of Mental Health and Developmental Disabilities, (907) 562-3717.

Military. Department of the Air Force, Headquarters, Alaskan Air Command, Elmendorf Air Force Base 99506; Department of the Army, Headquarters, U.S. Army Alaska, 600 Richardson Drive, Box 5900, Fort Richardson 99505; State Department of Military and Veterans Affairs, Box 5800, Fort Richardson 99505; Department of Transportation, U.S. Coast Guard, 17th Coast Guard District, P.O. Box 3-5000, Juneau 99802.

Mines and Petroleum. Alaska Miners Association, 501 W. Northern Lights Blvd., Suite 203, Anchorage 99503; Petroleum Information Corp., P.O. Box 102278, Anchorage 99510; State Division of Geological and Geophysical Surveys, 3601 C St., Anchorage 99503.

Permanent Fund Dividend. Anchorage Dividend Information Office, Box 25500, Juneau 99801.

Resorts/Lodges. Alaska National Park Connection, Box 221011, Anchorage 99522; (888) 277-2757. Hotline connects you with lodging and tour experts at Denali, Glacier Bay, Katmai, Kenai Fjords and Wrangell–St. Elias. E–mail wingsong@alaska.net.

River Running. Bureau of Land Management, 222 W. Seventh Ave., No. 13, Anchorage 99513; National Park Service, 2525 Gambell St., Anchorage 99503; U.S. Dept. of the Interior, Fish and Wildlife Service, 1011 E. Tudor Road, Anchorage 99503.

Senior Programs: Deborah Taylor, Anchorage, (907) 563-5654; elsewhere, (800) 478-9996.

Stranded Residents: Association for Stranded Rural Alaskans in Anchorage, 2606 C St., Suite 2B, Anchorage 99503; (907) 272-0643.

Travel and Visitor Information. Alaska Division of Tourism, Box 110801, Juneau 99811; Alaska Visitors Association, 3201 C St., Suite 403, Anchorage 99503; (907) 465-2010. Visit the Web site at http://www.alaskan.com or http://www.travel.org/alaska.html.

Weather Information: National Weather Service, (907) 456-0247; statewide, (907) 456-0389; Fairbanks, (907) 452-3553.

Inuit Circumpolar Conference
Started in Barrow in 1977, the Inuit Circumpolar Conference brings together Inuit from Greenland, Canada, Alaska and Chukotka (Russia) to address common concerns regarding environment, human rights, health and economic development. The ICC is prominent in national and international arenas, including the United Nations and circumpolar initiatives such as the eight-nation Arctic Environmental Protection Strategy. In Alaska, the ICC has supported international Native-to-Native agreements on managing shared wildlife resources such as polar bears.

National offices in each of the four countries represented by the ICC carry on the work of the organization, which is directed by triennial general assemblies, the sites of which rotate between countries. The next assembly will be held in Greenland in July 1998, and will bring together over 1,000 Inuit from around the Arctic.

Islands
Southeastern Alaska contains about 1,000 of the state's 1,800 named islands, rocks and reefs; several thousand remain unnamed. The Aleutian Island chain, stretching southwest from the mainland, contains more than 200 islands.

Of the state's 10 largest islands, six are in southeastern Alaska. Of the remainder, Unimak is in the Aleutians, Nunivak and St. Lawrence are in the Bering Sea off the west coast of Alaska, and Kodiak is in the Gulf of Alaska (*see* map, pages 8–9). The state's 10 largest islands, according to U.S. Geological Survey figures, are:

1. Kodiak, 3,588 sq. mi.
2. Prince of Wales, 2,731 sq. mi.
3. Chichagof, 2,062 sq. mi.
4. St. Lawrence, 1,780 sq. mi.
5. Admiralty, 1,709 sq. mi.
6. Baranof, 1,636 sq. mi.
7. Nunivak, 1,600 sq. mi. (estimate)
8. Unimak, 1,600 sq. mi.
9. Revillagigedo, 1,134 sq. mi.
10. Kupreanof, 1,084 sq. mi.

Ivory
Eskimos traditionally carved sea mammal ivory to make such implements as harpoon heads, dolls and ulu (fan-shaped knife) handles. For the past century, however, most carvings have been made to be sold. Etching on ivory originally was done with hand tools and the scratched designs were filled in with soot. Today power tools supplement the hand tools and carvers may color the etching with India ink, graphite, hematite or commercial coloring.

The large islands of the Bering Sea—St. Lawrence, Little Diomede and Nunivak—are home to the majority of Alaska's ivory carvers. Eskimos from King Island, renowned for their carving skill, now live in Nome along with talented artists from many other villages.

The bulk of the ivory used today comes from walrus tusks and teeth, seasoned for a few months. Old walrus ivory, often mistakenly called fossil ivory, is also used. This

Walrus. From *Alaska's Mammals* by Dave Smith (text) and Tom Walker (photos)

ivory has been buried in the ground or has been on beaches for years, and contact with various minerals has changed it from white to tan or any of a multitude of colors. Some highly prized old ivory exhibits rays of deep blue or areas of brown and gold that shine. Most old ivory comes from ancient sites or beaches on St. Lawrence Island and is sold by the pound to non-Native buyers, generally for use in some kind of artwork.

Mastodon tusks are often unearthed in the summer by miners or found eroding on river cutbanks where they have been buried for thousands of years. Although these tusks are enormous and their colorations often beautiful, the material cannot be used efficiently because it dries and then separates into narrow ridges. Various federal prohibitions govern the collection of old walrus, mammoth and mastodon ivory. Such materials may be gathered from private or

> The state-required notice of Workers' Compensation Coverage in every workplace in Alaska contains this notice: "Immediately (not later than 30 days from . . . death date) give your employer and the Alaska Workers' Compensation Board written notice of a job-related . . . death."

reservation lands, but may not be traded or sold if found on public lands. The taking of fresh walrus ivory is prohibited to non-Natives in accordance with the Marine Mammal Protection Act of 1972.

Walrus may be taken only by Alaska Natives (Aleuts, Eskimos and Indians) who dwell on the coast of the North Pacific Ocean or the Arctic Ocean, for subsistence purposes or for the creation and sale of authentic Native articles of handicrafts or clothing.

Raw walrus ivory and other parts can be sold only by an Alaska Native to an Alaska Native within Alaska, or to a registered agent for resale or transfer to an Alaska Native within the state. Only authentic Native-processed ivory articles of handicrafts or clothing may be sold or transferred to a non-Native, or sold in interstate commerce.

Beach ivory, which is found on the beach within a quartermile of the ocean, may, however, be kept by anyone. This ivory must be registered by all non-Natives with the U.S. Fish and Wildlife Service (USFWS) or the National Marine Fisheries Service within 30 days of discovery. Beach-found ivory must remain in the possession of the finder even if carved or scrimshawed.

Carved or scrimshawed walrus ivory (authentic Native handicraft) or other marine mammal parts made into clothing or other authentic Native handicrafts may be exported from the United States to a foreign country, but the exporter must first obtain an export permit from the USFWS. Even visitors from the Lower 48 simply traveling through, or stopping in Canada on their way home, are required to have a USFWS export and/or transit permit. Cost is $25. Mailing the carved ivory home will avoid the need for an export/transit permit. Importation of walrus or other marine mammal parts is illegal, except for scientific research purposes or for public display once a permit is granted. Because of ecological sensitivity to the use of elephant ivory, many carvers are switching to whalebone, recycled from the skeletons of harvested species.

For further information contact: Special Agent-in-Charge, U.S. Fish and Wildlife Service, 1011 E. Tudor Road, Anchorage 99503, (907) 786-3311; or Senior Resident, U.S. Fish and Wildlife Service, 1412 Airport Way, Fairbanks 99701; (907) 456-0239.

Jade

Most Alaskan jade is found near the Dall, Shungnak and Kobuk Rivers, and Jade Mountain, all north of the Arctic Circle. The stones occur in various shades of green, brown, black, yellow, white and even red. The most valuable are those that are marbled black, white and green. Gem-quality jade, about one-fourth of the total mined, is used in jewelry making. Fractured jade is used for clock faces, tabletops, bookends and other items. Jade is the Alaska state gem.

Juneau

Located on scenic Gastineau Channel, Juneau is the capital of Alaska. Established in 1880 as a mining camp, it was originally called Harrisburg after Richard Harris, who with his partner, Joseph Juneau, discovered gold and staked their claim in 1880. The camp quickly boomed.

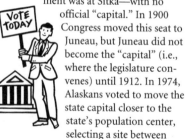

Under Russian rule, the seat of government was at Sitka—with no official "capital." In 1900 Congress moved this seat to Juneau, but Juneau did not become the "capital" (i.e., where the legislature convenes) until 1912. In 1974, Alaskans voted to move the state capital closer to the state's population center, selecting a site between Anchorage and Fairbanks at Willow. Juneau remained the capital after funding for transfer of government to Willow was defeated by voters in 1982. Of Southeast Alaska's 60,000 residents, half live in Juneau, Alaska's third-largest city.

Juneau is accessible only by boat, ferry or plane. No roads lead into or out of town. Often called "a little San Francisco," Juneau is tucked at the foot of Mount Juneau. The climate is wet and mild, with summer average daily maximum temperatures of 63°F and winter average daily minimum temperatures of 20°F, with an average annual snowfall of about 92 inches in the downtown area.

Sights include the Red Dog Saloon, the State Museum, the State Library and its archives, the State Office Building and the Governor's Mansion. Helicopter tours of the Juneau Icefield and tours to Glacier Bay National Park are popular activities, as are fishing, hiking and Inside Passage cruises.

Additional information is available from the Juneau Convention and Visitors Bureau, 134 Third St., Juneau 99801; (907) 586-2201. E-mail jcvb@ptialaska.net or view the visitor guide at http://www. juneau.com.

Kodiak

Kodiak, the oldest European settlement in Alaska, is located on Kodiak Island in the Gulf of Alaska, 252 air miles south of Anchorage and the Kenai Peninsula. Known as Alaska's "Emerald Isle," 100-mile-long Kodiak Island and its main city are accessible only by boat, ferry or plane.

After 7,500 years of Alutiiq occupation, Kodiak Island (the second-largest island in the U.S.) was "discovered" by Russian explorer Stephen Glotov in 1763. The town of Kodiak served as Russian Alaska's first capital city until 1804. In 1912, Kodiak was caught in drifting ash from the eruption of Novarupta Volcano on the Alaska Peninsula, which buried the town under 18 inches of pumice. On March 27, 1964, the biggest earthquake to shake North America (9.2 on the Richter scale) hit the Kodiak area and set off a tsunami that virtually destroyed downtown Kodiak, its fishing fleet, processing plants and more than 150 homes.

Today, more than 15,000 populate the Kodiak Island Borough. Commercial fishing is the island's main industry, with 2,600 vessels and an annual harvest exceeding $80 million—making Kodiak one of the top five commercial fishing ports in the U.S.

Timber activities and tourism are also important segments of the local economy. Kodiak is home to the U.S. Coast Guard's base for North Pacific operations, the nation's largest.

The city of Kodiak has two museums, the Baranov and the new Alutiiq Museum and Archaeological Repository. The Baranov Museum displays many items from the Russian era. The Alutiiq Museum chronicles the 8,000-year history of the indigenous Alutiiq people and the advent of the Russian fur trade. Icons, rare paintings and handmade brassworks can be seen at the Russian Orthodox Church.

It is estimated that more than 3,000 Kodiak bears inhabit the island. Kodiak National Wildlife Refuge (accessible only by floatplane or boat) was established in 1941 to preserve the natural habitat of the bear. Bears can be observed feeding on salmon during the summer in remote parts of the refuge.

For free maps, brochures, hunting and fishing information, contact the Kodiak Island Convention and Visitors Bureau,

Woman in a kuspuk with her child, fishing through the ice. From The Alaska Heritage Seafood Cookbook by Ann Chandonnet

100 Marine Way, Kodiak 99615; (907) 486-4782. Or point your browser to http://www.kodiak.org/kodiak.

Kuspuk
A *kuspuk* is an Eskimo woman's parka, often made with a loosely cut back so that an infant may be carried piggyback-style. Parkas are made from seal, marmot, ground squirrel, rabbit or fox skins; traditionally, the fur lining faces inward. The ruffs are generally made of wolverine or wolf fur. An outer shell, called a *qaspeg*, is worn over a fur parka to keep it clean and to prevent wear. This outer shell is usually made of brightly colored corduroy, cotton print or velveteenlike material, and may be trimmed with rickrack.

Labor and Employer Organizations
Alaska has local branches of dozens of unions, including unions for longshoremen, carpenters, restaurant employees, pulp and paper workers, electrical workers, aerospace workers, firefighters and others. For details, consult the *Alaska Labor Union Directory* of the Alaska State AFL-CIO; phone (907) 258-6284.

Lakes
There are 94 lakes with surface areas of more than 10 square miles among Alaska's more than 3 million lakes. According to the U.S. Geological Survey, the 10 largest natural freshwater lakes in square miles are: Iliamna, 1,150; Becharof, 458; Teshekpuk, 315; Naknek, 242; Tustumena, 117; Clark, 110; Dall, 100; Upper Ugashik, 75; Lower Ugashik, 72; and Kukaklek, 72.

Land Use
At first glance it seems odd that such a huge area as Alaska has not been more heavily settled. Thousands of acres of forest and tundra, miles and miles of rivers and streams, hidden valleys, bays, coves and mountains, are spread across an area so vast that it staggers the imagination. Yet, more than two-thirds of the population of Alaska remains clustered around two major centers of commerce and survival,

Anchorage and Fairbanks. Compared to the settlement of the western Lower 48, Alaska is not settled at all.

Visitors flying over the state are impressed by immense areas showing no sign of humanity. Current assessments indicate that approximately 160,000 acres of Alaska have been cleared, built on or otherwise directly altered by man, either by settlement or resource development, including mining, pipeline construction and agriculture. In comparison to the 365 million acres of land that make up the total of the state, the settled or altered area currently amounts to less than one-twentieth of 1 percent.

There are significant reasons for this lack of development in Alaska. Frozen for long periods in the Arctic, much of the land cannot support quantities of people or industry. Where the winters are "warm," the mountains, glaciers, rivers and oceans prevent easy access for commerce and trade.

The status of land is constantly changing, especially in Alaska. In most places, the free market affects patterns of land ownership, but in Alaska, all land ownership patterns until recently were the result of a century-long process of a single landowner, the United States government.

The Statehood Act signaled the beginning of a dramatic shift in land ownership patterns. It authorized the state to select a total of 104 million of the 365 million acres of land and inland waters in Alaska. (Under the Submerged Lands Act, the state has title to submerged lands under navigable inland waters.) In passing the Statehood Act, Congress cited economic independence and the need to open Alaska to economic development as the primary purposes for large Alaska land grants.

Alaska Native Claims Settlement Act.
The issue of the Native claims in Alaska was cleared up with the passage of the Alaska Native Claims Settlement Act (ANCSA) on Dec. 18, 1971. This act of Congress provided for the creation of Alaska Native village and regional corporations, and gave the Alaska Eskimos, Aleuts and Indians nearly $1 billion and the right to select 44 million acres from a land "pool" of some 115 million acres.

Immediately after the settlement act passed, and before Native lands and National Interest Lands were selected, the state filed to select an additional 77 million acres of land. In September 1972, the litigation initiated by the state was resolved by a settlement affirming state selection of an additional 41 million acres.

Section 17 of the settlement act, in addition to establishing a Joint Federal–State Land Use Planning Commission, directed the secretary of the interior to withdraw from public use up to 80 million acres of land in Alaska for study as possible national parks, wildlife refuges, forests, and wild and scenic rivers. These were the National Interest Lands Congress was to decide upon, as set forth in Section 17(d)(2) of the settlement act, by Dec. 18, 1978. The U.S. House of Representatives passed a bill (HR39) that would have designated 124 million acres of national parks, forests and wildlife refuges, and designated millions of acres of these and existing parks, forests and refuges as wilderness. Although a bill was reported out of committee, it failed to pass the Senate before Congress adjourned.

In November 1978, the secretary of the interior published a draft environmental impact supplement, which listed the actions that the executive branch of the federal government could take

Within two weeks of the opening of the new $168 million Alaska Native Hospital in Anchorage, hospital officials asked U.S. Fish & Wildlife Service biologists to consult on the problem of infectious diseases being tracked into the hospital because of the large amounts of wild goose droppings from the neighborhood flock.

to protect federal lands in Alaska until the 96th Congress could consider the creation of new parks, wildlife refuges, wild and scenic rivers and forests. In keeping with this objective, the secretary of the interior, under provisions of the 1976 Federal Land Policy and Management Act, withdrew about 114 million acres of land in Alaska from most public uses. On Dec. 1, 1978, the president, under the authority of the 1906 Antiquities Act, designated 56 million acres of these lands as national monuments.

In February 1980, the House of Representatives passed a modified HR39. In August 1980, the Senate passed a compromise version of the Alaska lands bill that created 106 million acres of new conservation units and affected a total of 131 million acres of land in Alaska. In November 1980, the House accepted the Senate version of the Alaska National Interest Lands Conservation Act (ANILCA), which President Jimmy Carter signed into law on Dec. 2, 1980. This is also known as the d-2 lands bill or the compromise HR39. (*See also* National Forests; National Parks, Preserves and Monuments; National Wild and Scenic Rivers; National Wilderness Areas; *and* National Wildlife Refuges)

Land use in Alaska will continue to be a controversial and complex subject for some time. Implementation of the d-2 bill, and distribution of land to the Native village and regional corporations, the state of Alaska and private citizens in the state will require time. Much of this work is being done by the Bureau of Land Management, which also surveys federal land before a patent is issued. The passage of ANILCA set the stage for long-term management of resources, and the BLM is now moving forward to establish fish, wildlife and recreation resources as critical and necessary ingredients in a multiple-use mix. Debate continues over issues such as Native sovereignty and subsistence rights.

130 years ago

In 1867, the United States purchased Alaska from Russia for $7.2 million.

Acquiring Land for Private Use.
The easiest and fastest way to acquire land for private use is by purchase from the private sector, through real estate agencies or directly from individuals. Because of speculation, land claim conflicts and delays involving Native, state and federal groups, however, private land is considered by many people to be in short supply and often is very expensive.

Private land in Alaska, excluding land held by Native corporations, is estimated to be more than 1 million acres, but less than 1 percent of the state. Much of this land passed into private hands through the federal Homestead Acts and other public land laws, as well as land disposal programs of the state, boroughs or communities. Most private land is located along Alaska's small road network. Compared to other categories of land, it is highly accessible and constitutes some of the prime settlement land.

All laws related to homesteading on federal land (as opposed to state land) in Alaska were repealed as of 1986. Federal land is not available for homesteading or trade and manufacturing sites.

Following are programs that are in effect for the sale of state land. A one-year residency (except for the auction program) and an age of at least 18 are required for all programs.

Only in Alaska...
Thar's gold in them thar nuggets. This is a fact—there are guys in Alaska who go out and collect moose droppings. They shellac them (if they are reputable and scrupulous moose nugget jewelry craftsmen) and then turn them into jewelry and other souvenirs for tourists. I've done research on this: In Australia they don't make bracelets out of kangaroo crap. In South Dakota, they don't make belt buckles out of buffalo chips . . . Only in Alaska. . . .—Mr. Whitekeys' Alaska Bizarre

Auction: The state has been selling land by public auction since statehood. The state may sell full surface rights, lease of surface or subsurface rights, or restricted title at an auction. There is a minimum bid of fair market value and the high bidder is the purchaser. Participants must be 18.

Homesite: The homesite program was passed in 1977 by the state legislature. Under its provisions, each Alaskan household is eligible for up to five acres. A person who has a homesite entry permit, purchase contract or patent may not apply for another homesite, and neither can any member of that person's household. The land is free, but the individual must pay the cost of the application filing fee ($10), survey and platting, and appraisal, if purchasing. Persons enrolled in this program must live on the homesite for 35 months within seven years of entry and construct a permanent, single-family dwelling on the site within five years. (This is called "proving up" on the land.) After the dwelling is completed and approved by the division, the permit holder may purchase the land at fair market value at the date of purchase. The occupancy requirement is then waived.

Remote Parcels: This remote parcel program replaced the old open-to-entry program. It permitted entry upon designated areas to stake a parcel of 5, 20 or 40 acres, depending on the area, and to lease the area for five years with the option of a five-year renewal.

The remote parcel program ended July 1, 1984, when it was replaced by the 1983 homesteading bill. Alaskans leasing remote parcels, but who have not yet purchased them, may continue under the remote parcel lease agreement program to obtain patent.

Lottery: One year of residency is required to participate in the lottery program. Successful applicants are determined by a drawing and pay the appraised fair market value of the land. They repay the state over a period of up to 20 years, with interest set at the current federal land loan bank rate. Lotteries require a 5 percent down payment.

The state offered 100,000 acres of land

Northwest Alaska. From *A Place Beyond* by Nick Jans

to private ownership in each fiscal year from July 1, 1979, to July 1, 1982. Disposal levels from that time forward have been based on an annual assessment of the demand for state land.

On April 1, 1983, the Department of Natural Resources discontinued a program that provided Alaska residents who were registered voters a 5-percent-per-year-of-residency discount (up to $25,000) on the sale of land purchased from the state. Recent legislation has changed U.S. military veteran benefits. A 90-day service now qualifies the veteran. Formerly, 15-year veteran residents had been eligible for up to $37,500 on this one-time program.

Homestead: Until 1995, any resident of at least one year, who was 18 years or older and a U.S. citizen, had a chance to receive up to 40 acres of nonagricultural land or up to 160 acres of agricultural land nearly free. To receive title, however, the homesteader was required to pay a $10 application fee and either survey or reimburse the state for survey costs, brush and stake the parcel boundary, build a dwelling, and occupy and improve the land in certain ways within specific time frames. This is called "proving up" on the homestead.

The last available parcel was won in a lottery in early 1997.

The state homestead act also allowed homesteaders to purchase parcels at fair market value without occupying or improving the property. In this category, some subdivision lots are left from a 1995 auction; even nonresidents may purchase these parcels.

Many of the original homesteaders were veterans who came to Alaska during the late 1940s and early 1950s. They had to brush up their boundaries within 90 days after issuance of the entry permit, complete an approved survey of the land within two or five years (depending on purchase option), erect a habitable permanent dwelling on the homestead within three years, and live on the parcel for 25 months within five years. If the parcel was classified for agricultural use, homesteaders labored mightily to clear and put into production or cultivation 25 percent of the land within five years.

Following is the amount of Alaska land owned by various entities as of October 1995:

Owner	Acreage (millions of acres)
U.S. Bureau of Land Management	87.9
State	88.1
U.S. Fish and Wildlife	75.3
National Park Service	52.7
Native	36.1
Forest Service	22.2
Military and other federal	2.1
Alaska Mental Health Trust Authority	1.0
Private	1.0

Source: U.S. Bureau of Land Management

Up-to-date information and applications for state programs are available from the Department of Natural Resources Public Information Office:

Northern Region, 3700 Airport Way, Fairbanks 99709.
Southcentral Region, 3601 C St., Suite 200, Anchorage 99503.
Southeastern Region, 400 Willoughby Ave., Suite 400, Juneau 99801.

Languages Besides English,
Alaska's languages include 20 Native American languages. Fifteen of these Native languages are at risk of extinction: Han, Haida, Eyak, Tanana, Tlingit, Dena'ina (or Tanaina), Ahtna, Ingalik, Holikachuk, Tsimshian, Koyukon, Upper Kuskokwim, Upper Tanana, Kutchin and Aleut. The Eskimo language group—Yupik, Central Yupik, Siberian Yupik and Inupiaq—is widely spoken by many Natives in western and northern Alaska.

Mammals (SEE ALSO BEARS; MUSK OXEN; AND WHALES AND WHALING)

Large Land Mammals. Black Bear: Highest densities are found in Southeast, Prince William Sound and southcentral coastal mountains and lowlands. Black bears also occur in interior and western Alaska, but are absent from Southeast islands north of Frederick Sound (primarily Admiralty, Baranof and Chichagof) and the Kodiak archipelago. They are not commonly found west of about Naknek Lake on the Alaska Peninsula, in the Aleutian Islands or on the open tundra sloping into the Bering Sea and Arctic Ocean. (See also Bears)

Brown/Grizzly Bear: These large omnivores are found in most of Alaska. The grizzly is not found in the Southeast islands south of Frederick Sound or in the Aleutians (except for Unimak Island). (See also Bears)

Caribou. From *A Place Beyond* by Nick Jans

Polar Bear: There are two groups in Alaska's Arctic rim: an eastern group found largely in the Beaufort Sea and a western group found in the Chukchi Sea between Alaska and Siberia. The latter group are the largest polar bears in the world. Old males can exceed 1,500 pounds. (*See also* Bears)

American Bison: In 1928, 23 bison were transplanted from Montana to Delta Junction to restore Alaska's bison population, which had died out some 500 years before. Today, several hundred bison graze near Delta Junction; other herds range at Farewell, at Chitina and along the lower Copper River.

Barren Ground Caribou: There are at least 13 distinct caribou herds, with some overlapping of ranges: Adak, Alaska Peninsula, Arctic, Beaver, Chisana, Delta, Kenai, McKinley, Mentasta, Mulchatna, Nelchina, Porcupine and Fortymile. Porcupine and Fortymile herds range into Canada. The Western Arctic herd is now about 450,000, the state's largest. Hunters of the 50 villages along its migration route take about 20,000 caribou annually for meat.

Sitka Black-tailed Deer: Sitka black-tailed deer range the coastal rain forests of southeastern Alaska. They have been successfully transplanted to the Yakutat area, Prince William Sound, and Kodiak and Afognak islands.

Roosevelt Elk: Alaska's only elk occur on Raspberry and Afognak islands, the result of 106 a 1928 transplant of Roosevelt elk from the Olympic Peninsula in Washington state. Other transplant attempts have failed.

Moose: Moose occur from the Unuk River in Southeast to the Arctic Slope, but are most abundant in second-growth birch forests, on timberline plateaus and along major rivers of Southcentral and Interior. They are not found on islands in Prince William Sound or the Bering Sea, on most major islands in Southeast or on Kodiak or the Aleutians groups.

> ### Horns and Antlers
> It's not so hard to remember: The Bovidae family (cows, sheep, goats and bison) has horns and the Cervidae family (moose, caribou, deer and elk) has antlers. Horns are slow growing and permanent . . . both male and female bovids have horns. Antlers fall off and grow back every year. In most cases, only males have antlers, but caribou and reindeer are exceptions.—Susan Ewing, *The Great Alaska Nature Factbook*

Mountain Goat: These white-coated animals are found in mountains throughout Southeast, and north and west along coastal mountains to Cook Inlet and Kenai Peninsula. They have been successfully transplanted to Kodiak and Baranof islands.

Musk Ox: These shaggy, long-haired mammals were eliminated from Alaska by hunters by 1865. The species was reintroduced and first transplanted to Nunivak Island, and from there to the Arctic Slope around Kavik, Seward Peninsula, Cape Thompson and Nelson Island. (*See also* Musk Oxen)

Reindeer: Introduced from Siberia just before the 20th century, reindeer roamed much of the Bering Sea Coast region but are now confined to St. George and Nunivak islands and the Seward Peninsula.

Dall Sheep: The only white, wild sheep in the world, Dall sheep are found in all major mountain ranges in Alaska except the Aleutian Range south of Iliamna Lake.

Wolf: Wolves are protected and managed as big game and valuable furbearers. Wolves are found throughout Alaska except Bering Sea islands, some Southeast and Prince William Sound islands, and the Aleutian Islands. The wolf succeeds in a variety of climates

> **If all the 18,177,000,000 nuggets produced yearly by Alaska's 166,000 moose were stacked on top of each other, the pile would be 98,181 times as high as Mount McKinley.**

Coping with the Cold

Most warm-blooded mammals put on weight and grow heavier coats in preparation for winter, but there are also other, more customized adaptations. In some large herbivores such as caribou and musk oxen, special nasal passages are designed to capture heat that would otherwise escape as steamy breath. Arctic wolves have specialized blood vessels in their paws that keep pad temperatures about 1 degree above freezing. . . . Some winter residents avoid the whole climate challenge by hibernating. Why do warm-blooded animals put up with the cold? Because even in winter, there is still enough food and burrow room to support a few extra members of the species. After all, an appropriate number of permanent residents keeps an ecosystem in equilibrium—like a skeleton crew on the job to keep things functioning during the slack season.—Susan Ewing, The Great Alaska Nature Factbook

and terrains. Because some biologists believe wolves must be culled to maintain caribou herd populations, controversial wolf kills, in which wolves are hunted by air, have taken place.

Wolverine: Shy, solitary creatures, wolverines are found throughout Alaska and on some Southeast islands. They are not abundant in comparison with other furbearers.

Furbearers. Beaver: These large vegetarian rodents are found in most of mainland Alaska from the Brooks Range to the middle of the Alaska Peninsula. Abundant in some major mainland river drainages in the Southeast and on Yakutat forelands, they have also been successfully transplanted to the Kodiak area. Beaver dams are sometimes destroyed to allow salmon upstream; however, the beavers can rebuild their dams quickly and usually do so on the same site.

Coyote: The coyote is a relative newcomer to Alaska, showing up shortly after the turn of the century, according to oldtimers and records. They are not abundant on a statewide basis, but are common in Tanana, Copper, Matanuska and Susitna river drainages and on Kenai Peninsula. The coyote is found as far west as Alaska Peninsula and the north side of Bristol Bay. Coyotes are increasingly seen near Anchorage.

Fox: *Arctic* (white and blue phases): Arctic foxes are found almost entirely along the Arctic coast as far south as the northwestern shore of Bristol Bay. They have been introduced to the Pribilof and Aleutian Islands, where the blue color phase, most popular with fox farmers, predominates. The white color phase occurs naturally on Saint Lawrence and Nunivak islands. *Red:* Its golden fur coveted by trappers, the red fox is found throughout Alaska except for most areas of Southeast and around Prince William Sound.

Lynx: These shy night-prowlers' main food source is the snowshoe hare. The lynx is found throughout Alaska, except on the Yukon–Kuskokwim Delta, southern Alaska Peninsula and along coastal tidelands. It is relatively scarce along the northern Gulf Coast and in southeastern Alaska.

Hoary Marmot: Present throughout most of the mountain regions of Alaska and along the Endicott Mountains east into Canada, the hoary marmot lives in the high country, especially the warm slopes near and above timberline.

Marten: The marten must have climax spruce forest to survive, and its habitat ranges throughout timbered Alaska, except north of the Brooks Range, on treeless sections of the Alaska Peninsula, and on the Yukon–Kuskokwim Delta. It has been successfully introduced to Prince of Wales, Baranof, Chichagof and Afognak Islands in this century.

Muskrat: Muskrats are found in greatest numbers around lakes, ponds, rivers and marshes throughout all of mainland Alaska south of the Brooks Range except for the

Alaska Peninsula west of the Ugashik lakes. They were introduced to Kodiak, Afognak and Raspberry Islands. Muskrats were traditionally an important early spring subsistence food for Native Alaskans.

River otter: A member of the weasel family, the river otter occurs throughout the state except on Aleutian Islands, Bering Sea islands and the Arctic coastal plain east of Point Lay. It is most abundant in southeastern Alaska, in Prince William Sound coastal areas and on the Yukon–Kuskokwim Delta. It is sometimes called the "land otter" to distinguish it from the sea otter.

Raccoon—The raccoon is not native to Alaska and is considered an undesirable

addition because of its impact on native wildlife. It is found on the west coast of Kodiak Island, on Japonski and Baranof Islands, and on other islands off Prince of Wales Island in Southeast.

Squirrel: *Northern flying:* These small nocturnal squirrels are found in interior, southcentral and southeastern Alaska where coniferous forests are sufficiently dense to provide suitable habitat. *Red:* These tree squirrels inhabit spruce forests, especially along rivers, from Southeast north to the Brooks Range. They are not found on the Seward Peninsula, Yukon–Kuskokwim Delta and Alaska Peninsula south of Naknek River.

Weasel: Least weasels and short-tailed weasels are found throughout Alaska, except for Bering Sea and Aleutian islands. Short-tailed weasels are brown with white underparts in summer, becoming snow-white in winter (designated ermine).

Other Small Mammals. Bat: There are five common bat species in Alaska.

Northern Hare (Arctic Hare or Tundra Hare): This large hare inhabits western and northern coastal Alaska, weighs 12 pounds or more and measures 2$^{1}/_{2}$ feet long.

Snowshoe Hare (or Varying Hare): In winter, these animals become pure white; in summer, their coats are grayish to brown. The snowshoe hare occurs throughout

Alaska except for the lower portion of Alaska Peninsula, the Arctic coast and most islands; it is scarce in southeastern Alaska. Cyclic population highs and lows of hares occur roughly every 10 years. Their big hind feet, covered with coarse hair in winter, act as snowshoes for easy travel over snow.

Brown Lemming: Lemmings are found throughout northern Alaska and the Alaska Peninsula; they are not present in Southeast, Southcentral or the Kodiak archipelago.

Collared Lemming: Resembling large meadow voles, collared lemmings range from the Brooks Range north and from the lower Kuskokwim River drainage north.

Northern Bog Lemming (sometimes called Lemming Mice): These tiny mammals, rarely observed, occur in meadows and bogs across most of Alaska.

Deer Mouse: These rodents inhabit timber and brush in southeastern Alaska.

House Mouse—Extremely adaptive, familiar house mice are found in Alaska seaports and large communities in south-central Alaska.

Meadow Jumping Mouse: These mice can jump 6 feet and are in the southern third of Alaska from the Alaska Range to the Gulf of Alaska.

Collared Pika: Members of the rabbit family, pikas are found in central and southern Alaska; they are most common in the Alaska Range.

Porcupine—These slow-moving rodents prefer forests and inhabit most wooded regions of mainland Alaska.

Norway Rat: The Norway rat came to Alaska on whaling ships in the mid-1800s, thriving in Aleutian ports (the Rat Islands group is named for the Norway rats). They are now found in virtually all Alaska sea-ports, and in Anchorage and Fairbanks and other population centers with open garbage dumps.

Shrew: Seven species of shrew range in Alaska.

Meadow Vole (or Meadow Mouse): Extremely adaptive, there are seven species of meadow vole attributed to Alaska that range throughout the state.

Red-backed Vole: The red-backed vole prefers cool, damp forests and is found throughout Alaska from Southeast to Norton Sound.

Woodchuck: These large, burrowing squirrels, also called groundhogs, are found in the eastern Interior between the Yukon and Tanana Rivers, from east of Fairbanks to the Alaska–Canada border.

Bushy-tailed Woodrat: Commonly called pack rats because they tend to carry off objects to their nests, woodrats are found along the mainland coast of southeastern Alaska.

Marine Mammals. Marine mammals found in Alaska waters are: **dolphin** (Grampus, Pacific white-sided and Risso's); **Pacific walrus; porpoise** (Dall and harbor); **sea otter; seal** (harbor, larga, northern elephant, northern fur, Pacific bearded or *oogruk*, ribbon, ringed and spotted); **Steller sea lion;** and **whale** (Baird's beaked or giant bottlenose, beluga, blue, narwhal, bowhead, Cuvier's beaked or goosebeaked, fin or finback, gray, humpback, killer, minke or little piked, northern right, pilot, sei, sperm and Bering Sea beaked or Stejneger's beaked). (*See also* Whales and Whaling)

The Marine Mammal Protection Act, passed by Congress on Dec. 21, 1972, provided for a complete moratorium on the taking and importation of all marine mammals. The purpose of the act was to

give protection to population stocks of marine mammals that "are, or may be, in danger of extinction or depletion as a result of man's activities." Congress further found that marine mammals have "proven themselves to be resources of great international significance, aesthetic and recreational as well as economic, and it is the sense of the Congress that they should be protected and encouraged to develop to the greatest extent feasible commensurate with sound policies of resource management and that the primary objective of their management should be to maintain the health and stability of the marine ecosystem. Whenever consistent with this primary objective, it should be the goal to obtain an optimum sustainable population keeping in mind the carrying capacity of the habitat."

At the present time, the U.S. Fish and Wildlife Service (Department of the Interior) is responsible for the management of polar bears, sea otters and walrus in Alaska. The National Marine Fisheries Service (Department of Commerce) is responsible for the management of all other marine mammals. The state of Alaska assumed management of walrus in April 1976, and relinquished it back to the USFWS in July 1979. However, an amendment to the Marine Mammal Protection Act in 1981 makes it easier for states to assume management of marine mammals, and Alaska is currently going through the necessary steps to assume management of its marine mammals.

Masks (SEE ALSO NATIVE ARTS AND CRAFTS) Masks are integral to the cultures of the Eskimos, coastal Indians and Aleuts of Alaska.

Eskimo. Eskimo masks rank among the finest tribal art in the world. Ceremonialism and the mask-making that accompanied it were highly developed and practiced widely by the time the first Russians established trading posts in southeast Alaska in the early 1800s.

The shaman used masks during certain ceremonies, sometimes in conjunction with wooden puppets, in ways that frightened and entertained participants. Dancers wore religious masks in festivals that honored the spirits of animals and birds to be hunted or that needed to be appeased. Each spirit was interpreted visually in a different mask and each mask was thought to have a spirit, or *inua,* of its own. This *inua* tied the mask to the stream of spiritual beliefs present in Eskimo religion. Not all masks were benign; some were surrealistic pieces that represented angry or dangerous spirits. Some had moving parts.

In 1996, the Anchorage Museum held a notable exhibit "Agayuliyararput–Our Way of Making Prayer: The Living Tradition of Yupik Masks," to demonstrate the interest of Yupik people in preserving their past and carrying the vital tradition of mask-making into the future. The exhibit went on to tour in New York City in 1997.

Indian. Several types of masks existed among the Tlingit and other coastal Indians of Alaska, including simple single-face

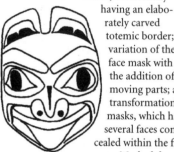

masks, occasionally having an elaborately carved totemic border; a variation of the face mask with the addition of moving parts; and transformation masks, which have several faces concealed within the first. Masked dancers were accompanied by a chorus of tribal singers who sang songs associated with the masks and reflecting the wealth of the host. Masks were the critical element in portraying the relationship of the tribe with spirits and projecting their power to spellbind their audiences.

Tlingit mask

Masks were always created to be worn, but not all members of the tribe held sufficient status or power to wear them. Ceremonial use of masks generally took place in the fall or winter, when the spirits of the other world were said to be nearby.

Northwest Coast Indian mask-makers primarily used alder, though red and yellow cedar were used at times.

Aleut. Examples of masks used on various islands of the Aleutian Chain for shamanistic and ceremonial purposes are reported as early as the mid-18th century. Some of these early masks represented animals. Many were apparently destroyed after use. Aleut legends maintain that some masks were associated with ancient inhabitants of the region, a people apparently considered unrelated.

On the Shumagin Islands, a group of cavelike chambers yielded important examples of Aleut masks late in the 19th century. A number of well-preserved masks, apparently associated with the burials of Aleut whalers, were found. All of them had once been painted. Some of them had attached ears and tooth grips. Pegs were used for inserting feathers or carved wooden appendages similar to those of Eskimo masks of southern Alaska today. Fragments of composite masks, those decorated with feathers, appendages or movable parts, have been found on Kagamil Island with earlier remains.

Early accounts of masked Aleut dances say each dance was accompanied by special songs. Most masks were apparently hidden in caves or secret places when the ceremony ended.

Today, modern Aleut mask-makers study the old traditions and reproduce masks from museum collections.

McNeil River State Game Sanctuary

Photographers, naturalists, wildlife enthusiasts and researchers come to McNeil River State Game Sanctuary for the opportunity to view the world's largest concentration of brown bears in their natural habitat. The Alaska Department of Fish and Game (ADF&G) manages the sanctuary's unique bear-viewing program, which allows visitors to watch the brown bears as they congregate to feed on migrating salmon. Small groups of visitors are escorted to a viewing area by an ADF&G guide, an area limited to 10 visitors a day. Despite the number of bears and the presence of humans, there have been no injuries to bears or humans in the 23 years of the program.

All visitors must apply for a permit to visit the sanctuary. In 1995, more than

1,500 people applied for a permit; 285 were granted by a lottery. Applications are available after January 1 and due March 1 for the upcoming visitor season. Contact the Alaska Department of Fish and Game, Division of Wildlife Conservation, 333 Raspberry Road, Anchorage 99518-1599, Attention: McNeil River.

Statistics on the bears in the sanctuary have been compiled since 1976 and include the following:

Most bears seen at one time at McNeil Falls—68

Most bears seen in one day at McNeil Falls—105

Most salmon seen caught in one day by one bear—90

Most salmon seen caught in one year by one bear—1,012

Most salmon seen caught in one year at McNeil Falls—15,455

Medal of Heroism

By a law enacted in 1965, the Alaska governor is authorized to award, in recognition of valorous and heroic deeds, a state medal of heroism to persons who have saved a life or, at risk to their lives, have served the state or community on behalf of the health, welfare or safety of other persons. The heroism medal is not necessarily given every year, and may be awarded posthumously.

Following are recipients of the Alaska Medal of Heroism:

Albert Rothfuss (1965), Ketchikan. Rescued a child from drowning in Ketchikan Creek.

Randy Blake Prinzing (1968), Soldotna. Saved two lives at Scout Lake.

Nancy Davis (1971), Seattle. A flight attendant who convinced an alleged hijacker to surrender.

Jeffrey Stone (1972), Fairbanks. Saved two youths from a burning apartment.

Gilbert Pelowook (1975), Savoonga. An Alaska state trooper who aided plane crash victims on St. Lawrence Island.

Residents of Gambell (1975). Provided aid and care for plane crash victims on St. Lawrence Island.

George Jackinsky (1978), Kasilof. Rescued two persons from a burning aircraft.

Mike Hancock (1980), Lima, Ohio. In 1977, rescued a victim of a plane crash that brought down high-voltage lines.

David Graham (1983), Kenai. Rescued a person from a burning car.

Robert Larson (1983), Anchorage. An employee of the Department of Public Safety who flew through hazardous conditions to rescue survivors of the crash that took John Stimson's life.

John Stimson (1983), Cordova. A first sergeant in the Division of Fish and Wildlife Protection who died in a helicopter accident during an attempt to rescue others.

Esther Farquhar (1984), Sitka. Tried to save other members of her family from a fire in their home; lost her life in the attempt.

Darren Olanna (1984),

The state of Alaska bought new $20,000 radar machines which display your speed in the hope that motorists who are speeding will slow down. The city of Anchorage had tried the machines several years ago near West High School but had discontinued the program after high school students began racing past the device to see how high they could get the machine to register.

Nome. Died while attempting to rescue a person from a burning house.

Billy Westlock (1986), Emmonak. Rescued a youngster from the Emmonak River.

Lieutenant Commander Whiddon, Lieutenant Breithaupt, ASM2 Tunks, AD1 Saylor, AT3 Milne (1987), Sitka. Rescued a man and his son from their sinking boat during high seas.

The Army and Air National Guard (1988), Gambell, Savoonga, Nome and Shishmaref. Searched for seven missing walrus hunters from Gambell.

Evans Geary, Johnny Sheldon, Jason Rutman, Jessee Ahkpuk Jr. and Carl Hadley (1989), Buckland. These youths rescued two friends who, while ice-skating on a frozen pond, had fallen through the ice.

Robert Cusack (1991), Lake Iliamna. Rescued a woman and a child who were trapped inside a floatplane that had crashed and sank in Lake Iliamna.

Clifford Comer, Robert Yerex, Gary Strebe, David Schron and Jeffery Waite (1992), Air Station Kodiak. Rescued a four-man fishing crew in adverse conditions.

Trooper Rose Edgren (1995), Delta Junction. Responding to a domestic violence call, Edgren and her partner were fired upon. Pushing her partner to safety, Edgren returned fire, shot the attacker, then administered lifesaving first aid.

Metric Conversions

As in the rest of the United States, metrics are slow in coming to Alaska. The conversion formulas on page 114 will help you to prepare for the metric system and to understand measurements in neighboring Yukon Territory.

Micro-Breweries

As in many parts of the United States, limited-edition stouts, ales and beers are a trend in Alaska. Many of the breweries offer dining plus window observation of the brewing process. Others offer tours and samples.

Alaskan Brewing & Bottling Company, 5429 Shaune Drive, Juneau 99801; tours and samples available.

Cusack's Brewpub, 598 W. Northern Lights Blvd., Anchorage 99503.

Glacier Brew House, 737 W. Fifth Ave., Anchorage 99501.

Railway Brewing Co., 421 W. First Ave., Anchorage 99501.

Raven's Ridge, 5690 Supply Road, Fairbanks 99701.

Snow Goose Restaurant/Sleeping Lady Brewing Co., 717 W. Third Ave., Anchorage 99501.

Mileage Chart

Driving Mileage Between Principal Points	Anchorage, AK	Dawson City, YT	Dawson Creek, BC	Fairbanks, AK	Haines, AK	Homer, AK	Prince Rupert, BC	Seattle, WA	Skagway, AK	Valdez, AK	Whitehorse, YT
Anchorage, AK		515	1608	358	775	226	1605	2435	832	304	724
Dawson City, YT	515		1195	393	578	741	1192	2022	435	441	327
Dawson Creek, BC	1608	1195		1486	1135	1834	706	827	992	1534	884
Fairbanks, AK	358	393	1486		653	584	1483	2313	710	284	602
Haines, AK	775	578	1135	653		1001	1132	1962	359	701	251
Homer, AK	226	741	1834	584	1001		1831	2661	1058	530	950
Prince Rupert, BC	1605	1192	706	1483	1132	1831		1033	989	1531	881
Seattle, WA	2435	2022	827	2313	1962	2661	1033		1819	2361	1711
Skagway, AK	832	435	992	710	359	1058	989	1819		758	108
Valdez, AK	304	441	1534	284	701	530	1531	2361	758		650
Whitehorse, YT	724	327	884	602	251	950	881	1711	108	650	

Metric Conversions (approximate)

	When you know:	You can find:	If you multiply by:
Length	inches	millimeters	25.4
	feet	centimeters	30.5
	yards	meters	0.9
	miles	kilometers	1.6
	millimeters	inches	0.04
	centimeters	inches	0.4
	meters	yards	1.1
	kilometers	miles	0.6
Area	square inches	square centimeters	6.5
	square feet	square meters	0.09
	square yards	square meters	0.8
	square miles	square kilometers	2.6
	acres	square hectometers (hectares)	0.4
	square centimeters	square inches	0.16
	square meters	square yards	1.2
	square kilometers	square miles	0.4
	square hectometers (hectares)	acres	2.5
Weight	ounces	grams	28.4
	pounds	kilograms	0.45
	short tons	megagrams (metric tons)	0.9
	grams	ounces	0.04
	kilograms	pounds	2.2
	megagrams (metric tons)	short tons	1.1
Liquid Volume	ounces	milliliters	29.6
	pints	liters	0.47
	quarts	liters	0.95
	gallons	liters	3.8
	milliliters	ounces	0.03
	liters	pints	2.1
	liters	quarts	1.06
	liters	gallons	0.26
Temperature	degrees Fahrenheit	degrees Celsius	5/9 (after subtracting 32)
	degrees Celsius	degrees Fahrenheit	9/5 (then add 32)

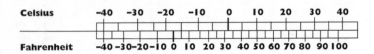

Celsius: -40 -30 -20 -10 0 10 20 30 40

Fahrenheit: -40 -30 -20 -10 0 10 20 30 40 50 60 70 80 90 100

Military

Until the rapid escalation of war in Europe in 1940–41, Congress saw little need for a strong military presence in the territory of Alaska. Spurred by World War II and a growing realization that Alaska could shorten the route to Asia for friend and foe, the government built and still maintains units of the Air Force, Army, Navy and Coast Guard at dozens of installations across the state and on floating units in Alaskan waters.

All branches of the military in Alaska are part of the Alaska Command (ALCOM). ALCOM is charged with maintaining air sovereignty, deploying forces for world-wide contingencies as directed by the Commander-in-Chief, Pacific Command, providing support to federal and state authorities during civil emergencies, and conducting joint training for the rapid deployment of combat forces. The combined forces of ALCOM include nearly 24,000 Air Force, Army, Navy and Coast Guard personnel, and 5,000 guardsmen and reservists.

At the state level are Air National Guard and Army National Guard units.

U.S. Army.

The Alaska District of the U.S. Army Corps of Engineers designs and

constructs buildings, runways, roads, utilities and other facilities for the Army, Air Force and National Guard in Alaska. The District develops and regulates water resources and has an increasing workload in environmental restoration. Elmendorf's new 430,000-square-foot, 110-bed medical center, was completed in 1997.

District headquarters are located at Elmendorf Air Force Base. Construction field offices are located at Forts Richardson and Wainwright. A project office has been established for Elmendorf's $160 million new medical center. A fifth office is located at the Chena River Lakes Flood Control project near Fairbanks. The Regulatory Branch has field offices in Juneau and Fairbanks.

District staff includes 20 Army engineer officers and 400 civilians representing skills in engineering, architecture, the natural sciences, real estate, contracting and administration.

The United States Army Alaska became the primary Army unit in Alaska upon the inactivation of the 6th Infantry Division (Light) in July 1994. The inactivation of the 6th and the activation of U.S. Army Alaska also marked the return of Army headquarters in the state from Fort Wainwright (Fairbanks) to Fort Richardson (Anchorage).

The brigade task force commander, a colonel, and his staff are located at Fort Wainwright. The senior Army commander in Alaska, a major general, and his staff, are at Fort Richardson.

Besides combat and combat support forces at those two posts, the U.S. Army Alaska has research facilities and training grounds at Fort Greely. The Alaska-based soldiers must be prepared to move quickly to support other troops as needed. In late 1990–91, more than 200 Alaska-based soldiers were deployed to the Persian Gulf.

The two primary elements of U.S. Army Alaska are the light infantry brigade task force, named the 1st Brigade, 6th Infantry Division (Light), and the Arctic Support Brigade. The 1st Brigade is headquartered with most of its forces at Fort Wainwright. The Arctic Support Brigade has its headquarters at Fort Richardson and has soldiers stationed at all three posts.

In addition, the 59th Signal Battalion oversees all Army communications in the state; the Northern Warfare Training Center at Fort Greely trains soldiers, guardsmen and representatives from other services in arctic combat and survival; and the Cold Regions Test Activity, also at Fort Greely, tests equipment for cold weather use.

The Army in Alaska conducts mid-winter training exercises each year for its soldiers and participates in multiservice exercises. Besides unit-level training in Alaska, soldiers train at the Joint Readiness Training Center at Fort Polk, Louisiana, the

Yakima Training Center in Washington state and at the National Training Center at Fort Irwin, California. Soldiers also participate in exercises in Thailand and Guam.

United States Army helicopters are stationed at Fort Wainwright and Fort Greely. Year-round training is conducted with infantry and support units with Blackhawk (UH-60) and Chinook (CH-47) helicopters under demanding arctic conditions. Medical evacuations of military and civilians in need are performed by the 283rd Medical Detachment, which participates in the Military Assistance to Safety and Traffic (MAST) program. The 283rd is stationed at Fort Wainwright and has a small team at Fort Greely. The High Altitude Rescue Team (HART) flies specially equipped Chinook helicopters in support of rescues on Mount McKinley and other remote peaks. Army helicopters also transport and

Captain Randy Acord, an Army Air Forces engineer flight test officer in World War II, holds the prop of a twin-engine P-38 fighter at Ladd Field near Fairbanks in 1944. From Heroes of the Horizon by Gerry Bruder

train with the Alaska National Guard throughout the state.

U.S. Air Force. The 11th Air Force (AF) provides forces to maintain air superiority in Alaska and support Alaska-based ground forces, and combat-ready air forces for employment by unified commanders to preserve the national sovereignty of the United States and defend U.S. interests overseas.

The commander of the 11th AF is the senior military officer in Alaska and also serves as the commander of the Alaskan Command and the Alaskan North American Aerospace Defense Region (NORAD).

The largest subordinate units in the 11th AF are the 3rd Wing at Elmendorf AFB, near Anchorage, and 354th Fighter Wing at Eielson AFB, near Fairbanks.

The 3rd Wing provides air defense and air superiority in Alaska, as well as supporting PACAF during contingencies in the Pacific Command area of responsibility. The 3rd is equipped with F-15C Eagles and F-15E Strike Eagles. The wing's F-15C aircraft stand active air defense alert 24 hours a day, year-round, in support of the NORAD mission.

Military airlift in Alaska is provided by the 3rd Wing's 517th Airlift Squadron at Elmendorf, with C-130 and C-12 aircraft. The 962nd Airborne Warning and Control Squadron flies the E-3 Sentry, a modified Boeing 707 equipped with a 30-foot-diameter rotodome mounted above the fuselage. The E-3 can direct friendly fighter aircraft to intercept and identify unknown aircraft as they enter U.S. airspace and also augment existing ground-based radar systems during peacetime by providing a survivable airborne radar platform during hostilities.

The 354th Fighter Wing uses the F-16 to provide close air support and battlefield air interdiction requirements of the 6th Infantry Division (Light) and Pacific Air Forces worldwide mobility commitments. The OA-10 Thunderbolt II provides forward air control for joint U.S. Army and Air Force contingencies.

Remote locations of the 11th AF are

operated by the 611th Air Support Group at Elmendorf AFB. These locations include Galena and King Salmon airports, Eareckson Air Force Station on Shemya Island and a network of 20 Air Force radar sites throughout Alaska.

Other major Air Force components in Alaska include the Air Mobility Command, Air Force Space Command and Air Force Intelligence Agency. When mobilized, the state's Air National Guard becomes an integral part of Alaskan Command's Air Force component. The Guard maintains KC-135 Tankers, C-130s and air rescue HH-60 Pavehawk helicopters.

Navy and Marine Corps. U.S. Navy officers and enlisted personnel are assigned to the Alaskan Command Headquarters staff. Although the Naval Component of the Alaskan Command, U.S. Naval Forces Alaska (USNAVAK), is primarily composed of 17th Coast Guard District personnel and forces, there are eight active-duty U.S. Navy personnel assigned to the USNAVAK staff. There are no Marines assigned to the Alaskan Command Headquarters or units.

The Navy and Marine Corps have commands and detachments located in Anchorage. Commands located in Anchorage include the Naval Security Group Activity; Military Sealift Command Office; Naval Reserve Center; Personnel Support Detachment, Company E, 4th Recon Battalion, 4th Marine Division; as well as several other small detachments. Naval Air Facility Adak is host command for the Naval Security Group Activity.

U.S. Coast Guard. The U.S. Coast Guard has been a part of Alaska since the mid-1800s, when it patrolled the extensive and unforgiving coastline with the wooden sailing and steam ships of its predecessor, the Revenue Cutter Service.

Since those early days, the service has changed names and those wooden ships have been replaced by today's

modern fleet of ships, boats and aircraft, operated and maintained by Alaska's Coast Guard men and women.

The 17th Coast Guard District encompasses the entire state of Alaska, or 33,904 miles of coastline—more than all other states combined. As the nation's smallest military service, the U.S. Coast Guard performs its many missions in Alaska with 2,100 military and civilian employees at 37 units. The district headquarters is located in Juneau, and the largest Coast Guard base in the country is in Kodiak.

Major responsibilities in Alaska include enforcing the 200-mile fisheries conservation zone where the majority of the fish caught are sold to foreign countries. Search and rescue in Alaska is another task performed by Coast Guard units. The service maintains aids to navigation, including Long-Range Aids to Navigation (LORAN) lighthouses and buoys. Marine environmental pollution is also a major responsibility. The Coast Guard served as the Federal On-Scene Coordinator for the cleanup of the *Exxon Valdez* oil spill.

The Coast Guard also has an active role in the defense of Alaska. The District Commander has recently been designated the Naval Component Commander for the Alaskan Command in addition to his responsibility as Commander, Maritime Defense Zone Sector Alaska. The Alaskan Command Naval component commander's mission complements that of Maritime Defense Zone Sector Alaska and Sector Aleutians.

National Guard. The Department of Military Affairs administers the Alaska Army National Guard and the Air National Guard. The guard is charged with performing military reconnaissance, surveillance and patrol operations in Alaska; providing special assistance to civil authorities

A recent graduate of the Alaska State Trooper's training school was quoted as saying, "This is great! They give you a gun, a badge, and enough money to buy beer *and* food!"

during natural disasters or civil disturbances; and augmenting regular Army and Air Force in times of national emergency. About 1,300 full-time employees work for the National Guard.

The Alaska Air National Guard has a headquarters unit located in Anchorage, a composite group made up of a tactical airlift squadron, an air refueling squadron and several support squadrons and flights. There are units based at Kulis Air National Guard Base on the west side of Anchorage International Airport, at Eielson Air Force Base in Fairbanks, and in Kotzebue, Bethel and Juneau.

Authorized staffing is 4,565 military personnel; about 35 percent are full-time technicians. When mobilized, the Air National Guard becomes an integral part of Alaska Command's Air Force component, and the Army National Guard becomes a part of Alaska Command's Army component.

The major unit of the Alaska Army National Guard, with a muster of 2,300, is the 207th Infantry Group, consisting of five Scout Battalions and detachments in almost 100 communities across the state. In addition, it has an airborne element, an air traffic control detachment and an aviation detachment.

Alaska Copper

In late summer 1900, a team of adventurous prospectors operating 200 miles north of the Gulf of Alaska along the Chitina River (a tributary of the Copper River) stumbled upon a massive cliff of green rock. When they analyzed samples, they discovered the ore was 70 percent copper and included some silver and gold as well. They had uncovered one of the earth's richest copper reserves. . . . Before the mine closed in 1938 it produced 1 billion tons of copper and 9.7 million ounces of silver worth a combined $300 million—a dollar sum practically equal to that produced by gold.
—Harry Ritter, Alaska's History

Military Population. Military services are a major industry in Alaska and have a significant impact on the Alaska economy. The total population of the active forces in Alaska as of June 1996 was approximately 51,437, or about 10 percent of Alaska's total population. Population figures include active-duty personnel, Department of Defense Civil Service employees, Nonappropriated Fund and Exchange personnel, and dependents. Of the total, 18,972 were active-duty uniformed personnel and 3,819 were Civil Service employees of the Department of Defense. Alaska was also home to 31 Canadian forces and 3,682 Reserve Forces.

On a per capita basis, Alaska's veteran population is one of the largest of any state.

Minerals and Mining (SEE ALSO COAL; GOLD; OIL AND GAS; AND ROCKS AND GEMS) The cumulative value of the Alaska mineral industry, as measured by the sum of exploration and development expenditures and value of production, exceeded $1 billion for the first time in 1996. The value surpassed the industry's 1995 total value by nearly 40 percent, setting an all-time record.

There were increases in all three mine-related activity categories: exploration increased 30 percent over the 1995 value to $44.5 million; development was up 165 percent to $393.8 million; and production increased nearly 10 percent to $591 million. This growth provided an additional 355 full-time equivalent jobs, bringing total mine-related jobs to 3,760, an increase of 10 percent from 1995.

Metals production accounted for 84 percent of total 1996 mineral industry value, and zinc was the mineral commodity of greatest total value produced in Alaska, accounting for more than half of total mineral production.

Zinc production in 1996 was 366,780 tons at $361.6 million, compared with gold production of 161,565 ounces valued at $60.97 million.

Red Dog Mine near Kotzebue was the largest producer; it is currently working on an expansion project that will increase its share of the world's zinc concentrate to 11 percent.

Gold production, languishing since World War II when gold was declared a nonstrategic metal, is being revived. The Nixon Fork mine near McGrath poured its first gold on Oct. 22, 1995, and is the first major hard rock gold mine to operate in Alaska since 1942. At full production, Nixon Fork is expected to produce 60,000 ounces a year. Fort Knox mine near Fairbanks poured its first three gold bars on Dec. 20, 1996. It is estimated that Fork Knox will add $76 million annually to state and local economies and produce more than 300,000 ounces of gold per year.

Kensington Gold Mine, north of Juneau, started construction in mid-1997, and is expected to peak at 200,000 ounces annually. Kennecott Greens Creek Mining Co. reopened the Greens Creek polymetallic mine near Juneau in July 1996. This underground operation operated from 1989-93, but closed due to low metal prices. It will produce silver, gold, zinc, lead and copper.

About 390 tons of copper was reported as a byproduct in two new hardrock mines, the first copper credited from Alaska in nearly four decades. Promising exploration projects include True North near Fairbanks, Donlin Creek near Flat, Pogo near Delta Junction, and Niblack polymetallic on Prince of Wales Island. Usibelli Coal mine near Healy is the state's only operating coal mine, and has been producing continuously since before WWII. Nearly half the annual production is used in Interior Alaska to generate electric power. The remainder is exported to South Korea. Coal reserves waiting to be developed include Wishbone Hill near Palmer (which Usibelli recently purchased) and Northwest Arctic Coal.

Other minerals produced for industrial and ornamental use include sand and gravel, building stone, nephrite jade and soapstone.

The total number of active Alaska state mining claims increased by 54 percent in 1996 to 38,200. The total number of active federal claims remained about the same at approximately 8,000.

Headnets provide some protection from thick clouds of mosquitoes. From The Alaska River Guide *by Karen Jettmar*

Mosquitoes

Alaska's ubiquitous mosquito is sometimes jokingly referred to as the "state bird." At least 25 species of mosquito are found in Alaska (the number may be as high as 40), the females of all species feeding on people, other mammals or birds. Males and females eat plant sugar, but only the females suck blood, which they use for egg production. The itch that follows the bite comes from an anticoagulant injected by the mosquito. No Alaska mosquitoes carry diseases. The insects are present from April through September in many areas of the state. Out in the bush they are often at their worst in June, tapering off in July. The mosquito plague usually passes by late August and September. From Cook Inlet south, they concentrate on coastal flats and forested valleys. In the Aleutian Islands, mosquitoes are absent or present only in small numbers. The most serious mosquito infestations occur in moist areas of slow-moving or standing water, of the type found in the fields, bogs and forests of interior Alaska, from Bristol Bay eastward.

Mosquitoes are most active at dusk and dawn; low temperatures and high winds decrease their activity. Mosquitoes can be controlled by draining their breeding areas or spraying with approved insecticides. When traveling in areas of heavy mosquito

(Continues on page 122)

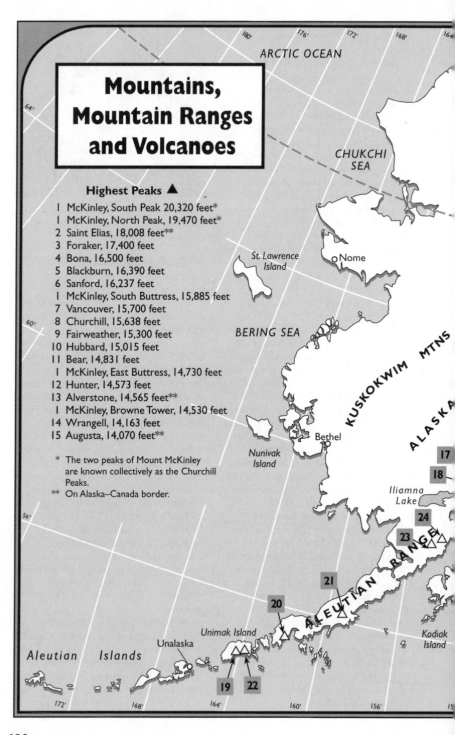

Mountains, Mountain Ranges and Volcanoes

Highest Peaks ▲

1 McKinley, South Peak 20,320 feet*
1 McKinley, North Peak, 19,470 feet*
2 Saint Elias, 18,008 feet**
3 Foraker, 17,400 feet
4 Bona, 16,500 feet
5 Blackburn, 16,390 feet
6 Sanford, 16,237 feet
1 McKinley, South Buttress, 15,885 feet
7 Vancouver, 15,700 feet
8 Churchill, 15,638 feet
9 Fairweather, 15,300 feet
10 Hubbard, 15,015 feet
11 Bear, 14,831 feet
1 McKinley, East Buttress, 14,730 feet
12 Hunter, 14,573 feet
13 Alverstone, 14,565 feet**
1 McKinley, Browne Tower, 14,530 feet
14 Wrangell, 14,163 feet
15 Augusta, 14,070 feet**

* The two peaks of Mount McKinley are known collectively as the Churchill Peaks.
** On Alaska–Canada border.

ARCTIC OCEAN

CHUKCHI SEA

St. Lawrence Island

Nome

BERING SEA

KUSKOKWIM MTNS

ALASKA

Bethel

Nunivak Island

Iliamna Lake

17

18

24

23

21

20

ALEUTIAN RANGE

Unimak Island

Unalaska

Aleutian Islands

19 22

Kodiak Island

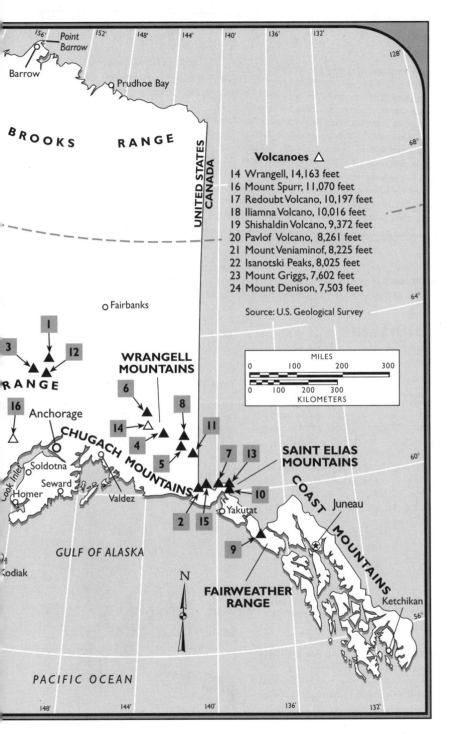

Volcanoes △

14 Wrangell, 14,163 feet
16 Mount Spurr, 11,070 feet
17 Redoubt Volcano, 10,197 feet
18 Iliamna Volcano, 10,016 feet
19 Shishaldin Volcano, 9,372 feet
20 Pavlof Volcano, 8,261 feet
21 Mount Veniaminof, 8,225 feet
22 Isanotski Peaks, 8,025 feet
23 Mount Griggs, 7,602 feet
24 Mount Denison, 7,503 feet

Source: U.S. Geological Survey

MILES
0   100   200   300

0   100   200   300
KILOMETERS

Point
Barrow

Barrow

Prudhoe Bay

BROOKS   RANGE

UNITED STATES
CANADA

Fairbanks

WRANGELL
MOUNTAINS

RANGE

Anchorage

CHUGACH MOUNTAINS

Soldotna

Cook Inlet

Seward

Homer

Valdez

SAINT ELIAS
MOUNTAINS

COAST

Juneau

Yakutat

MOUNTAINS

Kodiak

GULF OF ALASKA

N

FAIRWEATHER
RANGE

Ketchikan

PACIFIC OCEAN

The Sourdough Expedition

In 1906 explorer Frederick Cook announced that he and a companion had conquered Mount McKinley. Cook provided detailed reports of the alleged climb, as well as a photograph of himself at the summit. He was hailed by the gullible New York press [as] a celebrity. Cook's claims did not play well in the saloons of Fairbanks where, in late 1909, a group of miners led by Tom Lloyd decided no Easterner should be first to reach Denali's summit. Thus arose the "Sourdough Expedition." Lloyd and six partners—none with climbing experience—set off in the dead of winter. Before they reached the mountain a fist fight broke out, and three turned back. The remaining four began their assault in March 1910, without ropes and carrying a 14-foot flagpole to plant at the top. In a remarkable sustained climb of 18 hours, two of the party negotiated the final 9,000-foot ascent of McKinley's north peak, planted their pole, and came down—unaware that the south peak was actually 850 feet higher. Their exploit is still considered one of mountaineering's most astonishing feats.—Harry Ritter, *Alaska's History*

(Continued from page 119)
infestations, it is wise to wear protective clothing, carefully screen living areas and tents and use a good insect repellent.

Mountains
Of the 20 highest mountains in the United States, 17 are in Alaska, which has 19 peaks over 14,000 feet. (*See* map on pages 120–21)

Mount McKinley
Mount McKinley in the Alaska Range is the highest mountain on the North American continent. The South Peak is 20,320 feet high; the North Peak has an elevation of 19,470 feet. The mountain was named in 1896 for William McKinley of Ohio, who at the time was the Republican candidate for president. An earlier name had been Denali, an Athabascan word meaning "the high one." The state of Alaska officially renamed the mountain Denali in 1975 and the state Geographic Names Board claims the proper name for the mountain is Denali. However, the federal Board of Geographic Names has not taken any action and congressional legislation has been introduced to retain the name McKinley in perpetuity.

Mount McKinley is within Denali National Park and Preserve. The park entrance is about 237 miles north of Anchorage and 121 miles south of Fairbanks via the George Parks Highway. (A 90-mile gravel road runs west from the highway through the park; vehicle traffic on the park road is restricted.) The park is also accessible via the Alaska Railroad and by aircraft.

The mountain and its park are one of the top tourist attractions in Alaska. The finest times to see McKinley up close are on

West Buttress Route, Mount McKinley. From To the Top of Denali *by Bill Sherwonit*

summer mornings. August is best, according to statistics based on 13 summers of observation by park ranger Rick McIntyre. The mountain is rarely visible the entire day. The best view is from Eielson Visitor Center, located about 66 miles from the park entrance and 33 miles northeast of the summit. The center, open from early June through the second week in September, is accessible via shuttle bus provided by the park. There is a $30 bus fee. For more information about Denali National Park, call (907) 683-2294 or (907) 272-7275.

Eleven climbers perished on Mount McKinley in May 1992, making it the deadliest climbing season in the mountain's history. The 11 climbers, including one American mountaineering guide, died in five separate incidents on the mountain. Since 1932, when the National Park Service began keeping records of climbers attempting to reach the summit of Mount McKinley, 87 climbers have been killed on the mountain. Among the deadliest years on the mountain were 1981 and 1989, when six mountaineers were killed; 1967 and 1980, when eight mountaineers were killed, and 1992, when 11 died. Two climbers perished in 1996.

During the 1996 climbing season, 1,148 mountaineers from all over the world attempted to ascend McKinley's heights; about 43 percent or 489 climbers successfully reached the summit. The 42 percent success rate was the lowest since 1987, when only 30.7 percent of climbers reached the summit. This lower success rate was attributed to stormy weather on the mountain during the traditional 110-day season. The West Buttress remains the most popular route to the top of the mountain.

In 1996, 13 major rescue or recovery missions were conducted by the Talkeetna ranger staff and volunteers.

In 1995, for the first time in park history, climbers were charged a $150 fee to scale the mountain. Rescues in 1996 cost the National Park Service $143,943; military costs were $88,500.

The Park Service now requires climbers to register 60 days before a planned climb. Information on climbing Mount McKinley can be found on the National Park Service Web site at www.nps.gov/dena or call (907) 733-2231.

Mukluks

Mukluks are lightweight boots designed to provide warmth in extreme cold. Eskimo mukluks are traditionally made with *oogruk* (bearded seal) skin soles and leg uppers of caribou trimmed with fur. (Mukluk is also another name for *oogruk*.) Athabascan mukluks are traditionally made of moose hide and trimmed with fur and beadwork. Hay inner soles add insulation. The mukluks may be either calf-height or knee-height, with a leather drawstring in a casing around the top to keep out the wind and snow.

Eskimos of long ago sewed all their own clothing, mainly from the skins of animals and seabirds, including water-resistant mukluks. These mukluks were not worn in winter unless the weather was warm, for they were made from seal leather with the hair removed and *oogruk* soles. The *oogruk* was oiled very heavily to be water-resistant and no fur trim was used on the "water mukluks," as they were called. The skins of large fish, including salmon, were also used to make the water-resistant mukluks.

Any mukluks that have been exposed to water or dampness should be hung in a

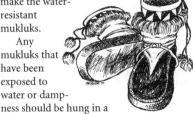

31 years ago

An eight-man climbing party, which included Alaskans Art Davidson, Dave Johnston and Ray Genet, successfully completed the first winter ascent of Mount McKinley in February 1967.

cool place to dry slowly; sudden heat could shrink them out of shape and make them hard and stiff.

Muktuk This Eskimo delicacy consists of outer skin layers and attached blubber of a whale. The two species of whale from which muktuk is most often sliced are the bowhead and the beluga, or white whale. The outer skin layers consist of a corky protective layer, the true skin and the blubber. In the case of beluga muktuk, the outer layer is white, the next layer is black and the blubber is pink. It may be eaten fresh, frozen, boiled or fermented.

Museums, Cultural Centers, Exhibits, Historic Parks, Historical Societies and Repositories

Visiting any of the following museums, historic sites, notable exhibits, archives or other repositories offers a look into the rich diversity of Alaskan culture and history. Many of the smaller museums are open only June through September. A selected number of visitor centers with exhibits have been included below.

In 1994 the Alaska Junior Theater presented a mime troupe from Los Angeles. The *Anchorage Daily News* announced that the "performance will be interpreted for the hearing impaired."

Alaska Aviation Heritage Museum, 4721 Aircraft Dr., Anchorage 99502; (907) 248-5325. Located on the south shore of Lake Hood, and features 30 vintage aircraft (including a Stinson A Trimotor and a Fairchild American Pilgrim), video and a military aviation gallery. On the observation deck you can watch takeoffs and landings from the largest floatplane base in the world.

Alaska Collection, Z. J. Loussac Library, 3600 Denali, Anchorage 99503; (907) 343-2832. Rare books, reference books, state records, microfilm of newspapers, catalogs of photographs at other archives in the state.

Alaska Experience Center, 705 W. Sixth Ave., Anchorage 99501; (907) 276-3730. *Alaska the Great Land* shows hourly on a 180-degree screen; in another exhibit, viewers "experience" a 4.5 earthquake.

Alaska Homestead and Historical Museum, Milepost 1415.4 Alaska Highway, Delta Junction 99737. Large collection of historical farming equipment; guided tours of authentic homestead farm.

Alaska Indian Arts, Inc., P.O. Box 271, Haines 99827; (907) 766-2160. Workshop with totem carvers, silversmiths and print-makers. Chilkat Dancers perform several times each week during the summer.

Alaska Public Lands Information Center, 605 W. Fourth, Anchorage 99501; (907) 271-2737. Features extensive displays and information on refuges, forests, parks and outdoor recreation lands in Alaska. Displays, video programs and computers permit self-help trip-planning. For on-line information, see www.nps.gov/aplic/center.

Alaska Public Lands Information Center, 250 N. Cushman St., Fairbanks 99701; (907) 456-0527. Provides information on Alaska's state parks, national parks, national forests, wildlife refuges, etc. Also a free museum featuring films on Alaska, interpretive programs, lectures, exhibits, artifacts, photographs and short video programs on each region of the state.

Alaska Resources Library, 222 W. Seventh Ave., Anchorage 99513; (907) 271-5025. Information on archaeology, Native land claims, environmental and natural resources of Alaska, ornithology and wildlife biology, fisheries biology and cold regions engineering.

Alaska SeaLife Center, P.O. Box 1329, Mile 0 Seward Highway, Seward 99664; (907) 224-3080. Live marine mammals and sea birds in habitat exhibits.

Alaska State Archives, Box 6, Juneau

99811. Photographs, documents, state government records.

Alaska State Museum, 395 Whittier St., Juneau 99801-1718; (907) 465-2901. E-mail jerryh@muskox.alaska.edu. Comprehensive  collections on Alaskan Natives, art, natural history, gold-rush days, archaeology, botany, contemporary gold-mining issues, geology and paleontology. Lectures, guided tours, workshops, films and demonstrations.

Alpine Historical Park, Box 266, Sutton 99674, access via Elementary School Road from Glenn Highway. Open-air museum featuring the concrete ruins of the Sutton Coal Washery (1920–22), historical buildings, perennial gardens, and picnic and playground facilities.

Alutiiq Musem and Archaeological Repository, Kodiak Area Native Association, 402 Center St., Kodiak 99615. Archaeological records and papers, artifacts from coastal sites around Kodiak Island.

American Bald Eagle Foundation, (Haines Highway and Second St.) Box 49, Haines 99827; (907) 766-3094. How birds interact with the environment; special programs and lectures.

Anchorage Museum of History and Art, 121 W. Seventh Ave., Anchorage 99501; (907) 343-4326. "Alaska Gallery" dioramas depict 10,000 years of Alaska history. Guided tours with docents available. "Art of the Far North" contains early engravings by artists who accompanied 18th-century explorers and features works of art from travelers, adventurers, early residents and Native artists.

Baranov Museum (Erskine House)/ Kodiak Historical Society, 101 Marine Way, Kodiak 99615; (907) 486-5920. Closed in February. Former Russian fur warehouse from early 1800s, oldest wooden building on the West Coast of the U.S. Exhibits offer an overview of Alutiiq, Russian and early American history. National historic landmark.

Begich-Boggs Visitor Center, Box 129, Girdwood 99587; (907) 783-2326. *See* Portage Glacier.

Big Delta State Historical Park, Mile 275 Richardson/Alaska Highway, Delta Junction 99737; (907) 895-4201. A glimpse of life in interior Alaska, 1904–47, the 10-acre park includes Rika's Roadhouse (built in 1910 and restored in 1986), an important way station on the Valdez-Fairbanks Trail, sod-roofed museum, ferryman's cabin and other historic structures. Guides are in period costumes.

Bristol Bay Historical Museum, Box 43, Naknek 99633; (907) 246-4432. "Living history museum" features regional archaeology, history, ethnology, commercial fishing and canning.

Carrie M. McLain Memorial Museum, Box 53, Nome 99762. Artifacts, photos and treasures; exhibits include the Nome gold rush (more than 6,000 gold rush photos), Eskimo culture and the Bering Land Bridge. Videos on the history of Nome shown during the summer season.

Circle District Museum/Circle District Historical Society, (Mile 127.7, Steese Highway) Box 1893, Central 99730. Permanent displays include a period cabin of the mining camps, the first printing press north of Juneau, equipment used in early-day mining and trapping, Yukon Quest Sled Dog Race sled display, research library with archives and photograph collection.

Clausen Memorial Museum, P.O. Box 708, Petersburg 99833; (907) 772-3598. Photos, Norwegian family items, cannery and fisheries items, fox farming, world's record king salmon and other mementoes from area's past.

Colony Museum, Greater Palmer Visitor Center, 723 S. Valley Way, Palmer 99645; (907) 745-2880. Scenes from 1935 farmers' colony: tools, housewares, handmade rakes and yokes, cash registers, manual typewriters.

Copper Center Lodge, Drawer J, Copper Center 99673; (907) 822-3245. Historic roadhouse opened in 1898. Museum exhibits, operating fish wheel.

Cordova Museum/Cordova Historical Society, P.O. Box 391, Cordova 99574;

(907) 424-7443. Exhibits of art, geology, fisheries and marine articles.

Corrington Museum, (Fifth and Broadway) P.O. Box 382, Skagway 99840; (907) 983-2580. Forty unique ivory exhibits tracing Alaska's history.

The Covered Bridge Museum, Old C Street Bridge, Anchorage 99501; (907) 278-5889. Gold panning, wooly mammoth and bison bones uncovered by dredges in Fairbanks area; smelting equipment, horse-drawn road grader.

Crow Creek Mine, Mile 3.1 Crow Creek Road, Girdwood 99587; (907) 278-8060. National historic site with eight original, fully restored buildings from 1898; daily gold panning, tools.

Dog Mushing Museum, Box 80-136, Fairbanks 99708; (907) 456-6874. Dog sleds, mushing paraphernalia.

Dorothy G. Page Museum and Old Wasilla Townsite Park, Box 870874, Wasilla 99654; (907) 373-9071. Historic buildings, including first schoolhouse (1917). Eskimo and Athabascan exhibits, gold mining exhibits, "Flying Dentist's" office.

Eagle Pioneer Museum/Eagle Historical Society, P.O. Box 23, Eagle 99738; (907) 547-2230. Restored courthouse, customs house and several Fort Egbert buildings. Daily walking tours and historical movies.

Eagle River Nature Center, Mile 12.7 Eagle River Road, Eagle 99738; (907) 694-2108. Interpretive displays, programs, guided daily hikes, outdoor telescopes, spectacular views. Entrance to walkable section of scenic Iditarod Trail.

Eklutna Historical Park, 165515 Centerfield Drive, Eagle River 99577; (907) 696-2828, located 25 miles north of Anchorage on the Glenn Highway. The park offers 30-minute tours and information about the blending of Athabascan and missionary cultures. Historic photos and objects. Unique grave monuments called "spirit houses," and St. Nicholas Russian Orthodox Church.

El Dorado Gold Camp, 1975 Discovery Drive, Fairbanks 99709; (907) 479-7613. Located at Mile 1.3 Elliott Highway, just past Fox, 9 miles north of Fairbanks. Tour of a working gold mine, permafrost tunnel, sluice box, assay office, gold panning.

Elmendorf Air Force Base Wildlife Museum, 4803 Eighth St., Anchorage 99507; (907) 552-2282, enter base through Boniface Parkway Gate. Habitat displays of Alaska wildlife: bear, musk oxen, Dall sheep, small mammals, extensive displays of fish and wildlife.

Ester Gold Camp, P.O. Box 109, Ester 99725; (800) 676-6925. Ester Camp was built in 1936 by the Fairbanks Exploration Company to support a large-scale gold dredge operation. It reopened in 1958 as a tourist attraction and is on the National Register of Historic Places.

Fairbanks Exploration Industrial Complex, Illinois St., Fairbanks; (907) 451-1920. Four houses for miners built in 1916 act as an inn. Visitors may watch gold pans being manufactured and see a machine shop complex where "time stands still."

Fairbanks Historical Preservation Foundation. *See* SS *Nenana.*

Fraternal Order of Alaska State Troopers, 320 W. Fifth Ave., Anchorage; (907) 279-5050. Law enforcement history from territorial days to statehood.

Fort Richardson Fish and Wildlife Center, Building 600, Fort Richardson 99505; (907) 384-0437 or 384-0823. Mounted animals and fish: moose family with calves, bear, musk oxen, birds, wolves and sea mammals. Guided tours by military personnel who specialize in wildlife biology.

Fourth Avenue Theatre, 630 W. Fourth Ave., Anchorage 99501; (907) 257-5600 or 257-5650. Art deco building from the 1940s houses museum photo display of old Anchorage on the lower level. On the main level, free Alaskan movies on the big screen. Dinner theater during the summer. Departure point for one-hour trolley tours of Anchorage.

George I. Ashby Memorial Museum/Copper Valley Historical Society, P.O. Box 84, Copper Center 99573; (907) 822-5555. Early mining of gold and copper, church and Native artifacts. Information about the unfortunate stampeders who tried to take the Valdez Glacier "All-Alaska" Trail to the Klondike in 1898.

George Otenna Museum, Wales 99783; (907) 664-3671. This Eskimo community of 143 persons is accessible only by air and dog sled. Museum features contemporary arts and crafts as well as Eskimo artifacts and the history of Wales and the surrounding area. Behind the present village is a burial mound of the Birnirk culture (500 A.D. to 900 A.D.), a National Historic Landmark.

Gold Dredge No. 8, Box 81941, Fairbanks 99708; (907) 547-6058. Millions of ounces of gold have been extracted by this dredge since 1928—the only gold dredge in Alaska open to the public. Listed in the National Register of Historic Sites, the dredge is a 250-foot vessel as tall as a 5-story building. Exhibits include mastodon and woolly mammoth bones and tusks.

Heritage Library Museum, Northern Lights and C St., Anchorage 99503; (907) 265-2834. Displays of Native baskets, ivory and artifacts plus photos, hunting implements, rare books and paintings; reference library.

Hoonah Cultural Center/Hoonah Indian Association, P.O. Box 144, Hoonah 99829. Features history and culture of local Tlingit Indians. Displays of Tlingit art and artifacts, totem poles, guided tours.

House of Wickersham, 123 Seventh St., Juneau 99801; (907) 586-9001. Built in 1898, the house was the residence of one of Alaska's first federal judges, James Wickersham. Educational tours and permanent collections.

Huslia Cultural Center, P.O. Box 70, Huslia 99746. Beadwork, arts and crafts.

Iditarod Trail Sled Dog Race Headquarters and Museum, Mile 2.2 Knik Road, Box 870800, Wasilla 99687; (907) 376-5155. Memorabilia, mushing films, full-size

replica of checkpoint cabin and cache. Of particular interest are the sleds that Susan Butcher and Joe Redington, Sr. used to mush to the top of Denali.

The Imaginarium Science Discovery Center, 737 W. Fifth Ave., Suite 140, Anchorage 99501; (907) 276-3179. Interactive (hands-on) scientific displays for children, planetarium bubble show, polar bear lair, physics of toys, arctic ecology. Monthly rotating exhibits.

Independence Mine State Historic Park, Hatcher Pass, near Palmer 99645; (907) 745-2827. Features restored gold mine buildings, mining machinery and a visitor center in spectacular mountain setting. Recreational gold panning permitted.

Indian Valley Mine, Mile 104 Seward Highway, Anchorage 99504; (907) 337-7749. National historic site offers gold panning and pictorial museum.

Institute of Alaska Native Arts (IANA), P.O. Box 80583, Fairbanks 99708.

Interior and Arctic Alaska Aeronautical Museum, P.O. Box 70437, Fairbanks 99707.

Inupiat Heritage Center, P.O. Box 69, Barrow 99723. This $12 million project broke ground in 1996. The 30,000-square-foot facility is scheduled to open in 1998 and will house a climate-controlled collection, library, offices and storage areas for artifacts. Exhibits may be shared with the New Bedford Whaling Park. Unusual aspects include a Traditional Room for an "Elders-in-Residence" program and a Skinning Room.

Isabel Miller Museum/Sitka Historical Society, 330 Harbor Drive, Sitka 99835; (907) 747-6455. Located in the Centennial Building near the cruise ship lightering dock, the exhibits include Tlingit baskets and carvings; the New Archangel Russian dancers and Noow Tlien Native dancers perform; and research library of manuscripts and photographs.

Juneau-Douglas City Museum, 155 S. Seward St., Juneau 99801; (907) 586-3572. Videos and exhibits highlight Juneau's colorful history and gold mining heritage; historic downtown walking tour.

Kake Tribal Heritage Foundation, P.O. Box 263, Juneau 99801.

Kasaan Totem Park, east side of Prince of Wales Island. Reached by charter plane or private boat. Part of a government-sponsored totem restoration program begun in 1937. Contains some examples moved from the Haida village of Old Kasaan.

Kenai Bicentennial Visitors and Cultural Center, 11471 Kenai Spur Highway, P.O. Box 1991, Kenai 99611; (907) 283-1991. Houses all the exhibits from Fort Kenay, plus a large eagle display.

Kenaitze Indian Tribe, Box 988, Kenai 99611. Archives of Kenai branch of Cook Inlet Athabascan Indians.

Kennecott Mine, Wrangell–St. Elias National Park, Kennicott 99588; (907) 582-5128. An abandoned copper mine with many buildings perched on steep slopes. Kennicott-McCarthy Wilderness Guides conducts historic tours of the mine and town, which ceased operating in 1938.

Klawock Totem Park/City of Klawock, P.O. Box 113, Klawock 99925. Historic site on west coast of Prince of Wales Island.

 Reached by air, private boat, state ferry. Park contains 21 totems—both replicas and originals—from the abandoned village of Tuxekan.

Klondike Gold Rush National Historical Park, P.O. Box 517, Skagway 99840. An unusual unit of this park is the Chilkoot Trail, a 33-mile trek through history, sometimes called "the longest museum in the world." Hundreds of relics (wagon wheels, coffee pots) left behind by the stampeders of '98 remain on the trail. Another unit of this park is in Pioneer Square in Seattle.

Knik Museum, Knik Road, Wasilla 99687; (907) 376-7755. Restored pool hall houses exhibits about fish camps, gold mines, dog mushers.

Kodiak Museum. *See* Alutiiq Museum and Archaeological Repository

Kodiak Tribal Council's Barabara, 713 Rezanof Drive, Kodiak 99615; (907) 486-4449. Authentic traditional Alutiiq

dwelling (sod house) used to stage presentations by the Kodiak Alutiiq Dancers.

Marine Education Center, Third and Railway, Box 730, Seward 99664; (907) 224-5261. Interpretive displays about northern seas, Resurrection Bay, marine animals; live saltwater tanks; movies shown on whales, salmon and other marine subjects. Operated by the University of Alaska.

Marine Works World War II Mini Museum, 2315 Airport Beach Road, Unalaska 99685; (907) 581-1749. Informal collection of articles from the Aleutian campaign of WWII.

Mascot Saloon Museum, National Park Service, Third and Broadway, Skagway 99840; (907) 983-2921. A typical saloon of 1898.

Museum of Alaska Transportation and Industry, Mile 47 Parks Highway, Wasilla 99687-0646; (907) 376-1211. Planes, trains, vehicles, tractors, tools, gold rush exhibit. Ten acres of neat old stuff.

Museum of Northern Adventure, Main St., Talkeetna 99676; (907) 733-2710 or 733-3999. Historic railroad building, exhibits about homesteading, prospecting, wildlife and famous Alaska characters.

NANA Museum of the Arctic, P.O. Box 49, Kotzebue 99752; (907) 442-3890. Collections reflect Eskimo ethnology and natural history of northwestern Alaska, plus wildlife exhibits, slide show. Cultural heritage demonstrations such as skin sewing, ivory carving, Eskimo dancing, Eskimo blanket toss. Winter hours by appointment.

National Archives, Alaska Region, 654 W. Third Ave., Anchorage 99501; (907) 271-2441. Contains more than 9,000 cubic feet of historical records, among them photographs, maps and architectural drawings, dating from about 1867 to the present. These records were created or received by the federal courts and over 30 federal agencies in Alaska. Both original records and microfilm are available for research.

National Bank of Alaska Heritage Library. *See* Heritage Library Museum

Nome Historical Park, c/o Nome Convention and Visitors Bureau, Box 240, Nome 99762; (907) 443-5535. Contains a nonworking gold dredge and mining equipment from the gold rush era.

Oil Pipeline Terminus, Valdez 99686; (907) 835-2686. Bus tours of pipeline terminal are available daily, May to September; reservations suggested. Entry restricted to authorized bus tours only.

Oscar Anderson House, 420 M St., Anchorage 99502; (907) 274-2336. The city's first wood frame house, built in 1915 by Swedish immigrant Oscar Anderson, was completely restored in 1982. Swedish Christmas celebration.

Pioneer Air Museum, Box 70437, Fairbanks 99707; (907) 451-0037. Located behind Civic Center at Alaskaland. Features antique aircraft and stories of their Alaskan pilots, with displays from 1913–48.

The Pioneers of Alaska Museum, (at Alaskaland) Airport Way and Peger Road, Fairbanks 99707; (907) 451-0037. Free guided historical walking tours. Park features Kitty Hensley house, Judge Wickersham house, first Presbyterian Church (1906); re-created Native village, gold rush town and paddle wheel riverboat.

Portage Glacier/Begich-Boggs Visitor Center, Box 129, Girdwood 99587; (907) 783-2326. Located 55 miles south of Anchorage off the Seward Highway. Exhibits on glaciers and ice caves. Theater shows 20-minute documentary *Voices from the Ice.* Interpretive programs during the summer.

Potter Section House and Historic Park, on Seward Highway, south of Anchorage; (907) 345-5014. Alaska Railroad historic site. Chugach State Park headquarters; maps, brochures, interpretive display, rotary snowplow, railroad cars.

Pratt Museum, 3779 Bartlett St., Homer 99603; (907) 235-8635. Natural and cultural

history of Kenai Peninsula. Displays include Eskimo, Indian and Aleut tools and clothing dioramas, whale skeletons; marine aquarium; botanical garden.

Rasmusson Library, University of Alaska Fairbanks 99775; (907) 474-7481. Extensive Alaska and Arctic archives and photograph collection available to researchers.

Resurrection Bay Historical Society Museum. *See* Marine Education Center

Russian Bishop's House, P.O. Box 944, Sitka 99835; (907) 747-6281. Located on Lincoln Street, a restored residence (built in 1842) with private chapel. One of only four Russian log structures remaining in North America. Both a unit of the Sitka National Historical Park and a National Historic Landmark. Exhibits describe Russian America.

Samuel K. Fox Museum (aka Dillingham Heritage Museum), P.O. Box 273, Dillingham 99576; (907) 842-5610 or 842-5521. Ethno-history museum featuring Yupik Eskimo culture of southwestern Alaska through contemporary and traditional arts, crafts and artifacts.

Saxman Totem Park and Tribal House, P.O. Box 8558, Ketchikan 99901. Historic site, 2.5 miles south of town. Park includes totems such as the famous Lincoln Pole, a carving center and Tlingit tribal house. Guided tours available.

Seward Marine Education Center. *See* Marine Education Center

Seward SeaLife Center, Seward 99664. Will open in Spring 1998. Combination aquarium, research center and rehab center for marine mammals and sea birds; partly funded by a settlement from the *Exxon Valdez* oil spill.

Sheldon Jackson Museum, 104 College Drive, Sitka 99835-7657; (907)

Alaskan households have the highest VCR ownership in the nation at 97 percent. Video tape rental choices generally follow national trends, except that Steven Segal movies are much more popular than anywhere else.

747-8981. Located on the campus of Sheldon Jackson College, Alaska's oldest museum has many exhibits of Tlingit artifacts, clothing, beadwork, art and carvings.

Sheldon Museum and Cultural Center, Box 269, Haines 99827; (907) 766-2366. Exhibits on the Dalton Trail, the overland freight route used to Fort Selkirk in the Klondike; Tlingit culture, Chilkat blankets, pioneer history.

Simon Paneak Memorial Museum, Box 21085, Anaktuvuk Pass 99721-0085; (907) 661-3413. Display of hunting tools and a description of the Paleo-Indian people who occupied the Mesa Site more than 11,000 years ago.

Sitka National Historical Park Visitor Center, 106 Metlakatla, Sitka 99835; (907) 747-6281. Displays of Tlingit history, totems, artifacts. Totem pole collection outside contains both original pieces collected 1901–03 and copies of originals lost to time and the elements.

Soldotna Historical Society Museum, P.O. Box 1986, Soldotna 99669; (907) 262-1337. Features wildlife museum and historic log village, including last territorial school (1958). Homesteading artifacts and photos.

Southcentral Alaska Museum of Natural History, 11723 Old Glenn Highway, Eagle River 99577; (907) 694-0819. Exhibits embrace geology, biology and anthropology of southcentral Alaska. "Fossil Forest" features elements of a newly discovered duck-billed dinosaur from the Talkeetna Mountains.

Southeast Alaska Indian Cultural Center, 106 Metlakatla, Sitka 99835. Housed in the Sitka National Park Visitor Center; visitors have a chance to talk to Native artists at work: beadworkers, carvers, printmakers, silversmiths.

SS *Nenana*/Fairbanks Historical Preservation Foundation, 2300 Airport Way, Cabin #1876, Box 70552, Fairbanks 99707; (907) 456-8848. Located at Alaskaland, a newly restored river steamer, a National Historic Landmark. Compelling 300-foot diorama takes visitors on a 2,400-mile voyage through the years 1847–1932 along the Yukon River system.

Talkeetna Historical Society Museum, P.O. Box 76, Talkeetna 99676; (907) 733-2487. Located one block off Main Street, the Talkeetna Townsite Historic District contains buildings reflecting a small 1917–40 gold mining community. Museum portrays lives of gold miners, early aviators and climbers of Mount McKinley.

Tanana Yukon Historical Society. *See* House of Wickersham

Tok Visitor Center, P.O. Box 335, Tok 99780; (907) 883-5887 or 883-5775. At the junction of Alaska and Glenn Highways, displays of Dall sheep, waterfowl, wolf, caribou, plus fossils and minerals. Open May to October.

Tongass Historical Museum, 629 Dock St., Ketchikan 99901; (907) 225-5600. Collection of Alaskana, Northwest Coast Native materials, photo archives and maritime history displays. Summer exhibit features the historic cannery town of Loring.

Totem Heritage Center, 601 Deermount St., Ketchikan 99901; (907) 225-5900. Large collection of original Tsimshian, Haida and Tlingit totems from surrounding islands.

Trail of '98 Museum, on Broadway, P.O. Box 415, Skagway 99840; (907) 983-2420. Houses fine collection of gold rush artifacts, all actually used by stampeders, and some personal belongings of notorious con man Soapy Smith. Photographs, historical records.

University of Alaska Archives and Manuscripts, Library, University of Alaska, 3211 Providence Drive, Anchorage 99508; (907) 786-1849 (Dennis Walle, archivist). Historic and contemporary papers, records, photographs; some artifacts. Open by appointment to researchers. Catalog of holdings available.

University of Alaska Museum, 907 Yukon Drive, Box 756960, Fairbanks 99775-1200; (907) 474-7505. Five galleries display Alaska's history, Native culture, art, natural phenomena, wildlife, birds, geology and prehistoric past, including the mummy of a 36,000-year-old Steppe bison, and a special display on the northern lights.

Hedgehogs and Deer

Like many Alaskans, I like to hunt and fish, and that includes hunting for mushrooms. In the fall I hunt for Sitka black-tailed deer. Where I hunt, there are large mossy areas with many hedgehogs, one of my favorite mushrooms. The mushrooms are well named—not only for the little spines that grow on them but also because they are large and meaty, the hogs of the fungus world. When I return to camp with a deer and some nice hedgehogs, I break out my cast-iron skillet, get it nice and hot over the campfire, throw in a small piece of deer fat, and wait till the skillet is shiny. I cut my hedgehogs in chunks, cooking them in the skillet until the water that comes out of them cooks off and they are tender. I set the hedgehogs aside, throw in another chunk of fat, and add thin slices of deer backstrap, frying them on each side. When they're done, I pile them on a plate smothered in hedgehogs. It's time to dig in! It can't get any better than that after a long day in the woods.—Bumpo Bremicker in Harriette Parker's *Alaska's Mushrooms*

Sculptures, totem poles, a Russian block-house and a nature trail with signs identifying local plants. Many special programs.

Valdez Museum and Historical Archive, 217 Egan St., Valdez 99686; (907) 835-2764. Permanent exhibits celebrate the 1898 gold rush route across Valdez Glacier. Restored 1907 Ahrens steam fire engine, log cabin, original Cape Hinchinbrook lighthouse lens, exhibits on the 1964 earthquake, the trans-Alaska oil pipeline and 1989 *Exxon Valdez* oil spill cleanup.

Veniaminov Museum, St. Herman's Russian Orthdox Theological Seminary, Mission Road, Kodiak 99615; (907) 486-3524. Archive of personal items belonging to Ivan Veniaminov (later Bishop Innocent), plus papers and documents (many in Russian) about Russian America and the Orthodox church in Russian America.

Wasilla–Knik–Willow Creek Historical Society. *See* Dorothy G. Page Museum

Wrangell Historical Society Museum, P.O. Box 1050, Wrangell 99929; (907) 874-3770. Housed in Wrangell's oldest building, displays include items from Wrangell history, Tlingit artifacts and petroglyphs.

Yugtarvik Regional Museum, Yupik Library and Cultural Center, P.O. Box 388, Bethel 99559. Located in historic Kilbuck Building on Hoffman Street, the museum displays traditional tools and clothing, hosts Native art classes, contains photo exhibits.

Yugtarvik means "a place for people's things."

Mushrooms
More than 500 species of mushroom grow in Alaska, and, while most are not common enough to be seen and collected readily by the amateur mycophile (mushroom hunter), many edible and choice species shoot up in any available patch of earth. Alaska's "giant arc of mushrooms" extends from Southeast's panhandle through Southcentral, the Alaska Peninsula and the Aleutian Chain and is prime mushroom habitat. Interior, western and northern Alaska also support mushrooms in abundance.

Mushroom seasons vary considerably according to temperature, humidity and available nutrients, but most occur from June through September. In a particularly cold or dry season, the crop will be scant.

There are relatively few poisonous mushrooms in relation to the number of species that occur throughout Alaska. Potentially fatal mushrooms, some of which occur in populated areas, include fly agaric (*Amanita muscaria*), poison pax (*Paxillus involutus*) and false morels. Easy-to-identify edible species include hedgehogs (*Hydnum repandum*) and shaggy manes (*Coprinus comatus*). Even edible mushrooms may disagree with one's digestion; the only test for an inedible or poisonous mushroom is positive identification. *If you can't identify it, don't eat it.*

Muskeg

Muskegs are bogs where little vegetation can grow except for sphagnum moss, black spruce, Sitka spruce, dwarf birch, tussocks and a few other shrubby plants. Such swampy areas cover much of Alaska.

Musk Oxen

Musk oxen are stocky, shaggy, long-haired mammals of the extreme northern latitudes. They remain in the open through Alaska's long winters. Their name is misleading, for they have no musk gland and are more closely related to sheep and goats than to cattle. Adult males may weigh 500 to 900 pounds, females 300 to 700 pounds. Both sexes have horns that droop down from their forehead and curve back up at the tips.

When threatened by wolves or other predators, musk oxen form circles or lines with their young in the middle. These defensive measures did not protect them from humans with guns.

Musk oxen were eliminated from Alaska in about 1865, when hunters shot and killed the last herd of 13. The species was reintroduced to the territory in the 1930s when 34 musk oxen were purchased from Greenland and brought to the University of Alaska Fairbanks. In 1935–36, the 31 remaining musk oxen at the university were shipped to

During extremely cold weather, musk oxen stand still to conserve energy. From Alaska's Mammals *by Dave Smith and Tom Walker*

Nunivak Island in the Bering Sea, where the herd eventually thrived. Animals from the Nunivak herd have been transplanted to areas along Alaska's western and northern coasts; at least five wild herds—approximately 3,000 musk oxen—exist in the state.

Indications are that musk oxen from Nelson Island are spreading to the mainland and that individuals from the eastern Arctic herd have wandered west into adjacent Canada.

The soft underhair of musk oxen is called qiviut and grows next to the skin, protected by long guard hairs. It is shed naturally every spring. The Musk Ox Development Corporation maintains a herd in Palmer and collects qiviut for the Oomingmak cooperative. The hair is spun into yarn in Rhode Island and sent back to Alaska, where the cooperative arranges for knitters in villages in western Alaska, where jobs are scarce, to knit the yarn into clothing at their own pace.

Each village keeps its own distinct signature pattern for scarves knitted from qiviut. Villagers also produce stoles, tunics, hats and smoke rings (circular scarves that fit a person's head like a hood). A total of 300 women are employed in this manner.

The domestic musk oxen farm in Palmer is open to the public. Guided tours operate daily from May to September and bring visitors face to face with these unique arctic animals. For more information, write: Musk Ox Development Corporation, P.O. Box 587, Palmer 99645.

National Forests (*SEE ALSO* LAND USE; NATIONAL PARKS, PRESERVES AND MONUMENTS; *AND* NATIONAL WILDERNESS AREAS)

Alaska has two national forests, the Tongass and the Chugach. The Tongass occupies the panhandle or southeastern portion of the state. The Chugach extends south and east of Anchorage along the southcentral Alaskan coast, encompassing most of the Prince William Sound area.

These two national forests are managed by the U.S. Forest Service for a variety of uses. They provide forest products for national and international markets, minerals, recreational opportunities, wilderness experiences and superb scenery and views for Alaska residents and visitors.

Nearly 200 public recreation cabins are maintained in the Tongass and Chugach National Forests. They accommodate visitors from all over the world and are a vacation bargain at $25 per night, including a boat on some freshwater lakes. (*See also* Cabins)

Wildlife and fisheries are important Forest Service programs in the national forests of Alaska. The Tongass and Chugach National Forests are also home to some of Alaska's most magnificent wildlife. It is here that the United States' national bird, the bald eagle, and large brown (grizzly) bears may be encountered in large numbers. Five species of Pacific salmon spawn in the rivers and streams of the forests, and smaller mammals and waterfowl abound. The Forest Service is charged with the management of this rich habitat; the Alaska Department of Fish and Game manages the wildlife species that this habitat supports.

There are many recreational opportunities in the national forests of Alaska, including backpacking, fishing, hunting, photography, boating, nature study and camping, to list just a few. For further information concerning recreational opportunities,

Old Growth

Old-growth forests are "multi-aged." Many age classes of trees are present, from saplings to old-timers, assuring a sustainable cycle of decay and regeneration. Instead of fire, periodic gales, usually from the Southeast, are the major disturbance to our coastal forests. —O'Clair, Armstrong and Carstensen, *The Nature of Southeast Alaska* ✎

contact the U.S. Forest Service office nearest the area you are visiting.

The Alaska National Interest Lands Conservation Act (ANILCA) created approximately 5.5 million acres of wilderness (divided into 14 units) within the 17-million-acre Tongass National Forest. It also added three new areas to the forest: the Juneau Icefield, Kates Needle and parts of the Barbazon Range, totaling more than 1 million acres. The Tongass Timber Reform Act (TTRA) of 1990 amended ANILCA and designated five additional wilderness areas and an addition to the existing Kootznoowoo Wilderness.

The lands bill also provided extensive additions to the Chugach National Forest. These additions, totaling about 2 million acres, include the Nellie Juan area east of Seward, College Fiord extension, Copper/Rude Rivers addition and a small extension at Controller Bay southeast of Cordova.

The following charts show the effect of the Alaska lands act on the Tongass and Chugach National Forests.

According to groundskeepers, approximately 50 percent of all new ornamental trees planted on the University of Alaska Anchorage campus are eaten by moose during the following winter.

Wilderness Units in Tongass National Forest   Acres

Wilderness Areas Established Dec. 2, 1980, by ANILCA

Coronation Island Wilderness	19,232
Endicott River Wilderness	98,729
Kootznoowoo Wilderness* (Admiralty Island National Monument)**	955,921
Maurelle Islands Wilderness	4,937
Misty Fiords National Monument**	2,142,243
Petersburg Creek–Duncan Salt Chuck Wilderness	46,777
Russell Fiord Wilderness	348,701
South Baranof Wilderness	319,568
South Prince of Wales Wilderness	90,996
Stikine–LeConte Wilderness	448,926
Tebenkof Bay Wilderness	66,839
Tracy Arm–Fords Terror Wilderness	653,179
Warren Island Wilderness	11,181
West Chichagof–Yakobi Wilderness	264,747

Wilderness Areas Established Nov. 28, 1990, by TTRA

Chuck River Wilderness	74,298
Karta Wilderness	39,889
Kuiu Wilderness	60,581
Pleasant–Lemusurier–Inian Islands Wilderness	23,096
South Etolin Wilderness	83,371

Total acreage 5,753,211

*Kootznoowoo Wilderness includes 18,486 acres (including 24 acres of non-national forest land) in the Young Lake Addition established by TTRA.
**Designated monuments under ANILCA; first areas so designated in the national forest system. These wildernesses include only the public lands above mean high tide.

National Forest Lands in Alaska	Tongass	Chugach
Total acreage before ANILCA	15,555,388	4,392,646
Total acreage after ANILCA	16,954,713	5,940,040*
Wilderness acreage created	5,753,211	None created
Wilderness study	None created	2,019,999 acres

*This lands act provides for additional transfers of national forest land to Native corporations, the state and the U.S. Fish and Game Department of an estimated 296,000 acres on Afognak Island, and an estimated 242,000 acres to the Chugach Native Corporation.

National Historic Places

(SEE ALSO ARCHAEOLOGY) A "place" on the National Register of Historic Places is a district, site, building, structure or object significant to the state for its history, architecture, archaeology or culture. The national register also includes National Historic Landmarks. NHLs are properties given special status by the secretary of the interior for their significance to the nation, as well as to the state. The register is an official list of properties recognized by the federal government as worthy of preservation. Listing on the register begins with owner's consent and entails a nomination process with reviews by the State Historic Preservation officer, the Alaska Historical Commission and the Keeper of the National Register. Limitations are *not* placed on a listed property. The federal government does not attach restrictive covenants to the property or seek to acquire it.

Listing on the register means that a property is accorded national recognition for its significance in American history or prehistory. Additional benefits include tax credits on income-producing properties and automatic qualification for federal matching funds for preservation, maintenance and restoration work when such funds are available. Listed properties are also guaranteed a full review process for potential adverse effects by federally funded, licensed or otherwise assisted projects. Such a review usually takes place while the project is in the planning stage. Alternatives are sought to avoid, if at all possible, damaging or destroying the particular property in question.

Southcentral. A.E.C. Cottage No. 23, Anchorage

Alaska Central Railroad Tunnel No. 1, Seward

Alaska Nellie's Homestead, Lawing vicinity

Alex (Mike) Cabin, Eklutna

American Cemetery, Kodiak

Anchorage Cemetery, Anchorage

Anchorage City Hall, Anchorage

Anderson (Oscar) House, Anchorage

Ascension of Our Lord Chapel, Karluk

Bailey Colony Farm, Palmer

Ballaine House, Seward

Beluga Point Archaeological Site, North Shore, Turnagain Arm

Bering Expedition Landing Site NHL, Kayak Island

Berry House, Palmer

Brown & Hawkins Store, Seward

Campus Center Site, Palmer

Cape St. Elias Lighthouse, Kayak Island

Chilkat Oil Company Refinery Site, Katalla

Chisana Historic District, Chisana

Chitina Tin Shop, Chitina

Chugachik Island Archaeological Site, Kachemak Bay

Coal Village Site, Kachemak Bay

Cooper Landing Historic District, Cooper Landing

Cooper Landing Post Office, Cooper Landing

Copper River and Northwestern Railway, Chitina vicinity

Cordova Post Office and Courthouse, Cordova

Crow Creek Mine, Girdwood

Cunningham-Hall PT–6 NC692W Aircraft, Palmer

Dakah De'nin's Village Site, Chitina

David (Leopold) House, Anchorage

Diversion Tunnel, Lowell Creek, Seward

Eklutna Power Plant, Eklutna vicinity

Federal Building–U.S. Courthouse (Old), Anchorage

Fourth Avenue Theatre, Anchorage

Gakona Roadhouse, Gakona

Government Cable Office, Seward

Herried House, Palmer

Hirshey Mine, Hope vicinity

Holm (Victor) Cabin, Cohoe

Holy Assumption Russian Orthodox Church NHL, Kenai

Fireweed at sunset, Kennecott Copper Mine. From Picture Journeys in Alaska's Wrangell– St. Elias *by George Herben*

Holy Resurrection Church, Kodiak
Holy Transfiguration of Our Lord Chapel, Ninilchik
Hope Historic District, Hope vicinity
Hyland Hotel, Palmer
Independence Mine Historic District, Hatcher Pass
Indian Valley Mine, Girdwood vicinity
Jesse Lee Home, Seward
KENI Radio Building, Anchorage
Kennecott Mines NHL, McCarthy vicinity
Kimball's Store, Anchorage
Knik Site, Knik vicinity
KOD-171 Archaeological Site, Kodiak
KOD-207 Archaeological Site, Kodiak
KOD-233 Archaeological Site, Kodiak
Kodiak Naval Operating Base (Fort Abercrombie and Fort Greely) NHL, Kodiak Island
Lauritsen Cabin, Seward Highway
Matanuska Colony Community Center, Palmer
McCarthy General Store, McCarthy
McCarthy Power Plant, McCarthy
Middle Bay Brick Kiln, Kodiak
Moose River Site, Naptowne, Kenai area
Nabesna Gold Mine, Nabesna area
Nativity of Holy Theotokos Church, Afognak Island
Nativity of Our Lord Chapel, Ouzinkie
Old St. Nicholas Russian Orthodox Church, Eklutna
Palmer Depot, Palmer
Palugvik Archaeological District, Hawkins Island
Patten Colony Farm, Palmer
Pioneer School House, Anchorage
Potter Section House, Anchorage
Protection of the Theotokos Chapel, Akhiok
Puhl House, Palmer
Rebarcheck (Raymond) Colony Farm, Palmer area
Reception Building, Cordova
Red Dragon Historic District, Cordova
Russian-American Company Magazin (Erskine House) NHL, Kodiak
St. Michael the Archangel Church, Cordova
St. Nicholas Chapel, Seldovia
St. Peter's Episcopal Church, Seward
Sts. Sergius and Herman of Valaam Chapel, Ouzinkie

Sts. Sergius and Herman of Valaam Church, English Bay
Selenie Lagoon Archaeological Site, Port Graham vicinity
Seward Depot, Seward
Susitna River Bridge, Alaska Railroad, Talkeetna vicinity
Swetman House, Seward
Tangle Lakes Archaeological District, Paxson vicinity
Teeland's Store, Wasilla
Three Saints Bay Site NHL, Kodiak Island
United Protestant Church, Palmer
Van Gilder Hotel, Seward
Wasilla Community Hall, Wasilla
Wasilla Depot, Wasilla
Wasilla Elementary School, Wasilla
Wendler Building, Anchorage
Yukon Island, Main Site NHL, Yukon Island

Southeast. Alaskan Hotel, Juneau
Alaska Native Brotherhood Hall NHL, Skagway
Alaska Steam Laundry, Juneau
Alaska Totems, Ketchikan
American Flag Raising Site NHL, Sitka
Bergmann Hotel, Juneau
Building No. 29 NHL, Sitka
Burkhart-Dibrell House, Ketchikan
Cable House and Station, Sitka
Cape Spencer Lighthouse, Cape Spencer
Chief Kushakes House, Saxman
Chief Shakes House, Wrangell
Chilkoot Trail and Dyea NHL, Skagway
Davis (J.M.) House, Juneau
Duncan (Father William) Cottage, Metlakatla
Eldred Rock Lighthouse, Lynn Canal
Emmons House, Sitka
Etolin Canoe, Etolin Island
First Lutheran Church, Ketchikan
Fort Durham NHL, Taku Harbor, Juneau vicinity
Fort William H. Seward NHL, Haines
Frances House, Juneau
Fries Miners Cabins, Juneau
Gilmore Building, Ketchikan
Government Indian School, Haines
Governor's Mansion, Juneau
Gruening (Ernest) Cabin, Juneau
Hanlon-Osbakken House, Sitka

Russian Bishop's House

The Russian Bishop's House in Sitka—the oldest intact building in Alaska—is the only one remaining from the Russian colonial era and one of only four original Russian structures still standing in North America. As a missionary in 1824, Father Ivan Veniaminov began fashioning an alphabet for the Aleuts, taught brickmaking and other trades, and took farflung kayak trips for months at a time to convert an estimated 10,000 Natives to his faith. American observers referred to him as Paul Bunyan in a cassock. The manse he lived in here has been restored. . . . The 1842 structure of squared spruce logs and planks features a first-floor museum of Russian-American artifacts; the second story has been authentically returned to its early grandeur. —Paul and Audrey Grescoe, *Alaska: The Cruise-Lover's Guide*

Holy Trinity Church, Juneau
Jualpa Mining Camp, Juneau
Ketchikan Ranger House, Ketchikan
Klondike Gold Rush National Historic Park, Skagway area
Mayflower School, Douglas
Mills (May) House, Sitka
Mills (W.P.) House, Sitka
Murray Apartments and Cottages, Sitka
New Russia Archaeological Site NHL, Yakutat
Old Sitka NHL, Sitka
Pleasant Camp, Haines Highway
Porcupine Historic District, Skagway vicinity
Russian Bishop's House NHL, Sitka
St. John the Baptist Church, Angoon
St. Michael the Archangel Cathedral NHL, Sitka
St. Nicholas Church (Russian Orthodox), Juneau
St. Peter's Church, Sitka
St. Philip's Episcopal Church, Wrangell

Saxman Totem Park, Ketchikan
See House, Sitka
Sheldon Jackson Museum, Sitka
Sitka National Historical Park, Sitka
Sitka Naval Operating Base NHL, Sitka
Sitka Pioneers' Home, Sitka
Skagway and White Pass Historic District NHL, Skagway vicinity
Sons of Norway Hall, Petersburg
The Star, Ketchikan
Totem Bight, Ketchikan
Twin Glacier Camp, Juneau
U.S. Army Corps of Engineers, Storehouse No. 3, Portland Canal
U.S. Army Corps of Engineers, Storehouse No. 4, Hyder
U.S. Coast and Geodetic Survey House, Sitka
Valentine Building, Juneau
Walker-Broderick House, Ketchikan
Wickersham (James) House, Juneau
Wrangell Public School, Wrangell
Ziegler House, Ketchikan

Western. Adak Army and Naval Operating Bases NHL, Adak
Anangula Site NHL, Aleutian Islands
Ananiuliak Island Archaeological District, Aleutian Islands
Anvil Creek Gold Discovery Site, Nome
Archaeological Site 49 AF 3, Katmai National Park and Preserve
Archaeological Site 49 MK 10, Katmai National Park and Preserve
Atka B-24 Liberator, Aleutian Islands
Attu Battlefield and U.S. Army and Navy Airfields NHL, Attu

St. Michael the Archangel Cathedral NHL, Sitka

Brooks River Archaeological District NHL, Katmai National Park and Preserve

Cape Field at Fort Glenn NHL, Aleutian Islands

Cape Krusenstern Archaeological District NHL, Kotzebue vicinity

Cape Nome Mining District Discovery Sites NHL, Nome

Cape Nome Roadhouse, Nome vicinity

Carrighar (Sally) House, Nome

Cathedral of the Holy Ascension of Christ NHL, Unalaska

Chaluka Site NHL, Umnak Island

Christ Church Mission, Anvik

Discovery Saloon, Nome

Dutch Harbor Operating Base and Fort Mears NHL, Aleutian Islands

Elevation of the Holy Cross Church, Naknek

Fairhaven Ditch, Imruk Lake

First Mission House, Bethel

Fort St. Michael Site, Unalakleet vicinity

Fure's Cabin, Katmai National Park and Preserve

Gambell Sites, Gambell

Holy Resurrection Church, Belkofski

Iyatayet Archaeological Site NHL, Norton Sound

Japanese Occupation Site, Kiska NHL, Aleutian Islands

Kaguyak Village Site, Katmai National Park and Preserve

Kijik Historic District, Lake Clark National Park and Preserve

Kolmakov Redoubt Site, Kuskokwim River, Aniak vicinity

Kukak Village, Katmai National Park and Preserve

Norge Storage Site, Teller

Old Savonoski Site, Katmai National Park and Preserve

Onion Portage Archaeological District NHL, Noatak vicinity

Pilgrim 100B N709Y Air-craft, Dillingham

Pilgrim Hot Springs, Seward Peninsula

Port Moller Hot Springs Village Site, Alaska Peninsula

Presentation of Our Lord Chapel, Nikolai

Redoubt St. Michael Site, Unalakleet vicinity

St. Alexander Nevsky Chapel, Akutan

St. George the Great Martyr Orthodox Church, St. George Island

St. Jacob's Church, Napaskiak

St. John the Baptist Chapel, Naknek

St. John the Theologian Church, Perry-ville

St. Nicholas Chapel, Ekuk

St. Nicholas Chapel, Igiugig

St. Nicholas Chapel, Nondalton

St. Nicholas Chapel, Pedro Bay

St. Nicholas Chapel, Sand Point

St. Nicholas Church, Kwethluk

St. Nicholas Church, Nikolski

St. Nicholas Church, Pilot Point

St. Seraphim Chapel, Lower Kalskag

St. Sergius Chapel, Chuathbaluk

Sts. Constantine and Helen Chapel, Lime Village

Sts. Peter and Paul Russian Orthodox Church, St. Paul Island

Savonoski River District, Katmai National Park and Preserve

Seal Islands Historic District NHL, Pribilof Islands

Sitka Spruce Plantation NHL, Amaknak Island

Snow Creek Placer Claim No. 1, Nome vicinity

Solomon Roadhouse, Solomon

Takli Island Archaeological District, Katmai National Park and Preserve

TEMNAC P-38G Lightning Aircraft, Aleutian Islands

Transfiguration of Our Lord Chapel, Nushagak

Ulatka Head, anti-aircraft installation overlooking Unalaska Bay

Wales Archaeological District NHL, Wales vicinity

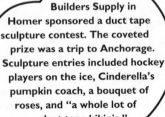

Spenard Builders Supply in Homer sponsored a duct tape sculpture contest. The coveted prize was a trip to Anchorage. Sculpture entries included hockey players on the ice, Cinderella's pumpkin coach, a bouquet of roses, and "a whole lot of duct tape bikinis."

Interior. Biederman (Ed) Fish Camp,
  Eagle area
Big Delta Historic District, Delta Junction
Campus Archaeological Site, Fairbanks
Central Roadhouse, Central
Chatanika Gold Camp, Chatanika
Chena Pump House, Fairbanks
Chugwater Archaeological Site, Fairbanks
Clay Street Cemetery, Fairbanks
Creamer's Dairy, Fairbanks
Curry Lookout, Talkeetna vicinity
Davis (Mary Lee) House, Fairbanks
Discovery Claim, Pedro Creek, Fairbanks
Dry Creek Archaeological Site NHL, Healy
  vicinity
Eagle Historic District NHL, Eagle
Ester Camp Historic District, Fairbanks
Ewe Creek Ranger Cabin No. 8, Denali
  National Park
Fairview Inn, Talkeetna
Federal Building, U.S. Post Office, Court-
  house (Old), Fairbanks
Goldstream Dredge No. 8, Mile 9, Old
  Steese Hwy., Ester
Harding Railroad Car, Alaskaland,
  Fairbanks
Igloo Creek Cabin No. 25, Denali National
  Park
Immaculate Conception Church, Fairbanks
Joslin (Falcon) House, Fairbanks
The Kink, Fortymile River
Lacey Street Theatre, Fairbanks
Ladd Field NHL (Fort Wainwright),
  Fairbanks
Lower East Fork Ranger Cabin No. 9,
  Denali National Park
Lower Toklat River Ranger Cabin No. 18,
  Denali National Park
Lower Windy Creek Ranger Cabin No. 15,
  Denali National Park
Main School, Fairbanks
Masonic Temple, Fairbanks
McGregor (George) Cabin, Eagle vicinity
Mission Church, Arctic Village
Mission House (Old), Fort Yukon
Moose Creek Ranger Cabin No. 19, Denali
  National Park
Mount McKinley National Park
  Headquarters, Denali National Park
Nenana Depot, Nenana
Oddfellows Hall (First Avenue Bathhouse),
  Fairbanks

Canoers on Wonder Lake with Mount McKinley
in the background. From *Discover Alaska* by
Alaska Northwest Books

Rainey's Cabin, Fairbanks
Riley Creek Ranger Cabin No. 20, Denali
  National Park
Rose Building, Fairbanks
Ruby Roadhouse, Ruby
Sanctuary River Cabin No. 31, Denali
  National Park
Slaven (Frank) Roadhouse, Eagle vicinity
Steele Creek Roadhouse, Fortymile
Sternwheeler *Nenana* NHL, Fairbanks
Sullivan's Roadhouse, Fort Greely
Sushana River Ranger Cabin No. 17, Denali
  National Park
Talkeetna Historic District, Talkeetna
Tanana Mission, Tanana
Taylor (James) Cabins, Eagle vicinity
Teklanika Archaeological District, Denali
  National Park and Preserve
Thomas (George C.) Memorial Library
  NHL, Fairbanks
Toklat Ranger Station (Pearson Cabin)
  No. 4, Denali National Park
Tolovana Roadhouse, Tanana vicinity
Upper East Fork Cabin No. 29, Denali
  National Park
Upper Savage River Cabin, Denali National
  Park
Upper Toklat River Ranger Cabin No. 24,
  Denali National Park
Upper Windy Creek Ranger Cabin No. 7,
  Denali National Park
Wickersham House, Fairbanks
Woodchopper Roadhouse, Eagle vicinity
Yukon River Lifeways District, Eagle vicinity

Far North. Aluakpak Site, Wainwright
vicinity
Anaktuuk Site, Wainwright vicinity
Atanik District, Wainwright vicinity
Avalitkuk Site, Wainwright vicinity
Birnirk Site NHL, Barrow
Gallagher Flint Station Archaeological Site
NHL, Sagwon
Ipiutak Archaeological District, Point
Hope
Ipiutak Site NHL, Point Hope
Ivishaat Site, Wainwright vicinity
Kanitch, Wainwright vicinity
Leffingwell Camp NHL, Flaxman Island
Napanik Site, Wainwright vicinity
Negilik Site, Barrow
Point Barrow Refuge, Cape Smythe
Utkeagvik Presbyterian Church Manse,
Barrow
Uyagaagruk, Wainwright vicinity
Whaling and Trading Station, Barrow
vicinity
Will Rogers–Wiley Post Crash Site, Barrow
vicinity

*A skier explores the Peters Hills, with Mount
McKinley in the distance. From Alaska's
Accessible Wilderness by Bill Sherwonit*

National Parks, Preserves and Monuments

The National
Park Service administers approximately
54 million acres of land in Alaska, consisting of 15 units classified as national parks,
national preserves and national monuments. The Alaska National Interest Lands
Conservation Act of 1980—also referred to
as ANILCA (*see* Land Use)—created 10 new
National Park Service units in Alaska and
changed the size and status of three existing
Park Service units: Denali National Park
and Preserve (formerly Mount McKinley
National Park); Glacier Bay National
Monument, now a national park and preserve; and Katmai National Monument,
now a national park and preserve. (*See* map,
pages 142–43)

In 1996, Alaska's national parks,
preserves and monuments entertained
1,649,849 visitors.

National parks are traditionally
managed to preserve scenic, wildlife and
recreational values; mining, cutting of
house logs, hunting and other resource
exploitation are carefully regulated within
park, monument and preserve boundaries,
and motorized access is restricted to
automobile traffic on authorized roads.
However, regulations for National Park
Service units in Alaska recognize that these
units contain lands traditionally occupied
and used by Alaska Natives and rural residents for subsistence activities. Therefore,
management of *some* parks, preserves and
monuments in Alaska provides for subsistence hunting, fishing and gathering
activities, and the use of such motorized
vehicles as snow machines, motorboats and
airplanes where such activities are customary. National preserves do permit sport
hunting.

Following is a list of National Park
Service parks, preserves and monuments.
The U.S. Forest Service manages another
two national monuments: Admiralty Island
National Monument, 937,000 acres; and
Misty Fiords National Monument, 2.1 mil-
lion acres. Both are in Southeast and part
of the National Wilderness Preservation
System. (*See also* National Wild and Scenic
Rivers *and* National Wilderness Areas)

Information on the parks, preserves and monuments is available at the Alaska Public Lands Information Centers: 605 W. Fourth Ave., Suite 105, Anchorage 99501, (907) 271-2737; 250 Cushman St., Suite 1A, Fairbanks 99701; and P.O. Box 359, Tok 99780. On-line information on each of the national parks can be found on the National Park Service home page at www.nps.gov.

National Park Service units are followed by address, acreage and major features or recreations:

Aniakchak National Monument and Preserve, Superintendent, Katmai National Park and Preserve, P.O. Box 7, King Salmon 99613 (603,000 acres). Aniakchak dry caldera.

Bering Land Bridge National Preserve, National Park Service, P.O. Box 220, Nome 99762 (2,785,000 acres). Lava fields, rare plants, archaeological sites, migratory waterfowl.

Cape Krusenstern National Monument, National Park Service, P.O. Box 1029, Kotzebue 99752 (660,000 acres). Archaeological sites.

Denali National Park and Preserve, National Park Service, P.O. Box 9, Denali Park 99755 (6,028,000 acres). Mount McKinley, abundant wildlife.

Gates of the Arctic National Park and Preserve, National Park Service, P.O. Box 74680, Fairbanks 99707 (8,472,000 acres). Brooks Range, wild and scenic rivers, wildlife.

Glacier Bay National Park and Preserve, National Park Service, Bartlett Cove, Gustavus 99826 (3,283,000 acres). Glaciers, marine wildlife.

Katmai National Park and Preserve, National Park Service, P.O. Box 7, King Salmon 99613 (4,090,000 acres). Valley of Ten Thousand Smokes, brown bears.

Kenai Fjords National Park, National Park Service, P.O. Box 1727, Seward 99664 (570,000 acres). Fjords, Harding Icefield, Exit Glacier, waterfowl, sea otters.

pop

years ago

The highest mountain in North America was named for William McKinley, the Republican presidential candidate from Ohio—a man who never set foot in Alaska.

Klondike Gold Rush National Historical Park, National Park Service, P.O. Box 517, Skagway 99840 (2,721 acres). Chilkoot Trail.

Kobuk Valley National Park, National Park Service, P.O. Box 1029, Kotzebue 99752 (1,750,000 acres). Archaeological sites, Great Kobuk Sand Dunes, river rafting.

Lake Clark National Park and Preserve, National Park Service, 4230 University Drive, Suite 311, Anchorage 99508 (4,044,000 acres). Backcountry recreation, fishing, scenery.

Noatak National Preserve, National Park Service, P.O. Box 1029, Kotzebue 99752 (6,574,000 acres). Abundant wildlife, river floating.

Sitka National Historical Park, National Park Service, P.O. Box 738, Sitka 99835 (106 acres). Russian Bishop's House, totems, trails.

Wrangell–St. Elias National Park and Preserve, National Park Service, P.O. Box 439, Copper Center 99573 (13,188,000 acres). Rugged peaks, glaciers, expansive wilderness.

Yukon-Charley Rivers National Preserve, National Park Service, P.O. Box 167, Eagle 99738 (2,523,000 acres). Backcountry recreation, river floating.

National Petroleum Reserve (SEE ALSO OIL AND GAS)

In 1923, President Warren G. Harding signed an executive order creating Naval Petroleum Reserve Number 4 (NPR-4), the last of four petroleum reserves to be placed under control of the U.S. Navy. The secretary of the Navy was charged to "explore, protect, conserve, develop, use, and operate the Naval Petroleum Reserves," including NPR-4, on Alaska's North Slope. (*See* map, pages 142–43)

The U.S. Geological Survey (USGS) had *(Continued on page 144)*

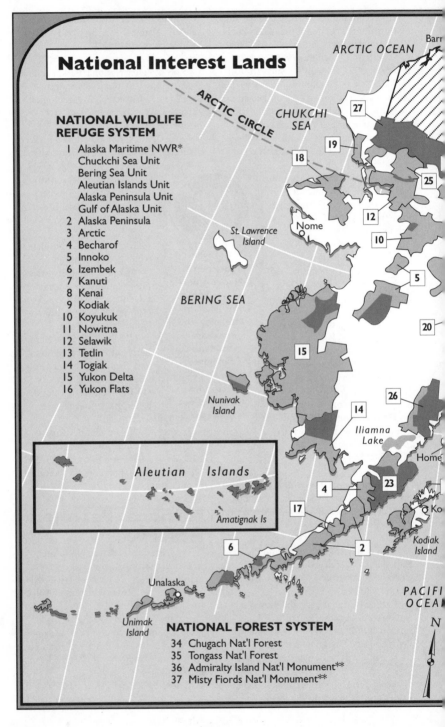

National Interest Lands

NATIONAL WILDLIFE REFUGE SYSTEM

1. Alaska Maritime NWR*
   Chuckchi Sea Unit
   Bering Sea Unit
   Aleutian Islands Unit
   Alaska Peninsula Unit
   Gulf of Alaska Unit
2. Alaska Peninsula
3. Arctic
4. Becharof
5. Innoko
6. Izembek
7. Kanuti
8. Kenai
9. Kodiak
10. Koyukuk
11. Nowitna
12. Selawik
13. Tetlin
14. Togiak
15. Yukon Delta
16. Yukon Flats

ARCTIC OCEAN

Barr

ARCTIC CIRCLE

CHUKCHI SEA

St. Lawrence Island

Nome

BERING SEA

Nunivak Island

Iliamna Lake

Home

Ko

Kodiak Island

Aleutian Islands

Amatignak Is

Unalaska

Unimak Island

PACIFI OCEA

N

NATIONAL FOREST SYSTEM

34. Chugach Nat'l Forest
35. Tongass Nat'l Forest
36. Admiralty Island Nat'l Monument**
37. Misty Fiords Nat'l Monument**

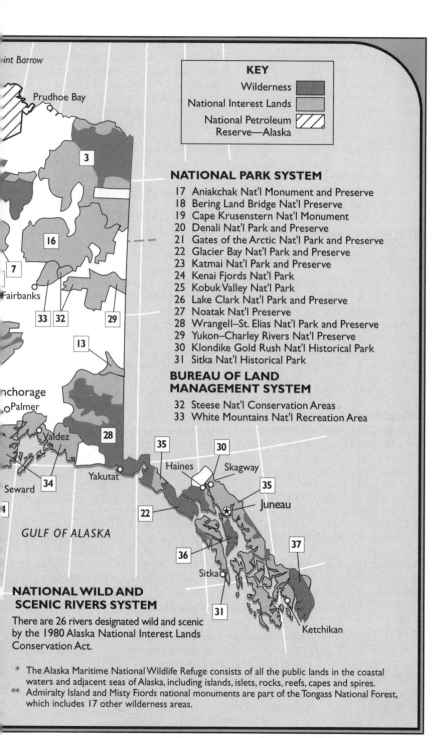

KEY

Wilderness	
National Interest Lands	
National Petroleum Reserve—Alaska	

NATIONAL PARK SYSTEM

17 Aniakchak Nat'l Monument and Preserve
18 Bering Land Bridge Nat'l Preserve
19 Cape Krusenstern Nat'l Monument
20 Denali Nat'l Park and Preserve
21 Gates of the Arctic Nat'l Park and Preserve
22 Glacier Bay Nat'l Park and Preserve
23 Katmai Nat'l Park and Preserve
24 Kenai Fjords Nat'l Park
25 Kobuk Valley Nat'l Park
26 Lake Clark Nat'l Park and Preserve
27 Noatak Nat'l Preserve
28 Wrangell–St. Elias Nat'l Park and Preserve
29 Yukon–Charley Rivers Nat'l Preserve
30 Klondike Gold Rush Nat'l Historical Park
31 Sitka Nat'l Historical Park

BUREAU OF LAND MANAGEMENT SYSTEM

32 Steese Nat'l Conservation Areas
33 White Mountains Nat'l Recreation Area

NATIONAL WILD AND SCENIC RIVERS SYSTEM

There are 26 rivers designated wild and scenic by the 1980 Alaska National Interest Lands Conservation Act.

* The Alaska Maritime National Wildlife Refuge consists of all the public lands in the coastal waters and adjacent seas of Alaska, including islands, islets, rocks, reefs, capes and spires.
** Admiralty Island and Misty Fiords national monuments are part of the Tongass National Forest, which includes 17 other wilderness areas.

(Continued from page 141)
begun surface exploration in the area in 1901; following creation of the 23-million-acre reserve, exploration programs were conducted by the Navy. From 1944 to 1953, extensive geological and geophysical surveys were conducted and 36 test wells were drilled. Nine oil and gas fields were discovered; the largest oil field, near Umiat, contains an estimated 70 million to 120 million barrels of recoverable oil. Active exploration was suspended in 1953.

In 1974, the Arab oil embargo, coupled with the knowledge of large petroleum reserves at nearby Prudhoe Bay, brought about renewed interest in NPR-4, and Congress directed the Navy to resume its exploration program.

In 1976, all lands within NPR-4 were redesignated the National Petroleum Reserve Alaska (NPR-A) and jurisdiction was transferred to the secretary of the interior. In 1980, Congress authorized the secretary of the interior to prescribe an expeditious program of competitive leasing of oil and gas tracts in the reserve, clearing the way for private development of the area's resources.

By mid-1983, three competitive bid lease sales, involving a total of 7.2 million acres of NPR-A, had been held. Dates of the sales and the number of acres involved were: January 1982, 1.5 million acres; May 1982, 3.5 million acres; and July 1983, 2.2 million acres. As oil prices have dropped, interest from the oil companies has lessened and leases have expired. As of mid-1993, there were only two leases covering 19,388 acres.

The Interior Department, through USGS, continued exploration of NPR-A into the 1980s. Past naval explorations and those conducted by USGS resulted in the discovery of oil at Umiat and Cape Simpson, and

several gas fields, including Walakpa, Gubic and Point Barrow. The North Slope Borough is developing the reserves in the Walakpa field to provide gas for heating and electrical generation for Barrow. The borough plans to drill up to eight wells to produce the gas. Data gathered indicates NPR-A may contain recoverable reserves of 1.85 billion barrels of crude oil and 3.74 trillion cubic feet of natural gas.

National Wild and Scenic Rivers (SEE ALSO

RIVERS) The Alaska National Interest Lands Conservation Act (ANILCA) of Dec. 2, 1980, gave wild and scenic river classification to 13 streams within the National Park System, six in the National Wildlife Refuge System and two in Bureau of Land Management Conservation and Recreation areas. (See map, pages 142–43) An additional five rivers are located outside designated preservation units. Twelve more rivers were designated for further study and possible wild and scenic classification.

The criteria for wild and scenic river classification covers more than just float trip possibilities. Scenic features, wilderness characteristics and recreational opportunities that would be impaired by alteration, development or impoundment are also considered.

Rivers are classified into three categories under the Wild and Scenic Rivers Act. The wild classification is most restrictive of development or incompatible uses—it stresses the wilderness aspect of the rivers. The scenic classification permits some intrusions upon the natural landscape, and the recreational classification is the least restrictive category. A specified amount of land back from the river's banks is also put in protected status to ensure access, use and the preservation of aesthetic values for the public.

The cost of living in Alaska has remained remarkably stable, according to the Spenard Index of Economic Indicators. In the year ending June 1997, the cost of a can of SPAM®, a roll of duct tape, a six-pack of cheap Oly beer, and a moose nugget swizzle stick rose less than 8 tenths of 1%!

A kayaker paddles across mirror-smooth Lake Beverley in Wood–Tikchik State Park. From *Alaska's Accessible Wilderness* by Bill Sherwonit

For those desiring to float these rivers, special consideration must be given to put-in and take-out points because most of the designated wild and scenic rivers are not accessible by road. This means that voyagers and their crafts have to be flown in and picked up by charter bush planes. Because Federal Aviation Administration regulations prohibit the lashing of canoes and kayaks to pontoons of floatplanes when carrying passengers, inflatable rafts and folding canvas or rubber kayaks are often more convenient and less expensive to transport.

Further information on rivers and river running can be obtained from the Alaska Public Lands Information Centers: 605 W. Fourth Ave., Suite 105, Anchorage 99501; 250 Cushman St., Suite 1A, Fairbanks 99701; 50 Main St., Ketchikan 99901; and P.O. Box 359, Tok 99780; the U.S. Fish and Wildlife Service, 1011 E. Tudor Road, Anchorage 99503; and the Bureau of Land Management, 222 W. Seventh Ave., No. 13, Anchorage 99513. Information for rivers within park units or managed by the National Park Service is also available from the particular park headquarters. (*See also* National Parks, Preserves and Monuments)

Rivers Within National Park Areas. Alagnak—Katmai National Preserve

Alatna—Gates of the Arctic National Park

Aniakchak—Aniakchak National Monument; Aniakchak National Preserve

Charley—Yukon–Charley Rivers National Preserve

Chilikadrotna—Lake Clark National Park and Preserve

John—Gates of the Arctic National Park and Preserve

Kobuk—Gates of the Arctic National Park and Preserve

Mulchatna—Lake Clark National Park and Preserve

Noatak—Gates of the Arctic National Park and Noatak National Preserve

North Fork Koyukuk—Gates of the Arctic National Park and Preserve

Salmon—Kobuk Valley National Park

Tinayguk—Gates of the Arctic National Park and Preserve

Tlikakila—Lake Clark National Park and Preserve

Rivers Within National Wildlife Refuges. Andreafsky—Yukon Delta National Wildlife Refuge

Ivishak—Arctic National Wildlife
Refuge
Nowitna—Nowitna National Wildlife
Refuge
Selawik—Selawik National Wildlife
Refuge
Sheenjek—Arctic National Wildlife
Refuge
Wind—Arctic National Wildlife Refuge
(General information on rivers not
listed in refuge brochures may be obtained
from respective refuge offices by addressing
queries to refuge managers. Addresses for
refuges are given in the brochures.)

Rivers Within Bureau of Land Management Units.
Beaver
Creek—The segment of the main stem
from confluence of Bear and Champion
Creeks within White Mountains National
Recreation Area to the Yukon Flats
National Wildlife Refuge boundary.

Birch Creek—The segment of the main
stem from the south side of Steese Highway
downstream to the bridge at Milepost 147.

Rivers Outside of Designated Preservation Units.
Alagnak—
Those segments or portions of the main stem
and Nonvianuk tributary lying outside and
westward of Katmai National Park and
Preserve.

Delta River—The segment from and
including all of the Tangle Lakes to a point
one-half mile north of Black Rapids.

Fortymile River—The main stem
within Alaska, plus tributaries.

Gulkana River—The main stem from
the outlet of Paxson Lake to the confluence
with Sourdough Creek; various segments of
the west fork and middle fork.

Unalakleet River—Approximately
80 miles of the main stem.

Rivers Designated for Study for Inclusion in Wild and Scenic Rivers System
Colville River
Etivluk–Nigu Rivers
Kanektok River
Kisaralik River
Koyuk River

Melozitna River
Porcupine River
Sheenjek River
(lower segment)
Situk River
Squirrel
River
Utukok
River
Yukon River (Rampart section)

National Wilderness Areas
Passage of the Alaska
National Interest Lands Conservation Act
(ANILCA) on Dec. 2, 1980, added millions
of acres to the National Wilderness Preservation System. Administration of these
wilderness areas is the responsibility of the
agency under whose jurisdiction the land is
situated. Agencies that administer wilderness areas in Alaska include the National
Park Service, U.S. Fish and Wildlife Service
and the U.S. Forest Service. Although the
Bureau of Land Management has authority
to manage wilderness in the public domain,
no BLM wilderness areas exist in Alaska.
(See map, pages 142–43)

In addition, passage of the Tongass
Timber Reform Act (TTRA) on Nov. 28,
1990, designated an additional 299,721
acres of the Tongass National Forest as
wilderness.

Wilderness allocations to different
agencies in Alaska are: U.S. Forest Service,
approximately 5,753,211 acres; National
Park Service, approximately 32,848,564
acres; and U.S. Fish and Wildlife Service,
approximately 18,676,320 acres.

Wilderness, according to the federal
Wilderness Act of 1964, is land sufficient
in size to enable the operation of natural
systems without undue influence from
human activities in surrounding areas
and should be places in which people are
visitors who do not remain. Alaska wilderness regulations follow the stipulations of
the Wilderness Act as amended by the
Alaska lands act. Specifically designed to
allow for Alaska conditions, the rules are
considerably more lenient about transportation access, human-made structures

and use of mechanized vehicles. The primary objective of a wilderness area continues to be the maintenance of the wilderness character of the land.

In Alaska wilderness areas, the following uses and activities are permitted:

• Fishing, hunting and trapping will continue on lands within the national forests, national wildlife refuges and national park preserves. National park wilderness does not allow sport hunting, or sport or commercial trapping.

• Subsistence uses, including hunting, fishing, trapping, berry gathering and use of timber for cabins and firewood, may be allowed but are not permitted in all wilderness areas. Contact the particular land manager for the most up-to-date rules on subsistence activity.

• Public recreation or safety cabins in wilderness areas in national forests, national wildlife refuges and national park preserves will continue to be maintained and may be replaced. A limited number of new public-use cabins may be added if needed.

• Existing special-use permits on all national forest wilderness lands for cabins, homesites or similar structures may continue. Use of temporary campsites, shelters and other temporary facilities and equipment related to hunting and fishing on national forest lands will continue.

• Fish habitat enhancement programs, including planting of vegetation, construction of buildings, fish weirs, fishways, spawning channels and other accepted means of maintaining, enhancing and rehabilitating fish stocks, may be allowed in national forest wilderness areas.

• Special-use permits for guides and outfitters operating within wilderness areas in the national forests and national wildlife refuges will continue.

• Private, state and Native lands surrounded by wilderness areas will be guaranteed access through the wilderness area.

• Use of

fixed-wing airplanes, motorboats, snow machines and nonmotorized methods of surface transportation for *traditional* activities and for access to villages and homesites will be allowed to continue.

National Wildlife Refuges
Currently, there are 76,385,000 acres of National Wildlife Refuge lands administered by the U.S. Fish and Wildlife Service.

However, the USFWS will soon complete a project to recalculate acres in refuges. Using modern geographic information system software and new topographic quadrangles, map technicians expect to find several million "new" acres, including new islands in the Alaska Maritime Refuge. These changes will be announced early in 1998. Wildlife refuges are designed to protect large segments of intact ecosystems that provide habitats for representative populations of birds, fish and mammals. The 16 refuges vary widely in size. (*See* map, pages 142–43)

Public use is limited as only two of the refuges—Kenai and Tetlin—are accessible by road. Among the public recreational uses permitted within national wildlife refuges are sightseeing, nature observation and photography, sport hunting and fishing (under state law), boating, camping, hiking and picnicking. Trapping can be carried out under applicable state and federal laws. Commercial fishing and related facilities (campsites, cabins, etc.) are authorized by special-use permits.

Subsistence activities are permitted. Use of snowmobiles, motorboats and other surface transportation for rural residents is generally permitted. Fixed-wing aircraft access may be allowed. Helicopter access requires a special permit.

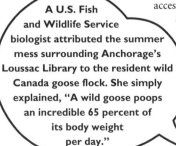

A U.S. Fish and Wildlife Service biologist attributed the summer mess surrounding Anchorage's Loussac Library to the resident wild Canada goose flock. She simply explained, "A wild goose poops an incredible 65 percent of its body weight per day."

National Wildlife Refuge administrative addresses are followed by acreage and pre-dominant wildlife:

Alaska Maritime National Wildlife Refuge, 2355 Kachemak Drive, Suite 101, Homer 99603 (3,435,639 acres). Seabirds, sea lions, sea otters, harbor seals, walrus.

Alaska Peninsula National Wildlife Refuge, P.O. Box 277, King Salmon 99613 (3,500,000 acres). Brown bears, caribou, moose, sea otters, bald eagles, peregrine falcons, wolves, wolverines, migrating whales.

Arctic National Wildlife Refuge, 101 12th Ave., Box 20, Fairbanks 99701 (19,285,923 acres). Caribou, polar bears, grizzly bears, wolves, Dall sheep, peregrine falcons, musk oxen, snowy owls.

Becharof National Wildlife Refuge, P.O. Box 277, King Salmon 99613 (1,200,018 acres). Brown bears, bald eagles, caribou, moose, salmon.

Innoko National Wildlife Refuge, P.O. Box 69, McGrath 99627 (3,850,000 acres). Migratory waterfowl, beaver, lynx, marten, moose.

Izembek National Wildlife Refuge, P.O. Box 127, Cold Bay 99571 (303,094 acres). Black brant (coastal geese), brown bears.

Kanuti National Wildlife Refuge, 101 12th Ave., Box 11, Fairbanks 99701 (1,430,002 acres). Waterfowl.

Kenai National Wildlife Refuge, Box 2139, Soldotna 99669 (1,904,752 acres). Moose, salmon, mountain goats, Dall sheep, bears, lynx, wolves.

Kodiak National Wildlife Refuge, 1390 Buskin River Road, Kodiak 99615 (1,656,363 acres). Brown bears, black-tailed deer, bald eagles, river otters.

Koyukuk National Wildlife Refuge, P.O. Box 287, Galena 99741 (3,550,000 acres). Wolves, bears, moose, waterfowl.

Nowitna National Wildlife Refuge, P.O. Box 287, Galena 99741 (1,560,000 acres). Migratory waterfowl, moose, bears, furbearers.

Selawik National Wildlife Refuge,

The First Bears

Long ago on the shores of the Arctic Ocean an Eskimo woman lived with her tribe. She already had several children but one day two children were born together. They were very strange twins, indeed. One was covered with long white fur while the other had a coat of brown fur. Since they were not like any of her other children the mother did not want them. So one day she took them far from the igloo and left them alone. When she had gone, the white-furred child got up and ran down to the beach and out across the frozen sea. The brown child turned his back to the sea and scrambled across the tundra and into the mountains. And there they have lived ever since. But people do not call them men. They are known as "Nanook" or Polar bear and Brown bear.

Some Eskimo still believe them to be their cousins. This is the reason why. One time a man went hunting far out on the frozen sea. A great wind arose causing the ice to break off from the shore and move out to sea carrying the hunter with it. For many days he wandered about on the ice, starving. When he was nearly dead he saw a great white bear coming towards him. It seemed friendly and more than that, it could talk. It found food for the lost hunter and stayed with him so that he did not die.

When the wind drove the ice back to the shore, the hunter asked the bear for something to prove to his friends that his story was true. The bear thereupon lifted his skin and the hunter saw that beneath it he wore clothes like an Eskimo. From his mukluk he took a string and gave it to the hunter. The Eskimo thanked the bear and it returned to the frozen sea.

When the hunter reached his village, he told his story. Of course nobody would believe him. Then he took out the string that the bear had given him. Not one among them had ever seen such a string. No Eskimo could tell how it was made or how it had been tanned. And so they knew that the hunter had spoken the truth.—Edward L. Keithahn, *Alaskan Igloo Tales*

P.O. Box 270, Kotzebue 99752 (2,150,000 acres). Caribou, migratory birds.
Tetlin National Wildlife Refuge, P.O. Box 779, Tok 99780 (700,009 acres). Migratory waterfowl, Dall sheep, moose, bears, ptarmigan.
Togiak National Wildlife Refuge, P.O. Box 270, Dillingham 99576 (4,097,432 acres). Caribou, walrus, seabirds, moose.
Yukon Delta National Wildlife Refuge, P.O. Box 346, Bethel 99559 (19,131,645 acres). Migratory birds, musk oxen and reindeer are found on Nunivak Island.
Yukon Flats National Wildlife Refuge, 101 12th Ave., Box 264, Fairbanks 99701 (8,630,000 acres). Waterfowl, moose, bears.

Native Arts and Crafts (*SEE ALSO* BALEEN; BASKETS; BEADWORK; IVORY; MASKS; NATIVE PEOPLE; POTLATCH; SKIN SEWING; *AND* TOTEMS)

The traditional arts and crafts of Alaska's Natives were produced for ceremonial and utilitarian reasons. These works were not thought of as art in the Western sense but as objects and designs to fulfill specific functions. Native art also reflected spiritual values and the physical environment each group inhabited. Alaska's Natives are known for their ingenious use and manipulation of natural materials to supply life's needs. Roots, bark, grasses, wood, fur, skins, feathers and the sea's resources are still used to produce containers, clothing, hunting implements, ceremonial regalia and many other items.

Today, most Native utilitarian objects are modern adaptations using plastic, metal and glass. But many traditional Native designs and natural materials are still used to create ceremonial objects, and Alaska Native arts and crafts are widely sought by collectors, museums and tourists. This new market for their work has proven beneficial to Native artists and therefore to Native culture as a whole, which is experiencing the transition from a subsistence lifestyle to a contemporary Western economy.

The Inupiat and Yupik Eskimo people, like all of the Alaska Native groups, are divided geographically and linguistically.

Haida blanket design

Because their coastal environment offers few forest resources, the Eskimo people have learned to rely on the tundra and the sea for cultural materials. The Inupiat of northern Alaska are known for making objects out of sea mammal parts—especially walrus ivory, baleen and whalebone. Their ivory carving and scrimshaw work is world renowned, and more contemporary work in which stiff baleen is coiled into elegant baskets is also gaining recognition.

The Yupik of western Alaska also utilize sea mammal materials in their art. In addition, they rely heavily on the coastal rye grass for their intricate coiled baskets and mat work. Yupik ceremonial masks, which are carved primarily of driftwood, assembled and painted, are distinctive in the global tribal mask-making tradition. Both the Inupiat and Yupik groups produce warm, beautiful clothing using the furs and skins of indigenous land and sea mammals.

The Aleut people of the Aleutian Islands also make beautiful baskets from rye grass, but they use a twining technique. The Aleut are known for their traditional capes made of sea mammal gut and their painted bentwood hunting hats and visors.

The Athabascan Indians of Alaska's Interior live in a region abundant with forest and river resources. They make decorative beaded clothing and other items, often on tanned, smoked moosehide, and they form the bark of the birch tree into lightweight canoes, baby cradles and containers. They are also known for their skill sewing skins into clothing.

The Tlingit, Haida and Tsimshian people of southeastern Alaska are part of the Pacific Northwest Coast Indian culture, which extends down the coast of British

Columbia and into Washington state. Each member of this culture is given at birth his or her own totemic crest—an animal form representing the family clan. These crests are reproduced in many art forms such as elaborate ceremonial regalia; carvings in wood, metal or stone; paintings or prints; and jewelry. The carvers of the Northwest Coast, best known for monumental totem poles, record legendary happenings and honor important people or events. Their artwork, which adheres to a complex, formal design system, is highly stylized and dramatic. Fine Northwest Coast pieces such as carved and painted wood hats, rattles, masks and bentwood boxes are sought worldwide by collectors and museums.

Native Peoples

Alaska's 94,027 Native people make up about 16 percent of the state's total population. Of those, the majority are Eskimo, Indian and Aleut. Although many live in widely scattered villages along the coastline and great rivers of Alaska, 16,540 Native persons lived in Anchorage as of July 1992.

Fairbanks had a Native population of 5,610.

At the time Europeans came in contact with the Natives of Alaska in 1741, the Eskimo, Indian and Aleut people lived within well-defined regions, with little mixing of ethnic groups. All were hunting and gathering people who did not practice agriculture.

In southeastern Alaska, the herring, salmon, deer and other plentiful foods permitted the Haida and Tlingit Indians to settle in permanent villages and develop a culture rich in art. The Athabascans lived chiefly in the Interior. They migrated from one seasonal subsistence camp to another to take advantage of seasonal abundance of fish, waterfowl and other game. The coastal Eskimo and Aleut subsisted primarily on the rich resources of the rivers and the sea.

Alaska's Tsimshian Indians moved in 1887 from their former home in British Columbia to Annette Island in Southeast Alaska, under Anglican minister Father William Duncan. About 1,200 Tsimshian now live in Metlakatla. They are primarily fishermen, as are most Southeasterners.

The Native Way of Life

In the traditional subsistence lifestyle of Native Americans, all food, clothing, shelter, tools, and fuel came from the natural. For at least 10,000 years, the Eskimo, Indian, and Aleut peoples of Alaska had lived off the land as skilled hunters and gathers.

The Athabascan Indians of the Interior were nomadic, following the food sources from season to season. At summer fish camps along major rivers, they caught and dried salmon and other fish. In fall hunting camps, they hunted caribou and moose, drying the meat for winter food and tanning the skins for clothing. In the winter, they trapped beaver and snared rabbits.

The Eskimo and Aleut peoples of Alaska's coastal regions relied primarily on the rich resources of the sea and the rivers. They hunted whales and other marine mammals seasonally, in spring gathered seabird eggs, and in summer harvested berries and edible plants. They made clothing from hides, gut, and fish skins. Animal bones were hewn into arrows, needles, and fish hooks. Stones were hollowed into oil lamps, and seal or whale oil was burned for light or heat.

The Northwest Coast Indians of Southeast Alaska and Northern Canada (Tlingit, Haida, and Tsimshian) enjoyed a moderate climate and settled in permanent villages. They gathered the plentiful salmon, herring, deer, shellfish, and edible plants. They made clothing from skins, feathers, cedar bark, and mountain goat hair. Rocks were fashioned into hammers and spearheads. Bark, roots, and grasses were woven into useful baskets.

In the subsistence way of life, all nature's offerings find a use and nothing goes to waste.

—Claire Murphy and Jane Haigh, Gold Rush Women

Traditional Native Distribution

Approximately 1,800 Haida live in Alaska, about 300 of whom live in Hydaburg on the south end of Prince of Wales Island. It is believed they migrated to Alaska from interior Canada in the 1700s. The Haida excel in the art of totem carving and are noted for skilled working of wood, bone, shell, stone and silver.

Today, about 13,900 Tlingit (KLINK-it) live throughout southeastern Alaska; approximately another 1,000 live in other parts of the state, primarily in the Anchorage area. The Tlingit, who migrated west from what is now Canada before the first European contact, commercially dominated the interior Canadian Indians, trading eulachon oil, copper pieces and Chilkat blankets for various furs and beaded clothing. Like the Haida and Tsimshian, they are part of the totem culture; totems provide a record of major events in family or clan history.

Athabascan Indians, who number approximately 13,700 in Alaska, occupied the vast area of Alaska's Interior. They were nomadic people whose principal sources of food were caribou, moose and fish. Hard times and famines were frequent for all Athabascans, except the Tanaina and Ahtna groups, who lived along the Gulf of Alaska and could rely on salmon as their basic food.

The Eskimo have traditionally lived in villages along the harsh Bering Sea and Arctic Ocean coastlines, and along a thin strip of the Gulf of Alaska coast, including Kodiak Island. They took salmon, waterfowl, berries, ptarmigan and a few caribou, but it was the sea and its whales, walruses and seals that provided the foundation for their existence. Houses were barabaras—dwellings built partially underground and covered with sod. They did not live in snow igloos.

Kate Carmack, a Tagish Tlingit, c. 1898, who helped discover the Klondike gold. From Gold Rush Women *by Claire Rudolph Murphy and Jane G. Haigh*

The Aleut have traditionally lived on the Alaska Peninsula and along the Aleutian Chain. When the Russians reached the Aleutians in the 1740s, practically every island was inhabited. Decimated by contact with the white man, only a few Aleut settlements remain, including two on the Pribilof Islands, where Natives handle seal herds for the federal government.

The Aleut lived in permanent villages, taking advantage of sea life and land mammals for food. Their original dwellings were large, communal structures, housing as many as 40 families. After Russian occupation they lived in smaller houses, many adopting the Russian-style log cabin. Today many Aleuts are commercial fishermen.

Rapid advances in communications, transportation and other services to remote villages have altered Native life in Alaska. Economic changes, from a subsistence to a cash economy, culminated in the passage of the Alaska Native Claims Settlement Act in 1971. It gave Alaska Natives $962.5 million and 44 million acres of land as compensation for the loss of lands historically occupied or used by their people.

NATIVE REGIONAL CORPORATIONS. Twelve regional business corporations were formed under the 1971 Alaska Native Claims Settlement Act to manage money and land received from the government. (*See* map, page 154) A 13th corporation was organized for those Natives residing outside Alaska. Following is a list of corporations and the area or region each administers:

Ahtna Incorporated (Copper River Basin), Drawer G, Copper Center 99573, or 2701 Fairbanks St., Anchorage 99503.

Aleut Corporation (Aleutian Islands), 1 Aleut Plaza, 4000 Old Seward Highway, Suite 300, Anchorage 99503.

Arctic Slope Regional Corporation (Arctic Alaska), P.O. Box 129, Barrow 99723, or 313 E St., Suite 5, Anchorage 99501.

Bering Straits Native Corporation (Seward Peninsula), P.O. Box 1008, Nome 99762.

Bristol Bay Native Corporation (Bristol Bay area), P.O. Box 198, Dillingham 99576, or P.O. Box 100220, Anchorage 99510.

Calista Corporation (Yukon–Kuskokwim Delta), P.O. Box 408, Bethel 99559, or 516 Denali St., Anchorage 99501.

Chugach Alaska Corporation (Prince William Sound), 560 E. 34th Ave., Anchorage 99503.

Cook Inlet Region, Incorporated (Cook Inlet region), 2525 C St., Anchorage 99503.

Doyon, Limited (interior Alaska), 201 First Ave., Suite 200, Fairbanks 99701.

Koniag Incorporated (Kodiak area), 4300 B St., Anchorage 99503.

NANA Regional Corporation (Kobuk region), P.O. Box 49, Kotzebue 99752, or 4706 Harding Drive, Anchorage 99503.

Sealaska Corporation (southeastern Alaska), One Sealaska Plaza, Juneau 99801.

Thirteenth Regional Corporation (outside Alaska), 13256 Northup Way, Suite 12, Bellevue, WA 98005.

Regional Nonprofit Corporations.

Aleutian–Pribilof Islands Association, Incorporated (Aleut Corporation), 1689 C St., Anchorage 99501.

Association of Village Council Presidents (Calista Corporation), P.O. Box 219, Bethel 99559.

Bristol Bay Native Association (Bristol Bay Native Corporation), P.O. Box 237, Dillingham 99756.

Central Council of Tlingit–Haida Indian Tribes (Sealaska Corporation), One Sealaska Plaza, Suite 200, Juneau 99801.

Cook Inlet Tribal Council (Cook Inlet Region, Incorporated), 670 W. Fireweed Lane, Anchorage 99503.

Copper River Native Association (Ahtna Incorporated), Drawer H, Copper Center 99573.

Inupiat Community of the Arctic Slope (Arctic Slope Regional Corporation), P.O. Box 437, Barrow 99723.

Kawerak, Incorporated (Bering Straits Native Corporation), P.O. Box 948, Nome 99762.

Kodiak Area Native Association (Koniag, Incorporated), P.O. Box 172, Kodiak 99615.

Maniilaq (formerly Mauneluk) Association (NANA Regional Corporation), P.O. Box 256, Kotzebue 99752.

North Pacific Rim Native Association (Chugach Alaska Corporation), 3000 A St., Suite 400, Anchorage 99503.

Ounalashka Corporation (Aleut Corporation), P.O. Box 149, Unalaska 99685.

Tanana Chiefs Conference (Doyon, Limited), 201 First Ave., Fairbanks 99701.

Other Native Organizations.

Alaska Eskimo Whaling Commission, P.O. Box 570, Barrow 99723.

Alaska Federation of Natives, 1577 C St., Anchorage 99501.

Alaska Native Brotherhood, P.O. Box 112, Juneau 99801.

Alaska Native Commission on Alcoholism and Drug Abuse, P.O. Box 4-2463, Anchorage 99509.

Alaska Native Cultural Arts Exchange, 117 W. Fourth Ave., Anchorage 99501.

Alaska Native Foundation, 3305 Arctic Blvd., Anchorage 99503.

Alaska Native Health Board, 4201 Tudor Centre Drive, Anchorage 99508.

Central Council of Tlingit and Haida Indian Tribes of Alaska, One Sealaska Plaza, Suite 200, Juneau 99801.

Eyak Corporation, P.O. Box 340, Cordova 99574.

Fairbanks Native Association, Incorporated, 310 First Ave., Fairbanks 99701.

Interior Village Association, 127 1/2 Minnie St., Fairbanks 99701.

Inuit Circumpolar Conference, Barrow 99723.

Norton Sound Health Corporation, P.O. Box 966, Nome 99762.

Qawalangin (Sons of the Sea Lion), Box 334, Unalaska 99685, is the federally recognized tribal government of the Unangan (Aleut) people of Unalaska.

Southeast Alaska Regional Health Corporation, P.O. Box 2800, Juneau 99803.

Yukon–Kuskokwim Health Corporation, P.O. Box 528, Bethel 99559.

Yupiktat Bista (a branch of the Association of Village Council Presidents), Bethel 99559.

Native Village Corporations.

In addition to the 12 regional corporations managing money and land received as part of the Alaska Native Claims Settlement Act, eligible Native villages were required to form corporations and to choose lands made available by the settlement act by December 1974. The 203 Native villages that formed village corporations eligible for land and money benefits are listed under their regional corporation.

The City of Bethel received notification from the *Time* magazine sweepstakes that "C. Bethel" was at the top of its list of prize winners. Since the city needed $1 million for a new sewage lagoon, officials voted to invest the price of a stamp to enter the contest. "C. Bethel" did not win, and honey bucket services are still flourishing.

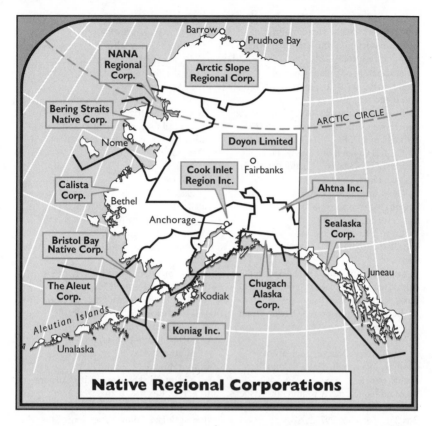

Native Regional Corporations

Ahtna Incorporated: Cantwell, Chistochina, Chitina, Copper Center, Gakona, Gulkana, Mentasta Lake, Tazlina.

Aleut Corporation: Akutan, Atka, Belkofski, False Pass, King Cove, Nelson Lagoon, Nikolski, St. George, St. Paul, Sand Point, Unalaska, Unga.

Arctic Slope Regional Corporation: Anaktuvuk Pass, Atkasook, Barrow, Kaktovik, Nuiqsut, Point Hope, Point Lay, Wainwright.

Bering Straits Native Corporation: Brevig Mission, Council, Golovin, Inalik/Diomede, King Island, Koyuk, Marys Igloo, Nome, St. Michael, Shaktoolik, Shishmaref, Stebbins, Teller, Unalakleet, Wales, White Mountain.

Bristol Bay Native Corporation: Aleknagik, Chignik, Chignik Lagoon, Chignik Lake, Clarks Point, Dillingham, Egegik, Ekuk, Ekwok, Igiugig, Iliamna, Ivanof Bay,

Kokhanok, Koliganek, Levelock, Manokotak, Naknek, Newhalen, New Stuyahok, Nondalton, Pedro Bay, Perryville, Pilot Point, Portage Creek, Port Heiden, South Naknek, Togiak, Twin Hills, Ugashik.

Calista Corporation: Akiachak, Akiak, Alakanuk, Andreafsky, Aniak, Atmautluak, Bethel, Bill Moores, Chefornak, Chevak, Chuathbaluk, Chuloonwick, Crooked Creek, Eek, Emmonak, Georgetown, Goodnews Bay, Hamilton, Hooper Bay, Kasigluk, Kipnuk, Kongiganak, Kotlik, Kwethluk, Kwigillingok, Lime Village, Lower Kalskag, Marshall, Mekoryuk, Mountain Village, Napaimiute, Napakiak, Napaskiak, Newtok, Nightmute, Nunapitchuk, Ohogamiut, Oscarville, Paimiut, Pilot Station, Pitkas Point, Platinum, Quinhagak, Red Devil, Russian Mission, St. Marys, Scammon Bay, Sheldons Point, Sleetmute, Stony River,

Toksook Bay, Tuluksak, Tuntutuliak, Tununak, Umkumiut, Upper Kalskag.

Chugach Natives, Incorporated: Chenaga, Eyak, Nanwalek, Port Graham, Tatitlek.

Cook Inlet Region, Incorporated: Chickaloon, Eklutna, Knik, Ninilchik, Seldovia, Tyonek.

Doyon, Limited: Alatna, Allakaket, Anvik, Beaver, Bettles Field, Birch Creek, Chalkyitsik, Circle, Dot Lake, Eagle, Fort Yukon, Galena, Grayling, Healy Lake, Holy Cross, Hughes, Huslia, Kaltag, Koyukuk, Manley Hot Springs, McGrath, Minto, Nenana, Nikolai, Northway, Nulato, Rampart, Ruby, Shageluk, Stevens Village, Takotna, Tanacross, Tanana, Telida.

Klukwan, Incorporated: Klukwan.

Koniag, Incorporated: Afognak, Akhiok, Kaguyak, Karluk, Larsen Bay, Old Harbor, Ouzinkie, Port Lions, Woody Island.

NANA Regional Corporation, Incorporated: Ambler, Buckland, Deering, Kiana, Kivalina, Kobuk, Kotzebue, Noatak, Noorvik, Selawik, Shungnak.

Sealaska Corporation: Angoon, Craig, Hoonah, Hydaburg, Kake, Kasaan, Klawock, Saxman, Yakutat.

Shee-Atika Corporation: Sitka.

Nenana Ice Classic

(*SEE ALSO* BREAKUP) The Ice Classic is a gigantic betting pool offering $300,000 in 1997 in cash prizes to the lucky winner who guessed the time, to the nearest minute, of the ice breakup on the Tanana River at the town of Nenana. Official breakup time each spring is established when the surging ice dislodges a four-legged "tripod" and breaks an attached line, which stops a clock set to Yukon standard time.

Tickets for the classic are sold for $2 each, entitling the holder to one guess. Ice Classic officials estimate over $7 million has been paid to lucky guessers through the years.

The primary intention of the Ice Classic was never as a fund-raiser for the town, but as a statewide lottery, which was officially sanctioned by the first state legislature in one of its first actions back in 1959.

Over the years the Ice Classic contest has benefited the town. Fifty percent of the gross proceeds goes to the winners. Nenana residents are paid salaries for ticket counting and compilation, and about 15 percent is earmarked for upkeep of the Nenana Civic Center and as donations to the local visitors center, the library and special events at the high school.

Top Five Regional Native Corporations

Ranked by most recent fiscal year gross revenues:

1) **Arctic Slope Regional Corporation**, Barrow. Gross revenues, $468.524 million; 7,200 shareholders; 22 subsidiaries

2) **Sealaska Corporation, Juneau.** Gross revenues, $236.9 million; 16,000 shareholders; 1 subsidiary

3) **Cook Inlet Region, Incorporated** (CIRI), Anchorage, $129.19 million; 6,800 shareholders; 12 subsidiaries

4) **Doyon, Limited,** Fairbanks, $50.78 million; 13,496 shareholders; 2 subsidiaries including Doyon Drilling

5) **NANA Regional Corporation,** Kotzebue, $46 million; 9,075 shareholders; 20-plus subsidiaries, including NANA Marriott, Maniilaq Limited and Akima

Compiled by *Alaska Journal of Commerce,* January 1997

The Internal Revenue Service also gets a large chunk of withholding taxes on the payroll and a huge bite of each winner's share. In 1997, 14 winners divided the $300,000 prize.

Another pool, the Kuskokwim Ice Classic, has been a tradition in Bethel since 1924. Initially, it was said that the winner was paid 20 fish or 20 furs, but stakes are considerably higher now, with the winner receiving 40 percent of the total ticket sales.

Breakup times for the Nenana Ice Classic from 1918 through 1997 are arranged in order of day and time of breakup (*see* chart below).

Newspapers and Periodicals (*Rates are subject to change*)

Air Guardian, 6000 Air Guard Road, Anchorage 99502. Monthly. Free.

Alaska Angler, Box 83550, Fairbanks 99708. Bimonthly. Annual rate: $49.

Alaska Bar Rag, 510 L St., No. 602, Anchorage 99501. Bimonthly. Annual rate: $25.

Alaska Boating Magazine, 205 E. Dimond Blvd., Suite 592, Anchorage 99515. Three times a year. Annual rate: $12.

Alaska Business Monthly, P.O. Box 241288, Anchorage 99524. Monthly. Annual rate: $21.95.

Alaska Commercial Fisherman, 3933 Geneva Place, Anchorage 99508.

Nenana Ice Classic, Breakup Times, 1918–1997

April	May	May
20, 1940— 3:27 P.M.	2, 1976—10:51 A.M.	8, 1933— 7:30 P.M.
23, 1993— 1:01 P.M.	2, 1960— 7:12 P.M.	8, 1968— 9:26 P.M.
24, 1990— 5:19 P.M.	3, 1941— 1:50 A.M.	8, 1986— 9:31 P.M.
26, 1995— 1:22 P.M.	3, 1919— 2:33 P.M.	8, 1971—10:50 P.M.
26, 1926— 4:03 P.M.	3, 1947— 5:53 P.M.	9, 1923— 2:00 P.M.
28, 1969—12:28 P.M.	4, 1967—11:55 A.M.	9, 1955— 2:31 P.M.
28, 1943— 7:22 P.M.	4, 1973—11:59 A.M.	9, 1984— 3:33 P.M.
29, 1939— 1:26 P.M.	4, 1944— 2:08 P.M.	10, 1931— 9:23 A.M.
29, 1958— 2:56 P.M.	4, 1970—10:37 P.M.	10, 1972—11:56 A.M.
29, 1953— 3:54 P.M.	5, 1957— 9:30 A.M.	10, 1975— 1:49 P.M.
29, 1983— 6:37 P.M.	5, 1961—11:31 A.M.	10, 1982— 5:36 P.M.
29, 1994—11:01 P.M.	5, 1996—12:32 p.m.	11, 1921— 6:42 A.M.
30, 1997—10:28 A.M.	5, 1987— 3:11 P.M.	11, 1918— 9:33 A.M.
30, 1936—12:58 P.M.	5, 1929— 3:41 P.M.	11, 1920—10:45 A.M.
30, 1980— 1:16 P.M.	5, 1946— 4:40 P.M.	11, 1985— 2:36 P.M.
30, 1942— 1:28 P.M.	5, 1963— 6:25 P.M.	11, 1924— 3:10 P.M.
30, 1934— 2:07 P.M.	6, 1977—12:46 P.M.	12, 1927— 5:42 A.M.
30, 1978— 3:18 P.M.	6, 1974— 3:44 P.M.	12, 1922— 1:20 P.M.
30, 1951— 5:54 P.M.	6, 1950— 4:14 P.M.	12, 1952— 5:04 P.M.
30, 1979— 6:16 P.M.	6, 1928— 4:25 P.M.	12, 1937— 8:04 P.M.
30, 1981— 6:44 P.M.	6, 1954— 6:01 P.M.	12, 1962—11:23 P.M.
	6, 1938— 8:14 P.M.	13, 1948—11:13 A.M.
May	7, 1925— 6:32 P.M.	14, 1992— 6:26 A.M.
1, 1991—12:04 A.M.	7, 1965— 7:01 P.M.	14, 1949—12:39 P.M.
1, 1932—10:15 A.M.	8, 1959—11:26 A.M.	15, 1935— 1:32 P.M.
1, 1956—11:24 A.M.	8, 1966—12:11 P.M.	16, 1945— 9:41 A.M.
1, 1989— 8:14 P.M.	8, 1930— 7:03 P.M.	20, 1964—11:41 A.M.

Biweekly. Annual rate: $30.

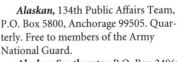

Alaska Digest, 3002 Spenard Road., #1, Anchorage 99503. Bimonthly. Free.

Alaska Directory of Attorneys, 203 W. 15th Ave., Suite 102, Anchorage 99501. Biannually. Annual rate: $25 per issue.

The Alaska Geographic Society, P.O. Box 93370, Anchorage 99509. Quarterly. Annual rates: $39; outside the U.S., $49.

Alaska International Trade Directory, Box 112955, Anchorage 99511-2955. Annually (July). Annual rate: $25.

Alaska Journal of Commerce, 4220 B St., Suite 210, Anchorage 99503. Weekly. Annual rates: $51; out of state, $75.

Alaska Justice Forum, 3211 Providence Drive, Anchorage 99508. Quarterly. Free.

ALASKA magazine, 4220 B St., Suite 210, Anchorage 99503. 10 issues a year. Subscriptions: (800) 288-5892.

Alaska Media Directory, 6828 Cape Lisburne Loop, Anchorage 99504. Annually. Annual rate: $68.

AlaskaMen, 205 E. Dimond, Suite 522, Anchorage 99515. Quarterly. Subscriptions: (800) MY-AK-MEN.

Alaska Miner, 501 W. Northern Lights Blvd., Suite 203, Anchorage 99503. Monthly. Mailed to members of Alaska Miners Association only.

Alaska Native Directory, 3002 Spenard Road, Anchorage 99503. Annually. Annual rate: $137.50.

Alaska Parenting Magazine, 3820 Lake Otis, Suite 214, Anchorage 99508. Monthly. Annual rate: $18.

Alaska People, Box 190648, Anchorage 99519. Quarterly. Annual rate: $19.95.

Alaska Traveler, P.O. Box 201894, Anchorage 99520. Three issues a year. Free.

Alaska View, 501 W. International Airport Road, Suite 16, Anchorage 99518. Monthly. Annual rate: $25.

Alaskan, 134th Public Affairs Team, P.O. Box 5800, Anchorage 99505. Quarterly. Free to members of the Army National Guard.

Alaskan Southeaster, P.O. Box 240667, Douglas 99824. Monthly. Annual rate: $28.

The All-Alaska Weekly, P.O. Box 70970, Fairbanks 99707. Weekly. Annual rate: $24.

Anchorage Chamber of Commerce Newsletter, 437 E St., Suite 300, Anchorage 99501. Monthly. Free to members only.

Anchorage Daily News, P.O. Box 149001, Anchorage 99514. Daily. Annual rates: Anchorage home delivery, $135; second-class mail, $390.

Anchorage Press, P.O. Box 243512, Anchorage 99524. Weekly. Free locally. Mailed subscription: $15.

Anchorage Visitors Guide, 524 W. Fifth Ave., Anchorage 99501. Home page: http://www.alaska.net/~acvb. April and October. Free.

Arctic Soldier Magazine, Public Affairs Office, HQ, U.S. Army Alaska, 600 Richardson Drive, #5900, Fort Richardson 99505. Quarterly. Free.

Arctic Sounder, P.O. Box 290, Kotzebue 99752. Weekly. Annual rates: Second-class mail, $45; first class, $90.

Arctic Star, Public Affairs Office, HQ, U.S. Army Alaska, 600 Richardson Drive, #5900, Fort Richardson 99505. Weekly. Free.

Boat Broker, 1910 Alex Holden Way, Juneau 99801. Monthly. Annual rates: Free; $12 if mailed.

Bristol BayTimes, P.O. Box 1129, Dillingham 99576. Weekly. Annual rates: Second-class mail, $45; first class, $90.

Capital City Weekly, 1910 Alex Holden Way, Juneau 99801. Weekly. Annual rates: Home delivery, free; $52 if mailed.

Chilkat Valley News, P.O. Box 630, Haines

The Kenai *Peninsula Clarion* advertised a $150,000 hilltop view house whose upper floor has "2 baloneys." There's nothing I enjoy more than watching a gorgeous sunset while I'm out sitting on my baloney!

99827. Weekly. Annual rates: $32 in Haines; $42 mailed in-state.

Chugiak–Eagle River Alaska Star, 16941 North Eagle River Loop, Eagle River 99577. Weekly. Annual rate: $20.

Copper River Country Journal, P.O. Box 336, Glennallen 99588. Bimonthly. Annual rate: $30.

Cordova Times, P.O. Box 200, Cordova 99574. Weekly. Annual rates: $45 for second-class mail; $90 first class.

Current Drift, Box 210430, Anchorage 99521. Monthly. Free to members of Alaska Boating Association.

Daily Sitka Sentinel, P.O. Box 799, Sitka 99835. Monday through Friday. Annual rates: $80; $90 mailed.

The Delta Wind, P.O. Box 986, Delta Junction 99737. Biweekly. Rate: 85 cents per issue.

Dutch Harbor Fisherman, Box 202, Unalaska 99685. Weekly. Annual rate: $45.

Eagles Call, PSC 486, Box 1202, FPO AP 96506. Monthly. Free.

Fairbanks Daily News–Miner, P.O. Box 70710, Fairbanks 99707. Daily, except Saturday. Annual rate: $270.

Fairbanks Magazine, 921 Woodway, Fairbanks 99709. June through October. Rate: $2.25 per issue.

The Frontiersman, 1261 Seward Meridian, Wasilla 99654. Biweekly. Annual rate: $60.

Great Lander Bush Mailer, 3110 Spenard Road, Anchorage 99503. Monthly. Free to rural villages.

Homer Alaska Tribune, 1266 Ocean Drive, Homer 99603. Weekly. Annual rate: $30.

Homer News, 3482 Landings St., Homer 99603. Weekly. Annual rate: Kenai Peninsula Borough, $35.

Interior Echo, P.O. Box 228, Aniak 99557. Bimonthly. Annual rate: $15.

Island News, P.O. Box 19430, Thorne Bay 99919. Weekly. Annual rate: $55.

Juneau Empire, 3100 Channel Drive, Juneau 99801. Monday through Friday, and Sunday. Annual rate: $115.50.

Kenai Peninsula Dispatch, 44619 Sterling Highway, #3, Soldotna 99669. Weekly. Free.

Ketchikan Daily News, P.O. Box 7900, Ketchikan 99901. Monday through Saturday. Annual rate: $92.

Kodiak Daily Mirror, 1419 Selig, Kodiak 99615. Monday through Friday. Annual rates: $85; $109 mailed in-state.

The Local Paper, 516 Steadman, Ketchikan 99901. Weekly. Free.

The MILEPOST®, Vernon Publications, 3000 Northup Way, Suite 200, Bellevue, WA 98004. Subscriptions: (800) 726-4707.

Mukluk News, P.O. Box 90, Tok 99780. Bimonthly. Annual rate: $20.

Mushing, P.O. Box 149, Ester 99725. Web site: http://www.polarnet.com/users/mushing. Bimonthly. Annual rate: $24.

Nome Nugget, P.O. Box 610, Nome 99762. Weekly. Annual rate: $55.

North Pole Independent, P.O. Box 55757, North Pole 99705. Weekly. Annual rate: $32.

North Slope Sentinel, Box 55757, North Pole 99705. Weekly. Annual rate: $45.

Northland News, P.O. Box 70710, Fairbanks 99707. Monthly. Free.

Peninsula Clarion, P.O. Box 3009, Kenai 99611. Monday through Friday. Annual rate: $64.

Petersburg Pilot, P.O. Box 930, Petersburg 99833. Weekly. Annual rate: $36.

Senior Voice, 325 E. Third Ave., Suite 300, Anchorage 99501. Monthly. Annual rates: $15 seniors; $20 under 55.

Seward Phoenix-Log, P.O. Box 89, Seward 99664. Weekly. Annual rate: $32.

Skagway News, P.O. Box 1898, Skagway 99840. Biweekly. Annual rate: $30.

Sourdough Sentinel, 3rd Wing, Public Affairs, 6920 12th St., Elmendorf Air Force Base 99506. Weekly. Free.

Southeast Alaska Business

Journal, 1910 Alex Holden Way, Juneau 99801. Monthly. Annual rate: $15.

Travelhost of Alaska, 376 S. Lane, Anchorage 99508; (907) 337-3620. More than 800,000 readers nationally, 25,000 locally. In-hotel room publication.

Tundra Drums, 660 Third Ave., Bethel 99559. Weekly. Annual rate: $45.

Valdez Star, P.O. Box 2949, Valdez 99686. Weekly. Annual rate: $30.

Valdez Vanguard, P.O. Box 980, Valdez 99686. Weekly. Annual rates: $45 second-class mail; $90 first class.

Valley Sun, 1261 Seward Meridian, Wasilla 99654. Weekly. Free to Matanuska–Susitna Borough box holders.

WHERE Alaska & the Yukon, 2208 Spruce St., Vancouver, B.C., Canada V6H 2P3; (604) 736-5586; e-mail 76632,716@compuserve.com. Complimentary in-room hotel publication, one of 41 *WHERE* magazines serving travelers around the world.

Wrangell Sentinel, P.O. Box 798, Wrangell 99929. Weekly. Annual rate: $27.50.

Wrangell–St. Elias News, McCarthy, Box MXY, Glennallen 99588. Bimonthly. Annual rate: $10.

Nome
Located on the shores of Norton Sound on the Seward Peninsula's south coast, Nome (population 4,021) is the transportation and commercial center for northwestern Alaska. Nome owes its name to a misinterpretation of "? name" on a chart in 1850. The question mark was taken as a "C" for cape, and the "A" in "name" was read as an "O." Originally the settlement was named Anvil City when gold was found in the Anvil Creek area in the summer of 1898.

The real gold stampede to Nome began in June 1899, when an estimated 30,000 miners rushed to Nome to stake their claims and pitch their tents along the beaches of the Bering Sea Coast. That year,

The "hell town" of Nome has lost its frontier character and become too "doggone civilized," old-timers complained in July 1946. For the first time in its history, Nome's churches outnumbered its saloons.

Nome was the largest city in the Alaska Territory. Miners quickly fled when their claims didn't pay, and by 1906 most of the gold and the prospectors were gone.

The mean average daily temperature in winter is –8°F and summer temperatures range from 40°F to 50°F. Mean annual snowfall (roughly late September through early June) is 53 inches.

A 3,350-foot-long granite wall built by the U.S. Army Corps of Engineers protects Nome from the sea. It is 65 feet wide at the base, 16 feet wide at its top, and 18 feet above mean low water.

Although not connected by road to the rest of the state, Nome boasts more than 300 miles of road in the area—the second-largest city road system in the state. (However, there is no winter maintenance of the roads.)

The city of Nome has several schools (including the Northwest College) and the distinction of having the state's oldest first-class school district. It also offers many churches, a library and museum (containing more than 6,000 photographs of the gold rush, Eskimo history and the Bering Land Bridge), and a historical park with a nonworking gold dredge and mining equipment from the gold rush days. For a fee, visitors can still try their luck panning the sands of the Nome beaches.

Throughout the year Nome offers many festivals and celebrations, including its most famous event—the finish of the Iditarod Trail Sled Dog Race. There's the Bering Sea Ice Classic Golf Tournament played on the frozen Bering Sea in March; a Polar Bear Swim on Memorial Day; a Midnight Sun Festival in June, featuring a raft race on the Nome River with many a strange craft taking part; a 12.5-mile run to the top of 1,977-foot Anvil Mountain on July 4; and a Labor Day Bathtub Race. Other celebrations include a reindeer fair, snowmobile races, snowshoe

softball games and the largest state basketball tournament.

The city today is a jumping-off point
for flights to Russia (only an hour-long
flight away), surrounding bush villages and
tours of the Arctic.

No-see-ums The words
describe a small biting two-winged midge.
In its usual swarms this tiny, gray-black,
silver-winged gnat is a most persistent
pest and annoys all creatures. But,
when alone, each insect is
difficult to see. While no-see-
ums don't transmit disease,
their bites are irritating.
Protective clothing, netting and a good
repellent are recommended while in dense
brush or near still-water ponds. Tents and
recreational vehicles should be well screened.

Officials

UNDER RUSSIA. *Emperor Paul of
Russia grants the Russian–American
Company an exclusive trade charter in
Alaska.*

Chief Managers, Russian-
American Company. Alexander
Andrevich Baranov, 1799–1818
Leontil Andreano-
  vich Hagemeiste,
  January–October
  1818
Semen Ivanovich
  Yanovski,
  1818–1820
Matxei I. Muravief,
  1820–1825
Peter Egorovich   *Alexander Baranov.*
  Chistiakov,   *From Alaska's History*
  1825–1830   *by Harry Ritter*
Baron Ferdinand P.
  von Wrangell, 1830–1835
Ivan Antonovich Kupreanof, 1835–1840
Adolph Karlovich Etolin, 1840–1845
Michael D. Tebenkof, 1845–1850
Nikolai Y. Rosenberg, 1850–1853
Alexander Ilich Rudakof, 1853–1854
Stephen Vasili Voevodski, 1854–1859
Ivan V. Furuhelm, 1859–1863
Prince Dmitri Maksoutoff, 1863–1867

UNDER UNITED STATES.
*United States purchases Alaska from Russia
in 1867; U.S. Army is given jurisdiction over
Department of Alaska.*

Army Commanding Officers.
Bvt. Maj. Gen. Jefferson C. Davis, Oct. 18,
  1867–Aug. 31, 1870
Bvt. Lt. Col. George K. Brady, Sept. 1,
  1870–Sept. 22, 1870
Maj. John C. Tidball, Sept. 23, 1870–
  Sept. 19, 1871
Maj. Harvey A. Allen, Sept. 20, 1871–
  Jan. 3, 1873
Maj. Joseph Stewart, Jan. 4, 1873–April 20,
  1874
Capt. George R. Rodney, April 21, 1874–
  Aug. 16, 1874
Capt. Joseph B. Campbell, Aug. 17, 1874–
  June 14, 1876
Capt. John Mendenhall, June 15, 1876–
  March 4, 1877
Capt. Arthur Morris, March 5, 1877–
  June 14, 1877

*U.S. Army troops leave Alaska in 1877; the
highest ranking federal official left in Alaska
is the U.S. collector of customs. Department
of Alaska is put under control of the U.S.
Treasury Department.*

U.S. Collectors of Customs.
Montgomery P. Berry, June 14, 1877–
  Aug. 13, 1877
H.C. DeAhna, Aug. 14, 1877–March 26, 1878
Mottrom D. Ball, March 27, 1878–
  June 13, 1879

*In 1879 the U.S. Navy is given jurisdiction
over the Department of Alaska.*

Navy Commanding Officers.
Capt. L.A. Beardslee, June 14, 1879–
  Sept. 12, 1880
Comdr. Henry Glass, Sept. 13, 1880–
  Aug. 9, 1881
Comdr. Edward Lull, Aug. 10, 1881–
  Oct. 18, 1881
Comdr. Henry Glass, Oct. 19, 1881–
  March 12, 1882
Comdr. Frederick Pearson, March 13,
  1882–Oct. 3, 1882

Comdr. Edgar C. Merriman, Oct. 4, 1882–Sept. 13, 1883

Comdr. Joseph B. Coghlan, Sept. 15, 1883–Sept. 13, 1884

Lt. Comdr. Henry E. Nichols, Sept. 14, 1884–Sept. 15, 1884

Congress provides civil government for the new District of Alaska in 1884; on Aug. 24, 1912, territorial status is given to Alaska. The U.S. president appoints territorial governors.

Presidential Appointments.

John H. Kinkead (President Arthur), July 4, 1884–May 7, 1885. (He did not reach Sitka until Sept. 15, 1884.)

Alfred P. Swineford (President Cleveland), May 7, 1885–April 20, 1889

Lyman E. Knapp (President Harrison), April 20, 1889–June 18, 1893

James Sheakley (President Cleveland), June 18, 1893–June 23, 1897

John G. Brady (President McKinley), June 23, 1897–March 2, 1906

Wilford B. Hoggatt (President Roosevelt), March 2, 1906–May 20, 1909

Walter E. Clark (President Taft), May 20, 1909–April 18, 1913

John F.A. Strong (President Wilson), April 18, 1913–April 12, 1918

Thomas Riggs Jr. (President Wilson), April 12, 1918–June 16, 1921

Scott C. Bone (President Harding), June 16, 1921–Aug. 16, 1925

George A. Parks (President Coolidge), Aug. 16, 1925–April 19, 1933

John W. Troy (President Roosevelt), April 19, 1933–Dec. 6, 1939

Ernest Gruening (President Roosevelt), Dec. 6, 1939–April 10, 1953

B. Frank Heintzleman (President Eisenhower), April 10, 1953–Jan. 3, 1957

Mike Stepovich (President Eisenhower), April 8, 1957–Aug. 9, 1958

Alaska becomes a state Jan. 3, 1959.

Elected Governors. William A.

Egan, Jan. 3, 1959–Dec. 5, 1966

Walter J. Hickel,* Dec. 5, 1966–Jan. 29, 1969

Keith H. Miller,* Jan. 29, 1969–Dec. 7, 1970

William A. Egan, Dec. 7, 1970–Dec. 2, 1974

Jay S. Hammond, Dec. 2, 1974–Dec. 6, 1982

Bill Sheffield, Dec. 6, 1982–Dec. 1, 1986

Steve Cowper, Dec. 1, 1986–Dec. 3, 1990

Walter J. Hickel, Dec. 3, 1990–Dec. 5, 1994

Tony Knowles, Dec. 5, 1994–

*Hickel resigned before completing his first full term as governor in order to accept the position of Secretary of the Interior. He was succeeded by Miller.

In 1906, Congress authorized Alaska to send a voteless delegate to the House of Representatives.

Delegates to Congress. Frank H.

Waskey, 1906–1907

Thomas Cale, 1907–1909

James Wickersham, 1909–1917

Charles A. Sulzer, 1917–contested election

James Wickersham, 1918, seated as delegate

Charles A. Sulzer, 1919, elected; died before taking office

George Grigsby, 1919, elected in a special election

James Wickersham, 1921, seated as delegate, having contested election of Grigsby

Dan A. Sutherland, 1921–1930

James Wickersham, 1931–1933

Anthony J. Dimond, 1933–1944

E.L. Bartlett, 1944–1958

Unofficial delegates to Congress to promote statehood, elected under a plan first devised by Tennessee. The Tennessee Plan delegates were not seated by Congress but did serve as lobbyists.

The Anchorage vote counting headquarters on Election Night, November 1996, was the Sullivan Arena. While politicos gathered to await the results, the electronic marquee outside the arena advertised an upcoming Pauly Shore appearance by continually flashing the words "Comedy at the Sullivan."

Where Does the Campaign Sticker Go on a Dogsled?

The campaign trail in Alaska takes many forms—frequently one that resembles a camping trip. Jerry Mackie rowed a skiff for three hours to campaign among a group of a half-dozen potential voters. "That was the only way I could think of to get there," he said. His opponent, Fred Zharoff, once did a balancing act across a shaky, rolling log bridge to meet a single voter. "I've traveled by boat along the Yukon River, I've gone by four-wheelers from community to community . . . I've been on the back of a sled plenty of times," remarked state Sen. Georgianna Lincoln, whose Interior district is about the size of Texas. Cheryl Davis of Nome, running for a House district covering part of western Alaska and Bering Sea islands, said candidates often pack a few days' supply of food so they don't have to impose on voters in remote communities, who are often living off the land and wildlife. She calls it "survival politics."—David Germain, The Associated Press

Senators. William Egan, 1956–1958
Ernest Gruening, 1956–1958

Representative. Ralph Rivers,
1956–1958

Alaska becomes 49th state in 1959 and sends two senators and one representative to U.S. Congress.

Senators. E.L. Bartlett, 1958–1968
Ernest Gruening, 1958–1968
Mike Gravel, 1968–1980
Ted Stevens, 1968–
Frank H. Murkowski, 1980–

Representatives. Ralph Rivers,
1958–1966
Howard Pollock, 1966–1970
Nicholas Begich, 1970–1972
Donald E. Young, 1972–

Correspondence Addresses.
The Honorable Tony Knowles, Office of the Governor, P.O. Box 110001, Juneau 99811
The Honorable Fran Ulmer, Office of the Lieutenant Governor, P.O. Box 110015, Juneau 99811

Alaska's Delegation in U.S. Congress. The Honorable Ted Stevens, United States Senate, 522 Hart Bldg., Washington, D.C. 20510

The Honorable Frank H. Murkowski, United States Senate, 709 Hart Bldg., Washington, D.C. 20510
The Honorable Donald E. Young, House of Representatives, 2331 Rayburn House Office Bldg., Washington, D.C. 20515

Alaska State Legislature.
Members of the Alaska Legislature as of the close of the 20th legislative session (June 1997) are listed below. During sessions, members of the legislature receive mail at the State Capitol, Juneau 99801-1182.

House of Representatives.
District 1: William Williams (D)
District 2: Ben Grussendorf (D)
District 3: Kim Elton (D)
District 4: Bill Hudson (R)
District 5: Albert Kookesh (D)
District 6: Alan Austerman (D)
District 7: Gail Phillips (R)
District 8: Gary "Lee" Davis (R)
District 9: Mark Hodgins (R)
District 10: Joseph Green (R)
District 11: Norman Rokeberg (R)
District 12: Mark Hanley (R)
District 13: Ethan Berkowitz (D)
District 14: Terry Martin (R)
District 15: Eric Croft (D)
District 16: Allen Kemplen (D)
District 17: John Cowdery (R)
District 18: Con "Ralph" Bunde (R)
District 19: Jerry Sanders (R)

District 20: Brian Porter (R)
District 21: Joe Ryan (R)
District 22: Ramona Barnes (R)
District 23: Eldon Mulder (R)
District 24: Pete Kott (R)
District 25: Fred Dyson (R)
District 26: Vic Kohring (R)
District 27: Scott Ogan (R)
District 28: Beverly Masek (R)
District 29: John Davies (D)
District 30: Tom Brice (D)
District 31: Pete Kelly (R)
District 32: Al Vezey (R)
District 33: Gene Therriault (R)
District 34: Jeanette James (R)
District 35: Gene Kubina (D)

District 36: Irene Nicholia (D)
District 37: Reggie Joule (D)
District 38: Richard Foster (D)
District 39: Ivan Ivan (D)
District 40: Carl Moses (D)

Senate. District A: Robin Taylor (R)
District B: Jim Duncan (D)
District C: Jerry Mackie (D)
District D: John Torgerson (R)
District E: Jerry Ward (R)
District F: Drue Pearce (R)
District G: Loren Leman (R)
District H: Johnny Ellis (D)
District I: Sean Parnell (R)
District J: Dave Donley (D)
District K: Tim Kelly (R)
District L: Randy Phillips (R)
District M: Rick Halford (R)
District N: Lyda Green (R)
District O: Gary Wilken (R)
District P: Bert Sharp (R)
District Q: Mike Miller (R)
District R: Georgianna Lincoln (D)
District S: Al Adams (D)
District T: Lyman Hoffman (D)

Oil and Gas (SEE ALSO

PIPELINE) Alaska's first exploratory oil well was drilled in 1898 on the Iniskin Peninsula, Cook Inlet, by Alaska Petroleum Company. Oil was encountered in this first hole at about 700 feet, but a water zone beneath the oil strata cut off the oil flow. Total depth of the well was approximately 1,000 feet.

The first commercial oil discovery was made in 1902 near Katalla, near the mouth of the Bering River east of Cordova. This field produced until 1933.

As early as 1921, oil companies surveyed land north of the Brooks Range for possible drilling sites. In 1923, the federal government created Naval Petroleum Reserve Number 4 (now known as National Petroleum Reserve Alaska; see National Petroleum Reserve), a 23-million-acre area of Alaska's North Slope. Wartime needs speeded up exploration. In 1944, the Navy began drilling operations on the petroleum reserve and continued until 1953, but made no significant oil discoveries. Since 1981, the U. S. Department of the Interior has leased out oil and gas tracts in the reserve.

Today, all of Alaska's oil is currently produced from two regions, North Slope and Cook Inlet.

Discovered in 1968, Prudhoe Bay was the first commercial North Slope oil field explored and the first to produce oil. Commercial production began in 1977, when Alyeska Pipeline Company completed the pipeline between Valdez and Prudhoe Bay.

A Denali Park ranger reported leading a hike to the top of a small mountain in an area where there were no trails. An apprehensive tourist asked, "If there are no trails, how will we know when we get to the top?"

Between discovery of oil and the start of commercial production, operators produced and refined small amounts of oil and gas for fuel to run the field equipment, and injected the residual oil back into the reservoir. North Slope fields produced a total of 11.6 billion barrels by the end of 1996, 82 percent of it from Prudhoe Bay, 12 percent from Kuparuk and 6 percent from other fields.

Three North Slope fields began production in 1993: Point McIntyre, by far the largest of the fields, North Prudhoe Bay State and West Beach. Niakuk pool began producing in 1994, and Milne Point production increased in late 1994 and 1995. These recent additions have somewhat offset regional decline in oil production.

Companies first discovered Cook Inlet oil at Swanson River on the Kenai Peninsula in 1957 and began production in 1959. In 1962, the first offshore oil in Cook Inlet was discovered, making the inlet one of three successful areas in the United States for offshore oil production. Currently, there are 15 production platforms in Cook Inlet, one of which produces only gas.

Regional production in Cook Inlet peaked in 1970 at 230,000 barrels per day (83 million barrels per year) and subsequently has declined to 42,000 barrels per day in 1996. By the end of 1996 Cook Inlet fields had produced a total of 1.2 billion barrels of oil, 48 percent of this from McArthur River, 18 percent from Swanson River and 34 percent from the other fields. Two fields, West McArthur River and Sunfish, were discovered in 1991. West McArthur River began production in 1993.

Projected Reserves and Production.

The Division of Oil and Gas (DO&G) estimates that Alaska's total reserves are: oil, 7.3 billion barrels; gas, 32.8 trillion cubic feet.

North Slope fields hold 98 percent of the oil and 94 percent of the state's gas reserves. The balance of reserves are in Cook Inlet.

Reserve estimates of oil for North Slope fields have increased through the years. In January 1986, Prudhoe Bay had produced 4.4 billion barrels and reserves were 5.8 billion barrels. By January 1997 the field had produced 9.5 billion barrels and reserves were estimated at 3.4 billion barrels. Much of the increase in ultimate recovery was due to improved technology, such as increased horizontal drilling and enhanced oil recovery. Technology may further increase future reserve estimates, but the main variable in recovering oil will be the perceived future price of oil.

North Slope oil production peaked in

1988 at 2 million barrels per day and subsequently declined to 1.5 million barrels per day in 1996. The DO&G estimates that the combined production from the presently operating fields and to-be-developed fields will decline to 292,000 barrels per day in the year 2020, and that cumulative production between 1997 and 2031 will be 7 billion barrels.

Cook Inlet fields will continue to produce well into the next century, but the DO&G estimates the region's production only to 2006, a shorter span than for the North Slope. Cook Inlet production depends on economic factors that cannot be reasonably estimated beyond that date. According to the DO&G estimates, regional production will decrease to 10,000 barrels per day in 2006, yielding a cumulative 71.2 million barrels between 1996 and 2006.

Gas. All Alaska gas is produced from the North Slope (mostly from the Prudhoe Bay area) and from Cook Inlet, the same two regions that produce all the state's oil. The production regimes of the two regions are very different because their markets are very different. The primary market for North Slope gas is Barrow, Alaska, as fuel for home heating oil production and related facilities. Most of the extracted gas is injected back into the reservoirs. That gas is available for sale if and when a market develops. North Slope fields had produced a cumulative net 3 trillion cubic feet by the end of 1996.

The Alaska Natural Gas Transportation System (a gas pipeline) was authorized by the federal government in 1977, but construction has not begun and a completion date not set for the foreseeable future due to problems in financing the $40 billion project. Most industry observers feel that the proposed gas pipeline is the most viable idea for transporting North Slope gas to Valdez for shipment to market. Gas production in the North Slope is expected to increase for the next several years, and has become an increasingly greater proportion of the field production.

Cook Inlet fields, however, lie near two gas processing plants and the Anchorage and Kenai commercial markets. Consequently, nearly all extracted gas has been consumed and very little has been injected. Regional production reached an all-time high of 221 billion cubic feet per year in 1996. Cook Inlet fields had produced a cumulative net 5.1 trillion cubic feet by the end of 1996.

Since 1987, Alaska and Texas have alternated as the number-one state in oil production. As of 1997 the top five oil-producing states are: Texas, Alaska, Louisiana, California and Oklahoma. According to the Alaska Oil and Gas Conservation Commission, Alaska currently provides about 23 percent of the nation's oil.

In fiscal year 1996, the state of Alaska received $1.87 million in royalties (includes previous revisions and settlements) from its oil and gas resources; approximately 87 percent of its general revenue comes from petroleum taxes and royalties. Since 1959, the state has collected about $40 billion in oil and gas revenues. The price of oil dropped in early 1986. Oil industry employment then declined, and the state government was in a more tenuous fiscal situation. Oil prices had improved by early 1990, but

---

Fossil Fuel

Scientists don't know exactly how oil is formed, but most believe that today's oil and gas were yesterday's marine microorganisms. As the tiny creatures died, their bodies collected on the seafloor, where they were covered with sediment. Eventually the sediment hardened into rock; over time, many layers of sediment could have been deposited. Heat and pressure from the covering rock layers are thought to have combined with bacterial processes to transform the sea creatures into petroleum. —Susan Ewing, The Great Alaska Nature Factbook

by then Prudhoe Bay production had begun to decline. In January 1994, crude oil prices sunk to a 10-year low, although they recovered midyear. It has been a difficult period for the state's oil and gas industry, which also suffered major layoffs in 1994 and 1995.

The oil industry received some good news in 1995 when the federal ban on exporting Alaska oil was lifted. Oil companies began exports in 1996. The Far East is the major international market for Alaska oil.

Oil and gas leasing on state land in Alaska is managed by the Department of Natural Resources, Division of Oil and Gas. The Secretary of the Interior is responsible for establishing oil and gas leasing on federal lands in Alaska, including the outer continental shelf. In 1986, Chevron, in partnership with a Native corporation, completed its well at Kaktovik on the coastal plain of the Arctic National Wildlife Refuge. The land was obtained in a swap with the U.S. Department of the Interior, but Congress will have to approve any further development within the boundaries of the refuge.

Alaska Oil and Natural Gas Liquid Production (in millions of barrels)

Year	Oil	Natural Gas
1986	681.3	1.302
1987	716.0	16.328
1988	738.1	21.029
1989	684.0	18.864
1990	647.3	18.171
1991	656.3	23.861
1992	627.3	26.845
1993	577.9	26.830
1994	568.9	25.867
1995	541.6	29.632
1996	544.2	33.198

Source: Alaska Dept. of Natural Resources, Division of Oil & Gas.

Oil Spill Prince William Sound was the site of the largest oil spill in U.S. history, when the 987-foot *Exxon Valdez* oil tanker, carrying a full cargo of 53,094,510 gallons of crude oil, struck Bligh Reef on March 24, 1989. Before the tanker leak could be stopped, more than 270,000 barrels, or more than 11.3 million gallons, of crude oil oozed into Prince William Sound. The oil, which poured out of the tanker at a rate of 42,488 barrels per hour, contaminated more than 1,500 miles of coastline in Prince William Sound, the Gulf of Alaska and lower Cook Inlet.

Shortly before the collision, the captain had changed course, veering from the normal shipping lane to avoid icebergs. At the time the tanker hit the reef, however, the third mate was piloting the tanker.

Within 15 hours of the spill, skimmer ships began to vacuum oil off the water's surface; booms were set up strategically to prevent the oil spill from contaminating salmon fisheries. Other fishing vessels assisted in attempts to capture oiled and wounded wildlife, and transport those animals to rehabilitation centers.

Four days after the spill, the oil slick covered a 300-square-mile area, hitting islands, beaches and fish hatcheries throughout the sound, an area known for its rich commercial herring and salmon hatcheries. Oil from the tanker also was found later to have fouled beaches on the Alaska Peninsula, almost 600 miles from the spill site.

Cleanup efforts involved armies of cleaning crews, who used techniques ranging from washing rocks by hand to washing the shore rocks with highly pressurized hot water. Bioremediation was another cleanup technique, which involved applying fertilizer to oiled shorelines to accelerate oil-metabolizing bacteria. Winter storms proved to assist the cleanup of many beaches throughout the oil spill area. Cleanup efforts were resumed in the spring of 1990 and continued into 1992.

Thousands of marine mammals, birds and other wildlife perished as a result of the oil spill. Carcasses of 1,011 sea otters were recovered from the sound in 1989, and estimates of the number of otters that died range from about 3,500 to 5,500. About 31,000 birds were reported to have been killed, caused by the spill.

But scientists believe these figures represent only a fraction of the total loss, since many birds were thought to have floated out to sea, sunk or simply have not been found. Preliminary figures fix the loss at between 350,000 and 390,000 birds, according to a report produced by the federal agencies, including the U.S. Department of Fish and Wildlife, in charge of damage assessment and restoration.

Exxon Corporation accepted full responsibility for the spill on March 25, 1989. More than 29,000 claims were filed for damages related to the oil spill. Many of the claims were from fishermen, canneries, Natives and business owners in the region whose livelihood was curtailed by the oil spill: in 1989, the red salmon season was canceled in Prince William Sound.

The state of Alaska sued Exxon and Alyeska Pipeline Service Company in 1989; Exxon countersued, alleging that state officials hampered cleanup efforts. In October 1991, the state of Alaska and the federal government settled their suits with Exxon, splitting $1.25 billion. Of this amount, $900 million in civil damages is to be paid over a 10-year period ending in September 2001.

In 1994, Exxon and 3,500 Alaska Natives reached an agreement in which Exxon agreed to pay $20 million for loss of subsistence hunting. Also that year a jury awarded commercial fishermen $286.8 million in damages. And a federal jury ordered Exxon to pay $5 billion in punitive damages. Litigation continues today as Exxon appeals the punitive damage award.

It is estimated that Exxon spent about $2.5 billion on the cleanup. During the peak of operations, 11,000 people worked on the cleanup, using 1,400 vessels and 85 aircraft. Environmental monitoring continues.

Exxon released its own scientific study on the oil spill in mid-1993, which concluded that no significant effects remain on the shoreline.

For further information, contact the Exxon Valdez Oil Spill Trustee Council, 645 G St., Anchorage 99501; (907) 278-8012. This public library specializes in materials on the *Exxon Valdez* oil spill.

The trans-Alaska oil pipeline was completed from Prudhoe Bay to the ice-free port of Valdez on Prince William Sound in 1977. The 800-mile overland pipeline carries oil over two mountain ranges and 350 rivers and streams.

Parka

Pronounced "PAR-kee" and sometimes spelled "parky," this over-the-head garment worn by Eskimos was one of their main pieces of clothing. Parka styles, materials used and ornamentation (such as pieced calfskin or beadwork trim) varied from village to village. The cut of parkas also changed from north to south.

The work parka was worn with the skin on the outside and the fur inside. Work parkas were not meant to be beautiful but serviceable. Often worn with pants made from skins, they provided excellent protection from the cold. These parkas usually used a second-hand worn ruff. Very poor persons did not have ruffs on their parkas at all, and if a person owned a parka without a ruff, he or she was given a ruff to use. When that person died, the ruff was cut off the parka and returned to the original owner.

A fancy parka, reserved for special occasions, used the skin of the male ground squirrel (the male offering larger, grayer pelts than the female). These decorated parkas had intricate fancywork with wolverine tassels and trims and were topped with a wide wolf ruff, made in layers so the ruff stood out from the face. The fancy parka had furs inside and out. A person's wealth was judged by the quality of his/her best parka.

The Aleut rain parka was made from *oogruk* (bearded seal) intestine. Instead of a fur ruff around the face of the hood, the rain parka had a folded *oogruk* piece which served as a sinew drawstring casing.

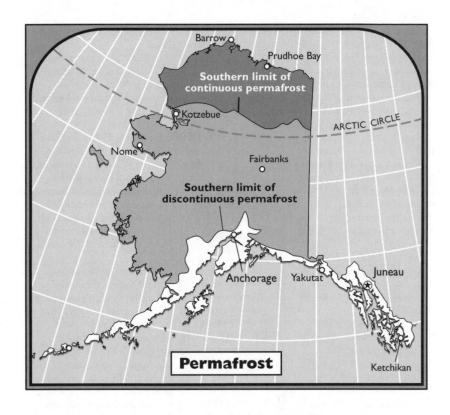

Permafrost

Eskimos used many animals skins for making parkas including seal, reindeer, caribou and ground squirrel. Wolf and wolverine were prized for ruffs. Also used to make parkas were fish (wolf fish) skins and bird skins—leaving the feathers on the outside—including those of murre, cormorants and diving fish ducks.

Permafrost

Permafrost is defined as ground that remains frozen for two or more years. In its continuous form, permafrost underlies the entire Arctic region to depths of 2,000 feet. In broad terms, continuous permafrost occurs north of the Brooks Range and in the alpine region of mountains (including those of the Lower 48).

Discontinuous permafrost occurs south of the Brooks Range and north of the Alaska Range. Much of the Interior and parts of southcentral Alaska are underlain by discontinuous permafrost.

Permafrost affects many man-made structures and natural bodies. It influences construction in the Arctic because building on it may cause the ground to thaw and if the ground is ice-rich, struc tures will sink. Arctic and subarctic rivers typically carry 55 percent to

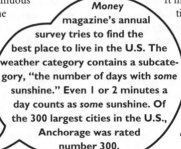

Money magazine's annual survey tries to find the best place to live in the U.S. The weather category contains a subcategory, "the number of days with *some* sunshine." Even 1 or 2 minutes a day counts as *some* sunshine. Of the 300 largest cities in the U.S., Anchorage was rated number 300.

Surviving the Cold

Many of the bird species that remain year-round in Alaska must adapt during the long winter to feed on few or different food items from their summer diet. Their winter foraging needs are further complicated by greatly reduced daylight in the Far North, less available habitat because of ice and snow cover, and the need to keep warm.

Blue grouse, for example, switch from a summer diet of succulent plants, seeds, berries, and insects to winter fare of buds and the fibrous needles of Sitka spruce trees. In winter, ptarmigan eat mostly willow twigs and buds. The digestive tracts of both of these species contain special bacteria that aid in the digestion of this tough material. Grouse and ptarmigan also have a crop—a food storage organ that can be filled while the birds are active during the short winter day, and then its contents can be digested later. . . .

Ptarmigan, ruffed grouse, and snow buntings may survive bitter winter storms and nights by plunging into and under the snow, where the temperature may be many degrees warmer than at the surface. Many birds conserve body heat by roosting together. . . .

Many northern-adapted bird species develop extra fat, more feathers, and a higher resting metabolic rate. Yet as we sit cozy and warm in our heated homes during a raging Alaskan winter storm, we can only marvel at the endurance and survival of birds that spend the winter with us, even though they have these and other adaptations.—Bob Armstrong, Alaska's Birds

65 percent of the precipitation that falls onto their watersheds, roughly 30 percent to 40 percent more than rivers of more temperate climates. Consequently, northern streams are prone to flooding and carry high silt loads. Permafrost is responsible for the thousands of shallow lakes dotting the arctic tundra because groundwater is held on the surface.

A tunnel excavated in permafrost near Fox, north of Fairbanks, during the early 1960s is maintained cooperatively by the University of Alaska Fairbanks and the U.S. Army Cold Regions Research and Engineering Laboratory. It is one of the few such tunnels in the world; it offers unique research opportunities on a 40,000-year-old accumulation of sediments and ice.

The tunnel is open to the general public from June 1 through August 31 each year, by appointment only, through the CRREL office.

Permanent Fund

In 1976, state voters approved a constitutional amendment to establish the Alaska Permanent Fund. This provides that a percentage of all mineral lease rentals, royalties, royalty sales proceeds, federal mineral revenue sharing payments and bonuses shall be placed in a Permanent Fund. Essentially a trust fund for all Alaskans, money in the fund must be invested and cannot be spent without a vote of the people. Income from the Permanent Fund is available for appropriation by the legislature.

In 1980, the legislature established a Permanent Fund dividend payment program that provides distribution of approximately one-half of the fund's earnings (interest dividends and capital gains) among the people of Alaska. Eligible residents were to receive a $50 dividend for each year of residency since 1959. The U.S. Supreme Court declared the 1980 program unconstitutional on the grounds that it discriminated against short-term residents, and in 1982 a new state program was signed into law. Under the plan, an initial $1,000 dividend was paid to applicants who had lived in the state for at least six months prior to applying. Since then, dividends have been distributed each year to every resident who applies by March 31 and qualifies. The amount is decided by adding together the fund's net income for the last five years, multiplying that number by 21 percent, and dividing that number in half.

If Alaska's Permanent Fund were a Fortune 500 company, it would rank in the top 5 percent in terms of net income. It is one of the 50 largest pools of money in the country, and the only fund that pays dividends to residents. In 1996, the Permanent Fund for the first time produced more net income for the state than the unrestricted oil revenues. As of March 31, 1997, the principal of the fund was $20.2 billion. The 1997 dividend payment to each qualified Alaska resident is anticipated to be in excess of $1,000.

Sitka Pioneers' Home

Pioneers' Homes

The first Pioneers' Home was established in Sitka in 1913 for "indigent prospectors and others who have spent their years in Alaska." At the arrival of statehood in 1959, there was only one home, the Sitka location. It had been opened to women in 1950; with the coming of statehood, it was opened to Natives as well.

Currently six state-supported Pioneers' Homes offer assisted-living care for a total of 600 older Alaskans. The homes offer a range of service levels, providing assistance with activities of daily living, intermittent health care and recreation depending upon residents' needs, with an emphasis on care of individuals with Alzheimer's disease and related disorders. Applicants must be

65 years of age or older, must have lived continuously in Alaska for one year immediately preceding application, must have a need for the

services provided in the homes and must agree to pay the rent established by the Department of Administration (if able to do so).

For additional information about Pioneers' Homes, contact the Director of the Division of Alaska Longevity Programs, P.O. Box 110211, Juneau 99811-0211; (907) 465-4400. Following are the six homes:

Anchorage Pioneers' Home, 923 W. 11th Ave., Anchorage 99501; (907) 276-3414.

Fairbanks Pioneers' Home, 2221 Eagan Ave., Fairbanks 99701; (907) 456-4372.

Juneau Pioneers' Home, 4675 Glacier Highway, Juneau 99801; (907) 780-6422.

Ketchikan Pioneers' Home, 141 Bryant, Ketchikan 99901; (907) 225-4111.

Palmer Pioneers' Home, 250 E. Fireweed, Palmer 99645; (907) 745-4241.

Sitka Pioneers' Home, 120 Katlian St., Sitka 99835; (907) 747-3213.

Pipeline

The trans-Alaska oil pipeline designer, builder and operator is Alyeska Pipeline Service Company, a consortium of seven oil companies:

BP Pipeline Company, 50.01 percent

ARCO Transportation Alaska, Inc., 21.35 percent

Exxon Pipeline Company, 20.34 percent

Mobil Alaska Pipeline Company, 4.08 percent

Amerada Hess Pipeline Corporation, 1.5 percent

Phillips Alaska Pipeline Corporation, 1.36 percent

Unocal Pipeline Company, 1.36 percent

Pipeline length: 800 miles; slightly less than half that length is buried, the remainder is on 78,000 aboveground supports, located 60 feet apart, built in a flexible zig-zag pattern. There are more than 800 river and stream crossings. Normal burial of pipe was used in stable soils and rock; aboveground pipe—insulated and jacketed—was used in thaw-unstable permafrost areas. Thermal devices prevent thawing around vertical supports. It has 151 stop-flow valves.

Pipe: Specially manufactured coated pipe with zinc anodes installed to prevent corrosion. Size is 48 inches in diameter, with thickness from 0.462 to 0.562 inch. Pipe sections before construction are in lengths of 40 and 60 feet.

Cost: $8 billion, which includes terminal at Valdez, but does not include interest on money raised for construction.

Amount of oil pumped through pipeline: At the end of 1995, 10.8 billion barrels of crude oil. The current flow represents about 25 percent of the total U.S. oil production. At any one moment, there are about 9 million barrels of oil in the line.

Operations: Control center at Valdez terminal and 11 operating pump stations along the line monitor and control pipeline.

Pipeline throughput: 1.4 million barrels a day, average, projected in 1996.

Estimated crude oil reserves recoverable on the North Slope: Approximately 6.2 billion barrels as of April 1996.

Terminal: 1,000-acre site at Port Valdez, northernmost ice-free harbor in the U.S., with 18 tanks providing storage capacity of 9,180,000 barrels of oil.

Valdez ship-loading capacity: 110,000 barrels per hour for each of three berths; 80,000 barrels per hour for one berth.

Length and cost of pipeline haul road built by Alyeska: 360 miles, from the Yukon River to Prudhoe Bay; $150 million.

Yukon River bridge: First bridge (2,290 feet long) to span the Yukon in Alaska.

Important dates: July 1968, Prudhoe Bay oil field discovery confirmed; 1970, suits filed to halt construction, Alyeska Pipeline Service Company formed; Nov. 16, 1973, presidential approval of pipeline legislation; April 29, 1974, construction begins on North Slope Haul Road (now the Dalton Highway) and is completed 154 days later; March 27, 1975, first pipe installed at Tonsina River; June 20, 1977, first oil leaves Prudhoe Bay, reaches Valdez terminal July 28; Aug. 1, 1977, first tanker load of oil shipped aboard the SS *ARCO Juneau*; June 13, 1979, tanker number 1,000 (SS *ARCO Heritage*) sails; July 15, 1983, 3 billionth barrel of oil leaves pump station; Sept. 15, 1986, 5 billionth barrel of oil leaves pump

The trans-Alaska oil pipeline 15 miles south of Livengood in the late 1970s. From Alaska's History by Harry Ritter

station; April 19, 1987, 7,000th tanker sails from Marine Terminal with Prudhoe Bay crude oil; Feb. 16, 1988, 6 billionth barrel arrives at the Marine Terminal; May 2, 1988, *Chevron Mississippi* is 8,000th tanker to load crude oil at Marine Terminal; June 30, 1989, 7 billionth barrel is loaded on the *Mobil Arctic,* and the 9,000th tanker sails from the Marine Terminal at Valdez with a full load of crude oil; Dec. 28, 1992, *Arco California,* 12,000th tanker to load; March 1994, 10 billionth barrel is pumped from the North Slope into the pipeline; April 1996, 22,000-gallon spill from defective valve.

Joint Pipeline Office: Because of concerns about spills from and corrosion of the trans-Alaska oil pipeline, the Joint Pipeline Office was established in 1990. The office is composed of nine state and federal regulatory and management agencies. Each agency has responsibilities either for issuing permits or for monitoring the operation and environmental safety of any and all pipelines operating in Alaska.

State agencies represented in the office include the Department of Natural Resources, the Department of Environmental Conservation, the Department of Fish and Game, and the Office of the Governor, Division of Governmental Coordination.

Place Names

Alaska has a rich international heritage of place names. Throughout the state, names of British (Barrow), Spanish (Valdez), Russian (Kotzebue), French (La Perouse), American (Fairbanks) and Native Alaskan (Sitka) origin dot the map. Some Alaska place names are quite common. There are about 70 streams called Bear Creek in Alaska (not to mention Bear Bay, Bear Bluff, Bear Canyon, Bear Cove and Bear Draw) and about 50 called Moose Creek. Many place names have an unusual history. Mount Ballyhoo (1,634 feet) in Unalaska is said to have been named by writer Jack London, who anchored here on his way to the gold fields of Nome.

For a comprehensive listing, description and history of Alaska's usual and unusual place names, from Aaron Creek to Zwinge Valley, see Donald Orth's *Dictionary of Alaska Place Names*, U.S. Geological Survey Professional Paper 567.

Poisonous Plants (SEE ALSO MUSHROOMS)

Alaska has few poisonous plants, considering the total number of plant species growing in the state. Nonetheless, some extremely poisonous plants are found in the state. Baneberry (*Actaea rubra*), water hemlock (*Cicuta douglasii* and *C. mackenzieana*), fly agaric mushroom (*Amanita muscaria*), monkshood (*Aconitum* species) and false hellebore (*Veratrum* species) are the most dangerous. Be sure

In the 1997 Nenana Ice Classic, 71 Alaskans paid money to bet that the ice would go out on April 31st—a day that doesn't even exist! In 1996, 80 people made the same bet. Alaskans have therefore gotten 11.3 percent smarter in the last year!

you have properly identified plants before harvesting for food.

Alaska has no poison ivy or poison oak, which are found in almost all other states. However, cow parsnip produces a photoreactive chemical which can cause blisters and burns.

Political Parties

There are four recognized political parties in Alaska. To become recognized in the state, a political party must be an organized group of voters that represents a particular political program and that nominated a candidate for governor who received at least 3 percent of the total votes cast at the preceding general election for governor.

Alaska's four political parties are:

Alaskan Independence Party, Chairperson Jack Coghill, P.O. Box 70007, Fairbanks 99707; (907) 457-1884.

Democratic Party of Alaska, Chair-Elect Deborah Bonito, Box 200445, Anchorage 99520; (907) 258-3050.

Green Party of Alaska, Chairman Tim Feller, 2611 Northrup Place, Anchorage 99504; (907) 278-7637.

Deadly Monkshood

They're so beautiful a flower, so innocent in appearance that it seems unkind to bandy about the nefarious ways these flowers have been used. But monkshood in particular is so deadly poisonous that it is essential foragers be aware of the hazard. . . . In medieval times, monkshood was called *thung* (a name for any deadly plant) and was used for warfare; the root was placed in water holes and wells to poison water supplies of pursuing armies. The Herb Book says that witches smeared the root on their broomsticks and bodies, took a dose of delirium-producing belladonna, and then went "flying." On a more mundane plane, the roots were mixed with toasted cheese to kill rats.—Janice Schofield, *Discovering Wild Plants*

Republican Party of Alaska, Chairperson Pete Hallgren, 1001 W. Fireweed Lane, Anchorage 99503; (907) 276-4467.

Populations and Zip Codes
According to the Alaska Department of Labor, many areas of Alaska grew in population between 1990 and 1996.

Between 1990 and 1994, Alaska's population increased by 10.2 percent, compared to a 4.7 percent increase in the U.S. population. The greatest overall growth occurred in Anchorage, which accounted for 49 percent of the state's population in 1996. Only the Yakutat Borough lost population over the 1990–94 period.

The populations for cities and communities in the following lists are taken from the Alaska Department of Labor, 1996 estimates. Entries lacking zip codes are communities without a U.S. post office. (NA=Not Available)

Community	Year Incorporated	Population	Zip
Adak Station	1972	596	96505
Afognak	—	—	99697
Akhiok (AH-key-ok)	1972	84	99615
Akiachak (ACK-ee-a-chuck)	—	554	99551
Akiak (ACK-ee-ack)	1970	328	99552
Akutan (ACK-oo-tan)	1979	414	99553
Alakanuk (a-LACK-a-nuk)	1969	633	99554
Aleknagik (a-LECK-nuh-gik)	1973	190	99555
Alexander	—	35	99695
Allakaket (alla-KAK-it)	1975	178	99720
Ambler	1971	307	99786
Anaktuvuk Pass (an-ak-TU-vuk)	1957	306	99721
Anchor Point	—	1,121	99556
Anchorage (Municipality)	1920	254,269	99510
Eastchester Station	—	—	99501
Fort Richardson	—	—	99505
Elmendorf Air Force Base	—	—	99506
Mountain View	—	—	99508
Spenard Station	—	—	99509
Downtown Station	—	—	99510
South Station	—	—	99511
Alyeska Pipeline Company	—	—	99512
Federal Building	—	—	99513
Anderson	1962	563	99744
Angoon	1963	605	99820
Aniak (AN-ee-ack)	1972	595	99557
Annette	—	49	99926
Anvik	1969	91	99558
Arctic Village	—	117	99722
Atka	1988	106	99502
Atmautluak (at-MAUT-loo-ack)	1976	311	99559
Atqasuk	1982	226	99791
Attu Coast Guard Station	—	24	99502
Auke Bay	—	NA	99821
Barrow	1959	4,276	99723
Beaver	—	104	99724

Community	Year Incorporated	Population	Zip
Bethel	1957	5,106	99559
Bettles City	1985	26	99726
Big Delta	—	496	99737
Big Lake	—	2,138	99652
Birch Creek	—	40	99790
Birch Hill	—	—	99710
Border	—	NA	99780
Brevig Mission	1969	261	99785
Buckland	1966	416	99727
Butte	—	2,374	NA
Cantwell	—	135	99729
Cape Yakataga	—	NA	99574
Central	—	51	99730
Chalkyitsik (chawl-KIT-sik)	—	92	99788
Chase	—	52	NA
Chefornak (cha-FOR-nack)	1974	393	99561
Chenega	—	95	99574
Chevak	1967	708	99563
Chickaloon	—	217	99674
Chicken	—	NA	99732
Chignik	1983	128	99564
Chignik Lagoon	—	80	99565
Chignik Lake	—	152	99564
Chiniak	—	75	99548
Chistochina	—	58	99615
Chitina (CHIT-nah)	—	82	99566
Chuathbaluk (chew-ATH-ba-luck)	1975	123	99557
Chugiak (CHOO-gee-ack)	—	*	99567
Circle	—	85	99733
Circle Hot Springs	—	29	NA
Clam Gulch	—	93	99568
Clarks Point	1971	66	99569
Clear	—	NA	99704
Coffman Cove	1989	241	99950
Cohoe	—	579	99669
Cold Bay	1982	90	99571
Coldfoot	—	31	99701
College	—	11,971	99708
Cooper Landing	—	272	99572
Copper Center	—	538	99573
Copperville	—	187	NA
Cordova**	1909	2,537	99574
Council	—	0	NA
Covenant Life	—	54	NA
Craig	1922	2,109	99921
Crooked Creek	—	136	99575
Crown Point	—	92	NA
Cube Cove	—	178	99850
Deadhorse	—	24	99734

*The population of Chugiak–Eagle River is counted as one unit, with 28,600 residents.
**Includes Eyak since 1993.

Community	Year Incorporated	Population	Zip
Deering	1970	141	99736
Delta Junction	1960	849	99737
Denali National Park	—	NA	99755
Dillingham	1963	2,226	99576
Diomede (DY-o-mede)	1970	172	99762
Dora Bay	—	0	99950
Dot Lake	—	74	99737
Douglas	1902	NA	99824
Dry Creek	—	112	NA
Dutch Harbor	1942	NA	99692
Eagle	1901	160	99738
Eagle River	—	*	99577
Eagle Village	—	33	NA
Eareckson Air Force Station	—	15	NA
Edna Bay	—	75	99825
Eek	1970	285	99578
Egegik (EEG-gah-gik)	—	139	99579
Eielson Air Force Base	—	5,604	99702
Ekwok (ECK-wok)	1974	84	99580
Elfin Cove	—	50	99825
Elim (EE-lum)	1970	284	99739
Emmonak (ee-MON-nuk)	1964	784	99581
Ester	—	218	99725
Evansville	—	24	99726
Eyak (see Cordova)	—	—	NA
Fairbanks (Municipality)	1903	31,633	9970–
Main Office	—	—	99701
Eielson Air Force Base	—	5,875	99702
Fort Wainwright	—	—	99703
Main Office Boxes	—	—	99706
Downtown Station	—	—	99707
College Branch	—	—	99708
Salcha	—	—	99714
False Pass	1990	70	99583
Ferry	—	66	NA
Flat	—	9	99584
Fort Greely	—	713	99790
Fort Wainwright	—	—	99703
Fort Yukon	1959	562	99740
Fox	—	309	99712
Fox River	—	422	NA
Freshwater Bay	—	0	99850
Fritz Creek	—	1,882	99603
Gakona (ga-KOH-na)	—	23	99586
Galena (ga-LEE-na)	1971	529	99741
Gambell	1963	636	99742
Game Creek	—	74	NA
Girdwood	—	NA	99587
Glennallen	—	491	99588
Gold Creek	—	—	99695

*The population of Chugiak–Eagle River is counted as one unit, with 28,6000 residents.

Community	Year Incorporated	Population	Zip
Golovin (GAWL-uh-vin)	1971	161	99762
Goodnews Bay	1970	253	99589
Grayling	1969	203	99590
Gulkana	—	100	99586
Gustavus (ga-STAY-vus)	—	345	99826
Haines	1910	1,400	99827
Halibut Cove	—	71	99603
Happy Valley	—	388	99950
Harding Lake	—	29	99714
Healy	—	578	99734
Healy Lake	—	59	NA
Hobart Bay	—	131	99850
Hollis	—	169	99950
Holy Cross	1968	261	99602
Homer	1964	4,064	99603
Hoonah	1946	900	99829
Hooper Bay	1966	996	99604
Hope	—	160	99605
Houston	1966	976	99694
Hughes	1973	55	99745
Huslia (HOOS-lee-a)	1969	240	99746
Hydaburg	1927	410	99922
Hyder	—	133	99923
Icy Bay	—	NA	99695
Iguigig	—	48	99613
Iliamna (ill-ee-YAM-nuh)	—	103	99606
Indian	—	NA	99540
Ivanof Bay	—	28	99502
Jakolof Bay (Red Mountain)	—	28	99603
Juneau (Municipality)	1900	29,524	99801
Main Office	—	—	99801
Juneau—Main Office Boxes	—	—	99802
Mendenhall Station	—	—	99803
State Government Offices	—	—	99811
Kachemak (CATCH-a-mack)	1961	404	99603
Kake	1952	712	99830
Kaktovik (kack-TOE-vik)	1971	223	99747
Kalifonsky	—	325	99669
Kalskag	1975	NA	99607
Kaltag	1969	232	99748
Karluk	—	57	99608
Kasaan (Ka-SAN)	1976	41	99924
Kasigluk (ka-SEEG-luk)	1982	512	99609
Kasilof (ka-SEE-loff)	—	523	99610
Kasitsna Bay	—	NA	99695
Kenai (KEEN-eye)	1960	6,950	99611
Kenny Lake	—	498	99695
Ketchikan	1900	8,729	99901
Kiana (Ky-AN-a)	1964	394	99749
King Cove City	1947	705	99612
King Salmon	—	467	99613

Community	Year Incorporated	Population	Zip
Kipnuk (KIP-nuck)	—	551	99614
Kivalina	1969	349	99750
Klawock (kla-WOCK)	1929	726	99925
Klukwan	—	140	99827
Knik	—	445	99687
Kobuk	1973	78	99751
Kodiak	1940	6,869	99615
U.S. Coast Guard Station	—	1,871	99619
Kokhanok (KO-ghan-ock)	—	166	99606
Koliganek (ko-LIG-a-neck)	—	210	99576
Kongiganak (kon-GIG-a-nuck)	—	322	99559
Kotlik	1970	517	99620
Kotzebue (KOT-sa-bue)	1958	2,821	99752
Koyuk	1970	280	99753
Koyukuk (KOY-yuh-kuck)	1973	131	99754
Kupreanof (ku-pree-AN-off)	1975	23	99833
Kwethluk (KWEETH-luck)	1975	627	99621
Kwigillingok (kwi-GILL-in-gock)	—	332	99622
Labouchere Bay	—	—	NA
Lake Minchumina (min-CHOO-min-a)	—	44	99757
Larsen Bay	1974	127	99624
Lazy Mountain	—	976	NA
Levelock (LEH-vuh-lock)	—	111	99625
Lignite	—	117	NA
Lime Village	—	44	99627
Long Island	—	—	99950
Loring	—	NA	99950
Lower Kalskag	1969	302	99626
Lutak	—	51	NA
Manley Hot Springs	—	100	99756
Manokotak (man-a-KO-tack)	1970	396	99628
Marshall	1970	304	99585
McCarthy	—	33	99588
McGrath	1975	466	99627
McKinley Park	—	174	99755
Meadow Lakes	—	4,685	NA
Mekoryuk (ma-KOR-ee-yuk)	1969	200	99630
Mendeltna	—	64	NA
Mentasta Lake	—	108	99780
Metlakatla	1944	1,587	99926
Meyers Chuck	—	37	99903
Minto	—	251	99758
Moose Creek	—	638	99705
Moose Pass	—	120	99631
Mosquito Lake	—	90	NA
Mountain Village	1967	724	99632
Naknek (NACK-neck)	—	627	99633
Nanwalek	—	167	99695
Napakiak (NAP-uh-keey-ack)	1970	341	99634
Napaskiak (na-PASS-kee-ack)	1971	420	99559
Naukati Bay	—	164	99950

The Changing Faces of Anchorage

The minority population in Alaska's largest city is growing quickly, with the number likely to jump within the next decade from one in four to nearly one in three, according to Anchorage statistician Sue Fison. The number of Hispanics has increased nearly four times faster than that of whites since 1990. The growth rate for Asians is more than twice that of whites.

Natives and African Americans each accounted for about 7 percent of Anchorage's population in 1995. Asians, primarily Filipino, Korean and Japanese, made up 5.7 percent of the city's population. Hispanics are estimated to represent about 5.4 percent of Anchorage's population, according to Fison. Anchorage's minority population is smaller proportionately and significantly different than that of the rest of the United States: the largest minority group in Anchorage is Native Americans, who account for less than 1 percent of the nation's population.

These population changes are likely to play a larger role in the city's future, Fison says. Some impacts are already clear: retailers have altered their stocks to reflect the population, devoting space to Asian and Hispanic foods, for example. Other impacts are evolving as minority communities work on becoming a political presence in future elections.

Community	Year Incorporated	Population	Zip
Nelson Lagoon	—	79	99571
Nenana (nee-NA-na)	1921	357	99760
New Stuyahok (STU-ya-hock)	1972	442	99636
Newhalen	1971	175	99606
Newtok	1976	273	99559
Nightmute	1974	199	99690
Nikiski	—	3,013	99635
Nikolaevsk	—	555	99556
Nikolai	1970	109	99691
Nikolski	—	27	99638
Ninilchik	—	643	99639
Noatak	—	413	99761
Nome	1901	3,511	99762
Nondalton	1971	237	99640
Noorvik	1964	575	99763
North Pole	1953	1,523	99705
Northway	—	125	99764
Northway Junction	—	114	NA
Northway Village	—	115	NA
Nuiqsut (noo-IK-sut)	1975	435	99789
Nulato	1963	349	99765
Nunapitchuk (NU-nuh-pit-CHUCK)	1969	474	99641
Old Harbor	1966	316	99643
Olga Bay	—	NA	99697
Ophir	—	NA	99695
Oscarville	—	57	99695
Ouzinkie (oo-ZINK-ee)	1967	259	99644
Palmer	1951	4,282	99645
Paxson	—	27	99737
Pedro Bay	—	45	99647
Pelican	1943	196	99832

Community	Year Incorporated	Population	Zip
Perryville	—	101	99648
Petersburg	1910	3,356	99833
Pilot Point	1992	80	99649
Pilot Station	1969	536	99650
Pitkas Point	—	153	99658
Platinum	1975	39	99651
Pleasant Valley	—	559	NA
Point Baker	—	53	99927
Point Hope	1966	764	99766
Point Lay	—	180	99759
Polk Inlet	—	90	NA
Port Alexander	1974	102	99836
Port Alice	—	2	99950
Port Alsworth	—	64	99653
Port Clarence	—	19	99762
Port Graham	—	176	99603
Port Heiden	1972	147	99549
Port Lions	1966	234	99550
Port Protection	—	55	99950
Portage Creek	—	6	NA
Primrose	—	62	NA
Prudhoe Bay	—	47	99734
Quinhagak (QUIN-a-gak)	1975	567	99655
Rampart	—	65	99767
Red Devil	—	65	99656
Red Dog	—	40	NA
Ridgeway	—	2,295	NA
Rowan Bay	—	22	99850
Ruby	1973	190	99768
Russian Mission	1970	284	99657
St. George	1983	157	99591
St. John Harbor	—	—	NA
St. Marys/Andreafsky	1967	501	99658
St. Michael	1969	329	99659
St. Paul	1971	739	99660
Salamatof	—	1,011	99611
Salcha	—	374	99714
Sand Point	1966	808	99661
Savoonga (suh-VOON-guh)	1969	615	99769
Saxman	1930	390	99901
Scammon Bay	1967	425	99662
Selawik (SELL-a-wick)	1977	665	99770
Seldovia	1945	272	99663
Seward	1912	2,914	99664
Shageluk (SHAG-a-look)	1970	139	99665
Shaktoolik (shack-TOO-lick)	1969	231	99771
Sheldon Point	1974	137	99666
Shishmaref (SHISH-muh-reff)	1969	537	99772
Shungnak (SHOONG-nack)	1967	249	99773
Sitka (City)	1963/1971	8,632	99835
Skagway	1900	767	99840

Community	Year Incorporated	Population	Zip
Skwentna	—	86	99667
Slana	—	61	99586
Sleetmute	—	109	99668
Soldotna	1967	3,968	99669
South Naknek	—	157	99670
Spenard	—	—	99503
Stebbins	1969	507	99671
Sterling	—	5,378	99472
Stevens Village	—	115	99774
Stony River	—	43	99557
Sutton	—	367	99674
Takotna (Tah-KOAT-nuh)	—	46	99675
Talkeetna (Tal-KEET-na)	—	342	99676
Tanacross	—	75	99776
Tanana (TAN-a-nah)	1961	293	99777
Tatitlek	—	125	99677
Telida	—	8	99695
Teller	1963	278	99778
Tenakee Springs	1971	114	99841
Tetlin	—	82	99779
Thorne Bay	1982	645	99919
Togiak (TOE-gee-yack)	1969	740	99678
Tok (TOKE)	—	1,210	99780
Toksook Bay	1972	488	99637
Tonsina	—	45	99573
Trapper Creek	—	310	99683
Tuluksak (tu-LOOK-sack)	1970	411	99679
Tuntutuliak (TUN-too-TOO-li-ack)	—	335	99680
Tununak	1975	327	99681
Twin Hills	—	67	99576
Two Rivers	—	632	99716
Tyonek (ty-O-neck)	—	148	99682
Ugashik	—	5	99695
Unalakleet (YOU-na-la-kleet)	1974	798	99684
Unalaska (UN-a-LAS-ka)	1942	4,087	99685
Upper Kalskag/Kalskag	1975	197	NA
Valdez (val-DEEZ)	1901	4,254	99686
Venetie (VEEN-a-tie)	—	213	99781
Wainwright	1962	563	99782
Wales	1964	165	99783
Wasilla (wah-SIL-luh)	1974	4,714	99687
Whale Pass	—	76	99950
White Mountain	1969	212	99784
Whitestone Logging Camp	—	198	NA
Whittier	1969	289	99693
Willow	—	419	99688
Wiseman	—	29	99790
Womens Bay	—	672	NA
Wrangell	1903	2,595	99929
Yakutat (YAK-a-tat)	1948/1992	802	99689

Census Populations of Major Cities

City	1900	1920	1940	1950	1970	1980	1996**
Anchorage	*	1,856	4,229	11,254	48,081	174,431	254,269
Barrow	*	*	*	*	2,104	2,207	4,276
Cordova	*	955	938	1,165	1,164	1,879	2,537
Fairbanks	*	1,155	3,455	5,771	14,771	22,645	31,633
Juneau	1,864	3,058	5,729	5,956	6,050	19,528	29,524
Kenai	290	332	303	321	3,533	4,324	6,950
Ketchikan	459	2,458	4,695	5,305	6,994	7,198	8,729
Kodiak	341	374	864	1,710	3,798	4,756	6,869
Nome	12,488	852	1,559	1,876	2,357	2,301	3,511
Petersburg	*	879	1,323	1,619	2,042	2,821	3,356
Seward	*	652	949	2,114	1,587	1,843	2,914
Sitka	1,396	1,175	1,987	1,985	6,075	7,803	8,632
Valdez	315	466	529	554	1,005	3,079	4,254
Wrangell	868	821	1,162	1,263	2,029	2,184	2,595

*Population figures unavailable
**Estimates. Source: Alaska Department of Labor, Research and Analysis Section

Population by Census Areas (See map next page)

Key	Census Area	1970	1980	1990	1996
	Alaska	302,583	401,851	550,043	615,900
1	North Slope Borough	3,451	4,199	5,979	7,157
2	Northwest Arctic Borough	4,048	4,831	6,113	6,525
3	Nome Census Area	5,749	6,537	8,288	9,085
4	Yukon–Koyukuk	7,045	6,471	6,681	6,353
5	Fairbanks North Star Borough	45,864	53,983	77,720	82,435
6	Southeast Fairbanks	4,308	5,676	5,913	6,248
7	Wade Hampton	3,917	4,665	5,791	6,721
8	Bethel	8,917	10,999	13,656	15,400
9	Dillingham	2,510	3,232	4,012	4,462
10	Bristol Bay Borough	1,147	1,094	1,410	1,254
11	Aleutian Islands	7,834	7,768	11,942	7,951
12	Matanuska–Susitna Borough	6,509	17,816	39,683	50,759
13	Anchorage Borough	126,385	174,431	226,338	254,269
14	Kenai Peninsula Borough	16,586	25,282	40,802	46,790
15	Kodiak Island Borough	9,409	9,939	13,309	14,028
16	Valdez–Cordova	4,979	8,348	9,952	10,558
17	Skagway–Hoonah–Angoon	2,792	3,478	4,385	3,816
18	Haines Borough	1,401	1,680	2,117	2,373
19	Juneau Borough	13,556	19,528	26,751	29,524
20	Sitka Borough	6,073	7,803	8,588	8,632
21	Wrangell–Petersburg	4,920	6,167	7,042	7,126
22	Prince of Wales–Outer Ketchikan	3,782	3,822	6,278	7,117
23	Ketchikan Gateway Borough	10,041	11,316	13,828	14,728
24	Lake and Peninsula Borough	1,362	1,384	1,668	1,852
25	Denali Borough	NA	1,402	1,792	1,835
26	Aleutians East Borough	1,301	1,643	2,464	2,183
27	Aleutians West Borough	6,533	6,125	9,478	5,768

Source: July 1, 1996, estimates, Alaska Department of Labor

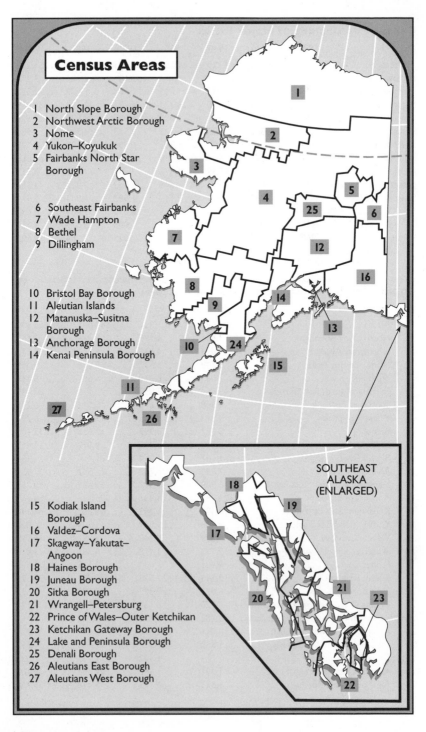

Census Areas

1 North Slope Borough
2 Northwest Arctic Borough
3 Nome
4 Yukon–Koyukuk
5 Fairbanks North Star
  Borough

6 Southeast Fairbanks
7 Wade Hampton
8 Bethel
9 Dillingham

10 Bristol Bay Borough
11 Aleutian Islands
12 Matanuska–Susitna
   Borough
13 Anchorage Borough
14 Kenai Peninsula Borough

SOUTHEAST
ALASKA
(ENLARGED)

15 Kodiak Island
   Borough
16 Valdez–Cordova
17 Skagway–Yakutat–
   Angoon
18 Haines Borough
19 Juneau Borough
20 Sitka Borough
21 Wrangell–Petersburg
22 Prince of Wales–Outer Ketchikan
23 Ketchikan Gateway Borough
24 Lake and Peninsula Borough
25 Denali Borough
26 Aleutians East Borough
27 Aleutians West Borough

Potlatch

This Native gathering, primarily an Indian custom, is held to commemorate major life events. Traditional Native foods are served, songs and dances are performed and gifts are distributed to everyone who attends. A funeral potlatch might result in the giving away of the deceased's possessions to relatives or to persons who had done favors for the deceased during his or her lifetime.

Before the U.S. and Canadian governments outlawed the practice in the 1880s, potlatches were a focal point of Native society. The host family might give away all its possessions in an attempt to demonstrate its wealth to the guests. Each guest in turn would feel an obligation to hold an even more sumptuous potlatch. The outlawing of potlatches resulted in the disintegration of many aspects of Native culture. Potlatch restrictions were repealed in 1951.

Radio Stations

Alaska's radio stations broadcast a variety of music, talk shows, and religious and educational programs. Many radio stations in Alaska also broadcast personal messages, long a popular and necessary form of communication in Alaska—especially in the bush. It was in consideration of these messages—and the importance of radio stations in providing the sole source of vital weather information to fishermen and hunters—that the United States and Canada agreed to grant some Alaska radio stations international communication status. The "clear channel" status provides protection against interference from foreign broadcasters. Personal message broadcasts are heard on:

Anchorage, KYAK's Bush Pipeline
Barrow, KBRW's Tundra Drum
Bethel, KYUK's Tundra Drums
Dillingham, KDLG's Bristol Bay Messenger
Fairbanks, KIAK's Pipeline of the North
Galena, KIYU's Yukon Wireless
Glennallen, KCAM's Caribou Clatter
Haines, KHNS's Listener Personals
Homer, KBBI's Bay Bush Lines
Ketchikan, KRBD's Muskeg Messenger; KTKN's Public Service Announcements
Kodiak, KVOK-KJJZ-FM's Highliner Crabbers
Kotzebue, KOTZ's Messages
McGrath, KSKO's Messages
Nome, KICY's Ptarmigan Telegraph; KNOM's Hot Lines
North Pole, KJNP's Trapline Chatter
Petersburg, KFSK's Muskeg Messages; KRSA's Channel Chatters
Sitka, KCAW-FM's Muskeg Messages
Soldotna, KSRM's Tundra Tom Tom
Wrangell, KSTK-FM's Radiograms

Statewide. APRN, 810 E. Ninth Ave., Anchorage 99501.

Bush Radio Network, Box 91941, Anchorage 99509.

Anchorage. KASH-FM 107.5 MHz; 800 E. Dimond Blvd., Suite 3-320, 99515.

KATB-FM 89.3 MHz; P.O. Box 210389, 99521.

KBFX-FM 100.5 MHz; 800 E. Dimond Blvd., Suite 3-320, 99515.

KBRJ-FM 104.1 MHz; 11259 Tower Road, 99515.

KBYR 700 kHz; **KNIK-FM** 105.3 MHz; 1007 W. 32nd Ave., 99503.

KEAG-FM 97.3 MHz; 3700 Woodland Park Drive, Suite 300, 99517.

KENI 550 kHz; 800 E. Dimond Blvd., Suite 3-320, 99515.

KFQD 750 kHz; **KWHL-FM** 106.5 MHz; 9200 Lake Otis Parkway, 99507.

Newsradio 750 KFQD advertised for news broadcasters in the *Anchorage Daily News* classifieds. According to the ad, "Applicants must have excellent reading and writing skills. . . . Radio or TV experience *required, but not necessary.*"

KGOT-FM 101.3 MHz; 500 L St., Suite 200, 99501.

KHAR 590 kHz; KBRJ-FM 104.1 MHz; 11259 Tower Road., 99515.

KJMM-FM 94.5 MHz; 3605 Arctic Blvd., Suite 945, 99503.

KKRO-FM 102.1 MHz; 11259 Tower Road, 99515.

KKSD 1080 kHz; 1300 E. 68th, Suite 208, 99518.

KLEF-FM 98.1 MHz; 3601 C St., Suite 290, 99503.

KMXS-FM 103.1 MHz; 9200 Lake Otis Parkway, 99507.

KNBA-FM 90.3 MHz; 810 E. Ninth Ave., 99501.

KOOL-FM 97.3 MHz; 3700 Woodland Park Drive, 99517.

KPXR-FM 102.1 MHz; 3700 Woodland Drive, No. 300, 99517.

KRUA-FM 88.1 MHz; 3211 Providence Drive, 99508.

KSKA-FM 91.1 MHz; 3877 University Drive, 99508.

KYAK 650 kHz; KGOT-FM 101.3 MHz; 2800 E. Dowling Road, 99507.

KYMG-FM 98.9 MHz; 500 L St., Suite 200, 99501.

Barrow. KBRW 680 kHz; P.O. Box 109, 99723.

Bethel. KYKD-FM 100.1 MHz; P.O. Box 2428, 99559.

KYUK 640 kHz; Pouch 468, 99559.

Chevak. KCUK 88.1 kHz; 985 KSD Way, 99563.

Cordova. KCHU-FM 88.1 MHz; P.O. Box 467, Valdez 99686.

KLAM 1450 kHz; P.O. Box 60, 99574.

Dillingham. KDLG 670 kHz; P.O. Box 670, 99576.

KRUP 99.3 MHz; Box 157, 99576.

Fairbanks. KAKQ-FM 101.1 MHz; 546 Ninth Ave., 99701.

KCBF 820 kHz; KXLR-FM 95.9 MHz; 3528 International Way, 99701.

KFAR 660 kHz; KWLF-FM 98.1 MHz;

P.O. Box 70910, 99707.

KIAK 970 kHz; KIAK-FM 1025 MHz; 546 Ninth Ave. 99701.

KSUA-FM 91.5 MHz; P.O. Box 750113, 99775.

KUAC-FM 104.7 MHz; University of Alaska, P.O. Box 755620, 99775.

KUWL-FM 103.9 MHz; P.O. Box 70910, 99707.

KWLF-FM 98.1 MHz; P.O. Box 70910, 99707.

Fort Yukon. KZPA-FM 900 MHz; P.O. Box 50, 99740.

Galena. KIYU 910 kHz; P.O. Box 165, 99741.

Glennallen. KCAM 790 kHz; P.O. Box 249, 99588.

KXGA-FM 90.5 MHz; mailing address: P.O. Box 467, Valdez 99686.

Haines/Klukwan/Skagway. KHNS-FM 102.3 MHz; P.O. Box 1109, 99827.

Homer. KBBI 890 kHz; 3913 Kachemak Way, 99603.

KGTL 620 kHz; KWVV-FM, 103.5 MHz; P.O. Box 109, 99603.

KPEN-FM 101.7 MHz; P.O. Box 109, 99603.

KWVV-FM 103.5 MHz; P.O. Box 109, 99603.

Juneau. KINY 800 kHz; 1107 W. Eighth St., Suite 2, 99801.

KJNO 630 kHz; 3161 Channel Drive, Suite 2, 99801.

KSUP-FM 106.3 MHz; 107.9 kHz; 1107 W. Eighth Ave., Suite 2, 99801.

KTKU-FM 105.1 MHz; 3161 Channel Drive, Suite 2, 99801.

KTOO-FM 104.3 MHz; 360 Egan Drive, 99801.

Kenai. KCZP-FM 91.9 MHz; P.O. Box 2111, 99611.

KDLL 91.9 kHz; Box 2111, 99611.

KPEN-FM 101.7 MHz; P.O. Box 109, Homer 99603.
KZXX 980 kHz; 6672 Kenai Spur Road, 99669.

Ketchikan. KFMJ 99.9 kHz; 516 Stedman St., 99901.
KGTW-FM 106.7 MHz; 526 Stedman St., 99901.
KRBD-FM 105.9 MHz; 123 Stedman St., 99901.
KTKN 930 kHz; KGTW-FM 106.7 MHz; 526 Stedman St., 99901.

Kodiak. KMXT-FM 100.1 MHz; 718 Mill Bay Road, 99615.
KRXX-FM 101.1 MHz; Box 708, 99615.
KVOK 560 kHz; KJJZ-FM 101.1 MHz; P.O. Box 708, 99615.

Kotzebue. KOTZ 720 kHz; P.O. Box 78, 99752.

McCarthy. KXKM-FM 89.7 MHz; mailing address: P.O. Box 467, Valdez 99686.

McGrath. KSKO 870 kHz; P.O. Box 70, 99627.

Naknek. KAKN-FM 100.9 MHz; P.O. Box 214, 99633.

Nenana. KIAM 630 kHz; P.O. Box 474, 99760.

Nome. KICY 850 kHz; KICY-FM 100.3 MHz; P.O. Box 820, 99762.
KNOM 780 kHz; P.O. Box 988, 99762.

North Pole. KJNP 1170 kHz; KJNP-FM 100.3 MHz; P.O. Box 56359, 99705.

Petersburg. KFSK-FM 100.9 MHz; P.O. Box 149, 99833.
KRSA 580 kHz; P.O. Box 650, 99833.

St. Paul. KUHB-FM 91.9 MHz; P.O. Box 905, 99660.

Sand Point. KSDP 830 kHz; P.O. Box 328, 99661.

Seward. KSWD 950 kHz; P.O. Box 405, 99664.

Sitka. KCAW-FM 104.7 MHz; 2-B Lincoln St., 99835.
KIFW 1230 kHz; KSBZ-FM 103.1 MHz; P.O. Box 299, 99835.

Soldotna. KKIS-FM, 96.5 Mhz; HC2, Box 852, 99669.
KSLD 1140 kHz; HC2, Box 852, 99669.
KSRM 920 kHz; KWHQ-FM 100.1 MHz; HC2, Box 852, 99669.

Talkeetna. KTNA-FM, 88.5 MHz; P.O. Box 300, 99676.

Unalakleet. KNSA 930 kHz; P.O. Box 178, 99684.

Unalaska. KIAL 1450 kHz; P.O. Box 181, 99685.

Valdez. KCHU 770 kHz; P.O. Box 467, 99686.
KVAK 1230 kHz; P.O. Box 367, 99686.

Wasilla. KMBQ-FM 99.7 MHz; P.O. Box 871526, 99687.

Whittier. KCHU-FM 88.3 MHz; P.O. Box 467, Valdez 99686.

Wrangell. KSTK-FM 101.7 MHz; P.O. Box 1141, 99929.

Yakutat. KJFP-FM 103.9 MHz; P.O. Box 388, 99689.

Railroads

The Alaska Railroad is the northernmost railroad in North America and was for many years the only one owned by the United States government. Ownership now belongs to the state of Alaska. The ARR rolls on 470 miles of mainline track from the ports of Seward and Whittier to Anchorage, Cook Inlet and Fairbanks in the Interior.

The Alaska Railroad began in 1912 when Congress appointed a commission to study transportation problems in Alaska.

In March 1914, the president authorized railroad lines in the territory of Alaska to connect open harbors on the southern coast of Alaska with the Interior. The Alaska Engineering Commission surveyed possible railroad routes in 1914 and, in April 1915, President Woodrow Wilson announced the selection of a route from Seward north 412 miles to the Tanana River (where Nenana is now located), with branch lines to Matanuska coal fields. The main line was later extended to Fairbanks. Construction of the railroad began in 1915 from a wilderness construction camp on Cook Inlet. Almost overnight, a tent city of 2,000 people sprang up and Anchorage was born.

On July 15, 1923, President Warren G. Harding drove in the golden spike at Nenana, signifying completion of the railroad.

The railroad offers year-round passenger, freight and vehicle service. The ARR features flag-stop service along the Anchorage-to-Fairbanks corridor, as well as summer express trains to Denali National Park and Preserve. Passenger service is daily between mid-May and mid-September, and in winter weekly service is available between Anchorage and Fairbanks. A one-day excursion to Seward is provided daily, mid-May to early September. Additionally, service to Whittier is offered daily from May through September and four days a week in winter. In 1996, a record 518,867 passengers rode the Alaska Railroad. For more information, contact The Alaska Railroad, P.O. Box 107500, Anchorage 99510; (800) 544-0552.

The privately owned White Pass & Yukon Route provided a narrow-gauge link between Skagway, Alaska, and Whitehorse, Yukon Territory. At the time it was built—1898 to 1900—it was the farthest north any railroad had operated in North America. The railway maintained one of the steepest railroad grades in North America, climbing to 2,885 feet at White Pass in only 20 miles of track.

The White Pass & Yukon Route provided both passenger and freight service until 1982, when it suspended service until 1988. The route can operate irregularly. Before planning a trip, contact the White Pass & Yukon Route, P.O. Box 435, Skagway 99840, for information.

Regions of Alaska
(SEE MAP, PAGES 8–9)

Southeast. Southeast, Alaska's panhandle, stretches approximately 500 miles from Icy Bay, northwest of Yakutat, to Dixon Entrance at the United States–Canada border beyond the southern tip of Prince of Wales Island. Massive ice fields, glacier-scoured peaks and steep valleys, more than a thousand named islands, and numerous unnamed islets and reefs characterize this vertical world where few flat expanses break the steepness. Spruce, hemlock and cedar, the basis for the region's timber industry, cover many of the mountainsides.

Average temperatures range from 50°F to 60°F in July and from 20°F to 40°F in January. Average annual precipitation varies from 80 to more than 200 inches. The area receives from 30 to 200 inches of snow in the lowlands and more than 400 inches in the high mountains.

The region's economy revolves around fishing and fish processing, timber and tourism. Mining is taking on increasing importance with development of a world-class molybdenum mine near Ketchikan.

Airplanes and boats provide the principal means of transportation. Only three communities in Southeast are connected to the road system: Haines via the Haines Highway to the Alaska Highway at Haines Junction; Skagway, via Klondike Highway 2 to the Alaska Highway; and Hyder, to the continental road system via the Cassiar Highway in British Columbia. Juneau, on the Southeast mainland, is the state capital; Sitka, on Baranof Island, was the capital of Russian America.

Southcentral/Gulf Coast. The Southcentral/Gulf Coast region curves 650 miles north and west of Southeast to Kodiak Island. About two-thirds of the state's residents live in the arc between the Gulf of Alaska on the south and the Alaska Range on the north, the region commonly called Southcentral. On the region's eastern boundary, only the Copper River valley breaches the mountainous barrier of the Chugach and St. Elias Mountains. On the west rise lofty peaks of the Aleutian Range. Within this mountainous perimeter course the Susitna and Matanuska Rivers.

The irregular plain of the Copper River lowland has a colder climate than the other major valley areas. The January average for Kenny Lake is –2°F. The January average for the Talkeetna airport is 10°F (measurements taken from 1970 to 1993). July temperatures average 50°F to 60°F in the region.

Regional precipitation ranges from a scant 17 inches annually in drier areas to more than 76 inches a year at Thompson Pass in the coastal mountains.

Small boy with king salmon, early 1920s. From *Alaska's History* by Harry Ritter

Vegetation varies from the spruce-hemlock forests of Prince William Sound to mixed spruce and birch forests in the Susitna Valley to tundra in the highlands of the Copper River–Nelchina Basin.

Alaska agriculture historically has been most thoroughly developed in the Matanuska Valley. The state's dairy industry is centered there and at a new project at Point MacKenzie across Knik Arm from Anchorage. Vegetables thrive in the area, which is well known for its giant cabbages.

Hub of the state's commerce, transportation and communications is Anchorage, on a narrow plain at the foot of the Chugach Mountains, and bounded by Knik Arm and Turnagain Arm, offshoots of Cook Inlet. The population of this, Alaska's largest city, is closely tied to shifts in the state's economy.

Alaska's major banks and oil companies have their headquarters in Anchorage, as does the Alaska Railroad. The city's port

Coca-Cola® has a toll-free hotline in Atlanta for information and complaints. When asked who calls this number, an operator replied, "People from Alaska call in the winter just to talk."

handles most of the shipping in and out of the state. Valdez, to the east of Anchorage on Prince Willam Sound, is the southern terminal of the trans-Alaska oil pipeline, which transports oil from Prudhoe Bay on the North Slope.

Interior. Great rivers have forged a broad lowland, known as the Interior, in the central part of the state between the Alaska Range on the south and the Brooks Range on the north. The Yukon River carves a swath across the entire state. In the Interior, the Tanana, Porcupine, Koyukuk and several other rivers join with the Yukon to create summer and winter "highways." South of the Yukon, the Kuskokwim River rises in the hills of the western Interior before beginning its meandering course across the Bering Sea coast region.

Winter temperatures in the Interior commonly drop to –50°F and –60°F. Ice fog sometimes hovers over Fairbanks and other low-lying communities when the temperature falls below zero. Controlled by the extremes of a continental climate, summers usually are warmer than in any other region; high temperatures are in the 80s and 90s. The climate is semiarid, with about 12 inches of precipitation recorded annually.

Immense forests of birch and aspen bring vibrant green and gold to the Interior's landscape. Spruce covers many of the slopes and cottonwoods thrive near river lowlands. But in northern and western reaches of the Interior, the North American taiga gives way to tundra. In highlands above tree line and in marshy lowlands, grasses and shrubs replace trees.

Gold lured the first large influx of non-Natives to Alaska's Interior. From 1903 to 1910, Fairbanks, the largest community in the region, was a booming gold-mining camp. Now the city on the banks of the Chena River is a transportation and supply center for eastern and northern Alaska. The main campus of the University of Alaska overlooks the city.

About 100 miles east of Fairbanks, farmers at the Delta project work to build a foundation for agriculture based on barley. At Healy, southwest of Fairbanks, the state's only operating coal mine produces coal used to generate electricity for the Interior. The rest of the Interior relies primarily on a subsistence economy, sometimes combined with a cash economy where fishing or seasonal government jobs are available.

Arctic. Beyond the Brooks Range, more than 80,000 square miles of tundra interlaced with meandering rivers and countless ponds spread out along the North Slope. In far northwestern Alaska, the Arctic curves south to take in Kotzebue and other villages of the Kobuk and Noatak River drainages.

Short, cool summers with temperatures usually between 30°F and 40°F allow the permanently frozen soil to thaw only a few inches. Winter temperatures range well below zero, but the Arctic Ocean moderates temperatures in coastal areas. Severe winds sweep along the coast and through mountain passes. The combination of cold and wind often drops the chill-factor temperature far below the actual temperature. Most areas receive less than 10 inches of precipitation a year, but the terrain is wet in summer because of little evaporation and frozen ground.

Traditionally the home of Inupiat Eskimos, the Arctic was inhabited by few non-Natives until oil was discovered at Prudhoe Bay in the 1960s. Today the region's economy is focused on Prudhoe Bay and neighboring Kuparuk oil fields. Petroleum-related jobs support most of the region's residents either directly or indirectly. Subsistence hunting and fishing fill

Alaska . . .
The name Alaska is probably an abbreviation of Unalaska, derived from the original Aleut word agunalaksh, which means "the shores where the sea breaks its back."—Corey Ford, *Where the Sea Breaks Its Back*

any economic holes left by the oil industry.

The largest Inupiat Eskimo community in the world, Barrow is the center of commerce and government activity for the region. Airplanes, the major means of transportation, fan out from there to the region's far-flung villages.

The Dalton Highway, formerly called the North Slope Haul Road, connects the Arctic with the Interior. The 416-mile road is open as far north as Disaster Creek, but only permit holders may travel the road. (*See* Dalton Highway)

Western/Bering Sea Coast.

Western Alaska extends along the Bering Sea coast from the Arctic Circle south to where the Alaska Peninsula joins the mainland near Naknek on Bristol Bay. Home of Inupiat and Yupik Eskimos, the region centers around the immense Yukon–Kuskokwim river delta, the Seward Peninsula to the north and Bristol Bay to the south.

Summer temperatures range from the 30s to low 60s. Winter readings generally range from just above zero to the low 30s. Wind chill lowers temperatures considerably. Total annual precipitation is about 20 inches, with northern regions drier than those to the south.

Much of the region is covered with tundra, although a band of forests covers the hills on the eastern end of the Seward Peninsula and Norton Sound. In the south near Bristol Bay, the tundra once again gives way to forests. In between, the marshy flatland of the great Yukon–Kuskokwim Delta spreads out for more than 200 miles.

Gold first attracted non-Natives to the hills and creeks of the Seward Peninsula. To the south, only a few anthropologists and wildlife biologists entered the world of the Yupik Eskimos of the delta. At the extreme south, fish, including the world's largest sockeye salmon run, drew fishermen to the riches of Bristol Bay.

The villages of western Alaska are linked by air and water, dogsled and snow machine. Commerce on the delta radiates

out from Bethel, largest community in western Alaska. To the north, Nome dominates commerce on the Seward Peninsula, while several fishing communities take their livelihood from the riches of Bristol Bay.

Southwestern/Alaska Peninsula and Aleutians.

Southwestern Alaska includes the Alaska Peninsula and Aleutian Islands. From Naknek Lake, the peninsula curves southwest about 500 miles to the first of the Aleutian Islands; the Aleutians continue south and west more than 1,000 miles. Primarily a mountainous region with about 50 volcanic peaks, only on the Bering Sea side of the peninsula does the terrain flatten out.

More than 200 islands, roughly 5,500 square miles in area, form the narrow arc of the Aleutians, which separate the North Pacific from the Bering Sea. Nearly the entire chain is in the Alaska Maritime National Wildlife Refuge. Unimak Island, closest to the Alaska Peninsula mainland, is 1,000 miles from Attu, the most distant island. Five major island groups make up the Aleutians, all of which are treeless except for a few scattered stands that have been transplanted on the islands.

The Aleutian climate is cool, with summer temperatures up to the 50s and winter readings in the 20s and lower. Winds are almost constant and fog is common. Precipitation ranges from 21 inches to more than 80 inches annually. The peninsula's climate is somewhat warmer than the islands' in summer and cooler in winter.

Aleuts, original inhabitants of the chain, still live at Atka, Atka Island; Nikolski, Umnak Island; Unalaska, Unalaska Island; Akutan, Akutan Island; and False Pass, Unimak Island.

The quest for furs first drew Russians to the islands and peninsula in the 1700s. The traders conquered the Aleuts and forced them to hunt marine mammals. After the United States purchased Alaska in 1867, fur traders switched their efforts to fox farming. Many foxes were turned loose on the islands, where they flourished and destroyed native wildlife. With the collapse of the fur market in the 1920s and 1930s, the islands were left to themselves. This relative isolation was broken during World War II when Japanese military forces bombed Dutch Harbor and landed on Attu and Kiska Islands. The United States military retook the islands, and after the war the government resettled Aleuts living in the western Aleutians to villages in the eastern Aleutians, closer to the mainland.

Today fishing provides the main economic base for the islands and the peninsula. Many Aleuts go to Bristol Bay or Unalaska (Dutch Harbor) to fish commercially in summer.

Religion
Nearly every religion practiced in American society is found in Alaska. Following is a list of addresses for some of the major ones:

Alaska Baptist Convention, 1750 O'Malley Road, Anchorage 99516.

Alaska Moravian Church, Bethel 99559.

Anchorage Friends Church (Quaker), 605 W. Tudor Road, Anchorage 99503.

Assemblies of God, 1048 W. International Airport Road, Anchorage 99502.

Baha'i Faith, 13501 Brayton Drive, Anchorage 99516.

Christian Science Church, 1347 L St., Anchorage 99501.

Church of God, 1711 S. Bragaw St., Anchorage 99508.

Church of Jesus Christ of Latter-day Saints, 13111 Brayton Drive, Anchorage 99516.

Congregation Beth Sholom, 7525 E. Northern Lights Blvd., Anchorage 99504.

Episcopal Diocese of Alaska, 1205 Denali Way, Fairbanks 99701.

The Anchorage Daily News carried a classified ad in the APPAREL FOR SALE section which read "Wedding dress. Worn once by mistake."

Evangelical Lutheran Church of America, 1836 W. Northern Lights Blvd., Anchorage 99517.

Jehovah's Witness, Foothills Congregation, 2552 E. 48th Ave., Anchorage 99507.

Lubavitch Jewish Center of Alaska, Congregation Shomrei Ohr, 1210 E. 26th Ave., Anchorage 99508.

Orthodox Church in America, Diocese of Alaska, St. Innocent Orthodox Cathedral, 6724 E. Fourth Ave., Anchorage 99504.

Presbyterian Churches, 616 W. 10th Ave., Anchorage 99501.

Roman Catholic Archdiocese of Anchorage, 225 Cordova, Anchorage 99501.

The Salvation Army, 726 E. Ninth Ave., Anchorage 99501.

United Methodist Church, Alaska Missionary Conference, 3402 Wesleyan Drive, Anchorage 99508.

Unity of Anchorage, 10821 Totem Road, Anchorage 99516.

Wat Lao Sayamungkhun (Buddhist), 2934 E. 42nd Ave., Anchorage 99508.

Reptiles
For all practical purposes, reptiles are not found in Alaska outside of captivity. The northern limits of North American reptilian species may be the latitude at which their embryos fail to develop during the summer. Three sightings of a species of garter snake, *Thamnophis sirtalis,* have been reported on the banks of the Taku River and Stikine River.

Rivers
(*SEE ALSO* NATIONAL WILD AND SCENIC RIVERS *AND* YUKON RIVER) There are more than 3,000 rivers in Alaska. The 10 longest rivers in Alaska are as follows:

Yukon River—1,400 miles in Alaska; the remainder is in Canada.

Porcupine River—555 miles. The Porcupine is a major tributary of the Yukon River.

Koyukuk—554 miles.

Kuskokwim—540 miles.

Tanana—531 miles.

Innoko—463 miles.

Colville—428 miles.

Many first-timers to the Nenana take a commercial white-water raft trip to the Gorge. From The Alaska River Guide *by Karen Jettmar*

Noatak—396 miles.

Kobuk—396 miles.

Birch Creek—314 miles.

The major navigable Alaska inland waterways are as follows:

Chilkat—Navigable by shallow-draft vessels to village of Klukwan, 25 miles above mouth.

Kobuk—Controlling channel depth is about 5 feet through Hotham Inlet, 3 feet to Ambler and 2 feet to Kobuk Village, about 210 river miles.

Koyukuk—Navigable to Allakaket by vessels drawing up to 3 feet during normally high river flow and to Bettles during occasional higher flows.

Kuskokwim—Navigable (June 1 to September 30) by 18-foot-draft ocean-going vessels from mouth upriver 65 miles to Bethel. Shallow-draft (4-foot) vessels can ascend river to mile 465. McGrath is at mile 400.

Kvichak—The river is navigable for vessels of 10-foot draft to Alaganak River, 22 miles above the mouth of Kvichak River. Remainder of this river (28 miles) navigable by craft drawing 2 to 4 feet, depending on the stage of the river. Drains into Lake Iliamna, which is navigable an additional 70 miles.

Naknek—Navigable for vessels of 12-foot draft for 12 miles with adequate

tide. Vessels with 3-foot draft can continue an additional 7.5 miles.

Noatak—Navigable (late May to mid-June) for shallow-draft barges to a point about 18 miles below Noatak village. Shallow-draft vessels can continue on to Noatak.

Nushagak—Navigable (June 1 to August 31) by small vessels of 2½-foot draft to Nunachuak, about 100 miles above the mouth. Shallow-draft, oceangoing vessels can navigate to mouth of Wood River at mile 84.

Porcupine—Navigable to Old Crow, Yukon Territory, by vessels drawing 3 feet, during spring runoff and fall rain floods.

Glacial Flour

Glacial rivers, such as the Knik River near Anchorage and the Nenana River of the Interior, appear milky from their heavy loads of silt, or "glacial flour," released into the river from melting glaciers. Fish live in the cloudy rivers, but usually move into clearer water to spawn. A Nenana River riverboat captain likes to say that glacial rivers are too dry to drink and too wet to plow. —Susan Ewing, The Great Alaska Nature Factbook

Stikine—Navigable (May 1 to October 15) from mouth 165 miles to Telegraph Creek, British Columbia, by shallow-draft, flat-bottom riverboats.

Susitna—Navigable by stern-wheelers and shallow-draft, flat-bottom riverboats to confluence of Talkeetna River, 75 miles upstream, but boats cannot cross bars at mouth of river. Not navigable by ocean-going vessels.

Tanana—Navigable by shallow-draft (4-foot), flat-bottom vessels and barges from the mouth to Nenana and by smaller river craft to the Chena River 201 miles above the mouth. Craft of 4-foot draft can navigate to Chena River on high water to University Avenue Bridge in Fairbanks.

Yukon—Navigable (June 1 to September 30) by shallow-draft, flat-bottom riverboats from the mouth to near the head of Lake Bennett. It cannot be entered or navigated by oceangoing vessels. Controlling depths are 7 feet to Stevens Village and 3 to 5 feet from there to Fort Yukon.

Roadhouses
An important part of Alaska history, roadhouses were modest quarters that offered bed and board to travelers along early-day Alaska trails. The majority provided accommodations for sled dog teams, as most travel occurred in winter. By 1920, there were roadhouses along every major transportation route in Alaska. Most roadhouses have vanished, though a few of the historic roadhouses survive, including Gakona Lodge on the Glenn Highway, Paxson Lodge at the junction of the Richardson and Denali Highways, and Talkeetna Roadhouse. The Cape Nome Roadhouse was a major stopover for dog teams, and also served as a temporary orphanage. Several roadhouses are included in the National Register of Historic Places. Some of these historic roadhouses are now occupied by modern businesses.

Rocks and Gems
(SEE ALSO GOLD; JADE; AND MINERALS AND MINING) Gemstones are not easy to find in Alaska. Rockhounds must hunt for them and often walk quite a distance. The easiest ones to collect are float-rocks that have been scattered by glaciation. These rocks are found on ocean beaches and railroad beds, and in creeks and rivers all over Alaska. In most rock-hunting areas, every instance of high water, wind, heavy rain and a melting patch of snow and ice uncovers a new layer, so you can hunt in the same area over and over and make new finds.

The easiest gemstones to search out are in the crypto-crystalline group of quartz minerals. These gems have crystals not visible to the naked eye. They are the jaspers, agates, cherts and flints.

Thunder eggs, geodes and agatized wood (all in the chalcedony classification) occur in Alaska. Thunder eggs have a jasper rind enclosing an agate core; harder-to-find geodes usually have an agate rind with a hollow core filled with crystals; agatized and petrified woods come in various colors and often show the plant's growth rings. Sometimes even the bark or limb structure is visible on agatized and petrified woods.

Crystalline varieties of quartz can also be found: amethyst (purple), citrine (yellow), rose quartz (pink), rock crystal (clear) and smoky quartz (brown).

Other gems to search for in Alaska are onyx, feldspar, porphyry, jade, serpentine, soapstone, garnet, rhodonite, sapphire, marble, staurolite, malachite and covelite (blue copper).

Russian Alaska
(SEE ALSO BARANOV, ALEXANDER; BERING, VITUS; HISTORY; AND SEWARD, WILLIAM H.) Russian presence in Alaska began with the 1741 voyages of Vitus Bering and Alexei Chirikof. Their exploration of the Aleutian Islands and the Alaska mainland spurred dozens of voyages by Russian fur hunters, or *promyshlenniki*. By the mid-1800s, Russians had explored most of the coast of southern and southwestern Alaska and some of the Interior. Their interest in Alaska lay primarily in exploiting the rich fur resources of the region, especially sea otters and fur seals. In 1799, the Russian post known today as Old Sitka was established. That same year, a trade charter was granted to the Russian-American

Russian Gold

The sea otter was the Golden Fleece which lured . . . Russian Argonauts across the North Pacific to the Aleutians and northwest America. Following the return of the St. Peter [in 1742], the first shipload of adventurers sailed from Kamchatka to Bering Island, returning with a cargo of 1,600 sea otters, 2,000 fur seals, and 2,000 blue Arctic foxes. Their success started a wild stampede to Alaska, greater than the Klondike gold rush which followed a century and a half later. Shipbuilding became the order of the day, though the Cossacks had no knowledge of naval architecture. Vessels were constructed of unseasoned timbers, hewn with axes from the forest. Rope had to be transported by packhorses from Kikutsk, and provisions purchased from Yakutsk at exorbitant prices. Men braved the stormy ocean in flatboats and barges and crude shitikus, native scows made of green planks held together with reindeer hide thongs instead of nails. The makeshift vessels were overcrowded, and so unseaworthy that they foundered at the first heavy gale. . . . Crews vanished without a trace in the fog . . . navigation was by guess or by God. Countless numbers were lost at sea, or starved to death on the shore of some barren island, but the fever of adventure gripped them, and they forgot all caution in their lust for the velvet booty.
—Corey Ford, *Where the Sea Breaks Its Back*

Company, a monopoly authorized by the czar in 1790 to control activities in Alaska.

During the entire Russian period, which lasted from 1741 to 1867, there were rarely more than about 500 Russians in Alaska at any one time. Nevertheless, the Aleut, Eskimo and Indians whom the Russians encountered felt the devastating effects of foreign contact. Native populations declined drastically from introduced diseases. The population of the Aleut people, the first to succumb to Russian occupation, was reduced to less than 20 percent of the precontact level through warfare, disease and starvation. The Tlingit, Haida and Chugach may have been reduced by 50 percent. The Russians also brought to the new land their customs, religion and language, which, through subjugation and the efforts of Orthodox missionaries, brought great changes in traditional technologies, social patterns and religious beliefs.

In 1867, facing increasing competition and frustrated in their efforts to expand its territory, the Russians sold Alaska to the United States for $7.2 million.

One of the foremost legacies of the Russian period is the Russian Orthodox Church, still a vital aspect of Native culture in Southwest, Southcentral and Southeast Alaska. Visitors to Kenai, Kodiak, Sitka and smaller Native communities can see the familiar onion-shaped domes of the Russian Orthodox churches.

School Districts (SEE ALSO EDUCATION)

Alaska's 54 public school districts served approximately 106,500 pre-elementary through 12th grade students in the 1995–96 school year. There are two types of school districts: city and borough school districts and Regional Educational Attendance Areas (REAA). The 34 city and borough school districts are located in municipalities, each contributing funds for the operation of its local schools. The 20 REAAs are located in the unorganized boroughs and have no local government to contribute funds to their schools. The REAAs are almost solely dependent upon state funds for school support. City and borough school districts are supported by about 66 percent state, 23 percent local and 11 percent federal funding.

The Alyeska Central School, Alaska Department of Education, 3134 Channel Drive, No. 100, Juneau 99801-7897, provides courses by correspondence to students in grades K–12.

Following are the names and addresses of Alaska's 54 public school districts:

Adak Region Schools, PSC 486, Box 1234, FPO AP 96506-1234, Intra-Alaska Mail, Adak.

Alaska Gateway Schools, Box 226, Tok 99780.

Aleutian Region Schools, Pouch 790, Unalaska 99685.

Aleutians East Borough Schools, P.O. Box 429, Sand Point 99661-0429.

Anchorage Schools, Box 196614, Anchorage 99519-6614.

Annette Island Schools, Box 7, Metlakatla 99926.

Bering Strait Schools, Box 225, Unalakleet 99684.

Bristol Bay Borough Schools, Box 169, Naknek 99633.

Chatham Schools, Box 109, Angoon 99820.

Chugach Schools, 165 E. 56th Ave., Suite D, Anchorage 99518.

Copper River Schools, Box 108, Glennallen 99588.

Cordova City Schools, Box 140, Cordova 99574-0140.

Craig City Schools, Box 800, Craig 99921.

Delta/Greely Schools, Box 527, Delta Junction 99737.

Denali Borough Schools, Box 280, Healy 99743.

Dillingham City Schools, Box 170, Dillingham 99576.

Fairbanks North Star Borough Schools, 520 Fifth Ave., Fairbanks 99707.

Galena City Schools, Box 299, Galena 99741.

Haines Borough Schools, Box 1289, Haines 99827.

Hoonah City Schools, Box 157, Hoonah 99829.

Hydaburg City Schools, Box 109, Hydaburg 99922.

Iditarod Area Schools, Box 90, McGrath 99627.

Juneau City Schools, 10014 Crazy Horse Drive, Juneau 99801.

Kake City Schools, Box 450, Kake 99830.

Kashunamiut School District, 985 KSD Way, Chevak 99563.

Kenai Peninsula Borough Schools, 148 N. Binkley St., Soldotna 99669.

Ketchikan Gateway Borough Schools, Pouch Z, Ketchikan 99901.

Klawock City Schools, Box 9, Klawock 99925.

Kodiak Island Borough Schools, 722 Mill Bay Road, Kodiak 99615.

Kuspuk Schools, Box 49, Aniak 99557.

Lake and Peninsula Schools, Box 498, King Salmon 99613.

Lower Kuskokwim Schools, Box 305, Bethel 99559.

Lower Yukon Schools, Box 32089, Mountain Village 99632.

Matanuska–Susitna Borough Schools, 125 W. Evergreen, Palmer 99645.

Nenana City Schools, Box 10, Nenana 99760.

Nome City Schools, Box 131, Nome 99762.

North Slope Borough Schools, Box 169, Barrow 99723.

Northwest Arctic Borough Schools, Box 51, Kotzebue 99752.

Pelican City Schools, Box 90, Pelican 99832.

Petersburg City Schools, Box 289, Petersburg 99833.

Pribilof Schools, Pouch 5, St. Paul Island 99660.

St. Marys School District, Box 171, St. Marys 99658.

Sitka Borough Schools, Box 179, Sitka 99835.

Skagway City Schools, Box 497, Skagway 99840.

Anchorage disc jockeys Radio Phill and Christina Campbell announced on April Fools' Day that Arnold Schwarzenegger was in town to blow up the abandoned eyesore McKay building in downtown Anchorage for a feature action film. Almost 100 people showed up to watch.

Southeast Island Schools, Box 8340, Ketchikan 99901.

Southwest Region Schools, Box 90, Dillingham 99576.

Tanana Schools, Box 89, Tanana 99777.

Unalaska City Schools, Pouch 260, Unalaska 99685.

Valdez City Schools, Box 398, Valdez 99686.

Wrangell City Schools, Box 2319, Wrangell 99929.

Yakutat City Schools, Box 427, Yakutat 99689.

Yukon Flats Schools, Box 359, Fort Yukon 99740.

Yukon/Koyukuk Schools, Box 309, Nenana 99760.

Yupiit Schools, Box 100, Akiachak 99551.

Seward, William H.

(SEE ALSO RUSSIAN ALASKA) William H. Seward, the man who negotiated the purchase of Alaska from Russia, was born in New York in 1801. He was admitted to the bar in 1822 and eventually became governor of New York for two terms (declining a third). Seward returned to his law practice until 1849, when he was elected to the United States Senate and served for two terms. In 1860 Seward was a candidate for the presidential nomination, but failing to receive it, he then supported Lincoln, whose cabinet he entered as secretary of state, a position he held from 1861 to 1869.

Due to the rapidly declining fur trade and the economizing and streamlining of the St. Petersburg regime, operations such as the Russian-America Company were deemed expendable. The Grand Duke Constantine urged the sale of Alaska to the United States in 1857, but the American Civil War in 1861 forestalled talks.

At the conclusion of the war, the czar's representative began immediate negotiations with Secretary of State Seward, who was eager to buy, and a selling price of $7.2 million was agreed upon—about 2 cents an acre. The sale was finalized on April 4, 1867. Angry newspaper editorials denounced the acquisition of the apparently worthless real estate and ridiculed the agreement as "Seward's folly," and caricatured Alaska as "Walrussia" and "Seward's icebox." After leaving office in 1869, Seward traveled around the world; he died in 1872.

Shipping Vehicles. Persons
shipping vehicles between Washington and Anchorage are advised to shop around for the carrier that offers the services and rates most suited to the shipper's needs. Not all carriers offer year-round service, and freight charges vary greatly depending upon the carrier and the weight and height of the vehicle. Rates quoted here are only approximate. Sample fares per unit: northbound, Washington to Anchorage, under 66 inches in height, $1,030.33; over 66 inches and under 87 inches, $1,317.98. Southbound, Anchorage to Washington, any unit under 84 inches, $730.27. Fuel surcharges and terminal handling charges may be applied.

Not all carriers accept rented moving trucks and trailers, and a few of those that do accept them require authorization from the rental company to carry its equipment to Alaska. Check with the carrier and your rental company before booking service.

Make your reservation at least two weeks in advance, and prepare to have the vehicle at the carrier's loading facility two days prior to sailing. Carriers differ on what items they allow to travel inside the vehicle, from nothing at all to goods packaged and addressed separately. Coast Guard regulations forbid the transport of vehicles holding more than one-quarter tank of gas, and none of the carriers listed allows owners to accompany their vehicles in transit. *Remember to have fresh antifreeze installed in your car or truck prior to sailing.*

At a lesser rate, you can ship your vehicle aboard a state ferry to southeastern ports. However, you must accompany your vehicle or arrange for someone to drive it on and off the ferry at departure and arrival ports.

Carriers that will ship cars, truck campers, house trailers and motor homes from Anchorage to Seattle/Tacoma include:

The Alaska Railroad, P.O. Box 107500, Anchorage 99510; (907) 265-2490.

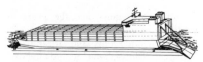

Sea-Land Freight Service, Inc., 1717 Tidewater Ave., Anchorage 99501; (907) 274-2671, or vehicle rates hotline (907) 263-5900.

Totem Ocean Trailer Express, 2511 Tidewater Ave., Anchorage 99501; (907) 276-5868.

In the Seattle/Tacoma area, contact: **A.A.D.A. Systems,** P.O. Box 2323, Auburn, WA 98071; (206) 762-7840.

Alaska Railroad, 2203 Airport Way S., Suite 215, Seattle, WA 98134; (206) 624-4234.

Sea-Land Service, Inc., 3600 Port of Tacoma Road, Tacoma, WA 98424; (206) 922-3100, or (800) 426-4512 (outside Washington state).

Totem Ocean Trailer Express, P.O. Box 24908, Seattle, WA 98124; (206) 628-9280 or (800) 426-0074 (outside Washington, Alaska and Hawaii).

Vehicle shipment between southeastern Alaska ports and Seattle is provided by: **Alaska Marine Lines,** 5615 W. Marginal Way SW, Seattle, WA 98106; (206) 763-4244 or (800) 443-4343 (serves Ketchikan, Wrangell, Petersburg, Sitka, Juneau, Haines, Skagway, Yakutat, Excursion Inlet and Hawk Inlet).

Boyer Alaska Barge Line, 7318 Fourth Ave. S., Seattle, WA 98108; (206) 763-8575 (serves Ketchikan and Wrangell).

For shipping to bush areas: **Alaska Bush Service,** Box 190827, Anchorage 99519; (907) 344-6690.

Household Goods and Personal Effects.

Many moving van lines have service to and from Alaska through their agency connections in most Alaska and Lower 48 cities. To initiate service, contact the van line agents nearest your starting point.

Northbound goods are shipped to Seattle and transferred through a port agent to a waterborne vessel for transportation to Alaska. Few shipments go over the road to Alaska. Southbound shipments are processed in a like manner through Alaska ports to Seattle, then on to the destination.

Haul-it-yourself companies provide service to Alaska for those who prefer to move their goods themselves. It is possible to ship a rented truck or trailer into southeastern Alaska aboard the carriers that accept privately owned vehicles (*see* Vehicles, *preceding*). A few of the carriers sailing between Seattle and Anchorage also carry rented equipment. However, shop around for this service, for it has not been common practice in the past—rates can be very high if the carrier does not yet have a specific tariff established for this type of shipment. *You will not be allowed to accompany the rented equipment.*

Sitka

The town of Sitka (population 8,632), one of the most scenic of Southeast Alaska's cities, is located on the west side of Baranof Island in the shadow of Mount Edgecumbe, about 95 miles southwest of Juneau.

Tlingit Indians originally occupied the townsite until Alexander Baranov, chief manager of the Russian-American Company, built a trading post and fort in 1799 just north of their settlement. The Indians burned down the fort, and in 1804 Baranov defeated the alliance of local Tlingits, driving them from their settlement and naming the site New Archangel Bay. By 1810, New Archangel was thriving as the capital of Russian Alaska. New Archangel was later renamed Sitka, meaning "by the sea" in the Tlingit language.

Today, tourism and commercial fishing are the mainstays of the town's economy.

The climate of Sitka is mild and wet, with an annual precipitation of 95 inches and an average daily temperature of 33°F in January and 55°F in July.

Among the many sights to visit in Sitka are Castle Hill, where Russia turned Alaska over to the United States in 1867; the Sitka Pioneers' Home (the first of six Pioneers' Homes built in Alaska); and Sitka National Historical Park, which reflects both the community's Tlingit heritage and its Russian past with two units: the Fort Site and the Russian Bishop's House. A replica of the old Russian Blockhouse, the original Russian Bishop's House (built in 1842) and the Indian Fort Site are preserved as part of the Sitka National Historical Park and are open to the public.

Visitors can see Sitka's historical roots in St. Michael's Cathedral, which contains priceless icons saved from a devastating fire that destroyed the cathedral in 1966 and was rebuilt from the original plans. The Sheldon Jackson Museum boasts the finest collection of Native arts and crafts in Alaska.

Located within walking distance from downtown Sitka is the Alaska Raptor Rehabilitation Center, offering self-guided or guided interpretive tours. The facility treats injured birds of prey so they can return to the wild.

Annual events include the Sitka Summer Music Festival, which draws international artists, and the Island Institute Writers' Conference in June. Alaska Day Celebration in October celebrates the transfer of Alaska from the Russians.

Contact the Sitka Convention and Visitors Bureau, Box 1226, Sitka 99835; (907) 747-5940, for more information.

Sitka Slippers

Also known as Alaska tennis shoes, Wrangell sneakers or Petersburg sneakers, Sitka slippers are heavy-duty rubber boots worn by residents of rainy southeastern Alaska.

Skagway (SEE ALSO CHILKOOT

TRAIL) Skagway, population 767, is found at the north end of Taiya Inlet on Lynn Canal in Southeast Alaska, about 90 air miles north of Juneau. The climate at Skagway averages 57°F in summer, 23°F in winter and the city has an annual precipitation of about 30 inches. Skagway serves as a gateway to the Alaska Highway in Southeast Alaska.

86
years ago

Darkness fell for three days on the Alaska Peninsula when the volcano named Mount Novarupta erupted on June 6, 1912, spewing 6 cubic miles of earth into the sky. Nearly 2 feet of ash fell on Kodiak, collapsing buildings and polluting water supplies.

Skagway began as a gold-rush town, springing up overnight as fortune-seekers made their way from Skagway, up the White Pass and Chilkoot Trails, to the Yukon gold fields.

In July 1897, Skagway was little more than a tent town. Within months, the town swelled to a population of more than 20,000, with dance halls and gambling houses, saloons and residences. Skagway was described as "hell on earth." Two years later the Klondike gold rush was over, and by 1903 Skagway's population had dwindled to 500 souls.

Today, tourism is Skagway's main economic activity. As a port, the town serves the Alaska State Ferry and many cruise ships, which bring more than 400,000 passengers each summer.

Skagway celebrations include the Buckwheat Ski Classic and an annual Windfest in March, and the Klondike Trail of '98 Road Relay from Skagway to Whitehorse in September.

Visitors can walk Skagway's historical district, with the false-fronted buildings and boardwalks of the Klondike Gold Rush National Historical Park. Other attractions include the Trail of '98 Museum and *The Days of 1898 Show with Soapy Smith*, which relates the history of the town in the days of one of its most notorious con men.

Prepared hikers can climb the 33-mile Chilkoot Trail, the historic route of the gold seekers over 3,739-foot Chilkoot Pass to Lake Bennett. Relics are still visible along the trail.

For more information on Skagway, write the Skagway Convention and Visitors Bureau, Box 415, Skagway 99840; (907) 983-2854.

Skiing Both cross-country and

downhill skiing are popular forms of outdoor recreation in Alaska from November through May. There are developed ski facilities in several Alaska communities, backcountry powder skiing is available by charter helicopter or ski-equipped aircraft and cross-country skiing opportunities are virtually limitless throughout the state. It is also possible to ski during the summer months by chartering a plane to reach glacier skiing spots.

Several cross-country ski races are held each year. The largest, the Alaska Nordic Ski Cup Series, determines contestants for the Arctic Winter Games and Junior Olympic competitions. The series of five races is held in Anchorage, Homer, Salcha and Fairbanks. The World Masters Cross Country Ski Championships were held in Anchorage in February 1992, and Valdez is now home to the World Extreme Ski Championships in April.

In the 1992 Winter Olympics, Hilary Lindh of Juneau turned all eyes to the state of Alaska when she won the silver medal for the downhill. This was the first individual-merit Olympic medal ever won by an Alaskan.

"Moe-mania" struck the state when Alaskan Tommy Moe captured the gold medal in the downhill and silver in the super-giant slalom at the 1994 Olympics in Lillehammer, Norway.

Anchorage. There are two major downhill ski areas in the Anchorage area: Alyeska Resort and Alpenglow at Arctic Valley. Alyeska Resort, 40 miles southeast of Anchorage, is the state's largest ski resort, offering five chairlifts with runs up to a mile long. Chair No. 3 is equipped for night skiing, and a fifth chairlift is reserved for racer training. The resort also has two rope tows and cross-country skiing.

Alyeska Prince Hotel, a seven-story, 300-room structure that opened in August 1994, includes six restaurants, an indoor pool, exercise and health facilities, and meeting rooms. The resort features a new, high-speed gondola capable of carrying 60 passengers at a time to a restaurant high on the slopes.

Alyeska is open year-round, with skiing from November through April and sight-seeing during the summer. Hours of operation depend on daylight, except for chair No. 3.

Alpenglow, a few miles from Anchorage, is owned and operated by the Anchorage Ski Club, a nonprofit corporation. Arctic Valley is open on winter weekends and holidays. Facilities include two double chairlifts, a T-bar/Poma lift combination and three rope tows on beginner slopes.

Several smaller alpine slopes maintained by the municipality of Anchorage include: Far North Bicentennial Park; Russian Jack Springs Park, with rope tows; and Hilltop, south of town, featuring the closest chairlift to the Anchorage area.

There are several popular cross-country ski trails in the Anchorage area in city parks that are maintained by the municipality. These include Russian Jack Springs, with nearly 5 miles of trails, all lighted; Kincaid Park, site of the first World Cup and U.S. National races in Alaska and the United States in March 1983, with 24 miles of trails, 6 miles lighted, and a warm-up chalet; Far North Bicentennial Park, with 3 miles of trails, about 2 miles lighted; Hillside Park, with 10.8 miles of trails, 1.5 miles lighted; Tony Knowles Coastal Trail, with 9 miles of trails, none lighted; and Chester Creek Greenbelt, with 6.2 miles of trails, none lighted.

Cross-country skiers also can find trails in Chugach State Park; in Hatcher Pass north of Anchorage and in the Turnagain Pass area; in Chugach National Forest, about 57 miles south of Anchorage; and at Sheep Mountain Lodge along the Glenn Highway. For information, contact the Nordic Skiing Association, (907) 561-0949.

Cordova. The Sheridan Ski Club operates the Mount Eyak Ski Hill about seven blocks from downtown Cordova. The season starts in December and extends until April, depending on snow conditions.

Fairbanks. Fairbanks has a few down-hill ski areas, but none as large as Alyeska Resort. Cleary Summit and Skiland, about

20 miles from town on the Steese Highway, both privately owned and operated, have rope tows, with a chairlift at Cleary Summit; Ski Boot Hill at Mile 4.2 on Farmer's Loop Road has a rope tow; Birch Hill, located on Fort Wainwright, is mainly for military use; the University of Alaska has a small slope and rope tow; and Chena Hot Springs Resort at Mile 57 on the Chena Hot Springs Road has a small alpine ski area that uses a tractor to transport skiers to the top of the hill.

Popular cross-country ski trails in the Fairbanks area include Birch Hill recreation area, about 3 miles north of town on the Steese Expressway to a well-marked turnoff, then 2 miles in; the University of Alaska Fairbanks, with 26 miles of trails that lead out to Ester Dome; Creamers Field trail near downtown; Salcha cross-country ski area, about 40 miles south of town on the Richardson Highway, with a fairly large trail system also used for ski races; Two Rivers trail area, near the elementary school at Mile 10 on the Chena Hot Springs Road; and Chena Hot Springs Resort, offering cross-country ski trails for both novice and more experienced skiers.

Southeast. Eaglecrest Ski Area on Douglas Island, 12 miles from Juneau, has a 4,800-foot-long chairlift, a Platter Pull lift, a 3,000-foot-long chairlift and a day lodge. Cross-country ski trails are also available. Eaglecrest is open from November to May. A few smaller alpine ski areas are located at Cordova, Valdez, Ketchikan and Homer. All have rope tows.

Kenai Peninsula. Most communities on the lower Kenai have trails or areas for skiing, including Anchor Point, Seldovia and Ninilchik. The best concentration of trails and slopes for Nordic, backcountry and downhill skiing exist in the Homer area. Among them are Baycrest–Diamond Ridge, Homestead Trail, Ohlson Mountain and McNeil Canyon. Skiing on glaciers (accessible by helicopter) is possible in the Kenai Mountains across Kachemak Bay

from Homer. Ski-joring (cross-country with a dog towing you) is increasingly popular in Homer.

Palmer. Hatcher Pass, site of the Independence Mine State Park, north of Palmer, is an excellent cross-country ski area with several maintained trails. The lodge has a coffee shop and warm-up area. The ski area is open from October through May.

Skin Sewing (SEE ALSO BEAD-WORK; MUKLUKS; AND PARKA)

The craft of sewing tanned hides and furs was a highly developed skill among Alaska's Natives. Although commercially made garments are now often worn by Eskimo villagers, women who are exceptional skin sewers still not only ensure the safety of family members who must face the harsh outdoors, but are regarded as a source of pride for the entire community.

Sewers place great importance on the use of specific materials, some of which are only available seasonally. For instance, winter-bleached sealskin can only be tanned during certain seasons. Blood, alder bark and red ochre are traditionally used for dyeing garments and footgear. Most sewers prefer sinew as thread, although in some areas sinew cannot be obtained and waxed thread or dental floss is substituted. Skins commonly used for making parkas and mukluks include seal, reindeer, caribou and ground squirrel. Wolf and wolverine are prized for ruffs.

An otter eats 25 percent of its body weight per day. If a 100-pound adult dines on its favorite Dungeness crab at the current market price of $6.95 per pound, it would need an annual income of $63,418.75, without counting melted butter, lemon, or a delicate little Semillon blanc.

Parka styles, materials used and ornamentation (such as pieced calfskin or beadwork trim) vary from village to village, and among Athabascan, Yupik, Inupiat and Siberian Yupik sewers. The cut of parkas changes from north to south.

In most regions, mukluk styles and material vary with changes in season and weather conditions. The mukluks advertise the skill of their makers and the villages where they were made.

The manufacture of moccasins and children's toys, primarily clothed dolls and intricately sewn balls, still reflects the traditional ingenuity of skin sewers.

Skookum
Skookum is a word meaning strong or serviceable. It originated with the Chehalis Indians of western Washington and was incorporated into the Chinook jargon, a trade language dating from the early 1800s.

A skookum chuck is a narrow passage between a saltwater lagoon and the open sea. In many areas of Alaska, because of extreme tides, skookum chucks may resemble fast-flowing river rapids during changes of the tide.

Soapstone
This soft, easily worked stone is often carved into art objects by Alaskans. Most of the stone, however, is imported. Alaska soapstone is mined in the Matanuska Valley by blasting. This process creates in the stone a tendency to fracture when being worked; therefore, it is not as desirable as imported soapstone.

Sourdough
Carried by many early-day pioneers, this versatile, yeasty

Alaska Sourdough Starter

Sourdough is a subject of much intrigue and debate here in the North. For a true sourdough, you should rely on naturally occurring yeast and lactobacilli in your kitchen. For a quicker version of sourdough, add a packet of active dry yeast to the following recipe, but it won't be a true sourdough.

Ingredients: 2 cups all-purpose flour and 2 cups warm distilled water

Mix the two ingredients in a glass or ceramic bowl or a plastic pitcher. (Never use metal when working with yeast.) Cover with cheesecloth and let the mixture rest in a warm, draft-free place in the kitchen for 48 hours. The mixture should be the consistency of pancake batter, slightly bubbly, and sour smelling. Stir the mixture and store, covered, in the refrigerator. Makes 2 cups.

Care and Feeding of a Sourdough Starter: Once you've made a sourdough starter, you can keep it going indefinitely.

Store your starter in the refrigerator, using any covered glass, ceramic or plastic container. To use the starter, remove as much from the container as you need and let it stand at room temperature until bubbly, about 1 hour. Replenish your starter by adding equal amounts of flour and water.

Feed your starter once every two weeks to a month. Do this by adding 1 cup each of flour and water to the starter. If you need a great deal of starter, increase its volume by adding up to 10 cups of flour per cup of starter and an equal amount of water. Let stand for 48 hours.

If a liquid forms on top of the sourdough, simply stir it back in. If the liquid becomes any color besides straw yellow, discard the sourdough.

Sourdough starter can be frozen for several months. The longer it is frozen, the more likely it is that changes will occur in bacterial cell structure. To use, remove the frozen sourdough from the freezer, thaw, replenish, and keep at room temperature for 24 hours.—Kirsten Dixon, The Riversong Lodge Cookbook

starter was used to make bread, doughnuts and hotcakes. Sourdough cookery remains popular in Alaska today. Because the sourdough supply is replenished after each use, it can remain active and fresh indefinitely. A popular claim of sourdough cooks is that their batches trace back to pioneers at the turn of the century. The name also came to be applied to any Alaska or Yukon old-timer.

Speed Limits

The basic speed law in Alaska states the speed limit is "no speed more than is prudent and reasonable."

The maximum speeds are 15 miles per hour in an alley, 20 miles per hour in a business district or school zone, 25 miles per hour in a residential area and 55 miles per hour on most roadways. The speed limit on portions of the Parks and Glenn Highways is 65 miles per hour.

Locally, municipalities and the state may, and often do, reduce or alter maximums as long as no maximum exceeds 55 miles per hour.

Squaw Candy

Squaw candy is salmon that has been dried or smoked for a long time until it's very chewy. It's a staple food in winter for rural Alaskans and their dogs. Contemporary terms for this food are "salmon jerky" or "strips."

State Forest

Created in 1983, the 1.81-million-acre Tanana Valley State Forest is located almost entirely within the Tanana River basin and includes 200 miles of the Tanana River. It extends from near the Canadian border approximately 265 miles west to Manley Hot Springs, encompasses areas as far south as Tok, and is interspersed with private and other state lands throughout the basin. The Bonanza Creek Experimental Forest near Nenana is located within the state forest.

Hardwood and hardwood-spruce trees dominate almost 90 percent of the forest, and 22 percent (392,000 acres) is suitable

for harvest. There are 44 rivers, streams and lakes within the forest with significant fish, wildlife, recreation and water values. Nearly all of the land will remain open for mineral development.

Approximately 85 percent of the forest is located within 20 miles of a highway, making it one of the more accessible public lands in the Interior. Rivers and trails throughout the river basin provide additional access to areas in the forest. The Eagle Trail State Recreation Site is the only developed facility in the Tanana Valley State Forest and has 40 campsites. For more information, contact the Regional Forester, Northcentral District, 3726 Airport Way, Fairbanks 99701.

State Park System

The Alaska State Park system began in July 1959 with the transfer of federally managed campgrounds and recreation sites from the Bureau of Land Management to the new state of Alaska. Since October 1970, these sites have been managed by the Division of Parks and Outdoor Recreation.

The Alaska State Park system consists of 132 individual units divided into seven park management areas. There are 46 recreation sites, 17 recreation areas, 6 historic parks, 3 historic sites, 2 state trails, 8 state parks (Afognak Island, Chugach, Denali, Chilkat, Kachemak Bay, Point Bridget, Shuyak Island and Wood-Tikchik), 1 wilderness park, 1 special management area, 1 preserve and 35 marine parks. The Kenai River Special Management Area is renowned for its salmon fishing. The 49,000-acre Chilkat Bald Eagle Preserve has the world's largest concentration of bald eagles. Wood-Tikchik State Park is Alaska's most remote state park and, with 1.5 million acres of wilderness, is the largest contiguous state park in the United States. All told, Alaska's State Park system embraces more than 3 million acres and hosts 5 million visitors a year.

Campsites are available on a first-come,
(Continued on page 204)

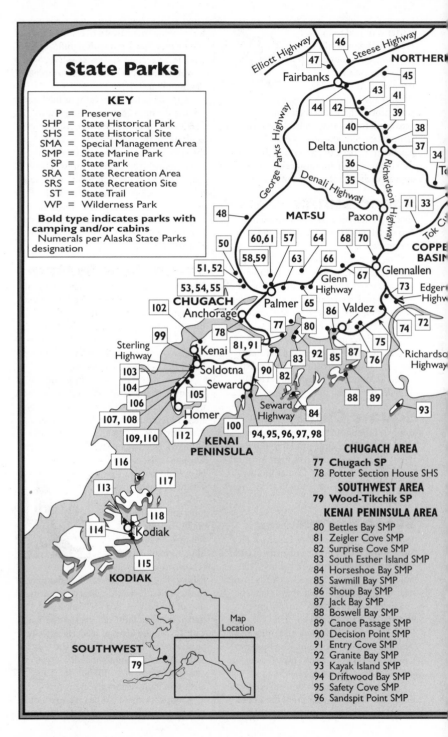

State Parks

KEY

P = Preserve
SHP = State Historical Park
SHS = State Historical Site
SMA = Special Management Area
SMP = State Marine Park
SP = State Park
SRA = State Recreation Area
SRS = State Recreation Site
ST = State Trail
WP = Wilderness Park

Bold type indicates parks with camping and/or cabins
Numerals per Alaska State Parks designation

Elliott Highway
Steese Highway
NORTHER
Fairbanks
George Parks Highway
Delta Junction
Richardson Highway
Denali Highway
Paxon
Tok C
COPPE
BASIN
MAT-SU
Glenn Highway
Glennallen
Edger
Highw
CHUGACH
Palmer
Valdez
Anchorage
Sterling Highway
Kenai
Soldotna
Richardso
Highway
Seward
Seward Highway
Homer
KENAI PENINSULA
SOUTHWEST
Map Location
Kodiak
KODIAK

CHUGACH AREA

77 **Chugach SP**
78 Potter Section House SHS

SOUTHWEST AREA

79 **Wood-Tikchik SP**

KENAI PENINSULA AREA

80 Bettles Bay SMP
81 Zeigler Cove SMP
82 Surprise Cove SMP
83 South Esther Island SMP
84 Horseshoe Bay SMP
85 Sawmill Bay SMP
86 Shoup Bay SMP
87 Jack Bay SMP
88 Boswell Bay SMP
89 Canoe Passage SMP
90 Decision Point SMP
91 Entry Cove SMP
92 Granite Bay SMP
93 Kayak Island SMP
94 Driftwood Bay SMP
95 Safety Cove SMP
96 Sandspit Point SMP

SOUTHEAST AREA

1 Totem Bight SHP
2 Refuge Cove SRS
3 Settlers Cove SRS
4 Pioneer Park SRS
5 Baranof Castle SHS
6 Halibut Point SRS
7 Old Sitka SHP
8 Juneau Trail Sys. ST
9 Johnson Creek SRS
10 Wickersham SHS
11 Point Bridget SP
12 Chilkoot Lake SRS
13 Portage Cove SRS
14 Chilkat SP
15 Chilkat Bald Eagle P
16 Mosquito Lake SRS
17 Gruening SHP
18 Dall Bay SMP

19 Thom's Place SMP
20 Beecher Pass SMP
21 Joe Mace Island SMP
22 Security Bay SMP
23 Taku Harbor SMP
24 Oliver Inlet SMP
25 Funter Bay SMP
26 Shelter Island SMP
27 St. James Bay SMP
28 Sullivan Island SMP
29 Chilkat Islands SMP
30 Magoun Islands SMP
31 Big Bear/Baby Bear SMP
49 Grindall Island SMP
56 Black Sands Beach SMP
62 Eagle Beach SRA

NORTHERN AREA

32 Tok River SRS
33 Eagle Trail SRS
34 Moon Lake SRS
35 Fielding Lake SRS
36 Donnelly Creek SRS
37 Clearwater SRS
38 Delta SRS

39 Big Delta SHP
40 Quartz Lake SRA
41 Birch Lake SRS
42 Harding Lake SRA
43 Salcha River SRS
44 Chena River SRS
45 Chena River SRA
46 Upper Chatanika River SRS
47 Lower Chatanika River SRA

MAT-SU/COPPER BASIN AREA

48 Denali SP
50 Willow Creek SRA
51 Nancy Lake SRA
52 Nancy Lake SRS
53 Rocky Lake SRS
54 Big Lake North SRS
55 Big Lake South SRS
57 Kepler-Bradley Lakes SRA
58 Finger Lake SRS
59 Wolf Lake SRS
60 Independence Mine SHP
61 Summit Lake SRS
63 King Mountain SRS
64 Bonnie Lake SRS
65 Long Lake SRS
66 Matanuska Glacier SRS
67 Little Nelchina SRS
68 Lake Louise SRA
70 Dry Creek SRS
71 Porcupine Creek SRS
72 Liberty Falls SRS
73 Squirrel Creek SRS
74 Little Tonsina SRS
75 Worthington Glacier SRS
76 Blueberry Lake SRS

97 Sunny Cove SMP
98 Thumb Cove SMP
99 Kenai River SMA
100 Caines Head SRA
102 Captain Cook SRA
103 Crooked Creek SRA
104 Kasilof River SRS
105 Johnson Lake SRA
106 Clam Gulch SRA
107 Ninilchik SRA
108 Deep Creek SRA
109 Stariski SRS
110 Anchor River SRA
112 Kachemak Bay SP&WP

KODIAK AREA

113 Fort Abercrombie SHP
114 Buskin River SRS
115 Pasagshak SRS
116 Shuyak Island SP
117 Afognak Island SP
118 Woody Island SRS

UNITED STATES
CANADA

Alaska Highway

Klondike Highway 2

Haines Highway

15 16 Skagway
12
13 11
Haines
14 28 62
29 8, 9, 10, 17
27 26 Juneau
23
25
24
4, 5, 6, 7
31 Sitka
30 22
20
Wrangell
19 1, 2, 3
21
SOUTHEAST
49 Ketchikan
56
18

(Continued from page 201)
first-served basis usually for $6, $8 or $10 per night. Fee exceptions are Eagle River Campground (Chugach State Park) and Chena River State Recreation Site for $15, and Byers Lake Campground (Denali State Park) for $12. Daily use of improved boat launches is $5. Use of sanitary dump stations is $5. These are located at Chena River SRS, Harding Lake SRA, Big Delta SHP, Eagle River Campground (Chugach SP) and Ninilchick SRA. There is free use of the dump station at Buskin River SRS. A daily parking fee of $3 to $5 is charged at selected park units. A yearly camping pass is also available for $75 for residents; $200 for nonresidents. A yearly boat launch pass is $75. A yearly parking pass is $25. A nonresident may purchase all three passes for $275, a discount of $25. An Alaska resident may purchase all three passes for $160, a discount of $15. A second pass of any kind may be purchased for a discount to the same resident family living at the same address. Second-pass prices are: camping, $40; boat launch, $40; daily parking, $15.

In addition to camping and picnicking, many units offer hiking trails, boating and fishing, as well as winter activities. Most developed campgrounds have picnic tables, firepits, water and latrines. General information on the state park system is available from Alaska State Park Information, 3601 C St., Suite 200, Anchorage 99503-5929.

State park units are managed by seven area offices and are listed below. (*See* map on pages 202–3)

Alaskans have the highest median household income in the nation, and are the second-highest per capita consumers of SPAM®!

Southeast Area, 400 Willoughby Building, Juneau 99801.
Northern Area, 3700 Airport Way, Fairbanks 99709.
Mat-Su/Valdez-Copper River Area, HC 32, Box 6706, Wasilla 99687.
Chugach/Southwest Area, HC 52, Box 8999, Indian 99540.
Kenai Peninsula Area, P.O. Box 1247, Soldotna 99669.
Kodiak Area, SR Box 3800, Kodiak 99615.
Southwest Area, 3601 C St., Suite 1200, Anchorage 99503.

State Symbols Flag.

Alaska's state flag was designed in 1926 by Benny Benson, a seventh-grade Aleut student who entered his design in a territorial flag contest. The Alaska Legislature adopted his design as the official flag of the Territory of Alaska on May 2, 1927.

The flag consists of eight gold stars—the Big Dipper and the North Star—on a field of blue. In Benny Benson's words, "The blue field is for the Alaska sky and the forget-me-not, an Alaska flower. The North Star is for the future state of Alaska, the most northerly of the Union. The Great Bear—symbolizing strength."

Alaska was proclaimed the 49th state of the Union on Jan. 3, 1959. The drafters of the constitution for Alaska stipulated that the flag of the territory would be the official flag of the state of Alaska. When the flag was first flown over the capital city on July 4, 1959, Benny Benson proudly led the parade that preceded the ceremony, carrying the flag of eight stars on a field of blue, which he had designed 33 years before.

Seal. The first governor of Alaska designed a seal for the then-District of Alaska in 1884. In 1910, Gov. Walter E. Clark redesigned the original seal, which became a symbol for the new Territory of Alaska in 1912. The constitution of Alaska adopted the territorial seal as the seal for the state of Alaska in 1959.

Represented in the state seal are icebergs, northern lights, mining, agriculture, fisheries, fur seal rookeries and a railroad. The seal is 2¹/₈ inches in diameter.

Song. *Alaska's Flag*
Eight stars of gold on a field of blue—
Alaska's flag.
May it mean to you the blue of the sea, the
evening sky,
The mountain lakes, and the flow'rs nearby;
The gold of the early sourdough's dreams,
The precious gold of the hills and streams;
The brilliant stars in the northern sky,
The "Bear"—the "Dipper"—and, shining
high,
The great North Star with its steady light,
Over land and sea a beacon bright.
Alaska's flag—to Alaskans dear,
The simple flag of a last frontier.

© University of Alaska

The lyrics were written by Marie Drake as a poem that first appeared on the cover of the October 1935 *School Bulletin,* a territorial Department of Education publication that she edited while assistant commissioner of education.

The music was written by Mrs. Elinor Dusenbury, whose husband, Col. Ralph Wayne Dusenbury, was commander of Chilkoot Barracks at Haines from 1933 to 1936. Mrs. Dusenbury wrote the music several years after leaving Alaska because, she was later quoted as saying, "I got so homesick for Alaska I couldn't stand it." She died Oct. 17, 1980, in Carlsbad, California.

The territorial legislature adopted *Alaska's Flag* as the official song in 1955.

Other State Symbols. Bird—Willow ptarmigan, *Lagopus lagopus,* a small arctic grouse that lives among willows and on open tundra and muskeg. Its plumage changes from brown in summer to white in winter; feathers develop in winter to cover the entire lower leg and foot. Common from southwestern Alaska into the Arctic. Adopted in 1955.

Fish—King salmon, *Oncorhynchus tshawytscha,* an important part of the Native subsistence fisheries and a significant species to the state's commercial salmon fishery. This anadromous fish ranges from beyond the southern extremes of Alaska to as far north as Point Hope. Adopted in 1962.

Flower—Forget-me-not (*Myosotis alpestris*). Adopted in 1949.

Fossil—Woolly mammoth. Adopted in 1986.

Gem—Jade. Adopted in 1968. (*See* Jade)

Insect—Four-spot skimmer dragonfly. Adopted in 1995.

Marine Mammal—Bowhead whale. Adopted in 1983. (*See* Whales and Whaling)

Mineral—Gold. Adopted in 1968. (*See* Gold)

Motto—North to the Future. Adopted in 1967.

Sport—Dog mushing. Adopted in 1972. (*See* Dog Mushing)

Tree—Sitka spruce, *Picea sitchensis,* the largest and one of the most valuable trees in Alaska. Sitka spruce grows to 160 feet in height and 3 to 5 feet in diameter. Its long, dark green needles surround twigs that bear cones. It is found throughout Southeast and the Kenai Peninsula, along the Gulf Coast, and along the west coast of Cook Inlet. Adopted in 1962.

Subsistence (SEE ALSO

WHALES AND WHALING) Alaska is unique among states in that it has established the subsistence use of fish and game as the highest-priority consumptive use of the resource. Alaska's legislature passed subsistence priority laws in 1978 and 1986. In addition, Congress passed a priority subsistence law in 1980 for federal lands in Alaska. Studies by the Alaska Department of Fish and Game have shown that many rural communities in Alaska depend upon subsistence hunting and fishing for a large portion of their diets and raw materials.

Subsistence, a controversial issue and a difficult concept to define, is defined by federal law as "the customary and traditional uses by rural Alaska residents of wild, renewable resources for direct personal or family consumption as food, shelter, fuel, clothing, tools or transportation; for the making and selling of handicraft articles out

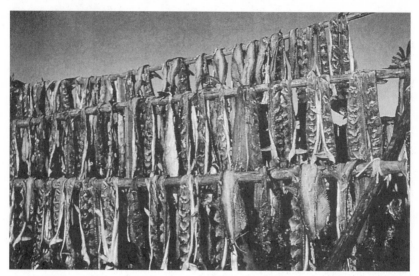

Subsistence fishers often dry fish along a river, then store it for winter. From *The Alaska River Guide* by Karen Jettmar

of nonedible by-products of fish and wild-life resources taken for personal or family consumption; and for the customary trade, barter or sharing for personal or family consumption."

According to the Alaska State Subsistence Statutes passed in 1986, only rural residents can be considered subsistence users. In addition to the rural requirement, subsistence uses can be identified by a variety of other criteria, such as long-term traditional use, local area use and frequent sharing of harvests. Subsistence also depends upon the biological status of fish and game resources, and is not authorized if harvesting will damage the resources.

In December 1989, the Alaska Supreme Court ruled that the rural subsistence preference in the state law was unconstitutional. This placed the state out of compliance with requirements of the federal law. As a result the federal government took over management of subsistence on federal lands in Alaska on July 1, 1990, and began to develop its own set of subsistence regulations. Although the state desires to regain this management authority, no resolution to the issue has been reached.

State subsistence fishing regulations are available as a separate pamphlet from the Alaska Department of Fish and Game,

Sheefish Delicacy

Sheefish, officially known as inconnu and also called Eskimo tarpon, are used as subsistence food for Alaska Natives and their dogs. In summer, sheefish are taken by seine and gill net as they move upstream. In winter, they were traditionally taken through holes in the ice by a jigging stick and hooks made of bear teeth and ivory, but modern rod and reel methods are now used.

Eskimos traditionally ate sheefish raw—but only after a slight preparation. First they buried the fish in leaf-lined pits and aged them for several weeks. They called this dish "stink fish." Its texture is described as cheese-like and its aroma as, well, stinky.—Robert H. Armstrong, *Alaska's Fish*

P.O. Box 25525, Juneau 99802. State subsistence hunting regulations are included with the annually published state hunting regulations, also available from the Alaska Department of Fish and Game.

Sundog
Sundogs are "mock suns" (parhelia) usually seen as bright, rainbow-hued spots on opposite sides of the winter sun. This optical phenomenon is created by the refraction of sunlight through tiny ice crystals suspended in the air. The ice crystals are commonly called "diamond dust."

Taiga
Taiga is a moist coniferous forest that begins where the tundra ends. Taken from a Russian word that means "land of little sticks," this name is applied to the spindly white spruce and black spruce forests found in much of southcentral and interior Alaska.

Telecommunications
History. Alaska's first telecommunications project, begun in the 1860s, was designed to serve New York, San Francisco and the capitals of Europe, not particularly the residents of Nome or Fairbanks. It was part of Western Union's ambitious plan to link California to Russian America (Alaska) with an intercontinental cable that would continue under the Bering Strait to Siberia and on to Europe. Men and material were brought together on both sides of the Bering Sea, but with the first successful Atlantic cable crossing in 1867, the trans-Siberian intercontinental line was abandoned.

The first operational telegraph link in Alaska was laid in September 1900, when 25 miles of line were stretched from military headquarters in Nome to an outpost at Port Safety. It was one part of a $450,000 plan by the Army Signal Corps to connect scattered military posts in the territory with the United States. By the end of 1903, land lines linked western Alaska, Prince William Sound, and interior and southeastern Alaska (where underwater cable was used).

Plagued by ice floes that repeatedly tore loose the underwater cables laid across Norton Sound, the military developed "wireless telegraphy" to span the icy water in 1903. It was the world's first application of radio-telegraph technology and marked the completion of a fragile network connecting all military stations in Alaska with the United States and each other. Sitka, Juneau, Haines and Valdez were connected by a line to Whitehorse, Yukon Territory. Nome, Fort St. Michael, Fort Gibbon (Tanana) and Fort Egbert (Eagle) were linked with Dawson, Yukon Territory. A line from Dawson to Whitehorse continued on to Vancouver, British Columbia, and Seattle.

In 1905, the 1,500 miles of land lines, 2,000 miles of submarine cables and the 107-mile wireless link became the Washington–Alaska Military Cable and Telegraph System. This, in turn, became the Alaska Communications System in 1935, reflecting a shift to greater civilian use and a system relying more heavily on wireless stations than land lines. The Alaska Communications System operated under the Department of Defense until RCA Corporation, through its division RCA Alascom, took control in 1971.

Alascom. Alascom, Inc., is the original long lines carrier for the state. On Oct. 27, 1982, Alascom launched its own telecommunications satellite, *Aurora*, into orbit from Cape Canaveral, Florida. The launching marked several firsts: it was the first telecommunications satellite dedicated to a single state, and it was the first completely solid-state satellite to be placed in orbit.

On May 29, 1991, Alascom launched its second satellite, *Aurora II*, from Cape Canaveral. Designed to replace the original *Aurora*, which had reached the end of its life span, *Aurora II* uses a similar design updated with modern technology to increase its life span.

In January 1997, AT&T began installing an all-digital communication system in rural Alaskan sites served by satellite. This new system eliminates the double satellite hop for most calls, allowing two remote locations to communicate directly without going through a third, "gateway," station. The result of these improvements is less time delay and clear reception on voice calls, plus improved performance for fax, data and Internet services.

Improvements over the past 10 years have made long-distance telephone service available to every community of 25 persons or more in Alaska. Live or same-day television is now available to 90 percent of the state's population.

General Communication Inc.

General Communication Inc. (GCI) provides local and long-distance telephone service to national and international destinations. In 1997, GCI began providing in-state cable television and cellular service to Alaska customers.

The company expects to offer Internet service within the next year.

Telephone Numbers in the Bush
Although most Alaskan bush communities now have full telephone service, a few villages still have only one telephone. For those villages, call the information number, 555-1212. The area code for all of Alaska is 907.

Television Stations

Television in Alaska's larger communities, such as Anchorage and Fairbanks, was available years before satellites were sent into orbit. The first satellite broadcast to the state was Neil Armstrong's moon walk in July 1969. Television reached the bush in the late 1970s with the construction of telephone earth stations that could receive television programming via satellite transmissions. The state funds Alaska Rural Communication Service (ARCS), which broadcasts general

and educational programming to more than 250 rural communities. For more information about ARCS, contact the Department of Administration, Information Services, 5900 E. Tudor Road, Anchorage 99507; (907) 269-5744.

Regular network programming (ABC, CBS, NBC and PBS) from the Lower 48

reaches Alaska on a time-delayed basis through the RATNet system. Most of the stations listed here carry a mixture of network programming, with local broadcasters specifying programming. Some stations, such as KJNP, carry locally produced programming.

Cable television is available from Sitka to Barrow. At least one cable system offers a complete satellite earth station and 24-hour programming. Local television viewing in Bethel, for example, includes Channel 4 (KYUK), which carries ITV programming such as PBS's *NOVA* series, *Sesame Street* and local news; cable Channel 8, which carries regular network programming; and a half-dozen other cable channels carrying specialized programming such as movies, news, weather, sports and specials.

The following list shows the commercial and public television stations in Alaska:

Anchorage. KAKM Channel 7 (public television); 3877 University Drive, 99508.

KCFT (UHF 20/Cable 20); P.O. Box 210830, 99521.

KDMD (Prime Cable 33); Box 143322, 99514.

KIMO Channel 13; 2700 E. Tudor Road, 99507.

KTBY Channel 4; 1840 S. Bragaw, Suite 101, 99508.

KTUU Channel 2; 701 E. Tudor Road, 99503.

KTVA Channel 11; 1007 W. 32nd Ave., 99503.

KYES Channel 5; 3700 Woodland Park Drive, No. 600, 99517.

Alaskans love sewage. At 20.2 percent, Alaska has the greatest percentage of households without complete plumbing. Various waste utilities in the state have adopted mottos like, "It may be sewage to you, but it's bread and butter to me."

Bethel. KYUK Channel 4 (public television); Pouch 468, 99559.

Fairbanks. KATN Channel 2; 516 Second Ave., Suite 400, 99701.
  KFXF Channel 7; 3650 Braddock St., 99701.
  KO7UU Channel 7; 3650 Braddock St., 99701.
  KTVF Channel 11; 3528 International Way, 99701.
  KUAC Channel 9 (public television); University of Alaska, P.O. Box 75560, 99775.
  KXD Channel 13; 3650 Braddock St., 99701.

Juneau. KJUD Channel 8; 1107 W. Eighth St., 99801.
  KTOO Channel 3 (public television); 360 Egan Drive, 99801.

Kenai. UHF Channel 17; P.O. Box 4665, 99611.

Ketchikan. KJMW (Cable 3); 501 Dock St., 99901.

Kodiak. KMXT Channel 9 (independent); 718 Mill Bay Road, 99615.

North Pole. KJNP Channel 4; P.O. Box 56359, 99705.

Sitka. KTNL Channel 13; P.O. Box 1309, 99835.
  KSCT Channel 5; 520 Lake St., 99835.

Unalaska. KO8IW Channel 8 (independent); Box 181, 99685.

Tides (SEE ALSO BORE TIDE) In southeastern Alaska, Prince William Sound, Cook Inlet and Bristol Bay, salt water undergoes extreme daily fluctuations, creating powerful tidal currents. Some bays may go totally dry at low tide.
  The second greatest tide range in North America occurs in upper Cook Inlet near Anchorage, where the maximum diurnal range during spring tides is 38.9 feet. (The greatest tide range in North America is Nova Scotia's Bay of Fundy, with spring tides over 50 feet.)
  Here are diurnal ranges for some coastal communities: Bethel, 4 feet; Cold Bay, 7.1 feet; Cordova, 12.4 feet; Haines, 16.8 feet; Herschel Island, 0.7 feet; Ketchikan, 15.4 feet; Kodiak, 8.5 feet; Naknek River entrance, 22.6 feet; Nikiski, 20.7 feet; Nome, 1.6 feet; Nushagak, 19.6 feet; Point Barrow, 0.4 feet; Port Heiden, 12.3 feet; Port Moller, 10.8 feet; Sand Point, 7.3 feet; Sitka, 9.9 feet; Valdez, 12 feet; Whittier, 12.3 feet; Wrangell, 15.7 feet; Yakutat, 10.1 feet.

Years ago

Russian settlers planted the first trees on the Aleutian Island of Unalaska. Three of the original spruce still survive— surrounded by countless seedlings.

Timber According to the U.S. Forest Service, Anchorage Forestry Sciences Lab, 129 million acres of Alaska's 365 million acres of land surface are forested, 15 million acres of which are classified as timberland. Timberland is defined as forest land capable of producing in excess of 20 cubic feet of industrial wood per acre per year in natural stands and not withdrawn from timber utilization.
  Alaska has two distinct forest ecosystems: the interior forest and the coastal rain forest. The vast interior forest covers 115 million acres, extending from the south slope of the Brooks Range to the Kenai Peninsula, and from Canada to Norton Sound. Nearly 10 million acres of white spruce, paper birch, quaking aspen, black cottonwood and balsam poplar stands are considered timberland, comparing favorably in size and growth with the forests of the lake states of Minnesota, Wisconsin and Michigan. There are an additional 3.4 million acres of forest land capable of producing more than 20 cubic feet per acre per year but are unavailable for harvest because they are in designated parks or wilderness.
  The interior's land management policies and the region's remoteness from large

markets have limited timber use to approximately 20 sawmills, a few of which have estimated capacities of 1 million to 5 million board feet per year, but most cutting less than 300,000 board feet per year. A mill with an estimated capacity of 70 million  board feet per year has been producing intermittently. There are some exports of sawlogs, cants and chips.

The coastal rain forests extend from Cook Inlet to the Alaska–Canada border south of Ketchikan, and they continue to provide the bulk of commercial timber volume in Alaska. Of the 13.7 million acres of forested land, 5 million acres are classified as timberland. An additional 2.6 million acres of timber stands are capable of producing more than 20 cubic feet per acre per year, but are in parks and wilderness and therefore are not available for harvest.

Western hemlock and Sitka spruce provide most of the timber harvest for domestic and export lumber and pulp markets. Western red cedar and Alaska cedar make up most of the balance, along with mountain hemlock, lodgepole pine and other species.

Lands from which substantial volumes of timber are harvested are divided into two distinct categories: privately owned by Native corporations and villages under the 1971 Native Claims Settlement Act, and publicly owned and managed federal, state and borough lands. Timber harvests from publicly owned lands are carried through short- and long-term sales offered by government agencies.

The forest products of Alaska are also divided somewhat along the same lines as land ownership. By federal law, timber harvested from federal lands (more than 85 percent of all timber harvested on public lands) cannot be exported without processing. Consequently, while processors dependent on federal lands produce rough-sawn lumber, pulpwood and chips, the Native corporations primarily produce round logs, which find more buyers along the Pacific Rim, especially Japan. Given that the Alaska forest products industry is almost entirely dependent on the Japanese market, the processing requirement has had considerable effect on some sections of the forest industry. Pulp mills provide a market for wood chips and for lower-quality timber from both public and private lands. A market for this utility wood is critical to all operators.

In 1995, more than 8.8 million board feet of timber were harvested on state lands, adding $250,000 to state revenues. Approximately 82 percent of the harvest was sawtimber. Timber harvested on federal lands was 223 million board feet. Timber exports in 1995 were valued at $572 million.

Time Zones (SEE MAP, PAGES 8–9) On Sept. 15, 1983, Transportation Secretary Elizabeth Dole signed a plan to reduce the number of time zones in Alaska from four to two. The plan, which became effective Oct. 30, 1983, when daylight saving time reverted to standard time, places 90 percent of Alaska residents on Alaska (same as Yukon) time, only one hour behind the West Coast. The far reaches of the Aleutian Islands and St. Lawrence Island enter Hawaii–Aleutian time.

Before the change, Alaska's time zones were Pacific time (southeastern Alaska), Yukon time (Yakutat) and Alaska time (from just east of Cold Bay and west of Yakutat northward, including Nome). The shift was accomplished to facilitate doing business in Alaska, improve communications and unify residents.

Totems (SEE ALSO NATIVE ARTS AND CRAFTS AND POTLATCH) In the prehistory of southeastern Alaska and the Pacific Northwest coast, the Native way of life was based on the rich natural resources of the land, on respect for all living things and on a unique and complex social structure. The totemic art of the Indians reflects this rich culture.

Totem poles, carved from the huge cedar trees of the northern coast, are a traditional art form among the Natives of the Pacific Northwest and southeastern Alaska. Although the best-known type of totem pole is tall and freestanding, totemic art also is applied to house frontal poles, houseposts and mortuary poles. Totem poles are bold statements that make public records of the lives and history of the people who had them carved; they represent pride in clans and ancestors.

Animals of the region are most often represented on the poles. Commonly depicted are eagles, ravens, frogs, bears, beavers, wolves and whales.

Also represented are figures from Native mythology: monsters with animal features, humanlike spirits and legendary ancestors. Occasionally included are objects, devices, masks and charms and, more rarely, art illustrating plants and sky phenomena.

The poles were traditionally painted with natural mineral and vegetable pigments. Salmon eggs were chewed with cedar bark to form the binder for the ground pigment. Traditional colors are black, white and red-brown; green, blue-green, blue and yellow are also used, depending on tribal convention. The range of colors broadened when modern paints became available. Totem art grew rapidly in the late 18th century, with the introduction of steel European tools acquired from explorers and through the fur trade. Large totem poles were a thriving cultural feature by the 1830s, having become a means by which the Natives displayed their social standing. For example, wealthy Tlingit often commissioned the Tsimshian to carve totems for them.

Totem pole carving almost died out between the 1880s and 1950s during the enforcement of a law forbidding the "potlatch," the core of Northwest Coast Indian culture. The potlatch is a ceremony in which major events are celebrated, such as marriages; guests are invited from near and far, dancing and feasting take place, property is given away and often poles are raised to commemorate the event. Since the anti-potlatching law was repealed in 1951, a revival of Native culture and the arts has taken place, and many tribes are actively carving and raising poles again. (See Potlatch)

Totem poles were left to stand as long as nature would permit, usually about 50 to 60 years. Once a pole became so rotten that it fell, it was left to decay naturally or used for firewood. Some totem poles still standing in parks today are 40 to 50 years old. Heavy precipitation and acid muskeg soils hasten decomposition, even though cedar is resistant to decay.

Collections of fine totem poles may be seen either outdoors or in museums in several Alaska communities, including Ketchikan, Wrangell and Sitka. Carvers can be seen practicing their art at cultural centers in those towns as well as in Haines.

Tourism Although Alaska has been attracting tourists for over 100 years, people are surprised that the visitor industry has quietly become the state's

Totem. From At Home in Hostel Territory by Janet Thomas

Alaska's Top 10 Most Visited Attractions

Attraction	Number of Visitors
1. Inside Passage	387,200
2. Portage Glacier	370,000
3. Ketchikan Totems	331,800
4. Mendenhall Glacier	331,800
5. Denali/McKinley	301,200
6. Skagway's Historic Gold Rush District	296,700
7. Glacier Bay	256,400
8. Anchorage Museum of History and Art	216,300
9. Trans-Alaska Pipeline	200,700
10. Sitka's Russian Church and Dancers	186,000

Source: Alaska Journal of Commerce, 1996

second-largest primary employer. The visitor industry employs 27,000 Alaskans directly during peak seasons and affects another 52,000 Alaskan jobs. Over 2,500 businesses in Alaska derive most of their income from visitor sales. In-state visitor spending reached nearly $775 million in 1996. Tourism is a renewable resource that brings dollars to all regions of Alaska. The visitor industry generates over $1.4 billion in revenues each year and is expected to continue to grow.

State government has long recognized the value of the visitor industry and supports this growing segment of the state's economy through the Division of Tourism.

For the fiscal year 1997, the Division of Tourism's projected budget was $2.404 million for international marketing, rural development and visitor inquiries. The Alaska Tourism Marketing Council's budget was $5.4 million for domestic marketing. The Legislature allocates these monies to promote Alaska as a visitor destination.

Alaska welcomed over 1.2 million nonresident visitors in 1996, an increase of 1 percent over the previous year. Summer visitor spending has grown 82 percent since 1985.

The continental United States provided 78 percent of Alaska's visitors in 1995, Canadian visitors formed 15 percent and 7 percent came from overseas. Of these travelers, 56 percent had independent itineraries while the remainder came on package tour programs. The most popular modes of entry for visitors were domestic air (52 percent), cruise ships (29 percent), personal vehicles (12 percent) and the ferry system (4 percent). The remainder arrived by international air (2 percent) and motor coach tours (1 percent).

Alaska's scenic beauty, trophy fish, abundant wildlife and colorful history remain its biggest attractions. The adventure travel market is growing in Alaska, with an increasing number of visitors participating in river rafting, backcountry trekking and other wilderness experiences.

Trees and Shrubs

According to the U.S. Department of Agriculture, the number of native tree species in Alaska is less than in any other state. Species of trees and shrubs in Alaska fall under the following families: yew, pine, cypress, willow, bayberry, birch, mistletoe, gooseberry, rose, maple, elaeagnus, ginseng, dogwood, crowberry, pyrola, heath, dispensia, honeysuckle and composite.

Commercial timber species include white spruce, Sitka spruce, western hemlock, mountain hemlock, western red cedar, Alaska cedar, balsam poplar, black cottonwood, quaking aspen and paper birch.

Rare tree species include the Pacific yew, Pacific silver fir, subalpine fir, silver willow and Hooker willow.

Tundra

Characteristic of arctic and subarctic regions, tundra is a treeless plain that consists of moisture-retaining soils and permanently frozen subsoil. Tundra climates, with frequent winds and low temperatures, are harsh on plant species attempting to grow there. Soils freeze around root systems and winds wear

---

Spruce (Picea spp.)

In the interior forests, white spruce is the most common tree. It occurs from near sea level to tree line at about 1,000 to 3,500 feet. Picea sitchensis (Sitka spruce), the largest tree of Alaska, is the state tree.

The pitch or gum from the spruce tree has been used for medicinal plasters. Spruce pitch's healing properties may be due to the fact that it keeps the wound clean, preventing infection during the natural healing process. The pitch should be clear and soft and it should be covered with a bandage. —Eleanor G. Viereck, Alaska's Wilderness Medicines

away portions exposed above rocks and snow. Consequently, the three distinct types of Alaska tundra—wet, moist and alpine—support low-growing vegetation that includes a variety of delicate flowers, mosses and lichens.

According to a report in *Alaska Science Nuggets*, every acre of arctic tundra contains more than 2 tons of live fungi that survive by feeding on, thus decomposing, dead organic matter. Since the recession of North Slope ice age glaciers 12,000 years ago, a vegetative residue has accumulated a layer of peat 3 to 6 feet thick overlying the tundra.

Ulu A traditional Eskimo woman's knife designed for scraping and chopping, this fan-shaped tool was originally made of stone with a bone handle. Today, an ulu is often shaped from an old saw blade and a wood handle is attached. The term derives from the Yupik word *uluaq* and the Siberian Yupik word *ulaaq*.

Umiak (*SEE ALSO* BAIDARKA) An umiak is a traditional Eskimo skin-covered boat, the design of which has changed little over the centuries. Although umiaks are mostly powered by outboard motors today, paddles are still used when stalking game and when ice might damage the propeller. Because umiaks must often be pulled for long distances over pack ice, the boats are designed to be lightweight and easily repairable. The frames are wood, often driftwood found on the beaches, and the covering can be sewn should it be punctured. The bottom is flat and the keel is bone, which prevents the skin from wearing out as it is pulled over the ice.

Female walrus skins are the preferred covering because they are the proper thickness when split (bull hides are too thick and often scarred) and because it only takes two to cover a boat. However, sometimes female walrus skins are unavailable, so the Eskimos substitute skins of the bearded seal, or *oogruk*. *Oogruk* skins are smaller and it takes six or seven skins to cover an umiak.

Umiak is the Inupiat word for skin boat and is commonly used by the coastal Eskimos throughout Alaska. The St. Lawrence Islanders, however, speak the Yupik dialect and their word for skin boat is *angyaq*.

56 *years ago*

In June 1942 the Japanese bombed the naval air base at Dutch Harbor and invaded the Aleutian islands of Attu and Kiska. In May 1943, American troops landed on Attu and defeated the Japanese in a battle that left 1,148 American casualties.

Unalaska/ Dutch Harbor

(*SEE ALSO* MILITARY AND WORLD WAR II) Located on Unalaska Island, the second-largest island in the Aleutian Chain, 800 miles southwest of Anchorage, Ounalashka, or Unalaska, was the Russian-American Company's headquarters for the sea otter fur trade in the 1700s. At the turn of the century, Unalaska was a major stop for ships heading to and from the Nome goldfields.

The international port of Dutch Harbor is located across a bridge from Unalaska on Amaknak Island. The U.S. Army and Navy began building installations there in 1939; in June 1942 the area was bombed by the Japanese and most of the local Aleut people were then evacuated.

A memorial to those killed in the Aleutians in World War II was recently moved to Memorial Park near the cemetery.

Unalaska/Dutch Harbor is a major port and the gateway to the Bering Sea region. The climate is referred to as the "Cradle of the Storms," where the warm Japan Current meets the colder air and water currents of the Bering Sea, creating an annual rainfall of 60.5 inches and colossal winds. Rare plants and birds and the historic Cathedral of the Holy Ascension of Christ draw visitors to the island. The Unalaska/Dutch Harbor area remains ice-free year-round and large canneries form the basis of the local economy, making it one of the most productive seafood processing ports in the United States.

Universities and Colleges

Higher education in Alaska is provided by the University of Alaska system and private institutions. The university system includes three regional multicampus universities, one community college and a network of services for rural Alaska. The three regional institutions are the University of Alaska Anchorage (UAA), the University of Alaska Fairbanks (UAF) and the University of Alaska Southeast (UAS). University of Alaska institutions enrolled 32,481 students in 1995.

Campuses of UAS are located in Juneau, Sitka and Ketchikan. The main UAA campus in Anchorage is supplemented by a network of extended colleges that includes Kenai Peninsula College, Kodiak College, Matanuska–Susitna College and Prince William Sound Community College, as well as the Chugiak–Eagle River Campus, a branch campus in Kachemak Bay and several military centers.

The UAA is the home of the Alaska Center for International Business/World Trade Center Alaska; Center for Alcohol and Addiction Studies; Center for Economic Development; Center for Economic Education; Center for Human Development, University Affiliated Program; Environment and Natural Resources Institute, which includes the Alaska Natural Heritage Program, Alaska State Climate Center and the Arctic Environmental Information and Data Center; Institute for Circumpolar Health Studies; Institute of Social and Economic Research; and the Justice Center.

The UAF is a land-, sea- and space-grant university that includes the main campus in Fairbanks; Bristol Bay Campus in Dillingham; Chukchi Campus in Kotzebue; Interior Campus with offices in Fairbanks and centers in Fort Yukon, McGrath, Tok and Unalaska; Kuskokwim Campus in Bethel; Northwest Campus in Nome; and Tanana Valley Campus in downtown Fairbanks.

The UAF research facilities include the Alaska Cooperative Fishery and Wildlife Research Unit, Alaska Native Language Center, Alaska Synthetic Aperture Radar Facility, Arctic Region Supercomputing Center, Center for Cross-Cultural Studies, Center for Global Change and Arctic Systems Research, Consortium for Research in Rural Alaska, Environmental Technology Laboratory, Fishery Industrial Technology Center, Forest Products Technology Center, Forest Soils Laboratory, Geophysical Institute, Georgeson Botanical Garden, Institute of Arctic Biology, Institute of Marine Science, Institute of Northern Engineering, Juneau Center for Fisheries and Ocean Sciences, Large Animal Research Station, Mineral Industry Resource Laboratory, Petroleum Development Laboratory, Poker Flat Research Range, Polar Ice Coring Office, Seismology Laboratory, Transportation Research Center, University of Alaska Museum, Water Research Center and West Coast National Undersea Research Center.

The Alaska Cooperative Extension and the Alaska Sea Grant College Program interpret and report some of the university's research results to the residents of Alaska.

For information on state colleges and universities, contact the following institutions:

University of Alaska Anchorage, 3211 Providence

> The University of Alaska Anchorage campus has 16 acres of roof, 17 acres of lawn, 26 acres of interior floor space, 46 acres of pavement, and uses 80 acres of toilet paper each year.

The Valley of Ten Thousand Smokes, circa 1917. From Alaska's History by Harry Ritter

Drive, Anchorage 99508; **Kenai Peninsula College,** 34820 College Drive, Soldotna 99669; **Kodiak College,** 117 Benny Benson Drive, Kodiak 99615; **Matanuska–Susitna College,** P.O. Box 2889, Palmer 99645; **Prince William Sound Community College,** P.O. Box 97, Valdez 99686.

University of Alaska Fairbanks, Fairbanks 99775; **Bristol Bay Campus,** P.O. Box 1070, Dillingham 99576; **Chukchi Campus,** P.O. Box 297, Kotzebue 99752; **Interior Aleutians Campus,** Box 248, Unalaska 99685; **Interior Campus,** P.O. Box 756720, Fairbanks 99775; **Kuskokwim Campus,** P.O. Box 368, Bethel 99559; **Northwest Campus,** Pouch 400, Nome 99762.

University of Alaska Southeast, Juneau Campus, 11120 Glacier Highway, Juneau 99801; **Ketchikan Campus, 2600** Seventh St., Ketchikan 99901; **Sitka Campus,** 1332 Seward Ave., Sitka 99835.

For information on private institutions of higher learning, contact the following:

Alaska Bible College, P.O. Box 289, Glennallen 99588.

Alaska Pacific University, 4101 University Drive, Anchorage 99508.

Sheldon Jackson College, 801 Lincoln St., Sitka 99835.

Many additional schools and institutes in Alaska offer religious, vocational and technical study. For a complete listing of these and other schools, write for the *Directory of Postsecondary Educational Institutions in Alaska,* Alaska Commission on Postsecondary Education, 3030 Vintage Blvd., Juneau 99801-7109.

Volcanoes
Volcanoes on the Aleutian Islands, on the Alaska Peninsula and in the Wrangell Mountains are part of the "Ring of Fire" that surrounds the Pacific Ocean basin. There are more than 80 potentially active volcanoes in Alaska, about half of which have had at least one eruption since 1760, the date of the earliest written record of eruptions. Pavlof Volcano is one of the most active of Alaskan volcanoes, having had more than 40 reported eruptions since 1790. One recent spectacular eruption of Pavlof in April 1986 sent ash 10 miles high, causing black snow to fall on Cold Bay; it continued being active through August 1988, producing lava and mud flows. The eruption of Augustine Volcano (elev. 4,025 feet) in lower Cook Inlet on March 27, 1986, sent ash 8 miles high and disrupted air traffic in southcentral Alaska for several days.

Most recently, Mount Redoubt erupted on Dec. 14, 1989, its first eruption since 1968. The biggest eruptions sent ash throughout most of southcentral Alaska and disrupted air traffic. This eruption continued until April 1990. Mount Spurr erupted in June, August and September

Alaska Tsunami Warning Center

Providing information, and timely warnings, on tsunamigenic earthquakes (those quakes measuring above 7.0 on the Richter scale and lasting 30 seconds or longer) is the job of the West Coast/ Alaska Tsunami Warning Center (WC/ATWC), located in Palmer. Established in 1967, the WC/ATWC covers Alaska, Canada and the West Coast of the United States, and ensures the avoidance of such a tragedy as the April 1, 1946, earthquake at Scotch Cap on Unimak Island, Alaska. Within minutes after the quake struck, waves measuring 100 feet high completely destroyed the lighthouse on the island, killing five people. Less than five hours later, the first wave hit Hawaii, killing 159 people. More recently, in March 1988, after a 7.6 quake in the Gulf of Alaska, tsunami warnings alerted coastal residents in plenty of time to take precautionary measures. Normally, tsunamis from remote Pacific sources will not cause damage in Alaska.

1992. Anchorage received the brunt of the ash fallout from the August eruption, which halted air traffic out of the city for several days. It was briefly interrupted again with the September eruption.

The most violent Alaskan eruption recorded occurred over a 60-hour period in June 1912 from Novarupta Volcano. The eruption darkened the sky over much of the Northern Hemisphere for several days, deposited almost a foot of ash on Kodiak, 100 miles away, and filled the Valley of Ten Thousand Smokes (now contained within Katmai National Park) with more than 2.5 cubic miles of ash during its brief but extremely explosive duration.

The state's 10 tallest volcanic peaks, nearly all of which are known to have erupted within the last 10,000 years are as follows (*see also* map on pages 120-21):

Mount Wrangell	14,163 feet
Mount Spurr	11,070 feet
Redoubt Volcano	10,197 feet
Iliamna Volcano	10,016 feet
Shishaldin Volcano	9,372 feet
Pavlof Volcano	8,261 feet
Mount Veniaminof	8,225 feet
Isanotski Peaks	8,025 feet
Mount Griggs	7,602 feet
Mount Denison	7,503 feet

Waves (SEE ALSO BORE TIDE; EARTHQUAKES; AND TIDES)

Alaska's recorded seismic history is very short, yet extremely active. Alaska responds to movement in the Aleutian–Alaska megathrust zone, where the edge of the Pacific plate descends under the North American plate. These vertical movements of the earth's crust result in vertical motion of the seafloor, which can produce great tsunamis. In fact, these crustal movements in the Alaska Peninsula, Aleutians and Gulf of Alaska can produce Pacific-wide tsunamis.

In southeastern Alaska, the Fairweather Fault lies inland. Though this fault has not triggered tectonic tsunamis as in other Alaskan areas, it can trigger nearby underwater landslides, which can cause tsunamis.

According to the West Coast/Alaska Tsunami Warning Center in Palmer, Alaska has had seven tsunamis that caused fatalities in recorded history. These were of local origin and occurred between 1788 and 1964. Tsunamis originating in Alaska Pacific waters have caused all of the fatalities reported on the West Coast and in Alaska, and most of those in Hawaii. The most recent damaging tsunami was in 1964 following the March 27, Good Friday earthquake. That wave completely destroyed three Alaskan villages before reaching Washington, Oregon and California, and continued to cause damage as far away as Hawaii, Chile and Japan.

Tsunami is taken from the Japanese words *tsu* meaning harbor and *nami* meaning great wave. Although often called tidal waves, tsunamis are not caused by tides. Generated by earthquakes occurring on or below the sea floor, tsunamis can race across the Pacific Ocean at speeds of up to

600 miles per hour. Tsunamis rarely cross the Atlantic. Traveling across the open ocean, the waves are only a few feet high and can be up to 100 miles from crest to crest. They cannot be seen from an airplane or felt in a ship at sea. Once they approach shore, however, shallower water causes the waves to grow taller by increasingly restricting their forward motion. Thus, a 2-foot wave traveling 500 miles per hour in deep water becomes a 100-foot killer at 30 miles per hour as it nears the shore. The wave action of a tsunami can repeat every 15 to 30 minutes, and the danger for a given area is generally not considered over until the area has been free from damaging waves for two hours.

Another type of wave action that occurs in Alaska is a seiche. A seiche is a long, rhythmic wave in a closed or partially closed body of water. Caused by earthquakes, winds, tidal currents or atmospheric pressure, the motion of a seiche resembles the back and forth movement of a tipped bowl of water. The water moves only up and down, and can remain active from a few minutes to several hours. The highest recorded wave in Alaska, 1,740 feet, was the result of a seiche that took place in Lituya Bay on July 9, 1958. This unusually high wave was due to an earthquake-induced landslide that stripped trees from the opposite side of the bay.

For more information about current earthquakes and tsunamis, contact the WC/ATWC Web page at http://www.alaska.net/~ATWC.

Whales and Whaling

(*SEE ALSO* BALEEN) Fifteen species of both toothed and baleen whales are found in Alaskan waters. Baleen refers to the hundreds of strips of flexible fingernail-like material that hang from the gum of the upper jaw. The strips are fringed and act as strainers that capture krill, the tiny shrimplike organisms upon which the whales feed. Once the baleen fills with krill, whales force water back out through the sides of their mouth, swallowing the food left behind. Baleen whale cows are usually larger than bulls.

Baleen whales that inhabit Alaskan waters include blue, bowhead, northern right, fin or finback, humpback, sei, minke or little piked and gray. Toothed whales include sperm, beluga, orca (or killer whale), pilot, beaked (three species), dolphins (two species) and porpoises (two species). Another toothed whale, the narwhal, a full-time resident of the arctic region, is almost never seen in Alaskan waters. St. Lawrence Islanders call narwhals *bousucktugutalik,* or "beluga with tusk," due to a tusk that grows from the left side of the upper jaw on bulls only. Spiraling in a left-hand direction, the tusk can reach lengths of 7 to 8 feet on an adult.

A few facts concerning three of the whales indigenous to Alaska, and the whales residents and tourists are most likely to see in Alaska's waters, are interesting to note. According to the Alaska Department of Fish and Game, gray whales have the distinction of being the most primitive of the living *mysticete* ("moustached") or baleen whales. They can regularly be observed in large numbers from Alaskan shores, and are found in the North Pacific Ocean and adjacent waters of the Arctic Ocean. There are two geographically isolated stocks: the Korean or western Pacific stock, and the California or eastern Pacific stock. The California stock migrates between Baja California and the Bering and Chukchi Seas, a round-trip distance of 10,000 miles, and the longest migration of any marine mammal.

One grocery chain in Fairbanks has designated SPAM® as a permanently discounted coupon item. They obviously know that people in that city need all the help they can get.

Grays are mottled gray in color and covered with scars, abrasions and clusters of parasitic barnacles that are most abundant on their heads and backs, the parts that are exposed to air when they breathe.

The estimated daily consumption of an adult gray whale is about 2,600 pounds. In the approximately five months spent in Alaskan waters, one whale eats about 396,000 pounds of food, primarily amphipod crustaceans. Gray whales feed on the bottom by sucking tube-dwelling amphipods out of the sandy sediment and leaving large oval feeding imprints behind. Scientists can study these imprints and gain knowledge about the feeding habits of these whales. Muddy feeding trails are often seen when gray whales surface after feeding dives. Gray whales were called "devil fish" by early whalers because they were so aggressive and protective of their young when hunted.

Adult grays are about 36 to 50 feet long and weigh from 16 to 45 tons, with females larger than males at any given age. They have been known to live up to 70 years, but the average life span is 40 to 50 years.

The beluga, or white whale, belongs to the *odontocetes* ("toothed") group, which includes sperm and killer whales, dolphins and porpoises. Its closest relative is the narwhal. Belugas range widely in arctic and subarctic waters, and two populations occur in Alaska. The Cook Inlet population can be found in Turnagain Arm and in the Shelikof Straits region, although some belugas have been seen east to Yakutat Bay and west to Kodiak Island. Belugas of the western Arctic population range throughout the Bering, Chukchi and Beaufort Seas. These whales winter in the ice of the Bering Sea, moving in summer over 1,500 miles to concentration areas along the coast from Bristol Bay to the Mackenzie River delta in northwestern Canada.

In Alaska, major concentrations occur in the Bristol Bay area, Norton Sound, Kotzebue Sound and Kasegaluk Lagoon. In Bristol Bay, they sometimes swim more than 100 miles per day.

Belugas are very vocal animals, producing a variety of grunts, clicks, chirps and

whistles, which are used for navigating, finding prey and communicating. Because of their talkative nature, they are known as "sea canaries." Belugas are also masters of echolocation, using their sophisticated sonar to detect fish and to navigate in shallow waters or among gill nets without getting stranded. Over 100 belugas were stranded overnight in August 1996, near Anchorage; four died. In some areas, they may dive more than 2,000 feet to feed on the bottom. At birth, belugas are dark blue-gray in color, lightening to white by the age of five or six. Adult males are 11 to 16 feet long and weigh 1,000 to 2,000 pounds; adult females are smaller, reaching 12 feet in length. Belugas can live up to 40 years.

Orcas, also known as killer whales, or blackfish, are the largest member of the dolphin family. They range from the Beaufort Sea to Antarctica and are most abundant off the Aleutians. It is thought that orcas migrate, riding cold currents south in the winter. The most unusual feature of the orca is the high dorsal fin, which has no muscle, but may serve the whale as a keel would a boat. The fin on older males can grow to 6 feet in height.

Orcas are considered very intelligent and to possess all mammalian senses except smell. To sleep, they take catnaps on the surface of the water, and they hunt in pods using complex, cooperative patterns of attack. Prey includes sea lions, salmon, seals, porpoises, halibut, shark, squid, belugas and other whales. Male killer whales average 23 feet in length, with females being smaller. Average life span is 30 to 40 years.

Whaling. Decimated by commercial whaling in the late 1880s, the bowhead whale population is now protected and growing. It is estimated that 199 whales are added to the stock yearly, with a total 1994 population of 8,000.

Bowhead whales have been protected from commercial whaling for decades by the actions of a number of conventions, including the Convention for the Regulation of Whaling (1931), the International Convention for the Regulation of Whaling (1947), and by the Marine Mammal Protection Act (1973) and the Endangered Species Act (1973). Right, blue and humpback whales are currently on Alaska's endangered species list.

Gray whales are also protected, with commercial whaling for grays banned by the International Convention for the Regulation of Whaling since 1947. However, these conventions and regulations do allow for subsistence harvest by Alaska Indians, Aleuts and Eskimos.

Since 1978, the International Whaling Commission (IWC) has regulated the taking of both bowheads and grays. The IWC reclassified the eastern stock of gray whales from a protected species to a sustained management stock with an annual catch limit of about 179 whales. The entire catch limit of grays and bowheads is reserved for taking by Natives or by member governments on behalf of Natives.

At a convention in Puerto Vallarta in May 1994, the IWC revised the bowhead catch limit for Alaska. Bowheads landed from 1995 to 1998 shall not exceed 204. Furthermore, it is forbidden to strike, land or kill calves or any bowhead accompanied by a calf.

Other species of large baleen whales, such as minke and fin whales, are occasionally taken by Alaska Eskimos for food. It is not necessary to report minke harvests. The only toothed whale taken by Eskimos is the beluga and its harvest is monitored by the Alaska and Beluga Whale Committee (ABWC), which is currently developing a management plan.

Beluga Whales Landed 1985–96

Year	Beluga
1985	256–352
1986	174–191
1987	140–192
1988	375–418
1989	247–266
1990	316–338
1991	306–316
1992	163–164
1993	301–321
1994	263–271
1995	163+
1996	298–311

Wildflowers

Wildflowers in Alaska are seldom showy; they are usually rather small and delicate. More than 1,500 plant species occur in the state, including trees, shrubs, ferns, grasses and sedges, as well as flowering plants.

Alpine regions are particularly rich in flora and some of the alpine species are rare. Anywhere there is tundra there is apt to be a bountiful population of flowers. The Steese Highway (Eagle Summit), Richardson Highway (Thompson Pass), Denali Highway (Maclaren Summit), Denali National Park and Preserve (Polychrome Pass), Seward Highway (Turnagain Pass), Glenn Highway just north of Anchorage (Eklutna Flats) and a locale near Wasilla (Hatcher Pass) are wonderful wildflower-viewing spots. These are all readily accessible by car. Less easily accessible floral Edens are some of the Aleutian Islands, Point Hope, Anvil Mountain and the Nome–Teller Road (both near Nome), Pribilof Islands and other remote areas.

Alaska's official flower, the forget-me-not (*Myosotis alpestris*), is a delicate little beauty found throughout much of the state in alpine meadows

Forget-me-not, Alaska's state flower

and along streams. Growing to 18 inches tall, forget-me-nots are recognized by their bright blue petals surrounding a yellow "eye." A northern "cousin," the arctic forget-me-not (*Eritrichium aretioides*), grows in sandy soil on the tundra, or in the mountains, and reaches only 4 inches in height.

Winds (*See also* Climate) Some

of Alaska's windiest weather has been recorded on the western islands of the Aleutian chain. Overall, the causes are the same as elsewhere, incorporating planet rotation and the tendency of the atmosphere to equalize the difference between high and low pressure fronts. A few winds occur often and significantly enough to be given names: chinook, taku and williwaws.

Chinook. Old-timers describe chinook winds as unseasonably warm winds that can cause a thaw in the middle of winter. What they also cause are power outages and property damage, especially in the Anchorage bowl, where in recent years hundreds of homes have sprung up on the Chugach Mountain hillsides over which the chinook winds howl. One such wind occurred on April Fool's Day in 1980, causing $25 million in property damage and nominating the city as a disaster area. Parts of Anchorage were without power for 60 hours.

Until recently, it was not possible to predict the coming of a chinook wind. Today, however, Anchorage meteorologists can tell if the winds are gathering, when they will arrive and their relative

strength. It was discerned that such a warm wind could only originate in Prince William Sound and that its speed had to be at least 55 miles per hour or faster just to cross the 3,500-foot Chugach Mountains. Other factors that need to be present are a storm near Bethel and relatively stable air over Anchorage. Meteorologists predict the coming of chinook winds 55 percent of the time.

Taku. Taku winds are the sudden, fierce gales that sweep down from the ice cap behind Juneau and Douglas, to plague residents there. Takus are shivering cold winds capable of reaching 100 miles per hour. They have been known to send a 2-by-4 timber flying through the wall of a frame house.

Williwaws. Williwaws are sudden gusts of wind that can reach 113 miles per hour after the wind "builds up" on one side of a mountain and suddenly spills over into what may appear to be a relatively protected area. Williwaws are considered the bane of Alaska mariners. The term was originally applied to a strong wind in the Strait of Magellan.

World Eskimo-Indian Olympics

An audience of thousands watches the annual gathering of several hundred Native athletes from Alaska and the circumpolar-nations competing in the World Eskimo-Indian Olympics (WEIO) in Fairbanks. Held over four days in July, the self-supporting games draw participants from all of Alaska's Native populations (Eskimo, Aleut, Athabascan, Tlingit, Haida and Tsimshian). Canadian, Greenlandic and Russian Eskimos are also invited to participate, as well as Native Americans from the contiguous 48 states.

Spectators thrill to the sight of such feats as the knuckle hop and the ear-weight competition. Other traditional Native sports and competitions include the greased pole walk, fish cutting, stick pull, Indian-Eskimo dancing, men's and women's blanket toss,

and the spectacular two-foot and one-foot high kicks. Some of the more boisterous games include a lively game of tug-of-war and the muktuk-eating contest.

Each year the judges choose a Native queen to reign over the four-day Olympics. She reigns through the year, making several appearances throughout the state, and represents the WEIO at the National Congress of American Indians. The judges also pick the most authentic Native costumes.

The games will be held July 15–18, 1998, at the Big Dipper Recreation Arena in Fairbanks. Advance tickets may be purchased from the World Eskimo-Indian Olympics Committee, P.O. Box 2433, Fairbanks 99707; (907) 452-6646.

In 1867, the United States purchased Alaska from Russia for $7.2 million— about 2 cents an acre.

1997 WORLD ESKIMO-INDIAN OLYMPIC GAMES, FIRST-PLACE WINNERS.

Men—Eskimo Stick Pull, Eki Kagak; **Indian Stick Pull,** Brian Randazzo; **Two-Foot High Kick,** Brad Weyiouanna, 7'5"; **One-Foot High Kick,** Tino Morrow, 8'8"; **Blanket Toss,** Calvin Lane; **Ear Pull,** Robert Okpeaha, Jr.; **Four-Man Carry,** Eli Kagak, 54–0.

Women—Eskimo Stick Pull, Tselane Angason; **Indian Stick Pull,** Janet Ahlaloot; **Ear Pull,** Noel Oksoktaruk; **Two-Foot High Kick,** Nicola Johnston, 70"; **One-Foot High Kick,** Nicola Lincoln, 6'2"; **Blanket Toss,** Christina Long; **Drop the Bomb,** Christina Long, 9–2.

Fur Eskimo Parka Contest, Etta Lord. **Muktuk Eating Contest,** Edith Nashourak. **Miss World Eskimo-Indian Olympics,** Holly Snowball.

World War II (SEE ALSO
MILITARY AND UNALASKA/DUTCH HARBOR)
World War II was a key event in promoting the development of modern Alaska. In May 1940 Congress authorized the construction of Fort Richardson outside of Anchorage. After the bombing of Pearl Harbor, Alaska's strategic importance as a staging area for supplying forces in the North Pacific was apparent. The construction of the Alaska Canada Military Highway (the Alcan) began in March 1942, providing an overland route from the Lower 48 into Alaska.

The Japanese bombed a small military base at Dutch Harbor on June 3, 1942, in an attack that was designed to divert American forces north while engaging the American fleet in the central Pacific at Midway. The diversion failed and the battle at Midway became a turning point in the Pacific war.

On June 7, 1942, 1,200 Japanese troops landed on the islands of Attu and Kiska, where they built an air base, bunkers and anti-aircraft emplacements with the intention of preventing the United States from using the Aleutians to launch an attack on Japan. Although the Japanese presence on the islands posed no real threat to the United States, it was unthinkable to accept foreign occupation. But the ensuing fight to drive the Japanese from the Aleutians was as much a battle against the bad weather as it was against enemy forces. More American aircraft were lost to the violent 120 mph winds, the dense fog and constant storms than to Japanese fire.

On May 11, 1943, after nearly a year of Japanese occupation, 11,000 American troops landed on Attu and engaged in a bloody battle with the 2,600 Japanese troops. At the end of the month, 550 Americans were dead and 1,148 were wounded. Of the Japanese, only 28 prisoners were taken; American soldiers buried 2,351 Japanese troops killed in combat, hundreds of others were presumed to have died and were buried in the hills or were thought to have committed suicide.

The battle for Kiska was different. On July 28, 1943, the 5,000-man Japanese garrison evacuated the island in dense fog. For three weeks, U.S. forces continued to bomb and shell the island, unaware that the island was abandoned. In August, 35,000 Allied soldiers arrived on the island, but found only a few stray Japanese dogs.

Yukon Quest International Sled Dog Race (SEE ALSO DOG MUSHING AND IDITAROD TRAIL SLED DOG RACE) The Yukon Quest International

Sled Dog Race was begun by Roger Williams and LeRoy Shank in November 1983, with the purpose of supporting a long-distance sled dog race of international character between Fairbanks, Alaska, and Whitehorse, Yukon Territory. The first race took place in February 1984, with 26 teams competing, and had a purse of $50,000.

Named for the old-time winter "Highway of the North," the Yukon River, the 1,000-mile trek takes between 11 and 14 days to complete, depending on weather and trail conditions. It is held in February and is known as one of the toughest sled dog races. During their journey between the two cities, the teams retrace the footsteps of

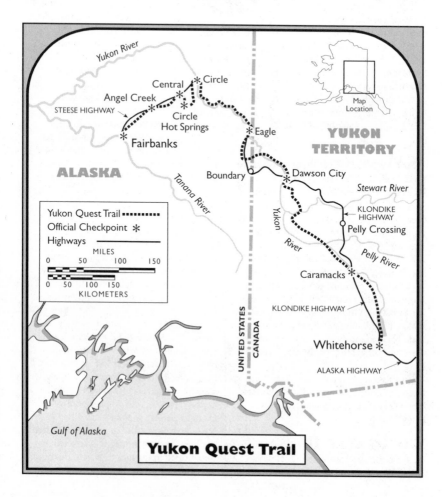

Yukon Quest Trail

gold rush trappers, miners, explorers and missionaries. They cross four major summits, over diverse and challenging terrain, travel 250 miles on the frozen Yukon River and cross the longest unguarded international border in the world.

The direction of the race alternates each year, and between the start and finish lines, there are six official checkpoints. The shortest distance between checkpoints is 10 miles, from Central to Circle Hot Springs, and the longest distance between checkpoints is 290 miles, from Dawson City to Carmacks. The only checkpoint at which a musher may receive help of any kind is at Dawson City, where a 36-hour layover is mandatory. Rules allow for eight dogs minimum and 14 dogs maximum at the start. Five dogs are the minimum allowed at the finish, and only four dogs can be

dropped during the course of the race. Each musher may use only one sled throughout the race, and mandatory equipment includes a sleeping bag, hand ax, snowshoes, promotional material and eight booties per dog.

In 1997, 18 mushers completed the race. Nine racers were scratched. The winner was Rick Mackey. Quest Rookie of the Year was Keizo Funatsu (*see* charts below).

For up-to-date information during the race, try Yukon Quest Online at www.newsminer.com/quest/.

Yukon River (*See also* Rivers)

The Yukon River is the longest river in Alaska, flowing in a 2,000-mile (1,400 miles in Alaska) arc from its British Columbia headwaters across the

Winners and Times

Year	Musher	Days	Hrs.	Min.	Prize
1984	Sonny Lindner, Johnson River	12	00	05	$15,000
1985	Joe Runyan, Nenana	11	11	55	15,000
1986	Bruce Johnson	14	09	17	15,000
1987	Bill Cotter, Nenana	12	04	34	15,000
1988	David Monson	12	05	06	20,000
1989	Jeff King, Denali	11	20	51	20,000
1990	Vern Halter, Trapper Creek	11	17	09	20,000
1991	Charlie Boulding, Nenana	10	21	12	25,000
1992	John Schandelmeier, Paxson	11	21	40	29,837
1993	Charlie Boulding, Nenana	10	19	09	25,000
1994	Lavonne Barve	10	22	44	20,000
1995	Frank Turner, Whitehorse, YT	10	16	20	20,000
1996	John Schandelmeier, Paxson	12	16	47	20,000
1997	Rick Mackey, Nenana	12	05	55	20,000

1997 Results

Place	Musher	Days	Hrs.	Min.
1	Rick Mackey, Nenana	12	05	55
2	Frank Turner, Whitehorse, YT	12	07	03
3	John Schandelmeier, Paxson	12	07	08
4	Mark May, North Pole	12	07	25
5	Keizo Funatsu, Osaka, Japan	12	16	12
6	Jerry Louden, Two Rivers	12	17	23
7	Dave Dalton, Fairbanks	12	23	32
8	Ned Cathers, Whitehorse, YT	13	02	28
9	David O'Farrell, Tagish, YT	13	12	05

Interior's forested hills, narrow mountain valleys and vast tundra flats to the Bering Sea. The fifth-largest river in North America, the third largest in the United States, the Yukon River watershed drains 330,000 square miles—a third of Alaska.

Archaeological evidence indicates that humans may have lived along the river more than 20,000 years ago. Historically, two Native groups occupied the Yukon valley: the Yupik Eskimos and the Athabascans. Most Native villages were established on the north bank of the river, apparently the preferred side of the river to fish for the millions of migrating king, coho and chum salmon that returned (and still return) to the river system to spawn. Fish traps and summer fish camps can still be seen along the river.

With the arrival of European trappers, the Yukon became a major supply route for the Interior. Travel was by steamboat during the summer and by dogsled from October to May, when the river was frozen.

The Yukon has never been dammed and is crossed by only one bridge. That bridge, on the Dalton Highway near Stevens Village, is just south of the Arctic Circle.

The Yukon River attracts canoeists, kayakers and others for float trips. Many commercial guides offer excursions, and the popular jumping-off point is at Eagle. A summer float trip downriver through Yukon–Charley Rivers National Preserve to Circle is 154 river miles and the trips average 5 to 10 days. Also available are float trips from Dawson City, Yukon Territory, to Circle which make a stop halfway at Eagle.

You can rent canoes in Eagle or choose a trip with a local commercial guide with gear supplied.

For more information on proper clothing, weather conditions and best time to make a float, contact the National Park Service, Box 167, Eagle 99378; (907) 547-2233.

The North American Butterfly Association's July 4 census showed Juneau to have the lowest number of butterflies in all of North America. Three counters spent 5 hours and saw only eight butterflies!

Zip Codes (SEE POPULATIONS AND ZIP CODES)

Yearly Highlights, 1996-97

The following is a collection of news events from mid-1996 to fall 1997. *The Alaska Almanac®* wishes to credit wire stories of the Associated Press, and stories printed in the *Anchorage Daily News, Alaska Journal of Commerce* and *Fairbanks Daily News–Miner* as the primary sources of information for Yearly Highlights.

Hundreds flee Mat-Su inferno. The most devastating fire in Alaska history burned nearly 40,000 acres and destroyed at least 344 buildings in the Matanuska–Susitna Valley during the first week of June 1996. The Miller's Reach fire started shortly before 5 P.M. on June 2 near Mile 59 of the Parks Highway. By the next day, although firefighters believed the blaze was under control, it found new life amid 40 mph gusts and continued to spread, leaping roads and waterways as it consumed forest, tundra, homes and businesses. By day three, some 500 evacuees found shelter at Big Lake Elementary School until fire threatened the building, and they were moved to Wasilla High School. Hundreds more fled their homes when the fire escalated and spread in various directions, whipped by dry, warm gusts of wind. After a week of losing ground, an army of 1,300 firefighters from throughout Alaska and the Lower 48 were aided by cooler weather and mild precipitation that slowed the fire's spread until it was under control. By June 9, damage estimates stood at nearly $9 million. Organizations and individuals statewide responded with an outpouring of cash, food, clothing and shelter while valley residents struggled to clean up and rebuild. More than 1,800 people had been turned out of their homes.

Postmaster murdered. The postmaster in the Yukon River village of Ruby was found beaten and dying on the floor of the post office June 20, 1996, one and a half hours after closing time. Agnes Wright, 32, left behind three children, including two toddlers. Cause of the murder seems to have been a robber seeking blank money orders. A suspect was not indicted until October, leaving the normally peaceful village of 200 in turmoil for some weeks.

Orthodox Bishop visits Kenai Peninsula villages. Bishop Innocent and several other Orthodox priests visited Port Graham and Nanwalek from Aug. 16–18, 1996. During this visit, the Bishop ordained John Moonin in Port Graham to sub-deacon status, and awarded him the St. Herman cross during Divine Liturgy. A Molieben service was held for school children. In Nanwalek, the Bishop tonsured Ephim Moonin to a reader and awarded him the St. Herman cross. The Nanwalek Seal Dancers performed for the Bishop and other visitors.

World-record lingcod caught. Charter boat captain Andy Mezirow caught the world-record lingcod in waters outside Resurrection Bay on Sept. 2, 1996. He later released the 43.26-pound female alive at the Seward small-boat harbor after weighing it in. Mezirow wouldn't say exactly where he caught it, but described his "fishing hole" as where a pinnacle of rock rises to within 14 feet of the surface. Lingcod can be exciting to catch because they're ferocious, Mezirow said.

Christmas in October. More than $335 million flowed into Alaskans' bank accounts when the Permanent Fund Corp. began disbursement of its annual dividend to state residents on Oct. 9, 1996. Nearly 300,000 people qualified for the $1,130.68 check. How do Alaskans spend their checks? On the Kenai Peninsula, residents used their money for automobiles, snowmachines, TVs, VCRs, electronics equipment or airplane tickets. Some paid their bills, or socked it away in savings.

Hunting the hunters. State Fish and Wildlife Protection officers cracked down on hunters during Kodiak Island's fall hunting season. Between Oct. 10 and

Nov. 15, 1996, the six-man post, beefed up by four off-island troopers, contacted 1,066 hunters and issued 35 citations. They patrolled by pickup, boat, floatplane and helicopter, checking kill sites for waste, among other violations.

Fairbanks hosts NCAA.

The University of Alaska Fairbanks hosted its first-ever NCAA Division I men's basketball tournament from Nov. 22–24, 1996, at the Carlson Center. The three-day basketball festival was a great success, with more than 21,000 fans attending. Alabama defeated Middle Tennessee State, 77–74, to win the championship. Other teams competing were Providence, Montana, Southern Illinois and Baylor.

Mines financing approved.

On Nov. 16, 1996, the Alaska Industrial Development and Export Authority's Board of Directors approved $157 million in financing to aid two Alaska mining projects:
   • an expansion of the Red Dog Mine north of Kotzebue; and
   • solid waste and sewage treatment facilities for the Fort Knox mine near Fairbanks.

The Red Dog project includes an $85 million expansion of the DeLong Mountain Transportation System, the Chukchi Sea port and a 60-mile service road.

For Fort Knox, the board approved $72 million in tax-free state revenue bonds in a unique arrangement allowed by the Internal Revenue Service.

Alaska skater captures gold.

Sydne Vogel of Anchorage, 17, conquered the world on Nov. 30, 1996, winning figure skating's World Junior Championship in Seoul, South Korea. Vogel was the first American female to win the title since Michelle Kwan's victory three years ago. Skating a program loaded with triple jumps, Vogel ousted first-day leader Elena Sokolova of Russia, who took home the silver.

Pavlof spouts off . . . again.

Pavlof Volcano, 590 miles southwest of Anchorage, erupted Dec. 10, 1996, for the second time this month. Located at the tip of the Alaska Peninsula, Pavlof is one of the most active volcanoes in the Aleutian volcanic arc, with nearly 40 documented eruptions dating back to 1790. Its latest spate of activity began in September and at one point sent an ash cloud to 30,000 feet.

Tug loses half of barge.

The back half of a 400-foot barge laden with empty railroad tank cars was spotted Jan. 4, 1997, adrift in Prince William Sound in waters frequented by oil tankers. A Coast Guard C-130 launched a search after a Seattle shipper reported its barge had broken in half while being towed from Whittier to Seattle. The barge was loaded with 30 empty tank cars belonging to the Alaska Railroad. The front section arrived without incident at Ward Cove, near Ketchikan. It was not immediately known what caused the 22-year-old flat-deck barge to divide.

Farewell to statehood champion.

Robert B. Atwood, *The Anchorage Times* publisher and statehood champion, 89, died in his sleep at home on Jan. 10, 1997. Congestive heart failure was the cause of death. Gov. Tony Knowles and Anchorage Mayor Rick Mystrom ordered flags flown at half-staff.

"From his championing of statehood to his forceful advocacy for this state's development, Bob left an indelible mark on the Last Frontier," Knowles said.

Atwood arrived in Anchorage 62 years ago, the husband of the banker's daughter, ambitious new owner of the only newspaper between Seward and Fairbanks. He survived the Depression, the 1964 earthquake and a 1986 attack by a gun-toting cab driver.

Journalism professor and historian John Strohmeyer knew Atwood for the past 12 years.

"I rank him ahead of William Allen White (the legendary Kansas boomer-publisher)," Strohmeyer commented. "I think Bob did more for Alaska as a civic journalism-type publisher than White did for Kansas."

Over the years, the $4 million Atwood

Foundation supported a variety of civic and cultural causes, including the Anchorage Concert Association and Alaska Pacific University.

Community activist shot by husband.

Domestic violence played a role in the murder and suicide of a noted Fairbanks community activist and her husband on Feb. 21, 1997. Annette Barnes, 43, was found dead in the downstairs room of her home. She was shot twice. Her husband, Tony Barnes, died in the same room of an apparently self-inflicted pistol shot. Ms. Barnes was active with the Martin Luther King Jr. Day Committee and was a board member of the Local March of Dimes. She worked for the state Department of Labor.

Same-day airborne hunts prohibited.

As of midnight Feb. 25, 1997, it became illegal for hunters and trappers in Alaska to land an airplane and shoot a wolf, fox, coyote, wolverine or lynx on the same day. Anyone who violates the law faces fines of up to $5,000 and imprisonment for up to a year. Furthermore, the state will not be able to conduct an aerial wolf-control program unless the Fish and Game commissioner makes a written finding that a biological emergency exists and that shooting wolves is the only suitable means the handling the emergency. State game officials said trappers have taken about 1,500 wolves annually over the past few years out of an estimated population of 7,000 to 9,000 animals.

Carnival brings in cool cash.

The 11-day carnival called Ice Art '97 brought Fairbanks nearly $1 million from March 6–16, 1997. An international roster of ice sculptors took part in the competition, which is an anchor event in the Interior's winter festivities. Sculptors come from Russia, Germany, Japan, France, Canada, Poland, Morocco, Mexico, Argentina and Colombia.

Ice Art has grown almost exponentially since its start in 1988 as a two-team demonstration sidebar to a snow sculpture competition. The Learning Channel's "How Do They Do That?" documented the event, and *Newsweek* in its Jan. 20 issue made mention of the competition.

Champ calls it quits.

Hilary Lindh of Juneau called it quits on March 13, 1997, ending one of the most spectacular careers in American skiing. Lindh, 27, is retiring while at the top of her sport. She departs as the world's reigning downhill champion and the country's most decorated female downhiller. A three-time Olympian, Lindh is the winner of more Olympic and World Championship downhill medals than any other woman in U.S. history. She claimed the gold medal at the World Championships in February, and would have been an automatic choice for next year's Olympic team.

"She's one of the all-time greatest American ski racers," said Paul Major, vice president of U.S. Skiing, who was among her coaches during her career.

Moe skis to gold.

Alaska skier Tommy Moe of Girdwood is the reigning Olympic downhill champ. But until March 20, 1997, he'd never won a national downhill title. Moe, 27, picked up the title that had eluded him for a decade at the U.S. Alpine Championships in Carrabassett, Maine. He won with a time of 1 minute, 23.26 seconds, nipping runner-up A. J. Kitt by two-tenths of a second. Anchorage skier Mike Makar was fifth in the men's race.

Moe's dry spell began when he blew out his knee near the end of the 1994–95 season. Last year he struggled, underwent more knee surgery—and injured his hand.

Incredible moose rescue.

Hollywood producers who glimpsed a home video of an Alaska moose rescue snapped up the footage for network television's "The World's Most Incredible Animal Rescues."

The action began March 26, 1997, when Fox Network executives phoned Department of Fish and Game biologist Ted Spraker in Kenai. Spraker was asked to narrate the video, which documents a heroic 1995 effort to rescue a moose that broke through ice near the Soldotna Bridge.

Videotaped by Bob Green, the footage shows an ad hoc rescue team including Spraker and a Homer Electric Association work crew. Rescuers retrieved the half-ton moose by fixing a rope around a utility pole and using an HEA truck to tow the wet, angry animal back to solid footing.

Said Spraker of his 15 minutes of fame, "That trip to Hollywood was more harrowing than pulling a moose out of the river."

Oldest Interior resident dies.

Moses Thomas was laid to rest in the old cemetery of Mansfield, in a handmade casket, wearing caribou skin boots and gloves for his final journey. He was at least 111 years old when he died at Tanacross on April 14, 1997.

Thomas was the sixth Athabascan Indian elder lost to Tanacross, population 110, in the last five years.

"I don't know what we're going to do," said Laura Sanford when she rose to speak at the funeral. "Seems like we're ghosts now."

Oil, gas lease sale trimmed.

On April 17, 1997, federal officials pared down a controversial lease sale in Cook Inlet to a sliver of its former self to appease the concerns of fishermen and environmental groups.

Outer Continental Shelf Lease Sale 149 is scheduled to be held June 11, the U.S. Department of the Interior's Minerals Management Service announced. The agency is offering 101 whole and partial blocks encompassing about 430,000 acres, down 78 percent from the original 402 blocks covering about 2 million acres.

"The decision to proceed with the sale was made after we considered all comments received from fishing groups, natural gas and oil companies, industry support companies, environmental organizations, state and local governments, and numerous local residents," MMS Director Cynthia Quarterman said in her April 17 statement. The MMS has spent about $2.6 million on environmental and socio-economic studies

preliminary to the sale, including a water-quality study.

New Tongass plan urged.

SJR 24, a bill sponsored by Sen. Jerry Mackie (D-Craig) passed the Alaska Senate by a vote of 19 to 2 on April 24, 1997. The resolution urges the U.S. Forest Service to bring the decade-long Tongass Land Management Plan to a conclusion and adopt a minimum harvest level of 300 million board feet, "enabling the people and communities of Southeast Alaska to move forward with more certainty in their economic and personal lives."

Western Steller sea lions endangered.

Steller sea lions off western regions of the Alaska coast received additional protection as of April 30, 1997, when they were reclassified as endangered under the federal Endangered Species Act. Populations of these marine mammals had declined steadily for 35 years; their numbers declined 19 percent between 1992 and 1996. The western population is now about 44,000.

The National Marine Fisheries Service predicts that there is a nearly 100 percent chance the western Steller sea lion will become extinct in the next 60 to 100 years. The classification affects sea lions from Prince William Sound to Kodiak, and down the Alaska Peninsula and Aleutian chain.

The oil keeps coming.

ARCO Alaska Inc. and BP Exploration (Alaska) Inc. announced plans April 30 and May 1, respectively, to develop two more North Slope oil fields, continuing the trend toward pursuit of a new generation of smaller accumulations in the vicinity of Alaska's hydrocarbon giants, Prudhoe Bay and Kuparuk. The new fields are Tarn and Liberty.

Tarn, located 10 miles from Kuparuk, is thought to contain 50 million barrels; startup will be in late 1998 or early 1999. Development cost will be $150 million.

Liberty is located 10 miles southeast of Endicott, to the east of Prudhoe Bay, five miles offshore in the Beaufort Sea. Reserves are estimated at 120 million barrels. Production here will start up by 2000.

In other news, a North Slope gas line has been proposed; the estimated cost for the project to become commercial is $12 billion.

Russian Far East flights begin.

Alaska Airlines and Reeve Aleutian Airways began new air service to Yuzhno-Sakhalinsk in the Russian Far East on May 1, 1997. Yuzhno-Sakhalinsk is the regional capital of the Russian island of Sakhalin. Reeve will make the flight once a week; Alaska has scheduled two flights per week.

Writer goes against the flow.

Ned Rozell, science writer for the University of Alaska Geophysical Institute in Fairbanks, began walking the trans-Alaska oil pipeline on May 4, 1997. Accompanied by Jane, his 10-year-old chocolate Lab, Rozell planned to walk the entire line from Valdez to Prudhoe Bay. There would be no need for bushwhacking; a well-defined gravel road known as "The Pad" follows the pipeline for 790 of its 800 miles, even when it goes underground.

Court rules for heirs.

A Native family that has been fighting the National Park Service for a quarter century has won an important court ruling in a clash over property in the middle of one of Alaska's prime brown bear-viewing sites.

The 80-acre parcel under dispute lies in Katmai National Park on the south bank of the Brooks River, next to a site where the Park Service planned to build a new lodge.

U.S. District Judge James Singleton ruled May 7, 1997, that the heirs of Palakia Melgenak have legal claim to the property. Melgenak began using the site in 1897 as a fishing camp and trapping area. In 1971, at the age of 92, she applied for the land under the 1906 Alaska Native Allotment Act. The suit charged that the Park Service actively resisted Mrs. Melgenak's use and occupancy of her land since at least 1950, insulted the family, and went as far as burning some of her buildings.

Alaska breathes easier.

Anti-smoking activists breathed easier May 10, 1997, after a close victory in the Alaska House for a huge tobacco-tax increase intended to put cigarettes out of teenagers' price range. The House approved a 71-cent increase, which will make Alaska's tax the nation's highest at $1 a pack. Taxes on cigars and other tobacco products will triple.

The victory followed a long, emotional House debate—a fitting end to a two-year fight for the tax. More than 23 percent of deaths of Alaskans 35 years of age or older are attributed to smoking. Eighty-three percent of adult smokers started smoking before the age of 20. Alaska Natives have some of the highest rates of tobacco use in the world, with 47 percent for men and 39 percent for women.

Canada's cigarette tax is nearly $2 a pack, and Denmark's is $4.26.

New Princess Lodge inaugurated.

The Mount McKinley Princess Lodge, a $30 million project, was opened on May 12, 1997. This creates 162 rooms coupled with an expansive lodge, located at Milepost 133 on the Parks Highway outside Trapper Creek.

Princess Lines contributes more than $147 million annually to Alaska from its successful marketing efforts. The company employs more than 1,500 Alaskans in full and seasonal positions throughout the state; the new lodge added 113 new positions. In 1996, Princess wrote paychecks for more than $10 million to Alaskans and contributed $3.6 million in taxes and user fees to the state's economy. Princess purchased in excess of $72 million in products from more than 1,300 Alaskan businesses and communities in 1996.

QVC broadcasts Anchorage.

Anchorage's Town Square was the site for more than 500 QVC fans watching a live broadcast on Saturday, May 24, 1997. QVC showed Alaska products and downtown Anchorage to an estimated 58 million viewers. Many of the 30-person crew stayed on after the broadcast to experience Alaska personally.

Fishing quota expands. Scores of villages in Western Alaska are about to cash in on a bottom-fish and crab harvest bonanza. By mid-1998, some 57 villages will share the rights to catch a share of yellowfin sole, Atka mackerel and Pacific cod as part of the latest expansion of the four-year-old federal Community Development Quota program. The move was announced on June 1, 1997.

That program already conveys more than $20 million a year into some of the state's poorest villages by giving them some of the pollock, halibut and black cod catches from the Bering Sea.

Turtle fossil discovered. On June 9, 1997, three students from Anchorage's Service High uncovered a turtle fossil dating back 55 million to 65 million years. It marks the first time a vertebrate has been found in the coal-bearing sedimentary rocks of the Chickaloon Formation and the first time a four-footed animal of the early Tertiary age has been found in Alaska. The fossil belongs to the genus *Protochelydra,* a forerunner of the common snapping turtle.

Amnesia victim found in Sitka. Twelve years after she was reported missing in Washington, former *Tacoma News Tribune* reporter Jody Roberts was discovered in Sitka leading a quiet life as a wife and mother. The mystery of the woman's disappearance was solved on July 15, 1997, when she was identified through an Internet photograph after her case was reopened as a homicide investigation. Roberts' earliest memory was walking out of a mall in Aurora, Colorado, in 1985. She didn't know where she was and carried no identification. After four months of hospitalization and a diagnosis of amnesia, Roberts was released. She found work and pursued a college degree without knowing that she already had one. Following her move to Sitka in 1989, Roberts married and gave birth to two sets of twin daughters. Anne Corning of Beaverton, Oregon, said her 39-year-old sister was overwhelmed by the news of her former identity and spent the first few days acquainting herself with her lost family.

Sailing with the Klondike Kings. A century ago, 68 weary prospectors disembarked from the steamer *Portland* when it arrived in Seattle on July 17, 1897. But they were rich men, every last one. Known as the Klondike Kings, their arrival from Yukon Territory signaled the start of the incredible gold rush to the Klondike. The Stampede of '98 attracted 100,000 fortune-seeking gold miners, but only about a third actually made it to Dawson.

In celebration of the 100th anniversary of the gold rush, in July the *Spirit of '98* reenacted the *Portland*'s historic journey. On board were descendants of Klondike stampeders, along with a more conservative shipment of gold. Due to security concerns, only a portion of the 3,000 ounces of gold—worth about $3 million—made the entire trip. Most of the shipment was brought on board just before its final call in Seattle.

Subsistence crisis nears deadline. State lawmakers continued to wrestle with Alaska's subsistence dilemma as a federally imposed deadline loomed over them. Without a state management plan in place by Oct. 1, the federal government would take over fisheries management in Alaska's navigable waters.

Alaska law and federal law are in conflict where subsistence hunting and fishing are concerned: State law allows preference for rural residents, while federal law requires equal access to fish and game for all residents.

In an attempt to stave off federal intervention, in early July a seven-member panel headed by Gov. Tony Knowles recommended a rural preference amendment to Alaska's constitution, along with several other proposals that were met with little support. However, among legislators, rural leaders, and sportsmen's groups, many believed the proposal was at least a move in the right direction. Any change in Alaska's constitution would require voter approval.

Suggested Reading

Alaska Northwest Books. *Alaska Wild Berry Guide & Cookbook*. Seattle: Alaska Northwest Books, 1982.

————. *Cooking Alaskan*. Seattle: Alaska Northwest Books, 1983.

————. *Discover Alaska: An Introduction to America's Last Frontier*. Seattle: Alaska Northwest Books, 1992.

Armstrong, Robert H. *Alaska's Birds: A Guide to Selected Species*. Seattle: Alaska Northwest Books, 1994.

————. *Alaska's Fish: A Guide to Selected Species*. Seattle: Alaska Northwest Books, 1996.

Black, Lydia T. *Glory Remembered: Wooden Headgear of Alaska Sea Hunters*. Juneau: Friends of the Alaska State Museum, 1991.

Blackman, Margaret B. *Sadie Brower Neakok: An Inupiaq Woman*. Seattle: University of Washington Press, 1989.

Bruder, Gerry. *Heroes of the Horizon: Flying Adventures of Alaska's Legendary Bush Pilots*. Seattle: Alaska Northwest Books, 1991.

Chandonnet, Ann. *The Alaska Heritage Seafood Cookbook*. Seattle: Alaska Northwest Books, 1995.

Cole, Dermot. *Amazing Pipeline Stories*. Seattle: Epicenter Press, 1997.

Collins, Julie, and Miki Collins. *Trapline Twins*. Seattle: Alaska Northwest Books, 1989.

Corral, Hannah, with Kim Corral and Roy Corral (photographs). *My Denali: Exploring Alaska's Favorite National Park*. Seattle: Alaska Northwest Books, 1995.

Davidson, Art. *In the Wake of the Exxon Valdez: The Devastating Impact of the Alaska Oil Spill*. San Francisco: Sierra Club Books, 1990.

Davis, Neil. *Caught in the Sluice: Tales from Alaska's Gold Camps*. Ester: McRoy & Blackburn, 1994.

Dixon, Kirsten. *The Riversong Lodge Cookbook: World-Class Cooking in the Alaskan Bush*. Seattle: Alaska Northwest Books, 1993.

Dumond, Don E. *The Eskimos and the Aleuts*. New York: Thames & Hudson, revised, 1987.

Dyson, George. *Baidarka: The Kayak*. Seattle: Alaska Northwest Books, 1986.

Eppenbach, Sarah. *Baked Alaska: Recipes for Sweet Comforts from the North Country*. Seattle: Alaska Northwest Books, 1997.

Ewing, Susan. *The Great Alaska Nature Factbook: A Guide to the State's Remarkable Animals, Plants, and Natural Features*. Seattle: Alaska Northwest Books, 1996.

Ferrell, Ed. *Strange Stories of Alaska and the Yukon*. Seattle: Epicenter Press, 1996.

Fitzhugh, William W., and Susan A. Kaplan. *Inua: Spirit World of the Bering Sea Eskimo*. Washington, D.C.: Smithsonian Institution Press, 1982.

Fobes, Natalie (photographs), Tom Jay and Brad Matsen (essays). *Reaching Home: Pacific Salmon, Pacific People*. Seattle: Alaska Northwest Books, 1994.

Ford, Corey. *Where the Sea Breaks Its Back: The Epic Story of Early Naturalist Georg Steller and the Russian Exploration of Alaska*. Seattle: Alaska Northwest Books, 1992.

Freedman, Lew, and Jeff Schultz. *Iditarod Silver: 25 Years of the Iditarod Trail Sled Dog Race*. Seattle: Epicenter Press, 1997.

Gilders, Michelle. *Crossing Alaska: A History of the Trans-Alaska Pipeline*. Portland, Ore.: Graphic Arts Center Publishing, 1997.

Grescoe, Paul, and Audrey Grescoe. *Alaska: The Cruise Lover's Guide*. Seattle: Alaska Northwest Books, 1994.

Haines, John. *The Stars, The Snow, The Fire: Twenty-five Years in the Northern Wilderness*. St. Paul, Minn.: Graywolf Press, 1989.

Heacox, Kim. *Alaska's Inside Passage*. Portland, Ore.: Graphic Arts Center Publishing, 1997.

Herben, George. *Picture Journeys in Alaska's Wrangell–St. Elias*. Seattle: Alaska Northwest Books, 1997.

Hirschmann, Fred (photographs), and Kim Heacox (text). *Bush Pilots of*

Alaska. Portland, Ore.: Graphic Arts Center Publishing Company, 1989.

Holm, Bill. *Spirit and Ancestor: A Century of Northwest Coast Indian Art at the Burke Museum.* Seattle: University of Washington Press, 1987.

Huntington, Sidney, as told to Jim Rearden. *Shadows on the Koyukuk: An Alaskan Native's Life Along the River.* Seattle: Alaska Northwest Books, 1993.

Jans, Nick. *A Place Beyond: Finding Home in Arctic Alaska.* Seattle: Alaska Northwest Books, 1996.

Jettmar, Karen. *The Alaska River Guide: Canoeing, Kayaking, and Rafting in the Last Frontier.* Seattle: Alaska Northwest Books, 1993.

———. *Alaska's Glacier Bay.* Seattle: Alaska Northwest Books, 1997.

Keithahn, Edward L. Illustrated by George Aden Ahgupuk. *Alaskan Igloo Tales.* Seattle: Alaska Northwest Books, 1974.

Kremers, Carolyn. *Place of the Pretend People: Gifts from a Yup'ik Eskimo Village.* Seattle: Alaska Northwest Books, 1996.

Lobb, Allan (text), Art Wolfe (photographs), and Barbara Paxson (illustrations). *Indian Baskets of the Pacific Northwest and Alaska.* Portland, Ore.: Graphic Arts Center Publishing Company, 1990.

Lopez, Barry. *Arctic Dreams: Imagination and Desire in a Northern Landscape.* New York: Charles Scribner's Sons, 1986.

Mattson, Ted. *Adventures of the Iditarod Air Force.* Seattle: Epicenter Press, 1997.

McPhee, John. *Coming into the Country.* New York: Farrar, Straus & Giroux, 1977.

Mergler, Wayne, editor. *The Last New Land: Stories of Alaska, Past and Present.* Seattle: Alaska Northwest Books, 1996.

Miller, Debbie. *Flight of the Golden Plover.* Seattle: Alaska Northwest Books, 1996.

Mr. Whitekeys. *Mr. Whitekeys' Alaska Bizarre: Direct from the Whale Fat Follies Revue in Anchorage.* Seattle: Alaska Northwest Books, 1995.

Muir, John. *Travels in Alaska.* Boston: Houghton Mifflin, 1915.

Murie, Margaret. *Two in the Far North.* Seattle: Alaska Northwest Books, 1978, 1997.

Murie, Olaus. *Journeys to the Far North.* Palo Alto: The Wilderness Society and American West Publishing, 1973.

Murphy, Claire Rudolf, and Jane G. Haigh. *Gold Rush Women.* Seattle: Alaska Northwest Books, 1997.

Murphy, Claire Rudolf (text), and Charles Mason (photographs). *A Child's Alaska.* Seattle: Alaska Northwest Books, 1994.

Nelson, Richard. *The Island Within.* San Francisco: North Point Press, 1989.

O'Clair, Rita, Robert Armstrong, and Richard Carstensen. *The Nature of Southeast Alaska.* Seattle: Alaska Northwest Books, 1992. Rev. 1997.

Parker, Harriette. *Alaska's Mushrooms: A Practical Guide.* Seattle: Alaska Northwest Books, 1994.

Paul, Frances Lackey (story), and Rie Muñoz (illustrations). *Kahtahah: A Tlingit Girl.* Seattle: Alaska Northwest Books, 1976, 1996.

Potter, Jean. *The Flying North: The Early Days of the Bush Pilots in Alaska.* Sausalito: Comstock Editions, 1986.

Ritter, Harry. *Alaska's History: The People, Land, and Events of the North Country.* Seattle: Alaska Northwest Books, 1993.

Schofield, Janice J. *Alaska's Wild Plants: A Guide to Alaska's Edible Harvest.* Seattle: Alaska Northwest Books, 1993.

Sherwonit, Bill. *Alaska's Accessible Wilderness: A Traveler's Guide to Alaska's State Parks.* Seattle: Alaska Northwest Books, 1996.

———. *To the Top of Denali: Climbing Adventures on North America's Highest Peak.* Seattle: Alaska Northwest Books, 1990.

Sherwonit, Bill (text), and Jeff Schultz (photographs). *Iditarod: The Great Race to Nome.* Seattle: Alaska Northwest Books, 1991.

Smith, Dave (text), and Tom Walker (photographs). *Alaska's Mammals: A Guide to Selected Species.* Seattle: Alaska Northwest Books, 1995.

Viereck, Eleanor G. *Alaska's Wilderness Medicines: Healthful Plants of the Far North.* Seattle: Alaska Northwest Books, 1987.

Permissions/Credits for Photos and Illustrations

Selected illustrations are by Val Paul Taylor and David Berger. Other credits are as follows:

Page 3, Mr. Whitekeys' photo by Randy Brandon. 15, courtesy of Carmen Jefford Fisher. 23, J. E. Thwaites, courtesy of the Anchorage Museum of History and Art. 25, Barbara Paxson, *Indian Baskets of the Pacific Northwest and Alaska.* 27, Bill Sherwonit. 31, 32, Robert H. Armstrong. 36, Bill Sherwonit. 41, Bill Sherwonit. 43, Picture Alaska Art Gallery, #199. 50, Robert Williamson. 59, Special Collections Division, University of Washington Libraries, #14501. 67, Port of Bellingham, Washington. 69, Joe Upton. 72, Ann Chandonnet. 78, U.S. National Archives. 84, Special Collections Division, University of Washington Libraries, Nowell photo #14507. 85, Alaska Historical Library, Mary Nan Gamble Collection, PCA 270-224. 87, *Indian Art and Culture of the Northwest Coast,* Della Kew and P. E. Goddard, Vancouver, B.C.: Hancock House, 1974. 91, Tom Walker. 100, Tom Walker. 102, Anchorage Museum of History and Art, B70.28.190. 105, Nick Jans. 106, Nick Jans. 116, courtesy of Randy Acord. 119, Karen Jettmar. 122, Bill Sherwonit. 132, Tom Walker. 135, George Herben. 139, Alissa Crandall. 140, Bill Sherwonit. 145, Bill Sherwonit. 152, Yukon Archives, Whitehorse. 160, Archives, Alaska and Polar Regions Dept., University of Alaska Fairbanks, Historical Photograph Collection, acc. #68-12-56N. 171, Special Collections Division, University of Washington Libraries, #14505. 187, Whatcom Museum of History and Art, J. W. Sandison Collection, #710. 191, Karen Jettmar. 206, Karen Jettmar. 215, Archives, Alaska and Polar Regions Dept., University of Alaska Fairbanks, Kirtley Fletcher Mather Collection, acc. #82-178-109.

See Suggested Reading for sources of photos, illustrations and text excerpts. Every attempt has been made to locate the owners of art and photos to obtain permission to reproduce them.

Index

eulachon (hooligan), 87
events and festivals: annual, 37–39; bird-
watching, 32; Fairbanks, 65–66; gold rush, 79;
Nome, 159–60; Sitka, 197; Skagway, 197. *See
also* Arctic Winter Games; World Eskimo-
Indian Olympics
exhibits, 124–31
exports and imports, 64–65
Extended Railbelt region, energy, 64. *See also*
Railbelt region
Exxon Valdez oil spill, 130, 166–67

Fairbanks, 65–66; air service, 15; average temperatures and precipitation, 46; daylight hours,
55; radio stations, 184; skiing, 198–99;
television stations, 209
Far North region, historic places, 140. *See also*
Arctic region
ferries, 66–67; annual numbers of passengers
and vehicles, 67; data on individual, 67;
information source, 98; nautical miles
between ports, 66–67. *See also* boating;
cruises
festivals and events. *See* events and festivals
fires on wild land, 67–69; acres burned annually
by, 68; largest in acreage, 68; largest in
economic toll, 68–69
fish, Alaska state, 205; individual state records
and best bait or lure, 72; per capita
consumption of, 127. *See also* fishing
fishing, 69–72; commercial, 69–71; sport, 71–72;
regulations, information source, 98;
regulations and licenses, sport, 72; value and
volume annually, 69–70. *See also* fish;
subsistence lifestyle
fish wheel, 72
flag, Alaska state, 204
float trips, Yukon River, 224
flower(s), Alaska state, 205, 219–20; wild, 219–20
flying, 13, 14; glacier, 132
food, cost of, 51
fossil, Alaska state, 205
fox, 108
frogs, 20
frostbite, 44
furs and trapping, 72–73; in Russian Alaska, 193

gas, 165–66; barrels produced annually, 166;
formation of, 165; and oil industry, 59–60,
62, 163–66; reserves and production, 164–65;
royalties, 165
gasoline, cost of, 51
gem, Alaska state, 205
gems and rocks, 192. *See also* gold; jade; minerals;
mining
genealogy, 77
General Communication Inc., 208
geographic center of Alaska, 73
geography, 73–74
glacial flour, 191
glacial rivers, 191
glacier flying, 132
glaciers, 74–76; largest and longest, 74–75
Glennallen, air service, 15; radio stations, 184
gold, 76–78; annual average price, 77; mining,

118–19; nugget, largest, 76; panning, information source, 98; panning, sluicing and
dredging, 76; production annually, 77.
See also gold mining; gold strikes and rushes;
history; minerals; mining
gold rush ancestors, 77
gold rush centennial, 79
gold strikes and rushes, 77–78, 79
golf and golf courses, 78–80
Good Friday earthquake, 20, 58, 59
goose (geese), 30, 31, 32; Emperor, 31
government: state and local, 80–81; tribal, 80.
See also court system; officials, government
governors, 161
gray whales, 217–18
grizzly bears. *See* bear(s)
groundfish: commercial harvest, 69–71; value
annually, 70
growing season, 12
Gulf Coast region, 187–88

Haida Indians, 150–51; arts and crafts, 149–50;
basketry, 26; distribution of, 151; effect of
Russians on, 193; traditional lifestyle, 150
Haines: air service, 15; radio stations, 184
halibut: commercial harvest, 69–70; value
annually, 70
handicapped access, information source, 98
hares, 109
Haul Road. *See* Dalton Highway.
health, information source, 98
health facilities, 87–89
herring: commercial harvest, 69; value annually,
70
highest mountains, 120–21
highest seiche (splash wave), 217
highest volcanoes, 216
highways, 81–83; information source, 98; major,
length, surface and times open, 81; map of,
82; total miles of, 81. *See also* Alaska
Highway; Dalton Highway
hiking, 83. *See also* Chilkoot Trail
historical archives, information source, 98
historical societies, 124–31
historic parks, 124–31
historic places, national, 134–40
history, 83–87. *See also* World War II
holidays in 1998, 87
home study, 61
Homer: average temperatures and precipitation,
46; radio stations, 184
homesteading, 104, 105–6. *See also* land use
hooligan, 87
horns and antlers, 107
hospitals, 87–89; military, 89; municipal, private
and state, 87–88; public health service, 88–89
hostels, 89–90
hot springs, 90–91
housing: cost of, 51; information source, 98
hunting, 91–93; regulations, information source,
98. *See also* subsistence lifestyle
hypothermia, 44, 93

icebergs, 93–94
ice fields, 74–76; map of major, 75